HISTORY OF THE AMERICAN

FILM INDUSTRY

from its beginnings to 1931

HISTORY OF THE AMERICAN

FILM INDUSTRY

from its beginnings to 1931

[FORMERLY TITLED: A HISTORY OF THE MOVIES]

Benjamin B. Hampton

WITH A NEW INTRODUCTION BY RICHARD GRIFFITH
CURATOR EMERITUS, THE MUSEUM OF MODERN ART
FILM LIBRARY

DOVER PUBLICATIONS, INC.
NEW YORK

This Dover edition, first published in 1970, is an unabridged and slightly corrected republication of the work
originally published by Covici, Friede, New York, in 1931
under the title *A History of the Movies*. A new Introduction has been written specially for this edition by Richard
Griffith.

Standard Book Number: 486-22403-1
Library of Congress Catalog Card Number: 71-94321

Manufactured in the United States of America
Dover Publications, Inc.
180 Varick Street
New York, N.Y. 10014

INTRODUCTION
TO THE DOVER EDITION

THREE early histories of the American film industry have stood the years till now—Terry Ramsaye's *A Million and One Nights,* first published in 1926; Lewis Jacobs' *The Rise of the American Film,* published in 1939; and Benjamin B. Hampton's *A History of the Movies,*[1] published between the other two, in 1931. Ramsaye's perpetually fascinating book reflects both his newspaper background and his peripheral involvement in all three branches of the motion picture industry, production, distribution, and exhibition. It is, in sum, romantic journalism of a high order. Jacobs' approach, at the end of the Depression, was much more sober and responsible, and it had a cause to plead—the double cause of the freedom of the screen and of its maximum social usefulness. But if, as a historian, he was also a special pleader, so half-consciously were both his predecessors, out of their much more direct experience of the movie maelstrom.

For Benjamin B. Hampton was a partisan too, of a point of view which finds comparatively few voices today. He was in love with American business enterprise—that "Promethean thrust," in Eric Hoffer's words, which until quite recently commanded the emotional allegiance of the great majority of Americans. Boldness had been the original watchword of business, but by 1900 it had

---

[1] In the present edition retitled *History of the American Film Industry.*

been largely succeeded by "efficiency." In selling its products business was still oriented toward the consumer, but the devising and the manufacture of those products business thought to be exclusively its own business—and increased profits were now seen to lie as much in the standardization and rationalization of production and sales as in buyer-appeal. But, also about 1900, there had appeared a new industry, of rapid growth and vast potential, which seemed to confute the whole industrial trend. By the time Hampton entered it in 1916, the movie business had already reached and passed its first major crisis. The mighty Thomas Edison's efforts to control an industry based on a machine of which he claimed to be the sole inventor, and to standardize its product in anticipation of predictable returns, had gone down to disastrous defeat. The defeat was the more humiliating because Edison and his cohorts had been beaten by a ragtag and bobtail of small-time operators who were mostly newcomers to these shores, and some of whom hardly knew enough English to read a financial statement. Efficiency they knew not, and boldness was their all-in-all. Their only assets were a gambling instinct and a penchant for "eccentric operations," both of which were abhorrent to the drawers-up of financial statements. To the lords of creation of the early century, the movies, besides their other doubtful qualities, seemed to fly in the face of a business philosophy based on shoveling out to a docile public a decoction of standard ingredients chosen at least as much for cheapness as for actual utility.

But the failure of Edison's bid for domination left the movie field wide open to all comers, and, after *The Birth of a Nation* in 1915, no one could any longer doubt that there was "real money" to be made out of the movies. Wall Street felt compelled to investigate the possibilities. One of the first to point to them was Benjamin B. Hampton. Hampton's original background was not unlike Terry Ramsaye's. Born in Macomber, Illinois, in 1875, he was a publisher and editor there and in New York until, in 1911, he joined the American Tobacco Company as a vice-president. Hampton had become interested in the movies before the Edison debacle; he followed the ensuing chaos with great attention, and in 1916 went to his boss, Percival S. Hill of American Tobacco, with a proposal typical of the business psychology of the period. Unwarned by the fate of the Edison "Trust," his solution for chaos was the merger of the eventually triumphant Paramount and the now-forgotten V L S E. The joining together of these two distributing organizations and the producers who released through them would at once bring about substantial reduction of both studio and distribution costs in a classic example of "efficiency." Such streamlining would cost money, but American Tobacco was perfectly willing to secure and invest the needed "fifteen to twenty million dollars"—an early instance of diversification and an embryonic form, perhaps, of conglomeration. Neither Hampton nor his well-heeled colleagues could see anything the matter with this scheme, but Hampton's subsequent education at the hands of Charlotte Pickford showed him once and for all that the best laid plans of men and magnates gang aft agley and, in the case of the movies, nearly always gang agley.

Oddly enough, it was not Mrs. Pickford and her fixation on money which finally foundered Hampton's bright scheme. The proximate cause was a sort of commercial idealism. The creator of the Paramount distributing company, W. W. Hodkinson, "sincerely believed that the three branches of motion pictures should be kept separate: the producer should concentrate on making pictures, the distributor on distribution, and the exhibitor on the ownership and management of theaters. He argued that such independence maintained interest and enthusiasm, and resulted in better pictures, better distribution, and better theater management than would be possible if all elements should be merged under one head." Such an argument must have fallen strangely on the ears of Hampton's financial backers when it was repeated to them, and Adolph Zukor would have none of it. If his Famous Players-Lasky producing company was to be swallowed up in the Paramount-V S L E merger, he wanted a dominating, if not a controlling, voice in the new corporation. That attitude seemed not unreasonable to the go-between Hampton. But not to Hodkinson. "He commented briefly that perhaps I was right: Zukor was certainly making good pictures, and he certainly had been clever enough to make Paramount pay him a good deal of money for them. Then he turned in his revolving chair, and gazed at the pigeons wheeling above the marble portico of the Astor Library. Silence settled on the room. He could not change his point of view."

That adamantine silence must have made a deeper impression on Hampton than he actually says in this book. It determined the whole of his movie career. When Zukor won and Hodkinson lost and was forced out of Paramount, it was Hodkinson whom Hampton followed. With no further attempts at mergers or other financial acrobatics, he became a small independent producer, releasing his films through the new distributing company which Hodkinson set up under his own name, and which futilely exemplified the virtues of production-distribution-exhibition autonomy. The result, for six years, was a steady stream of good-enough pictures, none of which seem memorable today. When Hodkinson, increasingly cut off from first-run screens as a result of the operations of the triumphant Zukor, finally gave up the struggle, Hampton had already preceded him into retirement. He became a sort of public apologist for the movies during the scandals of the early Twenties, and thereafter, when occasion arose, their skilful interpreter in high places. The last decade of his life (he died in 1932) he spent in reflection on the reasons why Hodkinson had proved to be wrong and Zukor right (at least for the time being), and the portent of those reasons for the business ethos and for democracy itself. Those reflections form the substance of this book, written apparently at the instigation of John Dewey.

For if Hampton himself was a sort of covert idealist, as he reveals himself to be here, his ideals expressed themselves in business terms. He subscribed to the doctrine that the public is to be served, that money is to be made in its service, and that you will make lots of money if you serve it quicker and better than the man who is breathing down your neck. The problem he and his like faced for the first time in dealing with the movies was that the "product" they brought for sale was emotion, a commodity as aery as the soul itself. That inconstant factor constantly threw out the whole business equation—yet business probity, business "sense," dictated an equally constant effort to bring the equation back in line, to justify investment, to rationalize risk. This struggle came to absorb Hampton, and forced him to take a new view of it, which is why this is no ordinary business history. That it is the best history of the movie business to date there can be no doubt. Ramsaye is far less exact, Jacobs far less complete, and neither conveys to the same extent the sense of being in the thick of events, and deeply affected by them, yet committed to a perspective based on the need to make an objective choice between competing business policies. This account of the defeat of the Trust, the rise of the star system, and the battle for the theatres does indeed show us just how the movies came to be lodged in the place they still occupy in the middle of American life. Sometimes the business details and the clash of personalities do obscure what Hampton mainly wants to say. We almost forget that movies exist on a screen as we follow the fight of Adolph Zukor, Lewis J. Selznick, Harry Aitken, W. W. Hodkinson, Charlotte Pickford, for the reins of the gilded chariot. But in the end Hampton never lets us forget that it was *Mary* Pickford, not her mother—and not even Miss Pickford herself, but the mere screen illusion of her—which determined into whose hands those reins would momentarily fall.

For what came to fascinate him most of all was the factor in the business equation which has been increasingly neglected by the business mind in the twentieth century, the "ultimate consumer." Initially it must have come as hard to Hampton as to his associates in the American Tobacco Company and in Wall Street to discover that "something unforeseen was happening to the mind of the mob. In some mysterious manner, millions of human beings were refuting the dogma that mass mentality could not, or would not, move ahead, but that it would always mill around in circles and get nowhere in the development of anything further than the desire for additional material possessions. Perhaps this philosophy remained as true as ever; perhaps the common people had no capacity to advance to a happy, wholesome civilization; nevertheless they were making remarkable progress in creating for themselves a form of entertainment that carried with it an immeasurable quantity of stimulation, enlightenment, and education. No so-called leaders of thought or of public opinion were influencing or guiding this unprecedented movement. There was no leadership of any sort. There was merely a ceaseless, irresistible drift of millions of plain people to little ticket-windows to buy amusement—cheap, flimsy amusement that aroused the disgust or scorn of the intelligentsia. But all the time the demand was for better and better pictures, and they had to be devised and manufactured, not by intellectuals, but by mere business men whose only purpose was to make money by selling better shows to their customers."

Hampton's conception of "better and better pictures" was limited by his own experience and allegiances. The French film historians Robert Brasillach and Maurice Bardèche quote him as saying of the 1925 version of *Ben Hur* and the 1927 *King of Kings:* "It is probable that they will stand permanently as the highest point of film production, and, if chemists should discover a way to preserve the photographic coating on celluloid, may be considered by future historians, together with Douglas Fairbanks' superb fantasy, 'The Thief of Bagdad,' as noteworthy achievements of the American civilization which inspired them." Bardèche and Brasillach add, "We should not have dared to go to these lengths, but since it is an American who speaks, that harsh judgment may be allowed to stand." But it is not Hampton's own tastes which are at issue here; the essence of his view is that the "common people" were "creating for themselves" the form of entertainment we think of as typical of the movie. To Hampton, it was a miracle that a public so lately a mere nickelodeon rabble—a world public, be it noted, not just an American one—should respond to *Ben Hur, The King of Kings,* and *The Thief of Bagdad,* "faithful, authentic, and awe-inspiring," to the extent of making the huge investments in these films profitable. And, questions of taste aside, the development of the movie under the commercial conditions of the early century *was* a miracle—as Hampton says, "the one triumph of democracy in creating an effective agency of its very own."

Today, accustomed to the miracle, we are more exacting. Fidelity and authenticity of themselves no longer inspire our awe; we look for something deeper. How are we to get it? Against all probability, the old movie system of big-scale production for mass audiences has survived the onslaught of television and of the other concomitants of affluence which now compete for leisure time and money. Many now place their faith in the break-up of the mass audience into a series of minority audiences, for which films of modest cost can be made with the reasonable expectation of a modest return. That ideal is not so very far from the Hampton-Hodkinson doctrine of the separation of powers of production, distribution, and exhibition which went down to defeat in the Twenties, and to make it successful today will require new distribution and exhibition methods, as well, in all probability, as new sources of production money. The trouble is that business men would still rather invest five million dollars in the expectation of getting back twenty-five million than put up two hundred thousand in the hope of a profit of a mere three hundred thousand. Their logic is unassailable; aside from the size of the sums involved, the one profit ratio is 1–5, the other 2–3. They have another objection. The cultivation of minority audiences is apt to be a wildcat affair, an emotional gamble, as opposed to the regulated manufacture of product for the big world audience which, seventy years of experience have "proved," is wedded to the eternal triangle of sex, violence, and religion—appropriately furnished out with authenticity, fidelity, and awesomeness. But if there is one thing Hampton learned in his adventures in the movie industry, it was that when the chips are down, the gamblers win, the conservatives lose. And gambles come in all sizes.

R<small>ICHARD</small> G<small>RIFFITH</small>

Winchester, Virginia
June, 1969

PREFACE

MANY years ago I began, reporter-like, to make notes on the movies, with the idea that some day I would write a book on this fascinating industry. As time went by the notes accumulated, and several magazine articles resulted. In 1921, James R. Quirk, editor of *Photoplay*, assigned to Terry Ramsaye the task of writing the story of motion pictures, and through several years Mr. Ramsaye's material appeared in *Photoplay*, taking final form in two splendid volumes, *A Million and One Nights*, published by Simon and Schuster in 1926. Mr. Ramsaye's work was a comprehensive history of the industry, and for the time I abandoned the plan of producing a book of my own.

In 1926, after eight years in Los Angeles, I returned to New York, and my old friends eagerly questioned me about motion pictures. Amos Pinchot was among the many who manifested a lively interest in the conditions that brought about the birth and the startlingly extensive development of films, and on numerous occasions he encouraged me to express my ideas. One evening at the Pinchot home, I talked for several hours to Dr. John Dewey and a dozen other men and women, and Dr. Dewey expressed the belief that my views on the movies should be put into book form. Thus encouraged by a philosopher and by an old friend, I started work on an undertaking that has lasted through five years.

At the end of four years I had produced a manuscript of approximately 300,000 words. The editorial board of one publishing house to whom it had been submitted suggested presenting it in three volumes! The mere thought of three volumes disheartened me so thoroughly that the manuscript was retired to my shelves. Then Harry Block, an editor who had read portions of the manuscript, returned from a year's absence abroad. He rescued the book from my library shelves, read it, and generously offered to assist me in reducing it to one-volume length. Thanks to him that work has been done. Without his enthusiasm, intelligence, and skill, I do not believe that the book could ever have been completed.

The list of those to whom I am indebted for help in gathering my material is too long to be included, but to them all I am deeply grateful. I am particularly indebted to James R. Quirk and the staff of *Photoplay* for many of the illustrations which they have generously loaned from their files, and to Will H. Hays, Maurice McKenzie, and Frank J. Wilstach, for obtaining the cooperation of many members of the motion picture industry in the considerable task of finding many rare and valuable pictures.

B. B. H.

CONTENTS

I. LIVING PICTURES AND PEEP SHOWS — 3

II. A NEW FORM OF THEATER — 29

III. QUANTITY *vs.* QUALITY — 49

IV. THE MOTION PICTURES PATENTS COMPANY — 64

V. THE STAR SYSTEM — 83

VI. FEATURE PICTURES — 101

VII. THE NEW ERA — 121

VIII. THE PICKFORD REVOLUTION — 146

IX. THE RISE OF FIRST NATIONAL — 170

X. THE POST-WAR BOOM — 197

XI. UNITED ARTISTS AND OTHER DEVELOPMENTS — 227

XII. THE BATTLE FOR THE THEATERS — 252

xiii. HOLLYWOOD SCANDALS AND CENSORSHIP   281

xiv. "BIGGER AND BETTER PICTURES"   304

xv. THE SILENT FILM'S APEX   326

xvi. IN FOREIGN LANDS   348

xvii. TALKIES   362

xviii. SOUND AND FURY   388

xix. TODAY AND TOMORROW   406

INDEX   435

ILLUSTRATIONS

PLATES 1-30   follow page 46

PLATES 31-62   142

PLATES 63-94   238

PLATES 95-125   334

HISTORY OF THE AMERICAN

FILM INDUSTRY

from its beginnings to 1931

CHAPTER ONE
LIVING PICTURES AND
PEEP SHOWS

MANY MEN, through many years, searched for ways to
make pictures appear to move. No one can be said to have
been the first to conceive the idea. Indeed, the scholarly mind
may trace static pictures and movies to a common source, and
see the progenitor of film shows in the first artist who scratched
images of animals and men and women on the walls of his
cave. For thousands of years, people have been interested in
pictures, and the desire to see representations of figures in motion is indicated by the drawings of the hunt discovered on
the walls of pre-historic homes and carved on bone and ivory.
Evidently the "chase" in pictures was one of the earliest forms
of entertainment, and as mankind moved along toward civilization the interest in pictures grew broader.

The invention of the "magic lantern" was a part of this search
for pictorial motion. Pictures painted on glass were placed in
front of the lantern in a dark room and appeared "magically"
on the opposite wall. In various forms, the magic lantern (or
stereopticon, as it is often called), attracted the attention of numerous experimenters, and the discovery of photography by the
Frenchman, Daguerre, and his associates, about 1830, gave im-

petus to the efforts to combine the magic lantern, or some of its principles, and photographic glass plates to obtain motion. From about 1850 to 1890, the urge for pictures in motion was so definite that many men in America and Europe—a few of them scientists, others artists, and others laymen—tinkered away at the problem; but an incident which greatly stimulated research came not from these specialists and amateurs, but from a disagreement among sportsmen as to the movement of a horse's legs.

Leland Stanford, capitalist and one-time governor of California, declared that a thoroughbred at full gallop lifts all four feet from the ground. Other horsemen and various anatomists, sculptors and painters disagreed with him, and Stanford, conceiving the idea of using the camera to establish the facts, employed a photographer named Eadweard Muybridge to do the work. Many photographs were taken in a series of experiments extending over several years, but the results were unsatisfactory until Stanford engaged an engineer, John D. Isaacs, who placed several cameras in a row and arranged an electrical device to open the shutter of each as the horse ran past. Thus a series of photographs was obtained, each picture showing the horse in a different position.

The photographs proved that Stanford was right—the racing horse does lift all four feet from the ground. Stanford was pleased. He had spent several years and much money in the experiments, but was more than repaid by the interest aroused by his photographs in America and Europe. In 1882, he published a book of the pictures, with analytical and descriptive text by J. D. B. Stillman.

The Stanford book and its revolutionary illustrations proved that motion could be photographed. Several inventors soon presented exhibitions of photographs on glass plates, using various stages of motion in a series of acts, and then arranging the plates so that an illusion of motion was created. One man photographed scenes of little plays on lantern slides, and by slipping one slide after another on the rack of a stereopticon produced a screen show in which there was an illusion of figures in motion. Others arranged their plates in drum-like racks placed before a light, so that as the racks revolved motion seemed to exist. Although none of these devices were perfect or even practical, their exhibition in halls and other public places aroused interest in the subject of photographing life in motion and encouraged further research.

The "zoopraxiscope"—nearly all of these early inventors insisted that they were scientists and to prove it selected long, unpronounceable Greek names for their apparatus—exhibited by Eadweard Muybridge at the Chicago World's Fair in 1893, was seen by many people and created widespread discussion of the possibilities of moving pictures. By 1893-4, the subject of photographing life in action appeared frequently in newspapers and technical journals and in the conversations of the many Americans constantly fascinated by visions of new inventions and discoveries.

Of course there is no motion whatever in a "motion picture." On the screen each successive photograph stands still for about one-sixteenth of a second, but the eye is tricked into believing that the flow of movement is continuous. The early experimenters were searching for the number of pictures per second necessary to create this illusion; some of the experiments were placed at as few as six per second and others as high as forty or fifty. Sixteen was finally established as producing the most satisfactory results.

But even though men might determine the number of photographs per second necessary to create an illusion of motion, there was no camera with which to take the pictures. Isaacs set up a row of cameras and the horse ran by them, and while this method was novel and interesting it could hardly be practically and generally applied. There was need of a camera that would hold enough glass plates to take a series of photographs. As quickly as one photograph was made, the plate had to be removed from the lens and another substituted in its place, and so on in a series of photographed images which, projected on a screen, would produce the desired illusion. Inventors tried to devise such a camera, but glass is so heavy and breakable that it was impossible to construct a machine to use it, and as long as the seekers continued to work with glass their search was hopeless. Sensitized papers and fabrics were tried as substitutes, and were unsatisfactory. Celluloid had been invented and experimenters in Europe and America were trying to discover a coating or "film" of chemicals which would enable them to use this tough, flexible, substance in photography instead of glass plates.

George Eastman and his associates at Rochester, New York, had developed the amateur camera, the Kodak, and if they could devise a substitute for glass plates or sensitized cloth or paper they were confident that photography would become very popular. Hannibal Goodwin, a New Jersey minister and chemist, and the Eastman group discovered methods of superimposing a film on celluloid about the same time, 1888-1890. The discovery became the subject of lengthy litigation; Goodwin died and his patents and processes passed to a corporation which brought suit against Eastman, which Eastman settled after many years. The Goodwin interests were never extensive manufacturers of film, and the Eastman company became the largest domestic or foreign maker of the product.

THOMAS ALVA EDISON, famous as the inventor of the incandescent lamp and many other marvels, was deeply interested in the phonograph, which he had produced and placed on the market in 1880-85, as a method of popular amusement. The "talking machine" was fixed into a cabinet, the mechanism of which was started by a coin, and a song or a speech was transmitted through tubes to the listener's ears. Men rented store-rooms and set rows of cabinets along the walls, and customers went from one to another, enjoying the new entertainment so much that the phonograph, even its early cabinet form, became a commercial success.

Edison always had watched nearly all fields of invention carefully, and the efforts of various experimenters to produce motion photography suggested the idea that animated pictures, united with music in his talking-machine cabinet, would provide a very popular amusement. The new preparation, celluloid with its coating of film, seemed to him to be the medium to use for motion photography. He had to design a camera that would roll the film to the lens, hold it there long enough for a photograph to be taken, and then roll it along so that a series might be registered. An exhibition cabinet had to be constructed to hold the phonograph and the motion picture film, with mechanism to operate them simultaneously, so that the auditor-spectator at the peep-hole could see the movies and hear the music at the same time.

Edison, deciding to produce a camera and a film-cabinet mechanism before attempting to unite talking-machine and motion picture, organized a department for the experiments in his laboratory at East Orange, New Jersey, and put one of his assistants, W. K. L. Dickson, in charge of the work. After three years of experiments, the result, in 1889, was the Edison "kinetoscope," a cabinet in which fifty feet of celluloid film revolved on spools. By dropping a coin in a slot, an electric light was flashed on the film, a tiny motor moved the spools, and the observer at the peep-hole was startled to see little pictures of humans and animals in motion. Although these first movies gave their brief shows in less than a minute, and the subjects were such simple things as a man sneezing, a girl dancing, a boxing-match, a horse eating hay, or baby taking a bath, people were enchanted by the novelty of motion in pictures.

Edison, deep in numerous laboratory experiments, was too far removed from the public to realize that his invention was anything more than a toy. His mind was so occupied with other research work which he regarded as more important that he did not even carry out his original intention to combine talking machine and movies, and let his business partners manage the kinetoscope department without giving it much of his own thought.

Edison phonographs were well distributed throughout the

United States when the kinetoscope reached the market, and movie peep-shows soon were everywhere installed by the side of talkie cabinets in the remodeled storerooms known as "phonograph parlors." Pictures of life in action attracted more attention and produced more entertainment than sounds transmitted through ear-pieces, and parlor proprietors noticed that the kinetoscope brought more customers than the phonograph.*

MEN with keener commercial sense than Edison, observing the enthusiasm of peep-show patrons, saw a field of money-making. This novelty, they believed, would yield profitable harvests of small coins, and if Edison was too busy to exploit his kinetoscope business, they were willing to grasp the opportunity he was neglecting. There soon appeared in America several peep-show cabinets with names, derived from Greek and Latin sources, suggesting motion, life, action, vision, record, or graphic portrayal —such as muto-scope, bio-scope, bio-graph.

The most alert competitors of the kinetoscope were the men who devised the "mutoscope," a peep-show cabinet, and later the "biograph," a system of screen movies. Biograph, as the company was known after a short time, was formed by Henry N. Marvin, scientist and college professor; Dickson, whom Edison had placed in charge of the experiments that produced the kinetoscope; E. B. Koopman, a dealer in small patented articles; and Herman Casler, an electrician and machinist. The mutoscope and the biograph harvested a large crop of small coins, and within a

---

* There are so many claims and counter-claims of priority of invention in motion pictures, that I have simplified the story by presenting only those events to which the passage of time has given importance. For example: In England, in or about 1890, several men attempted to create movies by rolling film from one spool to another, and their experiments afforded a foundation for declarations that they were as early as Edison in the field. However, no film, slipping from spool to spool, was uniformly successful. Edison was the "father of the movies" because of his use of perforated film, moved by a sprocket wheel, which insured regularity in starting and stopping for the fraction of a second while photographs were being registered or, later, projected to the screen.

few years the Biograph company became a substantial enterprise.

Edison patented his invention in the United States, but, regarding it as an unimportant plaything, refused to spend the few hundred dollars necessary to obtain foreign patents, and when his kinetoscope was exhibited abroad, Europeans were free to imitate it or to produce machines inspired by it. Robert Paul, in London, Lumière in Paris, and several other men in Europe soon made peep-show cabinets and cameras, and presently they began to export films to America. Lumière called his device the "cinematograph," and from that day the word "cinema" has been used in Europe to describe motion pictures.

The phonograph and kinetoscope parlors were now joined by another form of show shop—store-rooms from which windows and doors had been removed, or set back, the wide entrance hos pitably inviting passers-by to enter and enjoy the marvels of talking machines and animated pictures. Usually the entrance was decorated with garish, circus-like posters, and a mechanical piano or a giant music-box assisted a leather-lunged barker in advertising the entertainment. Pennies replaced nickels as the price and these show-shops became known as "penny arcades." Millions of pennies poured into the arcades and parlors; numerous men acquired snug profits by operating this new type of amusement house and by placing cabinets in billiard-rooms, shooting-galleries, cigar stores, railway stations and other places where people idled time away.

Soon the notion was born that if animated pictures could be taken from the cabinet and shown on a large curtain or screen, a new and profitable entertainment field would be discovered. This idea called for the invention of a projection machine which would have to be something more elaborate and more intricate than any magic lantern or the whirling spools of the kinetoscope. The strip of film would have to be moved forward to precisely the right point; then it must be stopped while an electric light back of it projected the picture through a lens to a screen; then it must move forward again, the moving and stopping process continuing with precision until all the photographs had passed through the lens; and as the film sped on its journey it must be unwound from one reel and rewound on another. The quantity and quality of light needed to obtain projection, and a method of preventing inflammable celluloid from being set afire by the heat of the electric lamp, were among the many obstacles to be overcome.

Frank R. Gammon and Norman C. Raff, associated with Edison in the phonograph and kinetoscope business, urged the scientist to heed the demand to transfer movies to the screen and to devise the necessary machinery. Phonograph and kinetoscope had built prestige for the Edison name in connection with entertainment, so that if Edison would produce a projection machine, his associates reasoned, it would become an immediate commercial success. Edison, however, persisting in his belief that the moving picture was a short-lived novelty, refused to consider the idea of screen shows, and the many mechanical and electrical difficulties involved in making them a reality were worked out by half a hundred other inventors.

The first two projection machines appeared in 1895, and were called "pantopticon" and "vitascope." The pantopticon was produced by the Lambda Company, organized by Major Woodville Latham, a Virginia professor living in New York, and his sons and several others, including for a while Dickson, who had been associated first with Edison and later with Biograph. In May, 1895, the pantopticon was set up in a store-room in New York and exhibited on the screen moving pictures of a prize fight, the show lasting less than five minutes.

The first pantopticon was, like all experimental machines, crude and imperfect; the film had not yet been adapted to the requirements of projection and the pictures flickered and wobbled blotchily. But they moved in life-size, life-like action, and that was the main thing. Major Latham had produced the illusion of living pictures. Mechanical and chemical smoothness and clarity were details that would be accomplished later.

In Washington, D. C., Thomas Armat and C. Francis Jenkins

each had worked independently on the idea of projecting motion pictures, but for a year or so they had been operating together. They produced the "vitascope" and gave exhibitions with it in the summer of 1895. That autumn, Jenkins withdrew from the association and later showed pictures with a machine which he called the "phantascope." Armat brought suit against him for infringement of patent rights, and in time the courts gave decisions in favor of Armat.*

Neither the Lambda Company nor Armat was equipped to produce projectors in quantity, and the progress of screen pictures was very slow until Gammon and Raff examined the vitascope and, convinced of its practicality, induced Edison to bring Armat into his organization and market the vitascope under the valuable Edison trade name. The Edison Company, with its manufacturing facilities, was able to produce projectors promptly in moderate quantities.

In April, 1896, the Edison Vitascope gave its premier public performance, at Koster and Bial's Music Hall, then the leading vaudeville theater in New York. When the tiny movies emerged from the peep-show cabinet and appeared life-size on the screen before the eyes of a large metropolitan audience, they were a smashing sensation. "Tremendous," "sensational," "enormous," —all the adjectives of the circus press-agent were used in describing the reception of this new form of amusement.

Vaudeville, or "variety" theaters, presenting entertainment to relatively sophisticated audiences paying fifty cents to a dollar and a half for admittance, were constantly seeking novelties, and, following the Koster and Bial exhibition, orders poured

* Here again I simplify by selecting only those events which developed later significance, omitting details of numerous statements that long befogged the history of the movies. Friends of C. Francis Jenkins have claimed for him the pioneer position in projection, saying that at his home in Richmond, Ind., in June, 1894, he showed on a sheet pictures of "Annabelle the Dancer." In December, 1895, Jenkins described his invention to the Franklin Institute of Pennsylvania and was awarded the Elliott Cresson medal. However, Latham's pantopticon presented the first recognized commercial exhibition of the screen, and the patents owned by Armat were those which were used by the Edison Company.

in to the Edison Company for vitascopes. "Living pictures" became known to theater audiences in all the principal American cities. Managers of some playhouses, assuming that movies were only a temporary sensation, lost interest in their projection machines in a short time, but films continued to hold a position on "variety bills" and in dime museums after more pretentious music halls concluded that the novelty had outlived its day.

Managers of phono-kineto parlors and arcades were keen to get possession of projectors, either by acquiring the discarded machines of music halls or by having machinists manufacture imitations of them. These showmen could take films from their peep-shows and paste them together to make up a reel of four or five hundred feet, giving a screen performance of five to eight minutes, which they presently extended to half an hour merely by adding more film to the reel. The rear part of the arcade was partitioned off, and, equipped with chairs and a screen, became a film "theater"; or the room above the store was converted into an exhibition hall, a miniature auditorium with seats for fifty, a hundred, or two hundred patrons.

The customers of the peep-shows were skeptical and suspicious. Barnum and his successors had convinced the common people that they were regarded as the legitimate prey of clever showmen, and they were constantly on guard against the humiliation of being swindled out of nickels and dimes by fake novelties and hokum mysteries. Some of them had heard of living pictures at high-priced theaters, but they had their doubts about arcades showing the genuine article for ten cents, and they dubiously regarded pitch-dark rooms "where pickpockets could go through you easy as an eel through water."

Thomas L. Tally, of Los Angeles, overcame skepticism by cutting a peep-hole in the wall of his phonograph parlor so patrons could look through and see for themselves the life-size images in motion on the screen in the dark rear room. After a brief glimpse, the doubters gave their dimes to the ticket-seller and rushed inside to enjoy a complete view of the marvel. Other showmen employed similar means of convincing suspicious patrons, and word of mouth advertising brought such throngs of customers to arcades and parlors that within a few months the demand for projectors and films far exceeded the supply.

No other invention of the mechanical age had created such widespread astonishment and interest. Other inventions had as their prosaic objectives the saving of labor and time. Steam engines manufactured cloth, lumber, metal wares and many other articles, and reduced the hardships and delays of travel by land and sea; hundreds of machines had been invented to take the drudgery out of life, and had been accepted as matters of fact. The telegraph, the telephone, the electric light, were comparatively new marvels. Each had created a sensation, but they had not entered into the lives of millions of people. The common man and his family still used kerosene lamps; none but the well to do had telephones; and the telegram was a form of communication seldom known in the average household except to announce serious illness or death.

But this new thing—this "living picture" affair—was not a prosaic tool to reduce labor or to save time; it was not an instrument to create more comfort and luxury for the well-to-do. It was a romantic device to bring entertainment to the common people. Other inventions had made their way slowly, the public becoming accustomed to them so gradually that there was not much general astonishment-value in any of them. But screen shows burst into the world with startling success. People did not at first associate the little film in the penny-arcade cabinet with "life-size living pictures" on a theater curtain, and the motion picture came into existence as a novelty almost equal to a miracle.

The subjects of the early screen shows were substantially the same as those in the fifty-foot films of the peep-cabinets, but spectators devoured them ravenously. People walking along a street, a dancer doing her turn, prize-fighters at work, a girl trying on shoes—anything served to thrill the arcade and parlor patrons and to send them home happy. When a camera man first produced a picture of a railroad train rushing headlong directly forward, many people screamed as the engine roared into their faces, and strong men sighed with genuine relief when it disappeared without wrecking the theater. Nothing in the million-dollar spectacles of later years ever excelled the punch delivered by this pioneer filmlet.

WHEN screen pictures spread from vaudeville theaters to the back-rooms and up-stairs halls of phono-kineto parlors and arcades, they passed into another, and much larger, section of human life. Perhaps a million, possibly two millions, of the hundred millions of people living in the United States were regular patrons of the various forms of theater entertainment—opera, spoken drama, musical comedy, vaudeville and burlesque—and perhaps another million enjoyed the stage occasionally. Ninety percent or more of the American population was not reached by any method of story-telling and character delineation by play-acting.

Three important obstacles prevented the populace from participation in theatrical amusements,—the cost of admittance, the infrequency of plays and other stage productions designed for the mental habits and moral viewpoints of the majority of the people, and ecclesiastical condemnation of theater-going.

The price of tickets ranged from $1.50 or $2 for orchestra seats, to 50 cents for the gallery, in metropolitan centers; and $1.50 to 25 cents in second-class houses or in smaller cities. The cost of the better seats was an insurmountable barrier to most families in the years when "a dollar a day was workingman's pay," and "white collar" households struggled to make both ends meet with incomes only slightly larger than laborer's wages. The lower price of the gallery was no great inducement, considering the noise of the mob and the annoyance of peanut shells, popcorn, and a variety of robust odors.

After 1880, the presentation of drama and melodrama or Negro minstrel shows at "popular prices" in second-class theaters in large cities attracted new groups of entertainment buyers, and traveling companies known as "repertoire troupes" toured the county seats and larger towns, appearing in "opera houses" and halls that were usually dark except for their sporadic visits. Ten, twenty, and thirty cents became generally standardized as their admittance fees, and the "rep troupes" acquired the nickname of "ten-twent-thirts."

The great public that existed beyond all theater doors received scant attention either from dramatists and managers who looked to the intellectual, or at least the sophisticated and well-to-do classes for patronage, or from the amusement purveyors who catered to those enjoying the frivolity of vaudeville or girl-and-music shows. Operas and plays were produced to please the elect who were to pay for them, and variety programs and light musical concoctions for the gayety-seekers who deplored a lack of tunefulness in grand opera and avoided the intellectual labor demanded by classical dramas and many of the "problem plays" endorsed by the intelligentsia between 1890 and 1910.

The moral views of very large sections of the American populace and the clerical ban upon theater-going were concentrated almost entirely on the subject of sex, although the portrayal of gambling and drinking and other vices was regarded as objectionable. Discussions of sex and exposures of feminine limbs were distinctly taboo, and for women and girls to appear on the stage in low-necked evening gowns was accepted in most homes as prima facie evidence of "looseness," to use one of the mildest phrases of the period. Stage girls presenting themselves in tights were past redemption; one-piece bathing suits were unknown either in the theater or on the beaches; even ballet dancers and chorus girls wore corsets almost as stiff as armor-plate.

However, so insistent was the hunger for entertainment and the desire for the delights of play-acting, that as the nineteenth century drew to a close more and more young people, broader-minded and more daring than their forebears, crept through the barriers erected by religious prejudice and enjoyed for themselves the plays presented by repertoire troupes. "Uncle Tom's Cabin," accepted as an exception to the evils of the stage, was a powerful factor in ameliorating the clerical attitude. Even rigid Baptists, Methodists, and Presbyterians approved of its propaganda against slavery and permitted themselves to enjoy the emotions aroused by half a hundred "Uncle Tom" troupes that played in halls and tents for forty years after slavery was abolished.

Through the gap made by "Uncle Tom" came "Ten Nights in a Bar Room," a temperance play, "Only a Farmer's Daughter," "Davy Crockett," Denman Thompson's "Old Homestead," James Herne's "Sag Harbor," "Uncle Josh Spruceby" and other plays "teaching wholesome lessons." "Ben Hur," accepted and endorsed as a religious play, was a reliable success for several decades, but owing to the tread-mill machinery needed in the chariot race, "Ben Hur's" activities never got beyond theaters in larger cities.

Little by little the church restrictions were relaxed—not formally by the authorities, but informally by the members—so that in the nineties of the last century multitudes of Americans were restlessly searching for entertainment. They knew they wanted something; they did not know what that thing was; they merely knew it must be enjoyable—and its price must be low. They had welcomed the phono- and kineto-parlors and arcades, and the comparatively scarce dime museums, as places of amusement within reach of their pocket books; and when living pictures reached these "cheap showshops," the masses soon overcame their suspicion of dark rooms and their skepticism of showmen's trickery, and flooded the ticket-sellers with their dimes and nickels.

To the great, non-theater-going public, life-size living pictures were not merely a novelty—they were a marvel that held in the background an elusive promise of something vague, indefinite, but full of encouraging possibilities. Vaudeville patrons enjoyed the newness of the first screen pictures, and enthusiastically welcomed succeeding unique film items such as the railroad train coming full speed into their eyes, or exceptionally interesting prize-fight or dancing pictures; but the customers of the arcades, parlors, and dime museums were the real devotees of movies. They could not see them often enough, and they wandered from one place to another, searching for films they had not seen before.

A new class of amusement buyers sprang into existence as quickly and apparently as magically as screen pictures themselves had appeared. In the cities in which show rooms had been opened, scores of thousands, swelling to hundreds of thousands, of men, women, and children daily and nightly appeared at ticket windows. From suburban and country towns were coming many calls for apparatus and films. Nothing comparable to the movement had ever happened before, and no one had anticipated or prepared for its advent.

Exhibitors, excited by incredible prospects of making money, exerted themselves to the utmost to rent or buy more projectors and films, and to obtain other and larger rooms to accommodate the picture-hungry masses. They could rent more halls and store rooms, but there were so few manufacturers of projection machines and producers of pictures that all of them together had not enough facilities to meet the ever-increasing demand. The youthful industry, with no experience or traditions to guide it, with insufficient machinery to satisfy the sudden, astonishing desire of the public—even without tools to build the machinery— and with no internal or external organization to give it direction or cohesion, was forced by the populace into a maelstrom of expansion that is without counterpart in business history.

PRIOR to the transformation of moving pictures to the screen, not many films of fifty-foot length were needed to supply the peep-shows, and as there had been no urgent demand for cameras, very few had been invented. The early Edison photographic apparatus—a huge dark-room mounted on a circular track to enable the camera to follow the sun—served its purpose until living pictures stimulated Edison engineers to produce a portable machine. Biograph's camera was smaller than the original Edison, but complicated, requiring expert operation. Lumière, in France, had invented a portable camera, but, unwilling to create competition for himself, guarded his secret zealously, and very few of his instruments had reached the market. Gaumont, Pathé, and other Frenchmen acquired photographic apparatus of their own, and Paul of London and others in America and Europe were experimenting with camera invention or imitation when living pictures aroused new audiences in the United States, but none had yet produced marketable equipment.

The Latham-Lambda company, failing to acquire the necessary organization and equipment to manufacture a steady supply of pantopticons, made only a few projectors and perhaps a few cameras, but never enough of either to win for itself a position in the new industry. The Edison Company, through alliance with Armat and his vitascope, was the foremost manufacturer, at home or abroad, of projectors, as well as films, but even a well-established institution such as this could not immediately fill all the many orders for projection machines. Edison was willing to rent projectors, and after a while another machine than Armat's vitascope was produced in the Edison shops and was sold outright to showmen; but the Edison Company would not sell or rent cameras, the intention being to control for itself the production and sale of pictures.

The Biograph company expanded to meet the requirements of screen entertainment, building on the foundation of its mutoscope cabinet operations. Biograph had obtained some financing from a bank, this being the only pioneer film project to receive assistance from capitalists, and Jeremiah J. Kennedy, an engineer experienced in important industrial undertakings, entered the corporation as representative of the banking interests. Percy Waters, an exhibitor and trader in films, also joined the organization, and its affairs were managed by Marvin, Kennedy and Waters.

Biograph's camera, designed to circumvent Edison's patents, used a film much larger than Edison film, and this difference in size carried with it similar differences in the mechanism of the projector. Biograph's large film registered good photographs which gave a superior quality of projection, but, as camera and projector were intricate instruments, requiring extreme care in operation, Biograph's early policy was to install its apparatus in theaters only when its own trained men could be in charge of operation; and of course its large film could not be used by exhibitors whose projectors were made in the Edison factory or were imitations of the Edison model.

THE PARADE of the movies in the first year or two of the screen was a bustling, hustling struggle of the paraders to keep abreast of the surge to exhibition rooms. Projection machines were coming too slowly from the Edison shops to satisfy the clamorous men who wanted to open shows, projectors were not for sale by Biograph and very few were obtainable from Lambda, still fewer were trickling into the market from abroad or from small new manufacturers at home. Edison and Biograph would neither rent nor sell cameras, and only an occasional French camera found its way across the Atlantic. No manufacturer anywhere was prepared to supply complete equipment for motion picture photography and screen exhibition. Film was obtainable from Edison and there was an increasing flow from abroad, but the demand was far in excess of the supply.

The longing of the people for amusement, now being satisfied for the first time in history by this weird novelty, caused more and more families to form the habit of visiting picture shows in back rooms and small upstairs halls. More and more of these show-shops were started in cities, and their apparent prompt success aroused desire in many men to obtain projectors and films and open exhibition rooms of their own. Other men, fascinated by the pictures themselves, became ambitious to obtain cameras and engage in photography. And still others were interested by the machines and wanted to try their hands at making cameras, projectors, and laboratory apparatus. Almost all of these ambitious, eager men were young; hardly one in a hundred had any money, or had access to capital; scarcely one of them was experienced in any commercial or industrial matters except those of the simplest nature; all of them were men of the people, or so closely associated with the people that they understood instinctively the public's deep desire for entertainment.

Where could they get the money to open a show, or buy a projector, or devise new machines? This was the great obstacle between them and attainment of their ambitions. Experienced, responsible men disdained the cheap show-shops. A request for funds to develop an idea for a camera or a projector would meet with nothing but laughter and scorn. Capitalists and bankers, if ever they had heard of living pictures, regarded them as something to amuse children; to invest money in any branch of such a business seemed to them absurd, and to run the risk of patent litigation with the powerful Edison interests by encouraging inventors was the height of folly.

However, despite all warnings and discouragements, in numerous small amateur shops, novices secretly labored to produce photographic and projection equipment, and while many of the results were thinly disguised imitations of the principles of Edison, Lambda, Armat, Biograph and Lumière, some of the experimenters created devices that were new and of real value, and the federal government granted many patents on arrangements of wheels and gears, sprockets and cams, loop devices to control the movement of film, shutters, lenses, and other contrivances. Due to the efforts of many ingenious minds, the mechanics and chemistry of motion pictures moved ahead, and within three years several new companies had entered the industry as makers of cameras and projectors or as producers of short pictures or as importers and traders in foreign films.

George Kleine, * importer and dealer in lenses and other optical wares, with headquarters in Chicago, was one of the first experienced, solidly established business men to recognize the commercial and social importance of living pictures; and he was, too, one of the first men of education and culture to partici-

* George Kleine died in New York in 1931.

pate in the affairs of the infant industry. He dealt in peep-show cabinets and films, and, when projection machines and cameras entered the market, added them to his line of merchandise, renting and selling both domestic and foreign products, including screen pictures, of which he became the largest importer. The necessities of his business kept him in touch with manufacturers of machinery and with producers and exhibitors of film in the United States and Europe, and his knowledge of pioneer conditions was broader than that of any other individual in the industry.

Edison, Biograph, and Kleine kept records of their operations, but other early manufacturers and traders were small and transient, and whatever records they may have made have since been lost, so that to establish exact dates and statistics of some details of screen history is difficult, if not impossible. In my investigations I have found George Kleine's records and data to be reliable, and he has told me that "1896 marked the beginning of all moving picture things in business."

For a year or two after 1896, the commerce depended largely on the rental and sale of Edison and Vitascope projectors, with a tiny stream from a few other inventors or imitators. The trade in films, at first confined to Edison and the American and foreign imitators of the kinetoscope, was expanded within two or three years by the entrance of a few new manufacturers at home and abroad. Little by little, under the pressure of increasing demand, a few cameras somehow came into existence, and anyone who could rent, buy, or borrow any form of "box" that would hold a lens and a roll of film could become a picture producer and enter immediately into the enjoyments of prosperity. The producer needed no experience or training in art, nor was he put to the trouble of engaging experienced actors or creating expensive artificial settings or scenic effects. All that was required was to set up the camera anywhere, "shoot" almost anything in motion, develop the negative, print the positives, and sell them at practically his own price.

Edison lawyers insisted that all inventors and manufacturers and all producers of films in America were operating in violation of Edison's patents. The lineage of each machine, they alleged, could be traced back to Edison's kinetoscope; and no matter how many devices might have been added, his machine was the father, or the grandfather, of the entire family. Threats of lawsuits did not, however, deter competition. The film industry had entered its first boom stage, and numerous men, deciding they would run the risk of litigation in preference to foregoing the opportunity of quick profits, continued their efforts to devise and manufacture machinery and to produce and trade in pictures.

Various moving picture projects bloomed quickly, and died so quickly as to leave almost no trace; impractical machines absorbed the slender capital of some of the promoters, a fire destroyed the models and patterns of one, and quarrels among partners disrupted others. A few individuals and small companies survived and wrote their names large on the early movie scroll.

JAMES STUART BLACKTON, a clever but none too prosperous painter, had two ways of adding to his income: one, which he called "chalk talks," consisted of a lecture and pictures rapidly drawn in view of the audience; and, when business was dull in lecture halls and on variety stages, and he was at home in New York waiting for engagements, he wrote special articles for newspapers and illustrated them with his own drawings. Tall, handsome, magnetic, with a rich, melodious baritone voice, Blackton always managed to keep busy at one or another of his occupations.

In lyceum and variety theater work he became acquainted with a youth named Albert Edward Smith, who followed the profession of public entertainer, usually as a magician; when stage engagements were not available, he fell back on his trade of book-binding. Smith was a quiet chap who liked to stay in his room at night, reading and thinking. After he and Blackton

became friends they did a lot of reading and walking and thinking and talking together. The earliest screen shows, coming at a
time when they had no stage engagements, received their earnest
attention, and, soon convinced that this form of entertainment
possessed almost unlimited possibilities, they searched for ways
and means of engaging in the alluring new business.

One day in 1897, Blackton went over to the Edison laboratory
in New Jersey to do a newspaper story, with pictures, about the
inventor, and before the interview ended Edison had agreed
to sell him a projector and an outfit of films for eight hundred
dollars. This was a huge sum of money for the two young men—
each was about twenty years old—to raise, and they had to beg
and borrow to get it; but they got it, and gave living-picture
exhibitions in theaters and halls in neighborhoods and cities in
which screen shows had not been opened.

Merely showing pictures did not satisfy them very long. Their
heads were full of ideas of pictures they would like to photograph, but no cameras were for sale or for rent. They talked
and thought, and thought and talked, and one day Albert Smith
made the discovery that the projection machine could be transformed into a camera—if he could invent several devices to make
it work properly. He invented the devices, the projector became
a camera, and Smith and Blackton were able to photograph
film.

Under the title of "Vitagraph," they became producers of motion pictures, photographing street parades, news incidents, prize
fights, dramatic episodes—any subject that would interest screen
patrons without involving the film-makers in too much expense
of production. Albert Smith's inventive mind kept at work and
evolved various improvements of the projecting machine as
well as the camera. Vitagraph had abundant energy and imagination, but it needed more capital to permit expansion.

In these years, Harlem was "way uptown," a district of quiet,
home-loving German and American families. One Hundred and
Twenty-fifth Street was its business center, and on this street
was a billiard and pool hall operated by William Rock, a cheer-

ful soul generally known as "Pop." Pop Rock was a showman himself, traveling summers and autumns with side-shows to country fairs, street carnivals and the like. He had been one of the first to sense the public interest in living pictures and had been showing them around the country in tents, halls, and small theaters. Smith, Blackton, and Rock merged their films and film machinery and cash in Vitagraph, as equal partners, their consolidated assets totaling perhaps three thousand dollars. This modest capital was enough to permit them to push their producing and trading activities vigorously.

Vitagraph instruments were based on the Edison system, and Vitagraph films therefore had an open, wide market with all showmen using the Edison type of projector. In time Biograph and all other manufacturers adopted the Edison film-size as standard, but in the early days, prior to this standardization, Vitagraph laid the foundations of a solid success.

While in New York Vitagraph was getting under way, in Chicago, two men, working separately, unknown to each other, were trying to invent cameras and projectors. One was William Selig, owner of a traveling minstrel show. The other was George K. Spoor, once a newsboy on a train, who had saved money and had become owner of a news-stand and had acquired interests in small theatrical ventures. Spoor had financed, to the extent of perhaps a hundred dollars, an inventor named Amet.

Sigmund Lubin, peddler of spectacles and optical wares and novelties, traveling the round of fairs and carnivals, had settled down in Philadelphia, and there was operating penny arcades and a small retail business in optical wares. With C. Francis Jenkins as his associate, Lubin was trying to devise projectors, cameras, and machines to print films.

Selig, Spoor, and Lubin each succeeded in manufacturing or acquiring his own instruments and each entered lustily into the business of producing screen movies, using film the size of Edison's.

Lumière, Gaumont, Pathé Frères, and Melies in France, and Paul and Charles Urban's Warwick Company in England, were rising to prominence as manufacturers of instruments and producers of films, and all throughout Central Europe other manufacturers of machines and makers of pictures were actively working to gain standing in the industry. European theater-goers enjoyed the novelty of living pictures, but as no arcade halls and back rooms were opened as cheap show-shops, the masses abroad had little opportunity to become acquainted with the new amusement, and European manufacturers looked across the Atlantic for the principal market for their short films.

WHILE the companies and individuals I have named were obsessed with the desire to make pictures, or to invent machines despite Edison's patents, scores of others were entering the business through the department of exhibition. Some of these were showmen who came from side-shows at circuses and county fairs and from small traveling dime museums, repertoire, and burlesque troupes. Some of them were ballyhoo artists and spielers who had become acquainted with country life in America through selling patent medicines from a buggy on small-town street corners, a gasoline torch supplying lighting effects, while the medicine vendor or his assistant drew the crowd with ventriloquism, magic, or songs.

Showmen of these classes were purveyors of novelties, real or alleged "genuine *new* novelties." They were perpetual wanderers, descendants in spirit of the mountebanks of previous centuries, and probably not one in a thousand of them ever had serious thoughts of settling down to the operation of a theater or any other business in one place. These men recognized in living pictures the novelty of their dreams. Here was the "quick clean-up" that would enable them to garner bushels of small coins, and their thoughts turned to exhibiting the new wonder in towns and villages where there were no music halls, parlors, and arcades. Anyone who could get a projection machine and a few films was sure of attracting throngs to small city theaters, town halls, lodge rooms, and country school houses. Some of the wanderers constructed tents with black tops—black to keep out the sunlight, thereby creating the darkness in which pictures could be shown—and made the rounds of county fairs and street carnivals. For a while black tops gathered in so many rural dimes that other side-shows suffered.

Many recruits to the exhibiting branch of the new industry came from New York's East Side, where scores of ambitious young Jews were restlessly searching for "access to the sources of wealth and power." They were quick to see the possibilities of the penny arcade and living pictures on the screen. Those who had money enough joined with partners in the purchase of arcades; those who lacked capital became ticket sellers, machine operators, ushers, anything in the show-shops to learn the business; and soon they were operating shows of their own.

Marcus Loew, a small fur merchant, bought a penny arcade; then a small theater, and another. He became acquainted with David Warfield, famous stage star, and Warfield listened with interest to Loew's enthusiastic predictions that living pictures would develop into an important industry. Warfield told his manager, David Belasco, of Loew's vision, and both invested money in Loew's project. Adolph Zukor, another modest trader in furs, put his savings, amounting to a few thousand dollars, into a partnership in arcade and parlor enterprises. A little later he became an associate of Marcus Loew, and presently embarked on operations of his own. William Fox, a garment worker on the East Side, was one of several partners in a picture show which prospered, and Fox left the garment factory to become an exhibitor himself.

Not only in New York, but in many other cities, were eager men fascinated by this new form of popular entertainment. Carl Laemmle was the manager of a clothing store in Wisconsin. His ambition to live in a large city and to operate a business of his own led him to Chicago to search for a suitable location. Out on the west side he found a vacant room that had housed a picture show. The location was satisfactory and the landlord offered to include in the lease the show's equipment of kitchen chairs, screen, and a batch of unused tickets, so that all the prospective tenant needed to make a theater owner of himself was to rent a projection machine and a mechanical piano.

The clothing man's business experience had been limited to retail shops, where it had always been necessary to "wrap something up for the customer to carry away." He was so startled by the idea that people would give money for something not represented by a parcel that far into the night he discussed with his wife the wisdom of attempting so odd a kind of merchandising. In the morning he sought the advice of Robert Cochrane, a bright young man who wrote advertisements and sold them "ready-made" with text and illustrations to clothing merchants. The advertising man encouraged him to rent the vacant show shop, and within a few days Laemmle was operating a theater. He kept it clean, he was polite to the customers. He succeeded so well that soon he had another house—and another.

During the earliest years of movie commerce, showmen bought the completed films outright from the manufacturers or importers, and "exchanged" films among themselves. For a few years this trading or exchanging of films among exhibitors was the only method of distributing motion pictures. Then men began to organize "exchanges," offices at which showmen could trade films they had used for films new to their patrons, and the practice of renting instead of buying pictures came into existence. The exchange became the jobber or distributor between manufacturer and retailer.

Joseph Brandt, clerk in a New York advertising agency, attended law school at night, and after admittance to the bar received one day a client engaged in the new film-exchange business. Brandt became so interested in the movies that he abandoned law and got a position with a small picture manufacturer. Two of his young cousins, Jack and Harry Cohn, starting as office boys in the agency, had progressed to important positions when the lure of the movies drew the older lad from the law, and the younger two followed their cousin in the search for success via the film route.

Tom Tally, Texas cowboy, rode into town one day after the round-up to see the sights and enjoy himself. A new kind of show attracted him—a phonograph parlor, with kinetoscope; Tally looked into each cabinet twice and heard every record several times before his astonishment subsided. He was a thrifty cowboy, and he left the ranch and put his money into a phonograph parlor. He prospered, and seeking a larger field, moved to Los Angeles and opened a parlor or two, and got into the exchange business on the side.

Patrick Ambrose Powers, born in up-state New York, became a salesman and then a dealer in mechanical pianos, phonographs, and other musical devices in Buffalo. Parlors and arcades lured him and he dropped his business to run peep-shows, soon moving into living pictures and exchange operations.

Richard Rowland had succeeded his father in the business of supplying calcium lights to theaters in the Pittsburgh district, this being in the days before electricity had replaced gas and calcium for stage lighting. When films made their appearance, he wisely adapted himself to changing conditions and used his connections with theaters to supply them with this new item of entertainment. Before long the calcium business had transformed itself into a movie exchange.

George Spoor opened an exchange in Chicago, Herbert and Harry Miles started one in San Francisco, and other men organized film-trading in other cities.

Producing, distributing, and exhibiting were beginning to develop into three distinct branches.

CHAPTER TWO

A NEW FORM OF THEATER

THE MANUFACTURERS of "raw stock" (unexposed negative and positive film), made their product primarily for amateur still cameras; motion photography remained an incident in their affairs for some time. The fifty-foot length established by the peep-shows was still being used, and the raw stock makers did not quickly provide laboratory equipment for longer strips. George Kleine places the achievement of long pictures—two hundred and fifty feet, or three to four minutes of exhibition—in 1900. Several producers immediately moved to the longer form, and material changes in screen shows took place.

Novel and ingenious incidents and events began to give way to pictures in which slender themes appeared, not constituting a real story, but marking a noteworthy advance in film technique. Street scenes, railroad trains, dancing, parades, were supplemented by storyettes: employer flirting with stenographer—kisses her—wife enters office and creates disturbance.... Dignified man strolling in garden with young lady, budding romance destroyed as man steps on hose which turns upward and splashes water in his face.... Magical pictures, produced by the double exposure of films, and other photographic tricks.... Automobile races.... Longer views of prize fights....

Slight as these changes seem, they required expansion of screen-producing organizations, and marked the first faint indication of a trend toward quality in pictures. Hitherto anyone could be an actor, almost any camera man could be his own director, and as no formal scenarios were needed for films of fifty feet, professional writers were unknown in the producers' small establishments. But now changes began to occur. Clever camera men or actors were designated as directors, and professional players were sought for leading rôles.

Henry Marvin of Biograph was in the forefront of the movement toward quality. He found or trained many of the best early photographers; actors to whom he entrusted the direction of playlets later became famous makers of photoplays; and he was, for instance, the first manufacturer to organize the writing of scenarios as a separate branch of production.

A young newspaper man, Roy McCardell, after seeing several living-picture shows, concluded that a new field of writing might lie back of the screen, and, calling at the Biograph office, asked Marvin if he did not need someone to prepare manuscripts.

"Indeed we do!" was the prompt answer. "Now we are depending for our stories on the momentary inspiration of directors, camera men, players or members of the office staff, and it's a great nuisance. If you can write ten scenarios a week for us I'll pay you ten dollars apiece, and if they are good I'll make the price fifteen."

"Let me have a typewriter and I'll do this week's ten now," said McCardell.

McCardell completed the week's requirements that afternoon, and became a member of Biograph's staff at a salary of $150— soon increased to $200—a week. At this time, early in 1900, newspaper wage scales gave reporters twenty-five to thirty-five dollars a week; none but the highest editors received such princely remunerations as $5,000 to $10,000 a year. The news of the gold field discovered by McCardell spread quickly among the scribes of the press, and thereafter they buzzed about the headquarters of film makers like flies around sugar barrels, and scenario writing soon became an occupation as definite as reporting.

For several years, two hundred and fifty to four hundred feet continued to be the customary length of screen playlets and storyettes, attempts to photograph anything more extensive being confined to reproductions of the Passion Play at Oberammergau or prize fights. Looking backward, it seems strange that the use of motion photography as a complete, definite, story-telling medium did not occur until 1903-5, eight or nine years after films became a screen show. Enthusiasts, enjoying the early living pictures, often wondered why producers did not expand into forms more ambitious than storyettes, and some of the alert young manufacturers were eager to experiment with complete plays, but the industry was so new and so unorganized that years had to pass before mass production of drama was realized.

In 1903, Edwin S. Porter of the Edison Company assembled a cast of players, borrowed a railroad train in New Jersey, and produced "The Great Train Robbery," a melodramatic story seven hundred and forty feet in length. Vitagraph and Biograph reached the market at about the same time with films that told stories, and other American, English, and French makers promptly followed.

Within a year or two the length of one thousand feet became standardized as "one reel," the screen time of a reel being about fourteen minutes, sufficient to present a short story or the essentials of a stage play. Mass production of the drama was accomplished by the one-reel movies. Crude, imperfect, cheap, made quickly and at low cost, they nevertheless contained the elements of drama—a story with a beginning, a middle, and an end; the characters represented by living beings, moving in natural action amid convincing surroundings, before the eyes of the spectators.

The obstacle of price was overcome by production in large quantities. Fifty, one hundred, any number of copies of a film play could be manufactured in a laboratory, packed into cans, and shipped to all parts of the globe, and a thousand or ten thousand screens could exhibit it. The machine-made drama could be retailed profitably for ten cents, the cost of admittance to a dime museum or a circus side-show.

In the early years there was no insistence upon quality in production or exhibition. The show-shops were adequate theaters; the audiences were not accustomed to the luxury of comfortable chairs, carpeted floors, and elaborate decorations; they came to see the pictures, not to admire the architecture and engineering. They didn't have to dress up to go to the movies and they didn't expect stylishness when they got there.

Any film that presented an interesting or amusing episode, or pictured a simple theme, was good enough to draw throngs to the store shows. For a while any camera that would expose film to a lens and produce any sort of wobbly, static-streaked negative would find buyers, and exhibitors had to be satisfied with projectors that would merely project. However, mechanical crudity did not last long; within a decade after film commerce had started, competent engineers and mechanics had smoothed out the roughest kinks in the instruments of the craft. The efficiency of cameras had been increased so that good photography in daylight was assured, and electric carbon lights had created acceptable photography within the simple picture factories. Projectors had been improved, and movies on the screen were ceasing to be "flickering monstrosities."

Changes in manufacturing methods were necessary to produce the long story-telling films of a thousand feet. Producers selected or so arranged scenarios so that as much of each picture as possible could be photographed outdoors, but more and more interior settings were needed as the playlets progressed in dramatic substance, and it became increasingly difficult for a director and camera man to "shoot the film" anywhere and everywhere. Factories—soon they were called studios—were needed; furniture and other properties had to be rented or bought; painted canvas scenery had to be stored when not in use; there had to be dressing-rooms for players, offices for directors and executives, and dark rooms in which negatives could be developed.

While a few producers organized themselves, with studios in loft buildings or large stables or warehouses or unused churches, to meet the requirements of the long films, other manufacturers continued with short subjects—episodes, comedies, and the like—of approximately three hundred to five hundred feet, and, depending on the momentary inspiration of the director, persisted in shooting wherever camera work was quickest and least expensive.

Numerous ambitious individuals, or small companies, attempted the production of pictures in and around New York, Chicago, Philadelphia and a few other cities. Usually these projects lived for a brief period, some times making only a few films before disappearing. But as soon as one passed from the scene another popped up.

The capital needed to become a movie producer was not increased much beyond the requirements of the first years of screen shows. When cameras became available—brought over from Europe or made in American machine shops—a producer could buy one, or occasionally he could hire a camera operator who owned his own instrument. The cost of scenarios did not advance materially, ten, fifteen, or twenty-five dollars remaining the standard price, and clever newspaper men could turn out more of them than they could sell readily. Some players were engaged by the week and received twenty-five to fifty dollars; the best of those employed from time to time were paid ten dollars a day, the rank and file getting five dollars, and "extras" —the men and women who appeared in "mob scenes"—two or three dollars.

The majority of the concerns were so casual, random, and unstable that orderly business methods were impossible. Each producer and each exchange fought lustily and unceremoniously to obtain for itself a big share of the golden flood; and commercial morals and ethics, as well as the laws of city, state, and nation, were forgotten by some of the contestants in their anxiety to secure and retain a foothold in this marvelous game of getting rich quickly.

THE Edison Company had not succeeded in its intent to control the manufacture of pictures through ownership of Edison's patents. While Thomas Alva Edison was indifferent to his kinetoscope toy and the screen shows that followed it, several other manufacturers and distributors obtained substantial footholds in the business, and when the Edison Company bestirred itself to active litigation against alleged infringers of its rights it had to meet the opposition of well-established concerns.

The Lambda company, which might have been organized to contend successfully with Edison, passed away before screen pictures became established, and in time its patents and claims were acquired by Biograph. Professor Latham disappeared from public view and died in poverty.

The most vigorous and progressive American competitors of Edison were Biograph and Vitagraph, each of which had equalled or surpassed the Edison studio in the production of films. Edison brought suits against them and against a dozen or so other smaller movie manufacturers in New York, later extending the litigation to include alleged infringers in Philadelphia, Chicago, and other cities.

Lubin was nimbly dodging around in Philadelphia and New York, manufacturing projectors and—so it was declared—cameras that used film the size of Edison's. He was printing positive films in a laboratory of his own with printing machines manufactured in his own shops, and was operating nickelodeons and trading in films.

William Selig, located in Chicago, was one of the most restless, alert, and persistent antagonists of Edison control. He had a sense of thrill-value that made his films successful. He was one of the pioneers in using cowboys, Indians, and other Wild West material, engaging an Oklahoma ranch foreman and town marshal, Tom Mix, to leave a position with Miller Brothers' 101 Ranch and Wild West Show to act in and direct one-reel westerns. Wild animals—lions, tigers, bears and wolves—were another source of Selig thrills, and he brought beautiful Kathlyn Williams to fame in a series of animal pictures in each of which

Kathlyn barely escaped with her screen life. In spite of the forays of Edison lawyers, Selig's business persisted in advancing. Max Aaronson, a vaudeville actor later known as G. M. Anderson, was one of the first to sense the demand for "westerns," and although never an expert horseman, his ambition and ingenuity made him internationally famous as a cowboy hero. His "Broncho Billy" films were shown on nearly all the screens in the world before Tom Mix or Bill Hart won their positions in the movies. "Broncho Billy" has another claim to fame, as he invented the "double" system in pictures in which the star appeared in the close-ups and a skilled cowboy or a trained athlete did the work of the exciting long shots. George K. Spoor and Anderson joined in organizing "Essanay" studios in Chicago, the name being formed from their initials, "S" and "A."

George Kleine became associated with a young newspaper man, Frank Marion, and an energetic sales manager, Samuel Long. With "K" from Kleine, "L" from Long, and "M" from Marion, they coined the word "Kalem" and made Kalem one of the foremost movie manufacturers. Kalem deserves its own niche in history for its production of "Ben Hur" in one reel, at a cost of a few hundred dollars, its action in using a novel and stage play without having obtained permission of the owners of the copyright resulting in a lawsuit and court decisions of noteworthy importance. Copyright laws, not having anticipated the advent of motion pictures, were very foggy for ten or a dozen years. Producers, following Shakespeare's method of taking their own wherever they found it, appropriated novels, short stories, and stage plays, and transferred them to celluloid versions without the formality of acquiring consent. Klaw and Erlanger, owners of the stage rights of "Ben Hur," and the heirs of General Lew Wallace, the author, brought suit against Kalem, obtaining an injunction against the exhibition of the picture. The higher courts decided that movie producers could not use copyrighted literary or dramatic material without consent of the owner.

IN THE get-rich-quick hurly-burly of these years, quantity was fundamental, and whenever quality appeared it was incidental and often accidental. The screen passed through three periods and entered the fourth before there was any systematic effort to attain quality.

While the novelty of pictures in motion was still drawing coins to peep-show cabinets in rural communities and city districts in which screen rooms had not been opened, movies entered into the second period of development, in which incidents were expanded or more scenes were photographed to acquire a greater length of film, but the type of subjects was not materially changed. Animation, action, speed, were the principal elements sought by the manufacturers.

This second period (films of two hundred and fifty to four hundred foot lengths), marked the development of the "chase" motif which has persisted for more than three decades as one of the surest methods of arousing spectators to a high pitch of excitement. A pursuit of any kind was sufficient to please picture patrons for a while, and chases covered a wide range, from hunters riding after a fox to comedy policemen racing after a grotesque tramp. However, the primitive enjoyment of mere pursuit was satisfied within a few years, and screen spectators demanded progress. The chase had to become a part of a theme or fragmentary story: the pursuit of Indians by white men, or of bandits by the sheriff's posse; or bound up with some exhibition of daring or heroism that aroused admiration of physical courage.

Almost equal to the chase in the affection of audiences were comedies, if the comedies were built on the situations and actions used as standard formulas for hundreds of years by clowns, jugglers, and mountebanks: a man hits another with barrel-stave; well-dressed man kicks hat under which a brick is concealed; dignified (preferably snobbish) man passes under ladder and bucket of paint falls on him; dude sits down in custard pie; waiter throws custard pie or any sticky mess at fellow workman, who dodges as well-dressed man suddenly enters scene and receives the pie in his face; and other similar situations. Physical embarrassment and downfall of dignity had been basic items in the recipes of funmakers for hundreds of years, and these elements were "sure-fire laugh-getters" when transferred to the screen.

Travel scenes in foreign lands were interesting, and so too were those classes of current events which later were definitely organized as "news reels" and became and have remained a standard feature of screen programs. Movie scenes of the Spanish-American War were a revelation, and in 1898-99 these were the first animated pictures to be seen by many people. A circular of the Edison Wargraph Company advertising "Edison's latest marvel, the Projectoscope" to exhibit the films at ten and twenty cents admittance, reveals the position of films during this period and the phraseology emphasizes the importance of novelty:

Edison's latest marvel, the Projectoscope. The giving of life to pictures so natural that life itself is no more real.

Life motion, realism, photographed from nature so true to life as to force the observer to believe that they are viewing the reality and not the reproduction.

If you have never seen animated pictures, don't fail to see this one. If you have seen them, see this one, the greatest of them all!

War views. All the best views of the Spanish-American War. Wonderfully realistic, thrilling and appalling.

Every American citizen should see this entertainment. Interspersed with the war views are many new and varied scenes of real life.

Satisfaction guaranteed.

Amusing—Instructive—Marvelous—bringing the whole world to your door.

"The Passion Play at Oberammergau" and its imitations manufactured in America and an occasional picture of a prize fight were almost the only attempts to produce movies of a thousand feet or more prior to 1903-4. The "Passion Play" was more than two thousand feet long, but this strain on the attention-capacity of audiences was regarded as justifiable because of the religious nature of the subject. Rather long prize fights (ten to twenty-five minutes), were exhibited because of the masculine interest in pugilism; and an occasional long magical story appeared, magic and fairy themes being regarded as involving no mental strain; but there is no indication that any pioneer movie manufacturer considered the possibility of popular demand for a secular story or drama as long as a thousand feet.

A marked change in the selection and treatment of subjects entered in the third period when pictures of three hundred to six hundred feet became common. Simple stories, or the framework of stories, began to appear, the central idea of producers continuing, however, to be the "instruction and amusement of the public with novel and ingenious" films.

Magical pictures and fairy stories, in which the camera was used to create illusions by double exposure of films and by various mechanical and chemical devices, won a moderate degree of popularity. The Jules Verne type of imaginative tale inspired fantasies such as "A Trip to the Moon."

The length and the subject matter of movies of 1902-03 are well represented by these descriptions, taken from advertisements of distributors:

"The Suburbanites," 718 feet; a comic film in seven scenes, which depict the experiences of Mr. Cityman and his family in looking for rest and happiness in the suburbs.

"The Lost Child," 538 feet; an exceedingly comical film, showing a series of laughable adventures which happened to a man suspected of stealing a baby.

"Impossible Voyage," 1075 feet. This exceptional film shows the fanciful adventures of a body of scientists, who take a trip on an impossible train under the sea.

"From Christiana to the North Cape," 426 feet; photographic reproduction of various places passed during a trip from Christiana to the North Cape. The film could be called "In the Land of the Mid-Night Sun," and shows some very artistic effects.

"The Adventures of Sandy McGregor," 292 feet. A very humorous subject showing the adventures of Sandy who is caught by two young ladies on a lonely beach while preparing to take his bath.

"Locomotive Races; Electricity vs. Steam," 266 feet; an unusual subject, showing the series of races between the powerful electric train which was tested by the New York Central Railway, and the regular Fast Mail Train. We consider this the most exciting as well as interesting railroad train scene that was ever made.

"A Race for a Kiss," 228 feet. This shows a pretty girl with rival lovers, one of them a jockey and the other a chauffeur. Both of them plead for a kiss and she proposes a race between the two for the prize. The race is run four times around the track with varying fortunes but the automobile finally gets the best of it, when a constable arrests the chauffeur for speeding, and the jockey wins the prize. Full of action and amusement.

"Avenging a Crime, or Burned at the Stake," 585 feet. This is a highly sensational film showing robbery and murder, the alarm, the chase, and final capture of the murderer, ending with the burning at the stake.

Romance and "sex appeal"—the latter term was unknown in the innocent opening years of this century—had not yet won for themselves a place on the screen. "A Race for a Kiss" was merely the chase motif flavored with a touch of romance. The following are other typical film offerings of the period, the titles of which clearly represent the contents:

"The Firebug, or a Night of Terrors." A highly sensational drama in moving pictures; 628 feet.

"Kit Carson"; 775 feet.

"The Moonshiners"; 960 feet.

"Indians and Cowboys"; 590 feet.

"The Trained Monkey"; 246 feet.

The various periods which I am indicating each overlapped the other, several years elapsing before the practices of one were entirely replaced by those of the next.

Porter's "The Great Train Robbery" and the story-telling pictures of Vitagraph and Biograph, appearing in 1903-4, may be used to designate the beginning of a fourth period, but story-telling pictures did not become general until 1906-08. From 1903 to 1910 the episodic films of the third period appeared on many screens; while on many others the new movies, telling a story in twelve or fourteen minutes, were gradually educating audiences to appreciation of longer, better entertainment. Improvement in quality had to come slowly or large sections of the public would have been driven away from the shows by complete stories or dramatic pictures before their minds were ready to receive them. While some audiences, or parts of audiences, were so far advanced that they wanted only long dramatic movies (twelve to fourteen minutes), many groups were not prepared for the mental concentration of anything more than three- to six-minute episodes and incidents for several years.

Picture makers and exhibitors were working in unexplored fields. No rules for their guidance were obtainable, and they had to experiment until they discovered formulas or patterns that pleased their patrons. The newspaper men and the actors who wrote scenarios for the first one-reel movies soon learned that experience in editorial rooms or on the stage was of limited value. Where formerly they had dealt with a few million minds approaching the top of the intellectual scale, they now had to arouse and satisfy tens of millions of mentalities that had been immune or semi-immune to the enlivening influence of the printed word and almost totally unacquainted with the spoken drama. The great usefulness of the screen proved to be that of supplying entertainment and stimulation to these middle and lower grades of minds. Had film quality advanced too quickly, vast groups would not have formed the habit of seeing the movies, and the story of modern American civilization might have been very different.

"Thrillers," principally those built around the chase motif, were the bridge across which audiences passed from episodes to story-telling. "The Great Train Robbery" and other action films were satisfying for awhile, and then the most active minds in audiences grew restless with repeated pursuits, and with comedies built on the crudest of antique structures, and with fairy and magical films. They wanted something different, and unless that something could be discovered and supplied many of them would cease to be customers of the little show-shops. The movie-makers blundered along until they discovered that romance was the recipe to sell more tickets at the box-office.

Woman—or, to be exact, girl, and a girl as pretty as possible

—ceased to be an incident in a chase, as typified by "A Race for a Kiss," and became the objective of the story. Stories of lawless years in the western states of America, when the white man was pushing his settlements across plains and mountains to the Pacific Ocean, supplied perfect material for a combination of pursuit, physical courage, and romance. There were villains, red and white, to supply menace to the heroine, and a wealth of obstacles could be placed in the path of the hero in his journey to save the damsel in distress. The "run to the rescue" could be filled with all the thrills of the chase plus all the emotions aroused by romance.

"Westerns," as they were soon designated by picture makers and screen followers, became the most popular form of entertainment ever known, although they did not reach the heights of success until 1909-10; and experiments in all sorts of themes were made in the intervening years. In a typical week in 1908, a large distributor handled eighteen pictures that were not westerns, and this was the division of subjects:

Human interest (or heart interest) dramas, one, of which this synopsis from the manufacturer's announcement is illustrative: "A little street vendor disposes of a box of matches to a well-to-do citizen, and unable to make change, leaves his wares in the latter's possession and hurries off to change the coin. On his return he is run over by a team and taken to his home, an attic room with a bed of straw, almost dead. As soon as he recovers consciousness he sends his little brother, a cripple, to return the change. The honesty of the lad brings a reward from the well-to-do citizen." This type of episode was the companion of stories told in Sunday School leaflets and religious journals.

Fairy and magical, three.

The Cinderella motif, two. These were often heavily soaked with human interest and heart interest to induce tears and sobs. Romance might be accompanied by melodrama, as in this subject:

A poor but proud maiden, reduced to poverty by misfortune, unable to secure work, is forced to beg in order to supply nourishment to her sick mother. At a resort she resents the familiarity of a man who has offered alms and is struck by the beauty of the maiden. She attempts suicide by asphyxiation, but the young man, overcome with remorse, follows her and is able to intercede in time to save her life. He leaves some coin with the mother and departs. The sincere repentance of the man wins the respect of the maid, and in the conclusion we see all principals of the story united in a happy home.

Travel, four.

Comedies: seven in which the ancient patterns were followed; four in which, in response to the new tendency, girls appeared prominently.

Changes in comedies were made very slowly, either in subject matter or technique. The comedy of situation—slapstick, custard pie, and other ingredients—made concessions to the comedy of character by including as players men and women with very fat or very lean bodies, crossed eyes and bulbous noses.

The length of comedies remained at three hundred to five hundred feet long after serious films were established at one thousand and two thousand feet. Many exhibitors believed that if children or sluggish-minded patrons were wearied by westerns and romances of twelve to twenty-five minutes screen-time, they would be refreshed and renewed by viewing six or eight minutes of comedy into which nothing new had crept since Noah led the animals off the ark.

Sex pictures were unknown in American studios, but naughty Europeans made experiments with this taboo subject in 1906-09. Any film touching on sex—to be exhibited in the United States— had to convey a wholesome, moral lesson, and this story indicates the technique of early movie makers in their efforts to introduce the problem drama to the screen:

A husband cruelly abandons his home, leaving wife and child to shift for themselves. The wife with the little daughter follows the husband and with abated (*sic*) breath are obliged to view him as he speaks of love to another woman, who is entirely oblivious of the misery she is unwittingly causing.

While the wife can endure no longer the perfidy of her husband, she comes forth with her child and confronts the guilty man. With the accusation against him ringing in his ears he sees his wife drop dead at his feet.

The love he craves is now denied him, and as atonement for his wrong he goes into seclusion.

The husband in this offering got away lightly, the almost inviolable rule of the screen being that a wrongdoer of any sort must pay a definite, severe penalty. Villains and crooks must be killed or at least captured and sent on the road to justice at the end of the film, or children did not get the wholesome, moral lesson assumed to be essential.

THESE episodes and simple stories were transferred to celluloid with the least expense possible. Scenario writers hustled their dramaturgical creations through the typewriters. Settings or sets—were obtained cheaply by painting scenes on canvas stretched across wooden frames, and were known as "flats." If a window, a clock, or a fireplace was needed it was daubed on the flat, and if a wind happened to blow through the studio while camera work was in progress, the fireplace, clock, and window waved gently on the screen. Directors assembled the best casts of players or near-players they could employ at low wages, and manufacturers were unhappy if more than a day or two was spent in shooting a film.

If any touch of quality happened to creep into the films—if the scenario was well written, if the director got an actor or an actress of ability, if the camera behaved nicely—no one objected to its appearance. There was no opposition to quality; there merely was no conscious effort to find superior stories, sets, acting, and directing. Writers, scene painters, players and directors were entirely free to do their work as effectively as they knew how, so long as their ambitions did not require any more film or cost any more money.

Films were sold by the foot; they were made by the foot; costs and profits were computed on a linear basis, and for a decade no one was ever bothered with the idea that perhaps audience intelligence might be moving toward an appreciation of something better.

SUPERLATIVES are needed to describe the success of the screen when films reached the story-telling length of a thousand feet. Living pictures had been eagerly accepted as a marvelous novelty, and now they had gone far beyond the bounds of novelty. An exhilarating form of entertainment had grown out of a mechanical plaything. Romance, adventure, comedy, thrills, and laughs, presented by living people in life size—this was fulfilment of the mysterious promise glimpsed by the populace when the first movies flickered blotchily on the screen. Their vague, indefinite dreams were coming true.

To the hundreds of thousands who had become screen enthusiasts in the years of episodes and storyettes, the story-telling motion pictures added millions. In every city and large town in the country so many customers appeared at ticket windows that there were not enough halls or upstairs rooms to seat them, and a new type of playhouse had to be created to accommodate the newcomers.

In the spring of 1902, Thomas L. Tally had opened the Electric Theater in Los Angeles, for moving pictures, the price of admittance being ten cents. Although the Electric was a success from the start, and other ten-cent "electric" theaters soon appeared in various parts of the country, it was merely the forerunner of a new, unique system of retailing popular entertainment.

Far away from the Pacific Coast, in the industrial districts of Pennsylvania, John P. Harris, trained in theater operation by his father, was managing a musée, curio hall, and variety show of his own in McKeesport, and was associated with his brother-in-law, Harry Davis of Pittsburgh, in various theatrical enterprises, when living pictures appeared. In April, 1897, they obtained a

Lumière cinematograph and introduced the new amusement to Pittsburgh and adjacent communities. The interest of both men in motion pictures carried them into continued exhibition and trading in films. Harris remodeled a store-room in McKeesport, giving it a gay, brightly colored, recessed front, and in June, 1905, opened it as a moving-picture theater, offering continuous performances from eight o'clock in the morning until midnight, at five cents admittance. In casting about for a name Harris merged "nickel," the popular term for the five-cent piece, and "odeon," the Greek word for theater.

The Nickel-Odeon presented a screen program of about twenty minutes' duration, accompanied by piano music, and the five cents admittance drew such throngs that the theater's ninety-six seats were constantly filled; on some days a thousand patrons would pack into the back of the auditorium and stand up to see the exhibition.

Harris' idea was immediately successful. From one end of America to the other, the common man and his wife and children literally poured into store rooms suddenly converted into theaters, and everywhere Harris' selection of a name, "nickel-odeon," was adopted by the public and became the general term for picture houses. *

Parlors and arcades were remodeled at moderate cost into nickelodeons by removing the peep-show cabinets and the partition across the back end of the room, and filling the entire store with kitchen chairs. If the front of the building had been taken out to make a wide-open entrance, the arcade owner now built a new front some distance back from the sidewalk line, thus making a large lobby in which posters could be displayed. The ticket booth was placed at the center of one side or the back, and when crowds besieged the theaters—as they usually did each evening—patrons could wait in the lobby or the mob could overflow to the sidewalk in the long lines that ever since then have been typical of movie theaters.

* The term "nickelette" was also extensively used.

Although no one can state precisely how many variety theaters were exhibiting motion pictures, or the number of halls and rooms that were offering film shows, when the nickelodeon craze swept the country, the reasonable estimate of the total would be a few hundred. Within a year after the opening of the first five-cent store show, a thousand or more nickelodeons were scattered throughout the country, and within four years there were eight or ten thousand.

With thousands of nickelodeons clamoring for films, exchanges multiplied rapidly, and soon there were a hundred or more wholesalers in about thirty-five cities in the United States. The demand for pictures was so great that distributors would buy almost anything from any producer, domestic or foreign, knowing that their rentals would yield a handsome profit.

Development of the exchange system established a route of communication from audience through exhibitor to distributor and producer, enabling the nickelodeon patrons to make their wishes known to the makers of pictures. If spectators enjoyed a film and applauded it, the nickelodeon owner scurried around and tried to get more like it, and if they grumbled as they left the show he passed on the complaints to the exchange, and the exchange told the manufacturer. In this simple way, and unconsciously, the American public began to take charge of the screen.

In addition to forming the habit of approval or disapproval of picture plays early in nickelodeon days, Americans discarded the Greek and Latin coined words used by inventors and manufacturers in describing their product. All the "kinetos" and "cinemas" and "vitas" and "bios" were set aside. "Living," "life motion," "animated," went too. "Movies," the American public named moving pictures on the screen, and this diminutive remained for many years the name of an entertainment enjoyed by more people than any other recreation in the long history of mankind.

"Movies,"—a new world for a nickel.

NOTE ON THE ILLUSTRATIONS

BETWEEN 1903, when the first story-telling film appeared, and the close of 1931, twenty-eight years have passed. During that period many thousands of motion pictures have been produced, almost any one of which contained scenes of interest. To choose an arbitrary number of stills from these thousands of pictures has been a fascinating, and difficult, task. The selection reproduced in the following pages has been made primarily to illustrate, in so far as it is possible by such means, the development of the motion picture in America, both as an industry and as an entertainment medium. The pictures were chosen to represent adequately the periods in which they were made, from the early days of one-reelers and open-air stages down to the great silent films of 1926 and 1927 and the talkies that followed them, as well as to illustrate my own text.

I can hardly hope that the selection will satisfy everyone, but with the wealth of material available in some instances, and the astonishing scarcity in others (where one had hoped for more), I have had to take what I could find and include as much as was practicable.

Credit is due *Photoplay Magazine* in all instances, save where another source is specifically mentioned.

I. THE FUNERAL OF PRESIDENT MCKINLEY, SEPTEMBER, 1901. THE FORERUNNER OF THE MODERN NEWS-REEL.

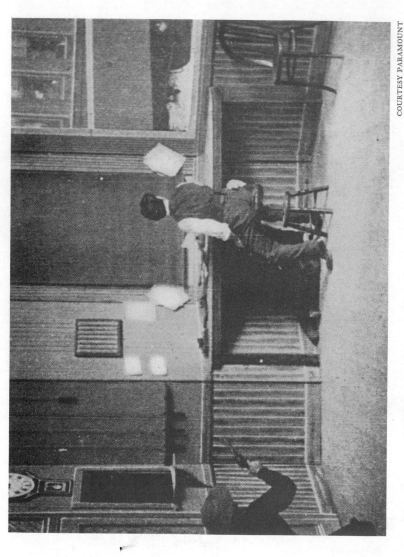

2. *The Great Train Robbery.* THE FIRST STORY-TELLING PICTURE EVER MADE, DIRECTED BY EDWIN S. PORTER FOR EDISON AND RELEASED IN 1903.

3. THE FIRST STUDIO OF THE BIOGRAPH COMPANY ON EAST FOURTEENTH STREET, NEW YORK, ABOUT 1908.

4. *Faust.* A ONE-REEL PRODUCTION MADE IN NEW ORLEANS, WITH JAMES MCGEE, JEAN WARD, HARRY TODD, AND TOM SANTSCHI. PRODUCED BY SELIG IN 1908.

5. THE FIRST SET IN CALIFORNIA, BUILT BY SELIG FOR A ONE-REEL PRODUCTION OF *Carmen*, 1908.

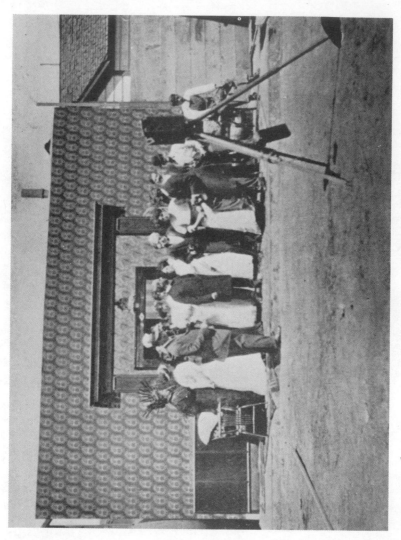

6. THE FIRST STUDIO IN CALIFORNIA, ESTABLISHED BY SELIG IN MARCH, 1908.

7A. *The Stage Rustler*. D. W. GRIFFITH (MAN WITH THE BARE ARM) DIRECTING AN EARLY BIOGRAPH PRODUCTION IN 1908.

7B. *The Italian Barber*, WITH MARY PICKFORD, MACK SENNETT, JOE GRAYBILL, AND MARION SUNSHINE. PRODUCED BY BIOGRAPH ABOUT 1908.

8. *The Life of Moses.* THE FIRST FIVE-REEL PICTURE MADE IN AMERICA. DIRECTED BY J. STUART BLACKTON. PRODUCED BY VITAGRAPH AND DISTRIBUTED BY GENERAL FILM CO. IN 1908.

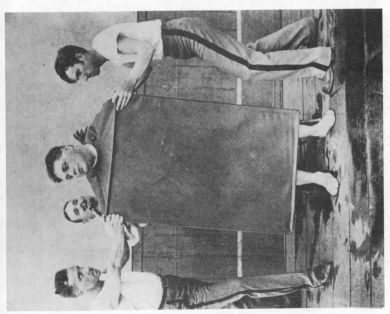

9A. *The Roman*, WITH HOBART BOSWORTH AND BETTY HARTE. THIS WAS BOSWORTH'S FIRST PICTURE, PRODUCED IN CALIFORNIA BY SELIG, 1908.

9B. *The Sanitarium*, WITH FATTY ARBUCKLE (IN HIS FIRST APPEARANCE) AND GEORGE HERNÁNDEZ. MADE IN 1909.

IOA. *Ramona,* WITH MARY PICKFORD. DIRECTED BY D. W. GRIFFITH.
PRODUCED BY BIOGRAPH IN 1908 OR 1909.

IOB. AN EARLY MARY PICKFORD PICTURE, WITH ARTHUR JOHNSON, DIRECTED
BY GRIFFITH FOR BIOGRAPH IN 1909.

11. UNIVERSAL'S FIRST OUTDOOR STUDIO, IN DYCKMAN STREET, NEW YORK, 1909.

12. MARIE DRESSLER IN A CHORUS-GIRL PICTURE OF THE PERIOD OF 1909 OR 1910.

13. *The Code of Honor*, WITH HOBART BOSWORTH AND ROBERT Z. LEONARD. PRODUCED BY SELIG IN 1909.

14. THE VITAGRAPH STUDIO IN BROOKLYN, NEW YORK, ABOUT 1910.

15A. *The Evil Men Do*, WITH MAURICE COSTELLO AND MARY CHARLESON.
PRODUCED BY VITAGRAPH IN 1909.

15B. *Dr. Lafleur's Theory*, WITH MAURICE COSTELLO AND CLARA KIMBALL
YOUNG. VITAGRAPH, ABOUT 1910.

16. THE WARDROBE-ROOM OF LUBIN'S PHILADELPHIA STUDIO, AROUND 1910.

17. SELIG'S CHICAGO STUDIO, 1910.

18A. *Ye Vengeful Vagabonds,* AN EARLY SELIG PICTURE, ABOUT 1909 OR 1910.

18B. *In the Days of the Thundering Herd.* TOM MIX IN ONE OF THE FIRST OF THE WESTERNS. PRODUCED BY SELIG, AROUND 1910.

19A. *The Fire Chief's Daughter*, WITH KATHLYN WILLIAMS. PRODUCED BY SELIG, 1910.

19B. AN EARLY "ALL-STAR" PICTURE, WITH HOBART BOSWORTH, TOM SANTSCHI, ART ACORD, EUGENIE BESSERER, HERBERT RAWLINSON, IRA SHEPARD, AND "DADDY" RICHARDSON. PRODUCED BY SELIG, ABOUT 1910.

20. A MEETING OF THE LEADERS OF THE GENERAL FILM COMPANY AND THE MOTION PICTURE PATENTS COMPANY. READING FROM LEFT TO RIGHT: 1. WILLIAM ROCK, 2. GEORGE K. SPOOR, 3. PETER HUBER, 4. J. A. BERST, 5. H. N. MARVIN, 6. SIGMUND LUBIN, 7. JEREMIAH J. KENNEDY, 8. ALBERT SMITH, 9. J. STUART BLACKTON, 10. WILLIAM SINGHI, 11. SAMUEL LONG, 12. THOMAS

21. REX INGRAM, LILLIAN WALKER, AND EARLE WILLIAMS, IN AN EARLY VITAGRAPH PICTURE, PROBABLY 1910 OR 1911.

22A. *Broncho Billy's Adventure*, WITH G. M. ANDERSON (BRONCHO BILLY). PRODUCED BY ESSANAY, 1911.

22B. *The Bearded Bandit*, WITH BRONCHO BILLY. ESSANAY, 1912.

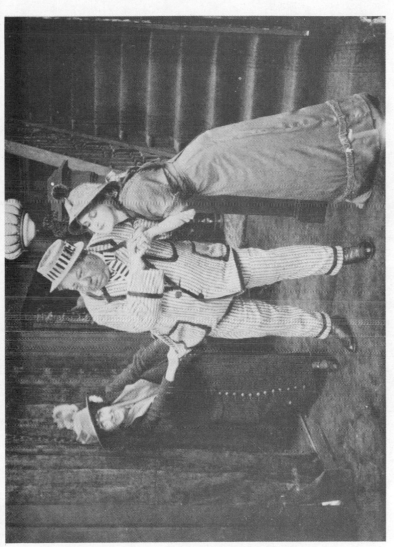

23. *Father's Flirtation,* WITH JOHN BUNNY, FLORA FINCH, AND MARY ANDERSON. PRODUCED BY VITAGRAPH IN 1912.

24. THE EDISON STUDIO IN 1912.

25. ESSANAY'S CHICAGO STUDIO STAFF, AROUND 1912. FRANCIS X. BUSHMAN, BEVERLY BAYNE, WALLACE BEERY, BEN TURPIN, AND OTHER STARS OF THE PERIOD APPEAR IN THIS PICTURE.

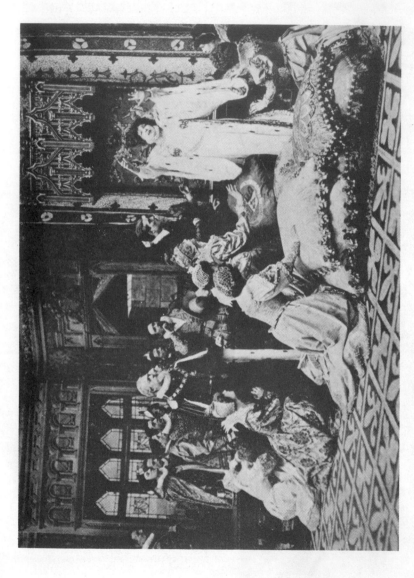

26. *Queen Elizabeth*, WITH SARAH BERNHARDT. THE FRENCH-MADE FOUR-REELER IMPORTED BY ZUKOR AND DISTRIBUTED AS HIS FIRST RELEASE IN 1912.

27A. *Judith of Bethulia*, WITH BLANCHE SWEET AND HENRY B. WALTHALL.
PRODUCED BY BIOGRAPH IN 1913.

27B. ANOTHER SCENE FROM *Judith of Bethulia*, WITH BLANCHE SWEET
AND KATE BRUCE.

28. JESSE L. LASKY'S FIRST STUDIO IN HOLLYWOOD, THE BARN DISCOVERED BY ROBERT W. BRUNTON IN 1913.

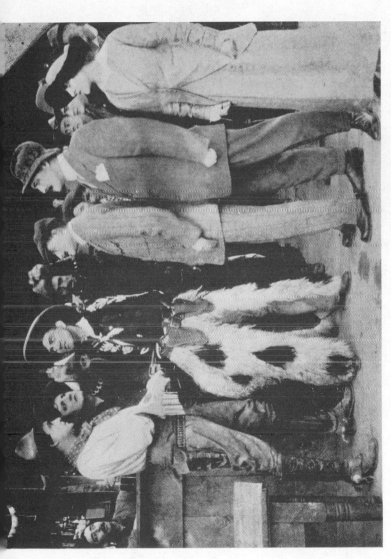

29. *The Squaw Man*, with Dustin Farnum, Winifred Kingston, Billy Elmer, Art Acord, and Monroe Salisbury. Directed by Cecil B. DeMille (His First Picture) and produced by Lasky in 1913.

30. *A Versatile Villain*, WITH LOUISE FAZENDA AND WILLIAM SHEER.
PRODUCED BY KEYSTONE, 1913.

FOR several years the nickelodeons were scarcely recognized by adults of the well-to-do classes, either as a form of entertainment or as a means of making money. While staid citizens and their wives ignored the store shows, or regarded them as undignified or foolish, their children accepted them joyously, and continually begged for the nickels necessary to obtain admittance. In the crowded, poorly ventilated nickelodeons, patrician youngsters sat with commoners and their offspring, democratically munching peanuts as they unconsciously created the great army of film fans that later was to dominate the screens of the world.

Successful business men, shrewd financiers, captains of industry, passed the movie gold mines day after day, and ignored them. They saw store fronts covered with noisy, gaudy posters, and that was all they saw. Vaudeville and stage producers and theater managers might easily have obtained important positions in the film industry in those early years, but with a few exceptions—such as John Harris and Harry Davis of Pennsylvania—they rejected it as a cheap, flimsy upstart, a nine-days' wonder that would repeat the history of the bicycle craze, sweeping the country off its feet and dying as quickly. They sneered at the "flickering monstrosities," and permitted the opportunity to pass by. Movies became the sole and exclusive property of those in the humbler walks of life.

Living pictures in arcade rooms and variety theaters had drawn hundreds of ambitious men into the new business, and had provided employment for a few hundred men and women, boys and girls, in film-producing studios and exchanges. But when, in 1905-10, the nickelodeon craze swept across America, and everywhere the nickels of millions of new theater-goers caused thousands of store shows to spring up, recruits were added to the industry by the thousands. The new theater owners and operators came from small retail stores, work benches, race tracks, newspaper offices, street carnivals, circus side-shows, "ten-twent'-thirt' " drama and minstrel troupes, law offices, railroads, garment factories, school teachers' desks, ministers' pulpits—from all sorts of modestly paid positions.

The distributors of pictures originated usually in the ranks of store-show owners, and the producers were men from these theaters or other small businesses. The scenario writers continued to come from newspapers or from traveling repertoire companies, and for several years the only actors and actresses who could be lured into studios were those unable to get regular employment on the stage, or stage-struck boys and girls.

These novices in the world of the theater sensed the deep desire of the populace for entertainment, and their very lack of experience caused them to create entertainment not too high in quality nor too high in price to satisfy their audiences. They had nothing to unlearn and, for the most part, were ignorant of the traditions they violated; they had no money with which to build fine theaters; and because of these very lacks, they served their patrons so satisfactorily that the movie business rushed ahead at lightning speed to become one of the most profitable industries in America, before those who had scorned its lowly beginnings had realized its importance.

CHAPTER THREE
QUANTITY VS. QUALITY

I N 1908-09, three individuals entered the motion picture world. So modestly did they arrive that no one suspected the influence they were to exert in changing the course of motion pictures from mere quantity production to a persistent search for quality in every department of screencraft.

One of the three was David Wark Griffith, a young man from Kentucky, who had been a newspaper reporter, an actor in traveling repertoire troupes, and had tried his hand at various other occupations. The others were a youthful Irish-Canadian widow, Charlotte Smith, and her daughter Gladys, who appeared under the professional name of Mary Pickford.

Biograph, having long since abandoned its wide negative for cameras of standard (i.e., Edison) size, thus making its films usable by all regular projection machines, was then an outstanding producer and its pictures were very popular. Griffith, with desire divided between writing and acting, had obtained employment at the studio as actor and scenario writer, and Henry Marvin, favorably impressed with his work, had given him an opportunity to direct some of the one-reel pictures that were a principal part of the company's output.

Before Griffith became a director, the industry had overcome many of its fundamental mechanical and chemical difficulties, and, although far from perfect, projectors, cameras, and other instruments were abundant; electric lamps for lighting indoor settings had been devised, and fairly good photography had become general. The principal energies of all studios had gone into intense efforts to keep abreast of the booming business, and while not much time or thought had been given to development of technical resources, these factors had made progress and were ready for a definite forward movement.

Scenic craftsmen had grown skilful, and were ambitious to build substantial settings, using lumber and solid composition boards instead of canvas flats that wobbled in a breeze. Some of them had dreams of screen productions more elaborate than anything possible under the limited conditions of the stage.

There were tools enough, there were material and personnel, there was a large, increasing market, but no master craftsman had arisen to consolidate tools, material, and personnel in the creation of better products. Griffith proved himself to be a master craftsman. His mind was stored with plots, situations, incidents, and his stage experience had taught him the tricks and the "business" of dramatic expression. As a director, he was daring in the use of his knowledge, never hesitating to try for the unattainable in story or dramatic effect.

Griffith was to work in a new medium: a strip of celluloid running through a box and registering sixteen photographs each second—still pictures, static portraits, each separate "frame" or section of film motionless in itself, but joined to hundreds of its fellows to create an illusion of motion. A trickery designed to fool the eye into believing that men and women were in action on the screen, when in reality six hundred and forty separate pictures were stopping and standing still and being illuminated each minute.

A still camera, aided by skilful lighting arrangements, can effectively conceal blemishes and lines, and can at least partially disguise unpleasant expressions. The portrait camera responds as cheerfully to the art of the photographer as does the society painter to the demands of the homely duchess. But the new brother of the still camera—this movie contraption, with its strip of celluloid clicking back of the lens—was a brutally honest thing that portrayed the duchess with her unmistakable wart, her eyes too close together, her big mouth and sloping chin.

Griffith had to deal with this inexorable iconoclast, this paradoxical device that created illusions of movement and destroyed delusions of personality. If he was to develop his art of studying man and presenting his studies to mankind through the medium of film, he must come to terms with the one-eyed magician in the box.

Many fascinating things were learned by the young director in his studies of the powers and the limitations of the movie camera. There was the interesting fact that each human being, unchanged by make-up or costume, presents at least three personalities: the man or woman talking with another, face to face, is not the person represented by the photograph registered in the still camera; and the movie camera, creating its illusion of motion by thrusting six hundred and forty portraits before the eye each minute, evolves a new personality differing wholly both from the actual person and from still pictures of him. The still camera was a marvel at concealing character; the movie camera was an uncanny instrument that impartially removed the masks from faces and revealed all sorts of hidden characteristics.

The camera was still as full of faults and distressing weaknesses as any intricate mechanical device in its early stages. Lens grinders had not learned how to acquire distance, speed, and clarity in their product. Film laboratories had to deal with the mysteries of chemistry. Special electric lamps had to be devised to light the players and the sets, so that the photography would result in good projection on the screen; and after electric lamps had been invented there were still unending experiments to be made in connection with lighting problems.

Camera angles presented another complicated study: the distance of the lens from the players so as to include the proper number of players to tell the story, point by point; the shifting of the camera from place to place, for the sake of emphasis; the use of the "close-up" in which the face or head of a single player is shown, for dramatic effect or to clarify the course of the story.

In addition to these purely mechanical problems, there was the difficulty of obtaining efficient players. Stagecraft was of some value, but Griffith soon found that its limitations were definitely marked. The primary object of the audience in a spoken theater is to *listen;* the mind cannot follow the speech of players and fully observe their expressions at the same time. Back of the footlights a pleasing voice, accompanied by appropriate movements of hands, head, and body, are usually enough to carry a rôle convincingly to the audience, even though the player's face has little range of expression.

When the close-up came into use, the motion picture camera revealed itself as an uncompromising realist that portrayed on the screen precisely what the lens found in front of it. The soft lighting of the stage, the skilful use of grease paint and rouge, the careful selection of wigs and costumes, enable the skilful actor to simulate youth long after he has passed his maturity. Sarah Bernhardt successfully presented "L'Aiglon" and other rôles at the age of sixty, and Eleanora Duse thrilled American theater-goers in the late autumn of her life. But the close-up ruined the reputations of the mature stage actresses who attempted romantic rôles on the screen.

Griffith's experiments convinced him that the best romantic screen artists would not be found among the famous heroes and heroines of the stage. He must get new material, young people whose youth and freshness could withstand the hard eye of the movie camera, and whose minds were not set in the rigid traditions of stagecraft; youthful faces, bodies, and minds that he could train into the new technique of the screen.

Chance brought to him a young stage actress, Mary Pickford, and Griffith was quick to recognize in her the combination of qualities for which he had been searching. The story of the most successful actress of the screen begins, however, not with

Griffith, nor with Mary herself, but with her mother, Charlotte Smith.

CHARLOTTE SMITH looked out of the windows of her small home in Toronto into a gray world. Her husband had just died; there was no money, and there were three babies that must be supplied with food and clothing and education, or the widow would lose them. A grim situation, enough to crush any young woman, but the Irish spirit in Charlotte Smith refused to be crushed. Her babies were more to her than all other things in life, and some way, somehow, she would earn money to support them.

She tried work of one sort and another, from sewing to keeping a small store, and always the wolf was close at her heels. By and by, there came the rumor that a small theatrical troupe needed an actress, and Charlotte, dressed in her best, applied for the position. Perhaps her perky smile, or the twist of the brogue as she declared to the manager "sure, I can act, and I can dance, and I can sing"; perhaps her small figure; perhaps all of these assisted. At any rate, Charlotte Smith went backstage and became a trouper.

Backstage with the young actress were the tiny Smiths, Lottie and Gladys and Jack. The two girls loved the life of make-believe and even as children often appeared in plays and helped their mother by looking after baby brother. Gladys' small fingers were always in the make-up boxes, and wigs and costumes were playthings with which to adorn her dolls. At the age of five, she was enjoying herself and assisting the family finances by playing parts.

There followed a procession of years in stock companies, when Charlotte Smith could rent rooms and make a temporary home for the children, and in traveling companies, when home-life was impossible; but she always carried her flock with her. The babies slept on wardrobe trunks in the dressing-rooms until the last curtain, and then Mrs. Smith would take them to hotel or boarding house and after tucking them into bed, would sew a dress for Lottie, or a shirt for Jack, or darn Gladys' stockings as she studied her part for next week's performance. After ten years of trouping, the Irish-Canadian actress found herself in a players' boarding house in New York. Gladys had become an experienced actress, and Lottie and Jack were seasoned players.

Charlotte had dropped "Smith," as lacking in box-office appeal, and the Smiths were known to the stage as "Pickford," a family name; "Mary" had been substituted for "Gladys." Each of the four had talent, and Mary had all the indications of the rare ability that sometimes manifests itself in a "child prodigy" and continues to grow with approaching maturity. She had developed stage personality. Not only was she pretty and possessed of a good figure—many girls have this equipment and do not succeed —but she had as well charm, magnetism, sweetness, "cuteness," and an uncanny knowledge of what to do to an audience to make it respond instantly to her demands. Living backstage from early childhood, busily absorbing the methods of the players with whom she worked, Mary never knew that she was learning to act. She acquired technical proficiency as naturally as she breathed, and part of her success on the screen was due to the complete absence of self-consciousness attained during the plastic years of childhood.

Charlotte Pickford believed in her children with the single-mindedness of a devoted mother, and dared to have great ambitions for them. The stage was her world and theirs, and in that world Lottie and Mary and Jack should succeed, and would succeed. Her own professional career was merely a means to an end; her rôle in life was to be a mother and put each of her children on the high road to fame. As her children's careers expanded, she took on the duties of manager, professional coach, and adviser, head of the household, administrator of finance and investments.

Mary, a veteran trouper at an age that finds most girls in grammar school, applied to David Belasco for a rôle and got it promptly. She continued on the stage for three years, all the time listening to backstage and boarding-house gossip about the new entertainment that was beginning to flourish in store shows. Mature troupers sneered at the tawdriness of the screen, "canned drama" being their most polite characterization of its offerings, and they all but ostracized the players who occasionally sneaked into studios and "picked up enough easy money" to satisfy a stony-hearted landlady. Mary Pickford listened, and gossiped, and heard all the trouper denunciations of films, and came to the conclusion that she liked the movies. She decided that the pictures made by Biograph were the ones she liked the best, and to Biograph she went to apply for a position.

Griffith met her, looked at her for a moment, and led her back to the set and put her to work—at five dollars a day. She instantly proved the soundness of the ambitious director's theory that he must bring youth, plasticity, and elasticity before the merciless eye of the camera. Mary had these qualities. Through her, Griffith was enabled to introduce into motion pictures the kind of acting especially suited to the camera, and between them they established standards that were of incalculable value in the development of screencraft.

Griffith worked with his scenario writers to smooth out the glaring implausibilities of their stories. His players were selected to "type" their parts, to look like the characters they were portraying. He directed seasoned stage actors away from the stilted, artificial, bombastic technique which had persisted in spoken drama from the days of Shakespeare, and younger players he trained in methods of naturalness, smoothness, and realism. His camera men, encouraged to push lens and film and lighting effects into unexplored territories, began to discover that the camera was not merely a means of photography but could be made to play an important part in the dramatization of a story.

Although the names of directors and players did not appear in the films nor in the advertising posters of those days, and there was no way to identify Griffith's work, so many nickelodeon patrons decided that Biograph's pictures were the best that Biograph forged ahead to a commanding position in the industry. Mary Pickford was so popular that before her name appeared in movies she was known to millions of admirers as "the girl with the long curls," or as "Little Mary," the character name most often used in her films. Mary Pickford was a "box-office drawing-card" before her name was spoken outside the Biograph studio.

Vitagraph was neck and neck with Biograph in the race for quality and supremacy, and the early directors and players of these two companies fill a large section of the movie hall of fame. Griffith discovered not only Mary Pickford, but Lillian and Dorothy Gish, Blanche Sweet, and a long list of other boys and girls afterwards to become celebrated players and directors. Florence Turner, Maurice Costello, John Bunny, Clara Kimball Young, Norma and Constance Talmadge, Anita Stewart and Alice Joyce are only a few of the many Vitagraph players who later achieved stardom.

WHILE efforts toward quality were thus beginning to replace novelty and quantity in the manufacture of movies, movements toward better methods in the exhibition of pictures and in the administration of the industry were also beginning to appear. At this time there was no co-ordination between any of the branches of the business. There existed, in fact, the exact opposite of co-ordination. All elements were running wild, with nothing resembling sober business conduct apparent anywhere except in the operations of the few large corporations. The industry as a whole was in a condition that might be described as anarchic save that anarchy presupposes the previous existence of some form of organization, and the film world had never known the meaning of organization.

During the brief dozen years of the screen's life, there never had been a moment that could be devoted to a consideration of organization of the elements composing the industry. From the time that movies made their first appearance in low-priced exhibition rooms, the public demand had increased so rapidly and persistently that every department of the infant business had been in a money-mad turmoil. Ten million—maybe twenty million; no one knew how many—new entertainment buyers had suddenly appeared in all parts of America, and were pouring their nickels into the ticket-windows. The small coins of the masses had created, within a decade, a business larger in volume than that of all spoken-drama theaters, dime museums, variety houses, lecture bureaus, concert halls, circuses, and street carnivals combined. Experienced purveyors of entertainment and amusement were dazed. There were no precedents by which such an extensive public movement could be appraised. Not only were movies new to the world, but this surge of millions of people to ticket-windows was something incomprehensible, incredible, fantastic. It could not be real—or if, by any chance, it was real, it could not endure. Soon the appetite of this vast new public would be satisfied, the craze would die, the nickelodeons would be empty, the movie business would be "busted flat." Everyone in the film business worked in feverish haste to grab a share of the golden floor of nickels before the inevitable day of reckoning. If anyone during the first decade of motion pictures made an analysis of the entertainment hunger of the great public and concluded that the movies had come to stay, he failed to leave a record of his observations.

By 1907-09, half a dozen film-producing corporations in America had become well organized, and in addition to these larger companies there were a hundred or more other concerns engaged in producing pictures, or importing them from Europe, or exchanging and trading in domestic and foreign pictures; still other companies and individuals were inventing and selling cameras, projectors and other instruments to photograph, develop, print, and exhibit film. Many of these manufacturers and traders were small, irresponsible, and transient, but each contributed his share to the confusion existent in the industry.

Movie factories operated in and around New York, Chicago, and Philadelphia, and occasional attempts were made to produce pictures in a score of other cities. Some of the larger manufacturers maintained exchanges of their own in the most important cities or established systems of steady operation with the more responsible distributors. Forty or fifty exchanges were equipped to function effectively, and scores of individuals always were trying to enter the business by getting a few films and cutting the prices of the "big fellows."

From the producer, through the exchanges, the pictures were exhibited to the public in ten thousand nickelodeons. A few spoken-drama theaters had been changed into movie houses, and several hundred variety theaters, beer gardens, and dime museums used films as added attractions. The utmost confusion permeated the exhibiting branch of the industry. Here and there, scattered throughout the country, were a few store-show owners of intelligence, good taste, and sound business sense, who were struggling to elevate the tone of the business. In competition with this handful of progressives were nine or ten thousand other exhibitors who were working their way up from the lowest levels of commercial and industrial experience. Quality in business or in anything else was a subject with which they were not familiar.

Many of the store-show owners were immigrants who had been operating cheap lunch rooms and restaurants, candy and cigar stores, and similar small retail shops when the film frenzy began to inundate America. Few of these foreigners could read or write English, and although many of them later learned the language of their adopted country, some of them were never able to read or write after they became millionaires. Foreigners and native-born alike followed parallel paths in entering the movie field. A small retailer, or a fiddler in a bar room orchestra, or a mechanic, or a bookkeeper, or a hanger on of racing stables, or a traveling salesman, or any other man of limited means, would decide that a nickelodeon could be made to pay in a certain locality, and would discuss the subject with one or two friends. They would calculate the cost: rent of the store room, rent or purchase of fifty or a hundred wooden chairs, a mechanical piano, a projection machine, rental of films. They could estimate the number of tickets that could be sold weekly. There seemed to be no doubt that the intake would exceed the outgo.

Often two or three or more men would "chip in" to raise the few hundred dollars needed for the undertaking. One partner would give up his wage-earning job, or sell his little store, and become manager of the theater, the others continuing with their customary methods of earning a living until the show-shop was firmly established. Then, they, too, became operators of five-cent houses, or went into exchanges, or into a new producing company.

Many of the nickelodeons were family affairs, managed by the father, with the daughter selling tickets and the mother taking them at the door, while the son ran the projection machine or directed patrons to vacant chairs. Whether partnerships or family projects, each store show had two to five people keenly interested in its weekly sales of tickets, and thus an army of perhaps forty thousand keen, money-hungry human beings were engaged in a mad-house scramble to acquire fortunes through this fascinating new business of selling cheap entertainment.

Suspicions, jealousies, hatreds, kept members of the army in daily turmoil among themselves and with the exchanges and manufacturers. There was no standard of film rental or film sale prices, and all the time each exhibitor suspected that a competitor was getting better terms than the exchanges charged him. Contentions, demands for rebates, and quarrels with exchange managers were daily events, and so, too, were suspicions that a partner was preparing to slip out and open a competing show and take the most efficient employees with him. Jealousy of the success of neighboring houses, constant scheming to be the first exhibitor to enter a new, desirable district, or to get a store show away from a competitor when his lease expired, filled any unoccupied corners in the showman's brain.

Knowledge of commercial ethics had to be acquired slowly by many members of all three branches of the industry, and for years their common willingness to take short cuts on the road to fortune made honorable business dealings extremely difficult for the manufacturers of equipment, producers of pictures, distributors, and exhibitors who wanted to be honest. One of the common practices of the early years was the "duping" of negatives: a distributor or exhibitor would rent a positive print (the duplicate of the negative, or original film); then he would send the positive to a crooked laboratory and have a negative photographed from the positive. The "duped," or duplicated, negative could be used to supply prints, which an exchange would sell or rent to exhibitors. To circumvent this practice, a few producers for a time tried the expedient of painting their trade marks on the sets and photographing them into their productions, hoping —in vain—that audience recognition of their product might frighten the "dupers" and shifty exhibitors into paths of commercial rectitude.

Another dodge of slippery exhibitors was the habit of "bicycling" prints. A group of theaters, under one ownership or associated for mutual profit, would rent a picture for exhibition at one theater, but would arrange the schedules of two or more screens so that a boy on a bicycle could race from one store show to another with the print under his arm. Thus, Theater A screened the film at 7; Theater B had it at 8, Theater C at 9, and with luck it reached Theater D at 10. The manufacturer and the distributor received rental on one theater; the exhibitors "grafted" the other showings.

There was need of quality in administration of the entire industry as well as need of quality in production. The need was felt by intelligent men in all departments, but no concerted effort was possible in a business national in scope, embracing thousands of separate units, each hostilely independent and bitterly suspicious of everyone and everything that threatened to hamper the progress of its individuals toward the goal of wealth and glory. Improvements could not come from the top—there was no top! They must come from the rank and file of the democratic mob that ruled the industry.

Griffith, steadily improving the quality of motion-picture production, had his counterparts in the nickelodeons and exchanges.

One of the most noteworthy of these youthful novices in the business of entertainment was William W. Hodkinson, a railroad telegraph operator in Ogden, Utah, and an ardent patron of the movies, who became convinced that if a store show was kept clean and fairly well ventilated, and if a reasonably efficient pianist replaced the amateurs and cynics who pounded the ivories, people would pay ten cents instead of a nickel for admittance. When he advanced his theory to nickelodeon proprietors they treated it with disdain. One exhibitor scornfully suggested that the telegraph operator buy a store show of his own, declaring he'd learn soon enough that a nickel was the limit people would pay. Hodkinson did that very thing. Pooling his savings with those of some friends, he bought a nickelodeon, cleaned it up, aired it out, discharged the honky-tonk pianist and his cold cigaret, and operated it in accordance with his own ideas.

To the intense surprise of most exhibitors, the "mob" that would not appreciate a "clean, decent show-shop if they had it" promptly responded to the Hodkinson idea, and soon Hodkinson's ten-cent theater was selling more tickets daily than the nickelodeons. Skeptical exhibitors quickly understood the message of doubled profits! The idea of quality in the form of better-managed theaters spread across the country, and in hundreds of houses the dime replaced the nickel as the price of admission.

The "plaything for children of all ages," the "cheap show for cheap people," the "flimsy amusement for the mob" (these are only a few of the disparaging terms used by critics of the period), had already grown to unbelievable proportions. Now, instead of losing its vast patronage when its cost was doubled, it tapped new and larger reservoirs of small coins. Not only did dimes instead of nickels pour into the better theaters, but more throngs of customers formed the habit of "going to the movies."

Better pictures, created by Griffith and other producers, and better exhibition, made possible by Hodkinson, Tally, Laemmle, and a few other men throughout the country, gave tremendous impetus to the infant industry and its infantile art. Newspapers had compared "the movie game" to a gold rush a few years before; now the glowing phrases of the press agent were inadequate to describe the movement. The volume of business increased, profits increased, the number of theaters increased, larger store shows began to appear, and new recruits poured into the ranks of manufacturers, producers, and distributors.

MEANWHILE, conditions in Europe were taking a different course from the development in America. Edison's neglect to register his kinetoscope patents abroad permitted foreign makers to copy his instruments without fear of litigation. French, English, Italian, and German manufacturers were rapidly making cameras and projectors, and their business was growing. Nevertheless, the rigid European social order operated very effectively to prevent anything like the extraordinary spread of movies that had occurred in America. Even more than in this country, the theater and the opera in Europe had always been exclusively upper-class entertainments, while the variety houses and music halls served for the middle class. In some countries, notably Italy and Germany, there was an abundance of cheap music in the wine shops and beer gardens. In Spain the bullfights supplied amusement for all classes, but nothing else in Europe even approached the idea of entertainment for all the people. The populace in general went without theater amusement, but as it had been trained for centuries to passive acceptance of its place in life, there was no searching for entertainment such as that which moved the restless American public to prompt adoption and development of screen shows.

When the film left the peepshow cabinet and appeared on the screen, thereby becoming the "cinema" in Europe, pictures became a part of variety-theater and music-hall programs. The price of tickets remained at the usual level of such houses and movies became no part of the common life. Nothing like the store-show movement or the nickelodeon ever occurred in Europe. Moreover, the Continental tax system would have defeated such a movement, as all theater tickets were highly taxed as a luxury, something that did not reach this country until after the World War was under way, and then only as an emergency measure. The home market thus remained relatively small for European producers and they were soon forced to look for new outlets abroad. For several years, most of their productions found their way to the United States, where, owing to the widespread and continually increasing popularity of pictures, the demand for films and film machinery was far in excess of the supply. But when Yankee manufacturers began to secure cameras and to produce American movies with American themes, the interest in foreign-made films soon subsided and the market declined. Pathé Frères sent J. A. Berst to this country to sell films and to investigate conditions in general; upon his recommendation, Pathé established a studio and laboratory in New Jersey and embarked on production and distribution in accordance with American methods. Melies, another French company, opened a New York branch to distribute its French product, and was successful until the demand for foreign films died out. Many European producers, directors, actors, and camera men came to the United States and entered the industry here.

The loss of the American market, combined with the absence of cheap theaters, brought the industry in Europe face to face with economic conditions that never obtained here. Some of the producers withdrew from the business. Others proceeded on entirely different lines, turning their energies to the making of photoplays for the classes rather than the masses, and thereby initiated a development which has been wholly different from the course of the American movie.

CHAPTER FOUR

THE MOTION PICTURES
PATENTS COMPANY

VIOLATIONS of Edison's patent rights, and allegations of
violations, increased in proportion to the general prosperity of
the industry in America. Cameras had to be acquired by men
who wanted to make pictures, and without projection machines
no screen show could operate. If cameras and projectors could be
obtained legally and at prices satisfactory to the buyers, they
would obtain them legally; if legal machines were hard to get,
or if the prices seemed too high, many men were willing to
traffic with illegal makers and dealers. "Bootleggers" of movie
equipment, raw stock, and completed films violated the patent
laws as nimbly and cheerily as the liquor oligarchy later scorned
the Volstead Act.

The Edison Company instituted lawsuits against all American inventors and manufacturers concerning whom it could obtain evidence of the use of alleged illegal cameras, projectors,
and other instruments, but the Edison lawyers might just as well
have attempted to enjoin a swarm of seven-year locusts against
entering a grain field. The irresponsible little offenders skipped
around like fleas, selling their machines and devices and films
to buyers who would take a chance of making profits before the

law could reach them. The several large manufacturers who had become successful and prosperous during the decade of strife and confusion in the industry had no such mobility; unable to evade process servers or fail to appear in court when their names were called, they were compelled to fight the Edison Company to the limit. If Edison's claims were sustained by judicial decisions, they would have to pay heavy damages and operate under licenses granted by the Edison Company, or else close their studios.

After Edison had lost interest in kinetoscope experiments, and Dickson, Latham, Armat, Albert Smith and other men had invented many devices to project pictures, to improve cameras, or to design new machines, most of the useful inventions had been acquired by the important studios, so that each principal producing company had become, in practical fact, a manufacturer of motion-picture instruments, in whole or in part, in addition to being a manufacturer of motion pictures. Each company, such as Biograph, Vitagraph, Selig, Essanay, Gaumont, Lumière, and Pathé, had a list of patents, and each contended that its patents gave it certain rights which enabled it to continue in business without the consent of Edison or any other patent holder. Some of these alleged rights were declared by Edison lawyers to be frail, but others were substantial, and until the Supreme Court could pass on the claims and counter-claims, the position of none of the litigants would be definitely established. In addition to the few real inventors and owners of legitimate patents, there were crooks who stole everything stealable. Cameras and other equipment were rented, borrowed, or stolen, and then taken to machine shops to be copied exactly or closely imitated.

The larger manufacturers, in addition to fighting against Edison, fought the crooks, and fought bitterly and constantly among themselves. A fourth of a producer's time and thought went to the making of pictures, and three-fourths were absorbed by legal battles with big and little competitors who sought to imitate his inventions or averred that he was stealing theirs. Every minor appliance and improvement became the subject of bitter controversy and litigation. The studios were turning out at least as many damage suits as movies. For a dozen years the industry was a battle ground, filled with intense hatreds and constant guerrilla warfare, and the mass of movie litigation grew to be so great that a regiment of lawyers was needed to follow its intricacies through the courts. The business itself was prosperous —people were anxious to see pictures—but inventors, producers, distributors, and exhibitors were so inflamed with enmities and bewildered with strife that administration of the industry became almost impossible.

When collapse, or total insanity, seemed to be the only end in sight, George Kleine suggested to Vitagraph, Edison, Biograph, Essanay, Kalem, and Selig that there was neither joy nor profit in spending their incomes on lawsuits.

"Why not pool our patents in one corporation and issue to ourselves licenses to manufacture motion pictures? Combinations in other industries are very successful. Isn't it good sense for us to end this warfare by getting together?"

After some months of discussions, this practical suggestion met with approval. A survey of the field indicated the desirability of including Sigmund Lubin, who claimed valuable patents and had created an important film-producing business in Philadelphia, and Pathé Frères and Melies, the two French companies that had opened branches in America and had patent claims and trade positions of value.

In January, 1909, these nine manufacturers, together with George Kleine, came together in the "Motion Pictures Patents Company," and turned into this corporation all of their patents. For mutual protection each of the nine parties acknowledged that Edison's kinetoscope patents were legal and fundamental and agreed to pay to Edison a royalty for the right to operate under them. Edison acknowledged the legality and soundness of various patents owned by other members of the merger, and all parties agreed to compensate the several owners for the use of their devices. The patents company issued licenses to the ten parties in the merger to manufacture movies under all the patents and with all devices owned by the corporation. No other licenses were to be granted.

There were other manufacturers and importers of machinery, equipment, and pictures in existence at the time; all told, perhaps fifty or a hundred others, but none of them was considered of sufficient importance to be included in the merger. An examination of inventions and patents by engineers and lawyers apparently proved that its control of machinery, equipment, processes, and patents was complete, or so nearly complete, that motion pictures could not be successfully photographed, developed, printed, or exhibited without consent of the Motion Picture Patents Company. Although the corporation was regarded as an "airtight trust," its lawyers declared that its formation was entirely legal, because it was founded on the rock of patents protection. Other industrial combinations might have to worry about the Sherman Anti-Trust Law, but, said its legal advisers, the Motion Pictures Patents Company might enjoy an impregnable monopoly in its field by virtue of the patent laws of the United States, Great Britain, France, Germany, Italy, and other countries.

The patents combination, born in a time of guerrilla warfare, was a fighting machine, and its owners did all in their power to enforce their monopoly and to enjoy its privileges to the utmost. It seemed to have a legal position and an industrial supremacy that the most ardent monopolist might envy. Apparently all that its members had to do was to sit tight, make movies, rent them at the highest possible price, and enjoy the profits. Theaters were crowded with patrons, and more shows were constantly being opened in stores and in outdoor summer places. Dimes were replacing nickels at the ticket-windows everywhere. Film commerce in America was growing at the rate of twenty-five million dollars or more a year, and American movie manufacturers were developing their export trade in Europe, Asia, Africa, and South America.

One reel had become the standard unit of the screen. The reel might consist of one play, or it might be a "split reel," composed half of comedy and half of travel or scenic pictures. Some exhibitors gave a show an hour in length, requiring four or five reels; others gave two-hour shows requiring seven to nine reels. The program in each theater was changed daily, so that about thirty to sixty reels a week represented the needs of exhibitors. This volume of pictures distributed among the ten manufacturers of the patents company necessitated the production or importation of three to six reels a week by each member.

To produce three to six reels each week, a manufacturer needed an adequate studio and a reliable organization, and, since the patents company had included in its membership all producers as well equipped as this, there seemed to be little or no chance of serious competition from any source. All of the producers omitted from the merger were small, and the quantity of their product was random and irregular. Some of the independents might have accomplished an output of one or two or three reels a week, but all of them joined together would have been unable to supply daily changes of program to all theaters. Exhibitors, therefore, apparently had no choice—they must accept the prices and terms of the patents company, or try to obtain from independents enough pictures to fill their screens each week. Those who acceded to the trust's stipulations were assured of an adequate supply to maintain their houses; those who did not were in danger of having nothing to exhibit to their patrons.

When trust officials analyzed the distributing branch of the industry, they found a number of well-organized exchanges in thirty or forty of the larger cities, and a motley crew of small film traders, each with a more or less irregular turn-over of reels obtained from small American producers or brought from Europe by importers. As in producing, there was a limited number of fairly sound business houses, and a noisy lot of ragged hangers-on.

Each of the manufacturers licensed by the patents company had his own arrangements with various exchanges, and for a while these distributing arrangements continued, but the patents company soon learned that regulation of the exchanges was extremely difficult. During the several years of unbridled competition, the many new producers constantly appearing in the industry, even though they lived to make only a few pictures, had enabled shrewd distributors to profit handsomely by playing one manufacturer against the over-abundance of others. Through its ability to influence, usually to determine, the price to be paid to the producers and the rentals to be charged to exhibitors, the wholesaling branch of the business had acquired the balance of power, and prosperous exchange owners were very unwilling to accede to any conditions that interfered with their freedom. They evaded or defied trust regulations, and many of them were suspected of giving preference whenever possible to manufacturers not licensed by the patents company.

For about a year Jeremiah J. Kennedy of Biograph, president of the trust, tried to bring the recalcitrants into line, and then the patents company decided it must create a distributing company under its own control, the profits to go to its licensed producers. The ten manufacturers organized the "General Film Company," each manufacturer owning one-tenth of the common, or voting stock, and each having equal representation in the board of ten directors. General Film officials permitted the rumor to spread through the industry that it planned to establish its own system of exchanges by purchasing wholesalers in some cities and by opening its own distributing offices in others.

General Film's survey of exchanges was so complete and accurate that some of the rebellious distributors, summoned to conference with trust officials, were startled to have the innermost records of their businesses spread before them. General Film offered to purchase the exchanges it regarded as the best, and about sixty owners accepted the offers. Independent distributors left out of General Film were compelled to look to independent producers for their films, or shut up shop.

The ten thousand or more exhibitors comprising the third branch of the industry did not inspire any deep respect in trust headquarters. The business men, engineers, lawyers, and scientists who were the real rulers of the patents-film combination regarded most of the show-shop keepers as a "rabble" of small retailers lacking ability or inclination to get together for united action on anything. Many of the exhibitors could be dismissed as "gypsies and bunco artists" recently graduated from circus and county-fair side-shows; the majority was regarded by trust officials as unworthy of any greater consideration than had been shown the small producers and distributors; the few solid, substantial men in the theaters were easily distinguishable, and of these the trust proposed to make friends, letting the rest shift for themselves.

Aside from the matter of quantity of daily or weekly film production, the patents company and General Film introduced regulations and methods that were extremely revolutionary in an industry that had never known anything but the wildest freedom.

Heretofore there had been no definite system of rental prices. Exhibitors and distributors haggled among themselves and bargained like horse traders or peddlers. Restrictions regarding "release dates"—specified days upon which films could be released for exhibition—had never been rigidly enforced. Film enthusiasts, always watching for a picture they had not seen, had formed the habit of giving their patronage to the theater that first showed a new movie in their neighborhood, and enterprising theaters paid a premium for the initial release in their district. Moreover, the new films were free from breaks and scratches, and the larger, better-managed houses insisted on getting film while it was in good condition. In their eagerness to be ahead of competitors, many exhibitors resorted to secret arrangements with exchange managers to secure first showing of new films; or a first-showing house associated with a second-showing one might slip a film along the line ahead of time. As a result, release dates were a source of constant bickering and dispute between theaters and exchanges.

General Film announced that all theaters would be classified, and each would pay a standard rental for film service. There would be no dickering or haggling; each exhibitor in a certain class would pay the same price as all others in that class, without deviation or favoritism. Its standard rental scale for a program, changed daily, was $100 to $125 a week for theaters in the best locations, graduating downward to $15 for small or out-of-the-way houses. Release dates were to be rigidly observed, and violation of this rule would result in instant withdrawal of film service.

No theater was to use projection machines or films made by any manufacturer not a member of the patents-film combination, and to make sure that no "outlaw" apparatus or pictures appeared in houses using its products, the trust announced that each exhibitor would be licensed, at a cost of two dollars a week. This license fee, unique in American business practice, was a successful method of money-gathering. One of the auditors of General Film told me that he used clothes-baskets to receive the two-dollar bills and money orders as mail clerks opened the weekly envelopes from ten thousand exhibitors. Eventually the number of contributors was more than twelve thousand, and the total yield amounted to twenty to twenty-five thousand dollars a week —a million or a million and a quarter a year—for license fees, exclusive of film rental bills.

The managers of General Film were too well acquainted with motion picture conditions to expect a calm acceptance of their dictates. They knew that a struggle would be necessary before they could harness the turbulent industry to sober business methods—and they were not disappointed. When the news of the trust's creation spread through the film world an instantaneous clamor arose. Manufacturers not included in the merger denounced the damnable octopus, and declared that not all its powerful tentacles could choke them. They would sue it for damages, they would form alliances with distributors and exhibitors, and they would manufacture cameras, projectors, and films and sell them in spite of all the threats that lawyers could invent.

The two-dollar-a-week tribute infuriated the theater owners. Much as the stamp tax levied on American colonies was in itself not a large thing, but produced the Boston Tea Party and kindled the flames that spread into the Revolutionary War, so the patents-trust license fee was regarded by exhibitors as an arrogant, dictatorial expression of the power of an oppressive monopoly.

Theater owners assembled in conventions throughout the country, and enthusiastically applauded speakers who denounced the patents combination and General Film as a merciless trust, determined to dominate all branches of the film business and to absorb for its members the profits hitherto enjoyed by the exhibitors. This menace could be removed, or at least reduced to harmlessness, declared orators and zealous promoters, by the formation of cooperative manufacturing and distributing companies by theater owners;—the films thus produced could earn their costs in the houses of the members of each company, and additional profits would accrue through rentals to other houses than their own.

If respect for the patents laws had been making headway in the industry,—and there is no evidence that any tendency in this direction had appeared save among the members of the patents company and their associates in distribution and exhibition—it certainly disappeared in the heat and clamor of these conventions.

As the result of the antagonism of exhibitors to the regulations of the patents company and General Film and the agitations aroused in meetings of protest, numerous producing companies, more or less cooperative in theory, invaded the trust's field of production and distribution, despite the perils of violating the patents laws. Nor were they fearful of the business or the technical menaces involved in movie-making, as in that formative period the commercial risks of film production were limited to the possible loss of a few hundred dollars in an unsold picture, and the artistic mysteries that later surrounded the craft simply did not exist.

Although all of these "mutual" producing and distributing ventures collapsed, or passed to the control of a few members within a short time—"cooperation" disintegrating because of internal jealousies and dissensions—some of the individuals connected with the independent movement persisted in determination to win success despite the protests and processes of a powerful trust. They were comparatively few in number, and at the start their capital accounts were limited to "shoestrings," but they were mighty in their desire for places in the sunlight of movie wealth and glory. They fought their great antagonist with every method hitherto used in film competition, and constantly bestirred their brains to devise new ways to injure the octopus, while evading its long, agile tentacles.

For five years, from 1909 to 1914, the battle between the patents-film combination and the independents was at fever heat. The patents company filed hundreds of lawsuits, it employed private detectives to search for evidences of violations of its patents, and called on the federal government for marshals to arrest the offenders, confiscate their equipment, and thrust them into jails. Ordinary processes of law sometimes gave way to physical violence. Cameras were seized and smashed. "Bootleg" laboratories and machine shops were raided whenever they could be found, and their films and equipment were destroyed. Exhibitors were threatened with the closing of their theaters if they used "outlaw" projectors or films.

In the course of time, several of the "outlaws"—and this was the most pleasant term used by General Film in describing independent producers and distributors—became very wealthy, eminently respectable gentlemen occupying high places in one of America's most important industries, honored in Wall Street, in Washington, and other seats of the mighty; but during the period of their great contest they fought the trust like demons. At times, some of them operated within legal boundaries, but by and large they made a football of patent laws and commercial ethics. They were out to get business. They were fighting a well-organized trust that used law and physical strength and rigorous business methods impartially to gain its ends. The devil was fought with fire, and each man decided for himself who the devil was and what sort of fire should be used in fighting him.

The independents were greatly assisted by Edison's failure to register his kinetoscope patents in foreign countries. The best of these instruments were based on the Edison device that stopped the film for a fraction of a second while a photograph was registered and then moved it forward for another exposure—a sprocket wheel similar to the device used in watch manufacturing, generally known as the "Swiss cross" or Swiss watch movement. Several foreign manufacturers used this device, and as long as the cameras remained abroad they were legal, but whenever one of them appeared in the United States the patents company denounced it as "outlaw" and tried to obtain possession of it. A few other cameras had been made in Europe and America without dependence on this important mechanism, but none of them was practical. They might take photographs occasionally, but usually they buckled or twisted the film or failed to move it precisely, so that with them photography was not a reliable art or craft but a sort of sporting event. These defective foreign cameras were, however, a principal means of keeping the American independents' alive during the years of vigorous trust litigation.

Nimble anti-trust producers evolved the ruse of buying a Bianchi, or other legitimate camera (i.e., one not based on Edison principles), and replacing its internal machinery with the mechanism of some camera containing the important Edison device. A genuine Bianchi would stand near the camera containing the imitation Edison equipment, and the trust detectives could not know without examination of the inside of the box which mechanism was legitimate and which could be declared outside the law. The only certain method was to arrest the operators, seize all cameras, and take them into court. This undertaking almost invariably resulted in a fight during which the doubtful camera disappeared and the defendant then appeared in court with a perfectly innocent instrument.

Another of the independents' annoying habits was the practice of hiring the most skilled employees of the trust. "Why waste time and money in experiments with directors, writers, and players," reasoned the shrewd independent, "when the well-established General Film studios have people who know the game backward and forward? I'll offer them a little higher wages than they're getting and they'll come on the run." Acting in accordance with this cheering thought, the outlaws combed the trust studios for desirable personnel, with the result that Biograph, Vitagraph, Edison, Selig, and other producers saw their staffs melting away almost as soon as men and women learned the rudiments of their work. The independents' product improved under this system of engaging the other fellows' expert craftsmen, and exhibitors were soon able to rent non-trust films of steadily improving quality.

Trust producers were infuriated but helpless. If a trust studio was paying a director $75 a week, for example—and that figure is fairly illustrative of salaries of the period—and an independent hired him at $125, the General Film producer had to let him go or raise all wages in the studio to conform to the higher figure. The independent, with a small organization, faced no such problem; he might have one or two or three directors, as contrasted with a dozen or two dozen in a General Film plant, and he could easily pay the higher price as insurance against the expensive delays and errors of inefficient craftsmen.

Lawsuits lost much of their terror for independents as soon as they began to make money enough to employ lawyers who knew how to take every advantage of the law's delays. The principal independents formed an association for mutual defense and protection, and, although they were never happy in one family, they paid their dues to the association's treasurer and more or less maintained the semblance of unity during the several years of trust litigation. Within two years after the formation of the patents combination enough independent projection machines were coming into the market, and there were enough films from independent studios to reduce the fear of exhibitors that the trust could darken their houses, and many of them began openly to defy the octopus by showing independent pictures whenever they chose to do so.

The patents company and General Film, prospering mightily, were nevertheless in a hazardous position unless the progress of competition—which they declared to be illegal—could be stopped.

Lawsuits were winding their snail-like way through the courts, and meanwhile the independents were marching farther and farther into the rich film field. Trust officials, casting about for methods to exterminate the outlaws, decided to leave lawyers and courts to their own slow processes, while they sought for direct, prompt results by stimulating the efforts of their detectives, spies, and plug-uglies to raid the users of non-licensed cameras and smash the instruments whenever seized.

This sort of action made life miserable for the independents. They might creep around injunctions, and the payment of court penalties could be postponed by appeals to higher tribunals, but without cameras they could not make pictures. To avoid trust detectives by hiding away in loft buildings or old mansions in the suburbs had become almost impossible. The conditions of easy, random film-making, under which producers might shift to new locations when pursued too closely, had disappeared when long, story-telling pictures had become generally established. Two-reel pictures had been introduced and this greater length was moving to popularity. Manufacturers of one and two reels, compelled to organize studios equipped with electric lights, heating plants for cold weather, and large quantities of scenery, properties, costumes, and other daily necessities, had too much paraphernalia for nomadism; they had to remain at their bases. Many quiet spots adjacent to New York, Chicago and Philadelphia were tried as locations for studios, but spies found ways to penetrate barriers even in a small town where the independents' guards were assumed to be able to watch every one.

Kalem, and one or two other General Film manufacturers had experimented with Florida as a site for movie-making, and Florida, a long distance from New York and the patents company, was tried by some of the independents. They found the winter climate satisfactory, but spring, summer, and autumn were too warm for working conditions, and, anyway, the trust detectives soon drifted down from New York. Florida was abandoned as a field for film production, as were other eastern and central southern states after a few experiments.

Los Angeles proved to be the haven for which harassed movie-makers were seeking and, likewise, the most difficult obstacle the trust had yet encountered. The glory of having discovered Los Angeles belongs to William Selig, who, in his traveling minstrel days, had become well acquainted with the west. When Edison lawyers—prior to the patents company—were pursuing all outlaw film-makers, Selig and Spoor, located in Chicago, were among the last to be attacked. When Edison litigation reached out for him, Selig's thoughts turned to the west, where he might produce pictures in places so remote that subpoena-servers and confiscators of cameras would have trouble in finding his troupes.

Then, too, just about this time, the outdoor film was becoming very popular, the earliest cowboy pictures having been instantaneous, smashing successes, sweeping over America and across the seven seas in whirlwind triumph. The foreign enthusiasm for American "westerns" was so great that two or three generations must pass before the Old World can be disabused of the belief that the common wearing-apparel of millions of Uncle Sam's sons is fringed buckskins, leather or sheepskin chaps, ten-gallon sombreros, repeating rifles and .45 calibre six-shooters.

The first westerns were made in the east and yielded quick harvests; several producers promptly bought stock-saddles, lariats, stage coaches and other properties necessary to the manufacture of the lurid little melodramas, which they filmed in the suburbs of New York, Chicago, and Philadelphia. Soon it became apparent that the nickelodeons would absorb all the westerns that could be manufactured, and when Edison pressure became severe, Selig journeyed west to refresh his memory of the country that he and others were immortalizing in film, the idea being that perhaps westerns could be made in the west as well as in the east.

He decided to try southern California, and there he found a mild climate, all the year round, and reliable, clear sunshine that assisted materially in obtaining a superior quality of photography. The genial climate reduced studio investment to a minimum—

a wooden platform with canvas sides and roof, arranged on pulleys to control the sunlight, made an adequate stage, and a bungalow or a hay barn could be transformed into dressing-rooms and offices. There were no winter heating problems and the heavy eastern expense of flooding stages with electric light was avoided except on rare foggy days. And above all, California was a long three thousand miles away from the Edison lawyers in New York City.

While Selig was quietly locating in Los Angeles, Broncho Billy, investigating the San Francisco district for Essanay operations, selected Niles Canyon, near Oakland, as his base, and soon was making his weekly pictures there. Although advantageous conditions were found in the vicinity of both San Francisco and Los Angeles, by all that is logical San Francisco should have become the capital of the motion-picture world, and the wealth and prestige now centered in Los Angeles should be the possession of the city by the Golden Gate. In 1908-09, San Francisco was the only metropolis of the Pacific coast. It had theaters, restaurants, and all the elements of metropolitan life, including a flourishing spoken stage and many cabarets from which film producers could draw players.

In the districts near the bay cities are innumerable "locations," as the movie people call the scenic spots in which their outdoor work is done: mountains, hills, valleys, plains, deserts, all more convincingly western than the back lots of Chicago or the hill sides near Englewood, New Jersey; and in San Francisco, Oakland, Berkeley, Burlingame and other towns of the north was available the assortment of residences, public buildings, factories, warehouses, etc., needed as exterior sets in photoplays.

Five hundred miles to the south lay the little city of Los Angeles. It had no better climate to offer, and it lacked many of San Francisco's advantages. Moreover, the character of the northern community was broad, tolerant, metropolitan, while that of the southern was distinctly Puritanical. Nevertheless, the deeply religious sentiment of Los Angeles and the gay, friendly spirit of San Francisco were both ignored by harassed independents.

Los Angeles had one advantage that out-weighed all others for the outlaws fleeing from subpoena servers and camera smashers. They investigated Selig's operations, and unhesitatingly settled in and near Los Angeles because it was close to the Mexican border. With a tight board fence around the lot on which a simple platform stage was built, and with a sentinel or two on guard at the corners, the movie maker could proceed in comfort with his labors. If suspicious strangers appeared down the road, a signal from the lookout was enough to cause the troupers to suspend work, hustle the precious cameras into a motor car (another new device which just at that time was proving to be useful and reliable), and dash across the border into Mexico, where Uncle Sam's marshals had no power.

Within a year or so, Los Angeles buzzed and sizzled with film folk and their contraptions. Motor cars rushed up to bungalows and stately dwellings, and discharged their loads of heroes, heroines, villains, trained nurses, policemen, and society gentlemen and ladies—all with faces painted a ghastly white save for lips as bright as slices of ripe water-melon—and a man in leather puttees and with a large megaphone to amplify a voice that seemed to require no amplification, began to shout orders.

Perhaps these film folk were defying Uncle Sam's solemn laws; perhaps they were bootleggers of the purest ray serene—General Film called them names much more violent than these—Puritan Los Angeles was not the least bit disturbed. The movie makers were fascinating to tourists and residents alike, and business men observed that they were bringing a lot of new money into the town. Los Angeles found them interesting, amusing, and profitable, and local public sentiment concerned itself not at all with the laws or the equities involved in the trust's battle.

Thus fortuitously was the fate of Los Angeles decided. In movie theaters everywhere people began to catch glimpses of streets filled with quaint little houses, of flower-filled patios, of palms and pepper trees, and eucalyptus. Stories were circulated of the everlasting summer, of the "bungalows" that could be rented so cheaply, of the romantic movie business that was a part of this enchanted town. No other city ever enjoyed the publicity that came to Los Angeles through the accident of its location near the Mexican border. From all over the country, tourists began to arrive. They came by thousands, tens of thousands, hundreds of thousands, and within a decade so many of them had remained that Los Angeles had grown from a little city to a great metropolis of a million and a quarter.

Not all of the independent producers and distributors that defied the trust were the "riff-raff" so colorfully described by its officers and lawyers. All the outlaw methods in the world would never have enabled the independents to battle long with an organization so solid and substantial as the Motion Picture Patents Company. The pirates and crooks who lived only by short cuts lacked the brains and stamina to go very far. They gradually disappeared, and the contestants who remained on the battlefield were alert, shrewd showmen who developed the ability to organize their affairs in accordance with common commercial practices. Of several dozen independent manufacturers and distributors who made of themselves a constantly increasing nuisance and menace to the trust, William Fox, Patrick A. Powers, Carl Laemmle, and the Mutual Film Company group became the most effective and most prominent.

William Fox, owner of several theaters and an exchange in New York, refused to accept General Film's offer for his distributing business. When General Film threatened to shut off his supply of pictures, he opened a studio of his own and started a national distributing system to handle his product. He prospered, and steadily increased his holdings of theaters in Greater New York, and soon was presenting popular-priced vaudeville in addition to pictures.

Winfield Sheehan, a Buffalo newspaper reporter, came to New York to work on the New York *World*. He left newspaper work to become secretary to the metropolitan police commission. While in charge of the issuance of theater licenses by the police department, he met William Fox and resigned from the city service to become Fox's chief lieutenant and to build a movie career that proved to be an unusually brilliant one.

Fox, violently disagreeing with the trust's attorneys that its patents afforded it immunity from attack under the Sherman Law, brought suit against the patents-film combination under the treble damages provision of this act—"treble damages" meaning that if the injured party could prove damages amounting to a certain sum the courts would award him an amount equal to thrice that sum. Other distributors followed Fox's example in filing suits, their claims eventually amounting to more than $20,000,000.

Patrick Powers, after producing in several small units for awhile, organized Universal Film Company, the trade name indicating a supply of all items needed by exhibitors for a complete program. Carl Laemmle and Robert Cochrane manufactured and distributed movies under the name of the Independent Motion Pictures Company, abbreviated to "Imp." Imp was impish in deed as well as in name. Cochrane's powerful and impudent advertisements in trade journals were an important factor in the final overthrow of the trust. Laemmle, Powers, and several other producers and a number of exchange owners in leading cities, merged their interests in Universal Film Company, remaining together during a few years of hectic internal strife, until Powers and the others sold their stock to Laemmle, placing him in control of the company, with Cochrane as his right-hand man. Powers, upon leaving Universal, continued in production and distribution under various corporate names.

Harry Aitken, salesman for a film exchange in Chicago, John R. Freuler, Milwaukee realtor, and Samuel S. Hutchinson, Chicago druggist, after some nickelodeon and exchange experience, formed the Mutual Film Company which eventually embraced Thanhauser and a dozen or more other producers who became well known and successful.

Adam Kessel and Charles Bauman, book-makers put out of business by the laws against race-track betting, became prominent film manufacturers, producing under several trade marks, one of the best known of which was "Bison." Their principal achievements were the creation of Keystone Comedies, directed by Mack Sennett, whom they lifted from obscurity in Biograph, and the discovery of a funny little Englishman named Charles Chaplin, brought to America to do a part in a music-hall sketch. One of their important directors was Thomas Harper Ince, a young repertoire trouper who later became a producer and the discoverer of many star writers, directors, and players.

Universal had studios near New York and in Los Angeles. Mutual's producers were around New York and Los Angeles, and Hutchinson built a studio, the American, at Santa Barbara, California. Kessel and Bauman produced on the east coast and the west coast. Universal and Mutual each established a national system of exchanges. Kessel and Bauman were members of Universal for awhile, and then allied themselves with Mutual.

CHAPTER FIVE

THE STAR SYSTEM

THE independents, lacking at the start the effective organization and large revenues of the trust, and handicapped constantly by the fierce litigation and smashing tactics of their opponents, nevertheless had one great advantage over the ten licensed manufacturers of the patents company—the "outlaws" were free to try all experiments that promised to please the public, while the trust producers were restricted by the footage-royalty system under which they operated.

The men at the head of the patents company had organized their enterprise in accordance with the best practices of mass production. Their conception of the desires and needs of the film-consuming public was good merchandise, of standard, reliable quality, manufactured in large quantities, and retailed at low prices. Confident they had assured the production of reliable quality, by the inclusion in the corporation of all capable manufacturers, they expected regularity and stability in their business. "Novel and ingenious films" would come regularly from the factories, and would be delivered promptly and in good condition to the exhibitors, who would pay reasonable, standardized rentals; audiences would see good shows for a nickel (later the trust modified its viewpoint to embrace a dime, but never more than a dime); the public would be pleased, exhibitors would make money, licensed manufacturers would earn reasonable profits, patents owners would receive proper royalties.

Quantity, based on the assumption of maintenance of standard quality, being the essence of mass production, the only method of dealing in pictures at this time was the footage system. The studios produced films by the reel of one thousand feet, and this unit was the foundation of operations among manufacturers, distributors, and playhouses. The exhibitor paid a rental fee for so many reels a day, and the studio's price to the distributor was measured in the reels, or the footage, of positive prints (the copies) taken by the exchanges.

The patents company and General Film fixed a price of ten cents per foot for the positive prints supplied by each of its producers. If, for example, fifty copies of a one-reel negative were used by the exchanges, the producer received approximately $100 per copy, or a total of about $5,000; if enough playhouses rented General Film's service, the demand might run to seventy-five, or one hundred, or even a larger number of prints, but the price of ten cents a foot did not vary. This figure of ten cents had not been determined arbitrarily; it represented the average costs of experienced producers plus an attainable commercial profit, and was based on wage scales that presumably would remain at about the existing levels, or would advance no more rapidly than wage scales in other industries.

The scale of rentals paid by exhibitors being similarly fixed, there was no elasticity, and producers had to regulate their studio costs to conform to earnings. Although too many human, material, climatic, and chemical conditions enter into the expense of pictures to permit perfect standardization, General Film manufacturers usually spent five hundred to a thousand dollars a reel in producing their negatives, and they had to keep pretty close to these figures or endanger their profits.

Competing producers, operating at least in theory on the General Film system of renting a daily program, and following approximately its scale of rentals, nevertheless were free to dicker and bargain with exhibitors. If an independent hit upon a popular idea in a series of pictures, he could try to induce theater owners to pay him a price above the normal, and if some of his films were not as good as others he could "sweeten the deal" by cutting rates on them. Exhibitors, by nature and training, were traders and bargainers, and, annoyed by the trust's insistence on stability and regularity, they broke away from its rigid rules whenever the temptation was sufficient, and dealt with the independents.

During the early years of the contest, the independents in addition to freedom to run wild, to hire employes away from any competitor, to sell or rent their films at whatever prices seemed best, to make the best trades, best bargains, whenever and however they could do so, enjoyed the incalculably great advantage of close contact with the public. Most of General Film's opponents had been exhibitors and they retained their interests in store shows after becoming producers. Through frequent visits to their theaters and daily reports of managers who often were partners they were constantly advised of audience reactions. They developed their sense of showmanship merely by observing the response of their patrons, in tears or laughter or indifference, as the story flowed across the screen, and by carefully listening to comments as the audience left the house.

The real rulers of the patents-film trust were not in touch with the consumers of their product. They never had been exhibitors, nor did they make any effort to discover what the public might happen to want. Several members of General Film were excellent showmen, but they were in the minority, and their suggestions and recommendations were overruled by the conservatives who could see no sense in departing from their industrial philosophy of standardization and regularity.

Before the novelty of one-reel story-telling pictures had worn off, alert exhibitors and their producer associates realized that screen enthusiasts were beginning to form habits of discrimination and selection. Interest in personalities manifested itself first, and theater patrons learned to identify various players long before their names appeared on the screen or in posters. "Little

Mary" quickly became popular, and people would ask ushers and ticket sellers, "When will you show another Biograph picture with that girl in it?" Those who wanted westerns called for "Broncho Billy" and Selig's thrillers, and those pleased with Vitagraphs learned to identify Maurice Costello, Florence Turner, and other favorites. Interest in personalities was followed by expressions of approval or disapproval of stories or certain types of stories, and presently people began to select one theater in preference to others because certain classes of stories were advertised on its posters.

Although this development was noticeable to acute exhibitors and exchange men, the heads of the patents company refused to accredit it. They were unable to believe that the populace was capable of any important progress toward appreciation of merit in cheap entertainment, and they dismissed as foolish and impracticable all suggestions that more expensive films would be welcomed by show-shop customers. Such notions were incompatible with their system of mass production and equalized distribution of standardized product; and, anyway, if carried out would prove too expensive for the movie trade to endure. Who would pay the price of better films? Surely screen patrons would not, because they could not; motion pictures were the poor man's show, and if admittance ever rose much above a nickel the business would quickly perish because of the public's inability to buy the output.

AUDIENCE interest in personalities did not definitely manifest itself until after the methods of the trust had become established and set. Favorable expressions regarding this pretty girl or that handsome hero were heard from time to time prior to 1908, but were not taken seriously by producers or exhibitors. "Little Mary's" films began to stir audiences definitely in 1909, and it is probable that she was the first player ever to register deeply and generally in the minds of screen patrons.

The star system had operated on the stage for more than a

century, but the screen was so distant from the stage that film producers had not applied this method of audience-attraction to their own business. Movies themselves, as an entertainment within the financial reach of the populace, had been all that was needed to build a large, highly profitable industry, and the exploitation of personalities had never been considered as a means of making more money. "Quality," "merit," and "art" as factors in "box-office appeal" now began to enter into calculations of possible larger revenue.

Griffith's analysis of quality had taken the form of better-written stories, more plausible plots, highly developed emotional elements, better direction of carefully selected players, and improved camera work, but the independent producers acquired more faith in the box-office appeal of individual players than in any assemblage of such abstract elements. Their contact with theater patrons convinced them that audiences liked some actors and actresses more than they did others, and from this observation arose the beginnings of star exploitation on the screen.

Imp, the Mutual producers, Powers and his associates, and other independents had already formed the habit of hiring skilled employes from trust studios, and as it seemed but an extension of this practice to lure some of the most appealing players away from General Film, Imp and Mutual each made experiments by obtaining Biograph or Vitagraph players, with gratifying results. Then one day Carl Laemmle and Cochrane got a hunch that "Little Mary" could be made into a star, and promptly followed the hunch by offering to double her wages. Her mother accepted the offer, Miss Pickford moved from Biograph to the Imp studio, and movie patrons soon learned that "Mary Pickford" was the name of the actress they had enjoyed so much in Biograph films.

Other independents selected other players and advertised them as stars. Enthusiastic movie patrons—just at this time they began to be called "fans"—now were able to demand pictures of their favorites by name, and audiences immediately displayed keen interest in the stars that pleased them. Before long, the showing of a new film of a popular star meant long lines outside the ticket-window of the fortunate theater, while competitors with less attractive offerings wondered why their houses were suddenly and strangely deserted. Movie stars were accepted into the public's affections to an extent the stage had never known. The principal stage players of the day continued to be known even to their most ardent admirers as Mr. Sothern, Miss Adams, Mrs. Fiske. But almost at once movie fans began to talk about "Mary" (Mary Pickford), "Bunny" (John Bunny) "Broncho Billy" (G. M. Anderson), "Tom" (Tom Mix), "Theda" (Theda Bara), etc.

This familiar attitude toward screen celebrities, contrasting sharply with the more formal custom of stage followers, is significant not only in revealing the emotional responses of American democracy, but in indicating the feeling of propinquity, of close, personal acquaintanceship, engendered by the screen and not by the stage. The shadow personalities presented by the film have seemed to spectators to be more real, more human, more intimately associated with themselves, than the flesh-and-blood players behind the footlights. Many players have, as shadow persons, penetrated into the thoughts and influenced the actions of audiences more deeply than the same artists have been able to accomplish in actual appearances on the stage.

Having learned the names of their favorites, theater patrons could not now see enough of them. Until death closed his career, John Bunny, Vitagraph's funny man, was welcomed in as many one-reelers as he could make—about two dozen a year. A weekly Broncho Billy film packed the theaters with his admirers, and presently Tom Mix was offering vigorous competition. Mary Pickford was appearing in about twenty pictures a year and her fans regretted that they could not see her every week instead of only twice a month.

The instantaneous spread of star interest astonished everyone in the industry—the trust as well as the independents. In response to an apparently insatiable public appetite, all sorts of hitherto obscure players were thrust into glory as quickly as their names could be inserted in credit titles and posters. The anonymous raw material of last month's canned celluloid was transformed into this month's celebrated artist. And so was born the press-agent's heaven, and the golden age of buncombe and hokum, in which screen celebrities were turned into sacred cows for their fans to worship at ever-increasing cost of adoration, began to spread its saccharine extravagances over the studios.

To imply that the independent producers sensed the deep interest of the public in movie personalities, and created the star system because of their superior acuteness, while General Film manufacturers were obtuse, would entirely misrepresent the situation. The fact is that the almost hysterical acceptance of personality exploitation by movie goers was a startling surprise to all factors and all factions in the screen world. No one had foreseen it, and no one was in any degree prepared for the results that followed its advent. The star system in films was in reality created by the public, and the public has had full and undisputed charge of its creation during every moment of its history.

NEARLY all independent producers were exhibitors or distributors before they became manufacturers, and nearly all theater owners and exchange managers accepted improvements in quality only when competition compelled them to do so. For years the majority of exhibitors steadily, and often noisily, resisted every attempt to move the movies upward, agreeing with the trust that five or ten cents was the top price for tickets and that a higher fee would close the door to millions of workingmen and their families. The exhibitors, as a class, insisted on flimsy, melodramatic stories, manufactured at low cost so their rental bills could be kept at the minimum. Progress had thus to contend with the opposition of most theater owners and the conservatism of the patents company. A few exceptional exhibitors and exchange men observed the improvement in public taste which inspired Griffith and a few others to search for quality in production, and Hodkinson, Tally, Mitchell Mark, Adolph Zukor and others to better exhibition methods—and sensed the unspoken desires of audiences illustrated dramatically by the eager acceptance of the star system when Laemmle and Cochrane tried their experiment with "Little Mary." Therefore a limited number of individuals were chiefly responsible for the rise of pictures and theaters to higher levels. But there was nothing mysterious or occult in their foresight;—they simply followed their "showman's hunch" that movies could be made better, and could be shown in better theaters, at higher prices of admittance.

Because of their standardized system of making and renting pictures, General Film manufacturers questioned the added expense involved in adoption of the star system, and for a little while they hesitated before plunging into this new scheme; while they hesitated independent producers acted promptly. They lured from trust studios players whom they suspected of having box-office appeal and in each instance announced stentoriously the capture of the greatest star ever known to the world. General Film studios soon swung into line and rushed forward every possible atom of star material in frantic efforts to gratify the public's longing for celebrities. Stars were manufactured with ease, or not at all, not even the shrewdest producer being able to predict in advance the success or failure of any given player. The only method was to make a picture or two and distribute them to the theaters. If they were successful, the producer might expect to gain a comfortable profit before a competitor outbid him for the new celebrity's services; and if the proposed star was a "flop" the employer merely hunted around for another player whom the populace might take to its bosom.

While everything in the industry was twisted out of kelter by the cyclonic popularity of the star system, forcing bewildering new methods into studios, exchanges, and theaters, the freedom and mobility of the independents gave them advantages over the trust that the brightest "outlaws" exploited to the utmost of their abilities. The sober, sensible business men, scientists and lawyers who ruled the patents company were annoyed and disgusted. The entire performance seemed so childish and silly, so unnecessary and ridiculous, so contrary to sane industrial practice and sound economics, that the well-trained brains of trust rulers denounced it as a fad, an exhibition of popular foolishness that would presently exhaust itself and depart without having affected their business seriously.

Although no factory—trust or independent—functioning on a system of a dollar-per-foot cost for negative film, could continue to operate comfortably when the ladies and gentlemen whose camera personalities were the raw material to be fabricated into dramatic strips of canned celluloid, unexpectedly announced that they could not express themselves unless wages were doubled or quadrupled, and that they must be regarded as artists instead of factory hands—although no studio could maintain any semblance of standardized sanity after star frenzy swept into the show-shops—the independent producers, never having been standardized or regulated in any way, rushed into all sorts of wild, apparently insane, experiments, while the members of General Film were restrained by the trust leaders' cautious adherence to the well-established rules of mass production for mass distribution. The difference between trust philosophy and independent practice was that the patents company rulers believed in giving the public what the trust thought the populace needed and the "outlaws" poignantly yearned to discover what the people wanted and to "pander to the public" by manufacturing the discovery and selling it at "the highest price the traffic would bear." (My quotations are from the current phrases of the period.)

These distinctively contrary viewpoints and the relentless battle of trust and anti-trust forces that raged behind the screen interested the populace not in the slightest degree. Public apathy to the rights or wrongs of the contest was one hundred percent complete, but universal enjoyment of the new delights of star personalities caused vast additions to the throngs of ticket buyers everywhere, and hugely augmented streams of nickels and dimes daily poured into the little show-shops, to the great enrichment of exhibitors, distributors, and producers. For a while the well-organized trust was the principal beneficiary of these swollen rivers of small coins, but the nimble outlaws were constantly diverting to their own bank accounts many rivulets that were rapidly enlarging.

What no one had foreseen was that all the rulers and leaders of the industry had suddenly lost control of their business. Nor did any one realize this important fact now; several years were to pass before the men at the head of the movies were brought face to face with the grim truth that as soon as the star system appeared on the screen the consumer had thrown the manufacturer and the exhibitor out of the driver's seat, and that ever thereafter the whimsical, mercurial, merciless populace would decide the course its entertainment should follow. The fans demanded pictures of their favorite—momentarily favorite—actors and actresses, and they cared not who made the pictures, nor why. The years of carefully built-up trade names, the bitter struggle of the independents against the trust for an unmolested place in the sun, were suddenly of no account. Biograph, Vitagraph, Selig, Essanay, Kalem, Universal, Mutual, Fox,—to the movie fans all trade names and "brands" were alike,—and many years were to elapse before the producers even partially emerged from the eclipse they themselves had established.

By 1910-11 the patronage of screen theaters had grown to ten million men, women and children—perhaps to twenty millions; inasmuch as no records of total American attendance were compiled until the federal government collected a war tax on tickets in 1918, the only figures available are the estimates of General Film pioneers. The operations of this unorganized, leaderless multitude continued along the simple, direct lines followed from the beginning of store shows: individuals merely decided that they liked this star, or did not like that one; and they bought tickets to see their favorites, and stayed at home when favorites failed to appear. This system was the acme of simplicity, and it proved to be extremely effective.

The movie army, in promptly endorsing the star system, had

unconsciously achieved its first great victory over all film rulers, and encouraged by this triumph it inspired many remarkable advances in its own form of entertainment within the next few years. Each forward step was won over the great obstacles erected by the conservatism of most manufacturers, distributors, and theater owners. Screen entertainment had been fixed, apparently permanently, on the system of a program of assorted subjects providing an hour or two hours of exhibition, and the maximum length of any one item seemed to be anchored at one reel (twelve to fifteen minutes).

Here and there, throughout the country, a few exhibitors, keeping closely in touch with patrons, insisted that sections of their audiences were reaching out for something better. In the studios were men who knew that carefully developed stories, presented by selected casts of players, with intelligent direction and good settings, would result in pictures whose quality would be superior to that possible in one-reel films; two reels would accomplish much and three reels would permit great advance. But production of these longer, better films would materially increase manufacturing expenses. The standard cost of one-reel negatives was fifty cents to a dollar a foot, or five hundred to a thousand dollars; two-reelers might add fifty cents or more per foot, and three-reelers might cost two dollars or more. As the earnings of pictures were definitely limited by the daily change of program, standard price system, under which one reel was the maximum possibility, trust producers who wanted to experiment with longer forms were pretty sure to lose money, if, indeed, they could succeed in persuading General Film to release the long picture.

The length of a picture was itself an obstacle of real importance. Exchanges and theaters alike were organized on a one-reel basis; a change to two reels would necessitate important modifications in business methods and exhibiting practices. And, moreover, most men in the industry were firmly committed to the belief that anything longer than a dozen minutes on the screen would throw such a burden on the mental capacity of audiences that many patrons, wearied and disgusted, would cease to visit the theaters. One reel, therefore, continued as the standard length of dramas and melodramas for several years after its introduction, and, when William Selig finally dared to produce a two-reeler, the industry was astonished by the prompt response of a large section of the public to the longer form. The demand for two-reelers was sufficient to cause several producers to advance to this length so quickly that afterwards they claimed to have antedated Selig.

The best of the two-reel films were really adequate mediums of story-telling by play-acting. In twenty-five to twenty-eight minutes, the essentials of a spoken play of three to five acts could be presented effectively, and with convincing delineations of character that were not possible in half this length. Very soon the more important, or more pretentious, themes appeared only in two reels. Westerns and other melodramas and less ambitious stories remained in one reel, and comedies, travels and "novelties" continued in split reels, comedies moving slowly from five hundred feet to a thousand.

However, even after the superior quality of these longer films had raised standards to a definitely higher level, and the more mentally active sections of the movie multitude were welcoming them, there remained the necessity of permitting the slower-minded groups of spectators to adjust themselves to the improvements. The screen theaters had created a democracy of opportunity in entertainment; five- and ten-cent admittance fees had leveled the cost so that practically everyone could afford to enjoy pictures; but, as there is never a democracy of mental development, while the quick minds were pushing ahead, the slower ones had to be carried safely from one era to another, or—as I have said before—the screen would have lost them.

The gap between split-reels and one-reel and the "long" pictures of two reels was bridged by a gradual evolution in exhibition methods. Whereas, in the beginning, all store shows had been alike, and nickelodeons had never pretended to be anything but cheap playhouses presenting uniform, standardized amusement, the better quality of two-reels soon brought about lines of demarcation, and theaters began to be classified by movie patrons and by exhibitors themselves.

As the production of two-reelers was more expensive than the making of two single reels, the rental prices of these better films were advanced considerably beyond the former scale. Many exhibitors—the majority of them—objecting strenuously to the higher rentals, clung to the programs of one-reel and split-reel, and permitted progressive houses to obtain the first showings of two-reelers. This minority of advancing showmen—usually located "downtown" or in neighborhoods where a large population could be drawn upon—made two-reelers the backbone of their program, filling in with shorter subjects. Presently they were attracting to their theaters such an important proportion of patronage that they were able to raise the admittance price from ten cents to fifteen, and here and there to twenty. And, too, they acquired the reputation of showing "first-class" pictures, while, by inference at least, other houses began to be marked as "second class."

Events soon proved that millions of the movie multitude had grown very alert, very quick to appreciate improvement in story-telling and to differentiate sharply in selection of player per-sonalities. By giving their patronage to the theaters that pre-sented first-class pictures, this vanguard in the movie army forced backward exhibitors into accepting two-reelers, and the conservative rulers of General Film, to meet the competition of independents, modified the trust's system far enough to permit the distribution of two-reelers as part of the standard program. However, when audiences and exhibitors demanded three-reelers, General Film refused flatly to permit any farther encroachment on standardization, and three-reelers were not included in the program.

DURING these gold-rush years of confusion and strife of manu-facturers, wholesalers, and retailers—years of frenzied competition and vigorous fighting never known in any other business—the accumulation of wealth by numerous individuals was proceeding at a pace and in such quantities as to stagger the very few bankers and industrial leaders who ever got glimpses behind the screen. Movies, established in opposition to the scorn and disdain of Wall Street and all sensible, well-placed commercial leaders—excepting the handful at the head of the Motion Picture Patents Company—were literally showering gold and glory on many men and women who had hitherto never dreamed of acquiring consideration from either fortune or fame.

The partners in little show-shops were blooming into well-to-do, substantial business men; and some of them were building bank accounts and making investments that startled their bankers. Shrewd independent producers and distributors were manifesting astonishing evidences of prosperity. And as to the members of the patents company and General Film, their fortunes were piling up at a rate that they themselves could not comprehend. James Stuart Blackton and Albert E. Smith had brought Vitagraph into existence in 1897 by scraping together a few hundred dollars and renting an office at $10 per month. By 1912-13 Vitagraph's gross income was between five and six million dollars a year, and the reports of a Wall Street firm of certified public accountants showed that, after deducting liberal salaries for the three partners, the net profits available for dividends, was a million to a million and a quarter dollars a year. By no stretch of the imagination could Vitagraph's original assets be given a value of more than $2,000 or $3,000. From the numerous inventions of its founder, the Edison Company has acquired large revenues, but it is improbable that from any source has it ever received a net income on each dollar of investment to compare with its profits from the movies. Each of the ten licensed manufacturers was, in theory, upon an equal footing; each was assumed to receive his share of the business, and insofar as possible this practice was followed for several years. The film trust poured into the pockets of its owners fifty or sixty millions of dollars of profits within the few years of its active life—and this corporation was a merger, accomplished without the employment of outside capital, of concerns that only a few years before had started with nothing but "shoestrings." American industrial history is filled with romantic stories of sudden rise to wealth, but there is no story to compare with this one.

The roar of the torrent of nickels and dimes, transforming themselves into gold as they sped into ticket windows throughout the country, deafened the rulers of the trust to the demands of progressive exhibitors that the public was advancing in appreciation and discernment, and that new methods of making and distributing and exhibiting pictures must replace the standardized practices established by the patents company. Such declarations from the battle front were pigeon-holed at General Film headquarters, but the information leaked through to the studios, and in several of them were ambitious young men, keen and daring, who yearned to go forward with the public, as far as audiences might want to go. At weekly meetings of General Film they presented their reasons for belief that the time had arrived for a loosening of the iron-clad rules that bound them to the daily-change program system, and soon they were vehemently insisting to their associates that the independents were forging ahead of General Film in public favor. To all such protests the rulers of the trust returned the same answer, "We have grown rich by following sane business practices; our wealth is continuing to increase. Why jeopardize our success? As sensible men let us leave well enough alone." And as the progressives and radicals in General Film viewed their monthly statements, and sent their huge checks to the banks, their arguments did somehow seem out of place.

The most advanced radical in General Film was William Wadsworth Hodkinson, the telegraph operator in Utah whose crazy dream of a well-managed nickelodeon had materialized so successfully that he had become owner of several small theaters and manager, from time to time, of various General Film exchanges, advancing finally to the important San Francisco office. Hodkinson believed in the future of pictures, and believed too in the practical justification for better pictures that cost more money to make. His formula was "meritorious pictures exhibited in attractive theaters," and he believed that greater business would result from the application of his formula. He regarded ten cents admittance as merely a step in the right direction, and declared the public willing to pay a quarter, a half-dollar, or even more, to see motion pictures whenever the quality justified the price. Standardization of films, a fixed rental scale, and the daily change of program had outlived their usefulness, he said, and now were retarding the entire industry. He zealously advocated introduction of a selective system, under which pictures would be graded and priced in accordance with the merit of each.

The daily program change destroyed a good picture's greatest asset, the "word-of-mouth" endorsement of those who happened to see it and advertised its merit to their friends. Unfortunately, when their friends arrived the following day, the film had already moved on to parts unknown, and a "sale" was lost. He insisted that the public would now keep an interesting film on a single screen for two or even three days, and soon, he predicted, "runs" of a week would prove successful. His logic seemed flawless. Given better pictures, audiences would pay higher prices; exhibitors, out of their increased profits, would build better theaters and pay higher rentals; out of the increased revenues, the producers would be enabled to make better pictures which, in turn, would draw upon ever-widening circles of the public and so continue the advance.

The trust rulers regarded Hodkinson's ideas as the ravings of an enthusiastic lunatic, but as he was a good salesman and an expert exchange manager, they merely smiled at his eccentricities and promised to consider his recommendations "later." Presently Hodkinson, concluding that "later" might be too far in the future, took matters into his own hands. Without waiting for approval from New York, he instituted reforms in the San Francisco exchange. Selecting from the daily programs the films he regarded as best, he rented them at higher prices to local exhibitors who put them on for two- and three-day runs.

His report created a turmoil among the ten manufacturers assembled in weekly conference in General Film headquarters. The manufacturers whose product he had graded as "first class" were gratified by his award of merit, and their earnings were increased by the higher rentals and longer runs. Naturally they regarded him as a talented manager deserving the whole-hearted endorsement of the board of directors; but their associates, whose pictures had been labeled "second class" and whose earnings had been decreased by the loss of daily-change rentals, denounced him as an anarchist who would wreck the company if permitted to remain in its employ.

The patents trust managers, having no confidence in the merit of their own merchandise and no belief in the public's capacity to appreciate or pay for quality, agreed with the conservatives and Hodkinson was rebuked for his flagrant violation of basic rules. He resigned from General Film and opened exchanges of his own in San Francisco and other western cities. As indicative of his point of view, he named his exchanges "Progressive"; and indicating the lack of unanimous belief in the wisdom of the trust's policies, Marion and Long of the Kalem Company quietly became his partners in the venture. Progressive obtained its supply of pictures from independent and foreign manufacturers, who applauded Hodkinson's policy of paying higher prices for selected quality.

Better music also occupied the thoughts of all ambitious exhibitors, and music remained a problem for the ten-cent playhouses until Thomas L. Tally of Los Angeles arrived at a solution. The success of Tally's "Electric Theater" enabled him to build, three years later, a larger and better house, designed in accordance with his analysis of the special needs of a movie audience. His own enjoyment of music caused him to give it a prominent place in the list of necessities. An orchestra was too expensive for a ten-cent theater and a piano was inadequate. A pipe organ would be ideal, but this instrument was so definitely associated with churches and large concert auditoriums that its use in a movie theater might seem sacrilegious or at least subject to criticism. Tally took a chance. He bought an expensive organ for his new theater and engaged a competent performer. The public endorsed this daring novelty so enthusiastically that all new movie houses followed Tally's example and pipe organs became as essential as chairs or screens.

Eugene Roth in San Francisco, Adolph Zukor in New York, Mitchell Mark in Buffalo, and other alert exhibitors scattered all over the country were struggling towards the same objective,— to satisfy the increasing public desire, of which they were acutely aware, for better entertainment. To win to the goal of the widest popular approval they were willing to risk their energy and money, and, if need be, to defy the dictates of a wealthy, auto- cratic and powerful trust.

CHAPTER SIX

FEATURE PICTURES

THE lawsuits of the patents company and its opponents dragged along, impeded by every delay known to lawyers who are not certain of a favorable decision; and in 1912 the federal courts decided against Thomas A. Edison Company in the suit brought by William Fox. True, the decision was technical, but its effect was greatly to encourage the independents. Edison, in his applications years previous, had claimed several points, some of which he had used in developing machines and one of which he had not used. The court decided that he should have "disclaimed" the point he did not use; and that the charges against alleged infringers should not have included the point he did not use; and therefore decision was rendered against the Edison interests. Edison and Motion Pictures Patents Company then took the necessary steps to correct the Edison patent papers, and a few years later the courts decided that Edison was entitled to the points he had claimed and had used. But however much the eventual victory meant to Edison as an inventor, the decision of 1912 was interpreted by the independents as a victory for their cause.

Outside of General Film there were, in 1912-13, several dozen manufacturers and distributors constantly clamoring for business, and while some of them were successful temporarily, the independent leaders continued to be Mutual and Universal with their groups of producers, and William Fox.

For several years Mutual, managed by Harry E. Aitken, John R. Freuler, and Samuel Hutchinson, was active, progressive and prosperous. Mutual had vision, courage, financial resources, energy and ability, and General Film keenly felt its competition. Aitken, gifted with unusual personal persuasiveness, was an exceptional promoter and business builder, with rare talent for persuading directors, players, bankers, and exhibitors to conform to his plans. Frueler was a substantial business man and careful executive. Hutchinson built and supervised operation of the American studios at Santa Barbara, California. Crawford Livingston, Wall Street banker and patron of the arts, became interested in financing the Mutual corporations and enlisted the assistance of Otto Kahn, of Kuhn, Loeb and Company, Wall Street bankers.

William Fox was the first movie man successfully to embrace in one organization all branches of the industry. If trust officials did not foresee the future importance of Fox, other men had confidence in his ability and backed him with their money. The first was a group of capitalists in Newark, New Jersey, prominent among whom was John F. Dryden, president of the Prudential Life Insurance Company; but although Fox obtained the support of capital the voting-power of Fox corporations always remained in his own hands.

Universal, starting business life as a cooperative or mutual organization of exhibitors, exchanges, and manufacturers, soon became a sprawling, quarrelsome democracy, its owners dissipating their energies fighting among themselves. It possessed, however, along with its squabbles, a faculty of clever showmanship, and Universal films were successfully made and distributed despite all the hubbub of the internal rows. When Laemmle bought out Powers and his other partners, he followed William Fox in creating an unlimited monarchy, with himself as king and Robert Cochrane as prime minister. Laemmle established his principal studios in Hollywood, later moving to a ranch north of Hollywood in the San Fernando Valley, where he built Universal City.

During the period of intense activity, while the industry was shaking off the restraints of the patents company and General Film and trying every conceivable experiment to capture the public's fancy, William Randolph Hearst, the only prominent newspaper publisher to enter the motion-picture field, organized the International Film Company and produced a film-news service in connection with William Selig, later transferring the service to Universal.

Edward A. McManus, a young Irishman graduated from the circulation department of *Hampton's Magazine* into the Metropolitan Newspaper Syndicate—then under the same ownership as *Hampton's*—conceived the idea that serial stories could be told on the screen as effectively as in periodicals. McManus joined Hearst International and for several years serial movies, consisting of a two-reel installment each week for three or four months, were extremely popular. The American Film Manufacturing Company, distributing through Mutual, created a sensation by paying Roy McCardell, who had abandoned newspaper work for scenario writing, $30,000 for the story and editorial supervision of a serial, "The Diamond from the Sky." Until this event writers had been receiving fifty to five hundred dollars for film stories, and no novelist or playwright had hitherto been paid more than a thousand dollars or so for the use of his material. American's fee to McCardell aroused the literary world, and authors and playwrights began to believe that the movies might become an important factor in their business affairs.

WHILE studios in the United States were intent on pleasing the store-room patrons, giving never a thought to intellectual and cultured classes, the comparatively few producers operating in Europe were striving to create photoplays that would be enjoyed by the very classes that Americans were neglecting. Euro-

peans, free from the infringement suits of Edison and the restraints of a trust, made broader experiments than were tried
in America, and the length of pictures in Italy, France, England,
and to some extent in Germany increased to from five to ten
reels while the two-reeler was a standard in the United States.
Italy was the leader in European development and Italian producers made some elaborate pictures, with great settings, huge
mob scenes, and spectacular effects; from about 1909 to 1914,
Italians seemed to possess a greater flair for the camera than any
other manufacturers in Europe.

The themes of these productions were usually classical,
or "highbrow," as befitted the custom of the houses in which
they were shown; or else spectacular and melodramatic on a
grand scale, as, for example, "Quo Vadis," in which the nude
girl on the bull's back in the arena scene caused audiences of
all classes to gasp in astonishment, or "Cabiria," in which a seductive young lady attended by a leopard introduced a foretaste of
sex appeal. Melodramatic thrills were supplied by such devices
as mobs of men engaged in battle, and the destruction of ships
by a fire started by a sun-glass.

George Kleine, keeping himself constantly advised of all
foreign picture-making, greatly desired to import some of these
elaborate films to the United States, and labored with the patents
company to bring about modifications of the trust's distribution
system so that long pictures could be handled. His efforts were
in vain, but nevertheless Kleine yielded to temptation and imported one film, "The Life of Moses," in five reels, which General Film agreed to distribute on its program at the rate of one
reel a week. Needless to say, the life of the Hebrew law-giver
was not a success when thus presented, and Kleine's ardor for
the trust was proportionately cooled.

As the independent movement grew in strength, pictures of
four reels or more occasionally found their way to America, and
were exhibited by theater-owners daring enough to find out if
audiences could live through a photoplay an hour or an hour
and a quarter in length. They learned that film spectators could

not only exist under the mental strain of this extensive concentration on a spectacular melodrama, but actually enjoyed the experience and clamored for more long films. Pictures longer than two or three reels came to be known in the trade as "features," to distinguish them from films sold as part of a program.

Occasionally an American would make a feature, or an ambitious director would smuggle one through a studio while his company's officers were so busy with commercial and legal battles that they could not watch him closely. Almost invariably these long films were successful with audiences. The home-grown plots, dealing with American themes, were "sure-fire" when they reached the screen in feature length. However, it was fatal to distribute such features as a part of the usual program as the greater cost of production could not be earned save by special handling. The extension from two or three reels to five was not merely an expansion of screen time; it necessitated a different and much more expensive technique permitting even more improvements in each department of production than were possible in the change from one reel to two.

One reel may be compared to a literary sketch, two reels to a short story, and a five-reel feature to the epitomization of a complete novel. Each important rôle in a feature length could be presented with sufficient detail to be clear and convincing; a larger amount of money could be spent on settings, furnishings, and costumes; directors could take time to rehearse players before photographing the scenes; camera men could experiment to get the best lighting effects and could re-shoot unsatisfactory sequences. Necessarily the costs of production advanced in proportion, the earliest American features involving a footage expense twenty-five to one hundred percent higher than one or two reel films.

From time to time a few General Film manufacturers yielded to the desire for feature length, but, distributing these productions on the footage basis, were unable to make a profit. One noteworthy experiment was "Judith of Bethulia," directed by Griffith for Biograph, in somewhat less than four thousand feet.

"Judith" was a fine production, and audiences enjoyed it, but under General Film's flat-price method it earned no more than any other film on the standard program.

"Judith" was the turning point in Biograph's career. This great pioneer producer then had in its studio many writers, directors, and players who were soon to make fortunes for manufacturers not yet firmly established or even in existence. Had this film been released as a feature its profits might easily have been so large that Biograph could have used its abundant talent in making long pictures regularly, and have continued permanently as one of the important companies. The commercial failure of "Judith" was interpreted by conservative stockholders of the corporation as convincing proof that long pictures of quality were not commercially practicable. Presently Griffith went to Mutual and the rest of Biograph's talented men and women were absorbed by other independents.

RADICAL exhibitors, observing the joyous public reception of infrequent features, declared that a great new era was waiting at theater doors, and urged General Film to provide a steady supply of long films, but their recommendations were ignored at trust headquarters. A few daring independent producers answered the demand by adding a few features to their program output, and these, with half a dozen acceptable long pictures from Europe, had to satisfy the advance guard of American enthusiasts through 1911-12-13.

If any one event could be selected as marking the beginning of a new period in the American industry, it would be the appearance in New York of "Quo Vadis," the Italian made nine-reel photoplay from Henry Sienkiewicz's famous novel. George Kleine, discouraged by General Film's handling of "The Life of Moses," nevertheless persisted in believing that long pictures would be accepted by the public, and when, on one of his journeys to Europe, he saw "Quo Vadis," he determined to exhibit it in America, with or without the assistance of his associates.

He bought the American rights, and when the picture reached New York, gathered the manufacturers and officials of the patents company and General Film and a number of prominent exhibitors into the company's projection room and screened it for them. With the exception of one man, the audience remained through the entire nine reels and agreed that "Quo Vadis" was a remarkable photoplay, but the rulers of the trust declined to modify their system and permit "Quo Vadis" to be distributed apart from the program.

The man who left the projection room before the completion of the picture was Marcus Loew, one of the most important New York theater-owners. Loew agreed with the trust conservatives that an audience could not maintain its interest throughout a long film. Within ten years, Loew's Metro-Goldwyn-Mayer studios were making no films shorter than six reels and some of them ran to twelve.

Kleine, anticipating rejection by General Film, had already concluded to rent a Broadway theater and attempt to accomplish the impossible by showing "Quo Vadis" as an entertainment equal to stage plays. The renting of a theater proved unnecessary, for when Sam Harris, play producer, saw "Quo Vadis," his enthusiasm was as great as Kleine's. George Cohan and Harris booked the picture for the Astor Theater on a percentage basis, Kleine receiving forty percent of the gross receipts.

"Quo Vadis" opened at the Astor on April 21, 1913, at a dollar admission. A photoplay at a dollar was a daring innovation. Kleine and Cohan and Harris were rewarded with enormous success. The Astor was packed with appreciative audiences from spring until autumn, and by the middle of the summer twenty-two "road shows" were exhibiting the picture in stage theaters in all sections of the United States and Canada. The overwhelming popularity of "Quo Vadis" convinced progressives of the soundness of their contentions that the public was ready and willing to accept and pay for any kind of movies that it considered worth the price.

ON THE west coast was one young man, and on the east coast another; neither knew the other for several years; each was driven by the same urge to supply audiences with finer entertainment than was believed to be possible or practical. They were William W. Hodkinson, operating independent exchanges in the west and searching constantly for meritorious pictures, and Adolph Zukor, who had left a furrier's store to become an associate of Marcus Loew in nickelodeons and vaudeville-film theaters in New York, and to operate picture shows of his own.

Studying audiences constantly, Zukor became convinced that many people wanted better pictures than they were getting, and while trust and independent producers were concentrating on the daily grind of making and marketing one- and two-reel films, he decided that expensive features would be accepted by the movie masses, and in time would dominate the theaters.

This was Hodkinson's belief, but while Hodkinson had no desire to make pictures himself—his ambition being to procure and distribute the best films—Zukor determined to risk his savings in becoming a producer of nothing but feature pictures. At this time, when three reels were a doubtful length and five reels were foolhardy, no American manufacturer had shown any inclination to jeopardize his well-being in exclusively feature production, and Zukor received little encouragement from his acquaintances in his wild scheme.

Marcus Loew's thoughts were concentrated entirely on theaters, and although Zukor was one of his partners, he was unable to endorse the feature idea. Loew was already famous in the industry, the head of an important chain of houses, a genial, well-liked man of magnetic personality. Zukor was practically unknown outside a small circle of exhibitors and exchange men in New York; he was merely an obscure fellow with a crazy idea and a burning desire to try it out.

The first problem for Zukor to solve was distribution, or he might find himself operating a studio and losing money through lack of sales. Universal, Mutual, and Fox each had organized a national system of exchanges, but each rarely handled any product except its own. In addition to these, and General Film, there had arisen half a hundred other distributors, known as "state's rights exchanges." Hodkinson, operating in San Francisco and Los Angeles, was one of these, and there were others in each of the thirty or thirty-five "key" cities throughout the country. Few of these distributors had exchanges in more than one city. The film maker would sell to an exchange in each key city the right to exhibit his picture in his district or state, and hence the designation "state's rights" had become a trade term.

Some of the state's rights dealers, notably Hodkinson and a few others, were well established and responsible, but many of them were unsubstantial and unreliable. Zukor desired to persuade General Film to let him use its exchanges, but to distribute his features separate from the regular program output. He knew that General Film was besieged by producers seeking distribution, and this privilege had been obtained occasionally for short films by arrangement with one of the licensed manufacturers; and he knew, too, that progressive members of the trust were advocating a more liberal policy and methods of distribution to permit longer pictures to make money. But so far the company's conservative rulers had given no indication of relaxing their rigid rules; nevertheless, Zukor determined to present his proposal.

For many weeks, he called at General Film headquarters to interview the haughty magnates who seemed to him the biggest big business men in the world, but got no farther than the singularly uncomfortable reception room where only the most patient souls ever lingered long. "There came a day," to quote an oft-used movie title, when a friendly assistant secretary promised to bring his petition to the president's attention. Quiet, patient and persistent, Zukor sat hour after hour on one of the hard benches. As morning dragged past noon, his shoulders drooped, the corners of his mouth drooped, the hat held in his limp hands drooped; he had every appearance of hopeless humility.

As usual, the session in the board room had been spent in ardent disagreements, and soon after five o'clock two or three of the weary directors, deciding that the quarrels of the day were nearly concluded, arose from their chairs and moved toward the door. The assistant secretary, remembering his promise to the patient man in the reception hall, whispered to the president, who asked his associates if they would listen to the petitioner. Zukor was known to one of them as a former partner of Marcus Loew and a cheap nickelodeon owner. At the secretary's information that Zukor was planning to produce five-reel pictures, the directors laughed and one of them predicted that he would "soon be back making button-holes." As they passed through the waiting-room, none gave a glance at the quiet man standing, hat in hand, hoping for a word of encouragement or a nod of recognition.

Rebuffed by the trust, Zukor was compelled to enter the producing field through state's-rights distribution. His first venture was to purchase, in 1912, the American rights of a four-reel French photoplay, "Queen Elizabeth," in which Sarah Bernhardt was the star. His handling of this feature was successful, and he concluded that the time was ripe for the launching of his own producing company. He proceeded to create an organization. As chief of staff he selected Edwin S. Porter, who had made the first story film, "The Great Train Robbery," in 1903. Benjamin P. Schulberg, a young newspaper man, was placed in charge of stories and adaptations, and Elek John Ludvigh, at that time attorney for Marcus Loew theaters, was engaged as legal adviser.

Zukor's thoughts turned toward the spoken stage for his acting personnel and Famous Players Company was the corporate expression of the idea. The counsel, influence, and prestige of Daniel Frohman, producer of stage plays, were enlisted, and for years Frohman's name was used in presenting the Famous Players films.

The first feature produced and distributed by Famous Players was "The Prisoner of Zenda," made from the dramatized version of Anthony Hope's novel, with James K. Hackett, famous theatrical star. Although the picture required an outlay of nearly $20,000, equal to the cost of several standard two-reel films, it was a success. Al Lichtman, a hustling sales manager, placed it with the best state's rights exchanges throughout the country, progressive theaters exhibited it, and audiences welcomed it with enthusiasm. "Zenda" was followed by other pictures at intervals of about a month.

Zukor's patience, persistence, and willingness to learn made him a clever producer as well as a clever business man. During the early years of Famous Players he acquired a sixth sense of anticipating the wishes of audiences in stories and stars, in selecting directors, writers, and camera men, and in combining these materials into successful productions. He soon abandoned the idea of using stage players in his films. The merciless lens of the movie camera too often revealed the matinée idol as long past his romantic youth, and movie audiences declined to be impressed with these middle-aged lovers, however great their stage reputations. Youth and beauty were the essentials of romance on the screen, and soon Zukor's famous players were being replaced by unknown youngsters, Mary Pickford among them, who satisfied the popular demand.

In 1913, movie studios throbbed with activity in New York, Chicago, Philadelphia, Los Angeles, San Diego, Santa Barbara, and Oakland. New York was the headquarters of distribution and finance, and in New York and its suburbs most of the pictures were being made.

Two dozen or more inexpensive picture plants, consisting of open-air stages and board-and-batten dressing-rooms and offices, were scattered about Los Angeles, and many films were being photographed in the clear sunshine and gentle climate of California, but there was no indication that Los Angeles would ever become the producing capital of the entire industry.

In the country immediately adjoining the city on the north-west, real-estate men, a few years prior to 1913, had bought land and mapped out blocks and streets to transform the district into a residential suburb. The abundance of holly and live-oak trees suggested the name of "Hollywood," and the section had at-tracted many home-builders.

Peaceful Hollywood had seen a few film folk, who oc-casionally traveled its country-lane "boulevards" seeking outdoor settings in groves and gardens, or using its old ranch houses and barns as locations for rural scenes; but nothing had ever occurred to sound the tiniest warning that it was soon to be lifted from obscurity and made famous throughout the world.

One Sunday, a Scotchman named Robert Brunton, strolling along Sunset Boulevard, noticed a barn that appeared to have possibilities, and in that moment Destiny took Hollywood in hand. Brunton, as a youth, had been a landscape painter in his native city of Edinburgh, and business in landscapes being notably slow, had gone to London and found employment in painting scenery for Sir Henry Irving's Drury Lane Theater. Irving, then in the full swing of his career, prided himself on his elaborate productions; all his scenery was painted, and many of his sets and properties were built, in his own shop.

The painter from Edinburgh became an expert in all branches of stagecraft, and Sir Henry, visiting America a few years later, brought Brunton with him as stage manager. By the time the troupe reached Los Angeles, Brunton had concluded that the Yankee invention, the cinema, was to be his road to fortune. He resigned from Sir Henry's company and sought a connection in the studios.

Frugal of speech, unwilling and unable to be a typical hand-shaking, back-slapping good fellow, Brunton had many more downs than ups in his first months in the free and easy west. His sound craftsmanship often collided with the flimsy film practices of the day, and his opinions were delivered with such brief but biting sarcasm that although, from time to time, he obtained positions, he was frequently discharged before he had time to resign.

Between periods of employment in studios, he worked as stage manager, scene painter and what-not in local theaters, and filled in odd hours by making plans and drawings of ideal studio stages, dressing-rooms, scene docks, sets, and so forth. The barn in Hollywood became, on his sketch block, a workable small studio. All that Brunton needed was a producer with money; he was prepared to tell him about the barn, and to build sets in it and on the lot around it, and to find the necessary players and camera men, prop boys, carpenters, and electricians.

Back East, in New York, Destiny had selected the other members of the cast that was to start Hollywood on its journey to fame. The title of the troupe was "Jesse L. Lasky Feature Play Company." Jesse Lasky brought to the movies an unusual equipment of experience, temperament and personality. In boyhood, in San Francisco, he was educated for a career in music, and entered professional life as a cornetist in an orchestra. Then the stage attracted him and he became a vaudeville performer in association with his sister Blanche. Soon he was a producer of vaudeville acts, and was so successful that he engaged in an ambitious, but disastrous attempt to establish a music hall, "Folies Bergères," in New York City.

Folies Bergères devoured the savings of several years, and Lasky turned to producing vaudeville acts and musical shows, often writing the words and music of his productions, and rehearsing the players, thus developing himself all around the circle of showmanship. He watched the movement of the movies upward, and as feature pictures intermittently appeared on screens, began to wonder if this new field of entertainment was not worthy of investigation.

A young human dynamo, disguised as a traveling salesman for a glove factory, saw Blanche Lasky on the vaudeville stage, and persuaded her to become Mrs. Samuel Goldfish.

Arthur Friend looked out from his law practice in New York

and decided that the world was hungering for more feature pictures than were being made.

Blanche Goldfish made a similar observation about the same time. As a result, Lasky, Goldfish, and Friend were formed into a corporation. They engaged as director, Cecil B. DeMille, son of Henry C. DeMille, a well-known playwright. The older son, William C., was already prominent as the author of "The Warrens of Virginia," "Strongheart," and other successful plays; Cecil had been through the training of a trouper with road shows, as stage manager, writer of plays and musical comedies, and was eager to try his hand at screen production.

Lasky, Goldfish, Friend and DeMille were young men, with financial resources limited to their personal savings; their company started with their own subscriptions of a few thousand dollars and loans of a few thousand more. Dustin Farnum, stage star, had won a large metropolitan following by his work in "The Squaw Man," which impressed the Lasky group as fine material for a feature picture, and arrangements were made with Farnum for use of the play and his services as its star.

One morning, as he read his breakfast newspaper, Brunton saw a burst of publicity dealing with Jesse Lasky, Samuel Goldfish, Cecil B. DeMille, Dustin Farnum, and other celebrities "now present in Los Angeles for the purpose of making feature pictures."

"That barn in Hollywood——" Brunton started to say to himself, but saved finishing the sentence by walking promptly to the Alexandria, taking his sketches with him. The most active man on the oriental rug in the Alexandria lobby was Samuel Goldfish, and the Scotchman attached himself to the movie producer who had been a glove salesman a few weeks earlier.

"I've got just the place you want for a studio," said Brunton.

"Does it cost much?"

"Cost nothing, or nearly nothing."

"Take me to it." Goldfish hustled Brunton to a motor-car, and they sped to Hollywood.

On Sunset Boulevard at Gower Street, a tumble-down old

road-house and out-buildings had been converted into a studio for making short films and comedies by David Horsley and Al Christie, and Universal's old open-air stages and shacks, in a field across the road, appeared to Goldfish's keen eyes as demonstrations of Brunton's "cost-nothing-or-nearly-nothing" statement.

The price of the land in the district then was three or four hundred dollars an acre. The cost of lumber was low and the wages of carpenters and other mechanics was twenty-five to fifty percent less than in New York. The pleasant climate made construction work possible every week in the year. Extras— men, women, and children for mob scenes—were available at two or three dollars a day, and thrifty producers sometimes obtained big mobs merely by providing a barbecue lunch and giving the amateurs the fun of working in the movies.

The cost of creating a studio plant in Hollywood and the expense of operation were so much less than the investment required in the east as to make comparisons difficult. One producer told me that pictures made in his Hollywood studio were better photographed—electricity had not then taken the place of sunlight—and that costs were one-third to one-half lower than in his New York plant.

The Lasky-Goldfish-DeMille organization's slender capital did not permit the purchase of any land when Goldfish made his first journey along Sunset Boulevard, but they rented the barn and adjacent building at Sunset and Vine Streets, and pushed "The Squaw Man" to completion rapidly. It was sold promptly and profitably to state's rights exchanges, and with the money thus obtained, the Lasky company started on its second picture and on its career of success. Its original cash capital, about six thousand dollars, expanded within three years to a valuation of nearer four millions.

The spectacular progress of the Lasky Company advertised Hollywood to other movie producers, and as the low cost of barns and dwellings and land made possible the organization of studio plants at minimum expense, many other manufacturers soon appeared in the district. Hollywood became the producing center of the world. Unknown in 1912, it was famous the world over ten years later.

The Lasky company bought eight or ten acres at Sunset and Vine and a large ranch over the mountains in San Fernando Valley; its studio organization grew to be one of the largest in America. The Hollywood buildings were demolished in 1927, the land that had been bought for a few thousands of dollars having advanced in value to hundreds of thousands as sites for apartment houses, hotels, mercantile buildings and theaters. The Zukor-Lasky organization then moved to Melrose Avenue, Hollywood, to a plant originally built by Brunton for Paralta Pictures, to which Robert Brunton Studio Corporation succeeded in 1918.

The Brunton company sold the property in 1922 to the United Studios Corporation of Joseph Schenck and M. C. Levee, and Brunton went back to Edinburgh. Destiny threw the dice against him, and this able craftsman, who had made important contributions to the development of studio technique, died in London within a year.

By the autumn of 1913, all the factors for a new epoch in the industry were once more in readiness, but no one had assembled them into order. The situation was comparable to that of 1908-09, when Biograph gave Griffith an opportunity to coordinate the elements in movie-making and start the search for quality production, and when Hodkinson, seeking for quality exhibition, had tried his experiment of turning a nickelodeon into a clean, well-managed ten-cent theater.

Advanced sections of American audiences were ready for the movies to abandon infantile habits and enter into a period of vigorous adolescence. The five-reel (and longer) photoplays made in Europe and the few features produced in the United States, had broadened their vision of screen possibilities, convincing them that two- and three-reel pictures should be superseded by the longer forms.

Existing theaters were being remodeled, and in a dozen large cities exhibitors were planning large houses to be constructed especially for motion pictures. The most remarkable of these projects was that of Mitchell L. Mark, who, entering the movies in penny-arcade days, had built up a chain of theaters in Buffalo and other eastern cities. Mark was a man of extraordinary vision and a showman who almost invariably guessed what his audiences wanted. He startled the film industry and theatrical circles in 1913 by beginning to build the Strand Theater in Longacre Square, New York, announcing that it would have nearly three thousand seats on only two floors and would be devoted solely to motion pictures. A scattered few applauded his judgment and courage, but otherwise he was regarded as an over-optimistic enthusiast.

Hodkinson, Zukor, Tally, Mitchell Mark, Lasky-Goldfish-DeMille, Aitken, Griffith and other progressives were insisting that features must supplant short films. Hodkinson had spread his gospel of better theaters and better pictures wherever he had operated, from Denver to California, and numerous theater owners in the west, east and north were now ready to exhibit features constantly.

What, then, was the obstacle that prevented a real, forward-sweeping development in the industry? Hodkinson concluded that distribution was the defective part of movie mechanism. General Film, the principal distributor, Mutual, Universal, Fox, and all other national exchanges, were still operating on the system of a program of short subjects, changed daily or every other day. General Film resolutely ignored features, and other producing-distributing groups handled them as items incidental to their short subjects.

Scattered over the country were a few state's rights buyers who, Hodkinson knew, had prospered whenever they could get a good feature to exploit. Perhaps a dozen or more features of fair quality had been offered to such distributors in 1913. Hodkinson believed that these exchanges could handle one five-reel film a week, increasing to two a week, provided the pictures were made in America and based on American themes.

Analysis of the producer's side of the situation revealed several items for consideration, the first being that manufacturers, aside from those connected with the large companies, lacked the capital needed to make five-reel pictures regularly. The cost of feature negatives, $10,000 to $20,000 each, involved a larger investment than they could afford. In 1913, very few bankers or financiers had any knowledge of or confidence in the movie industry, and producers had to depend on their own finances or obtain loans or subscriptions from friends. Another item was that under the state's rights system the producer usually sold his picture for a specified sum. If, therefore, the photoplay was a large success, the exchanges reaped the major portion of the profits, and the producer was unhappy because his reward seemed to him insufficient.

Several state's rights distributors had prospered during the several years of battle with the trust, and were now in a position to advance money for projects they considered sound. Numerous theater owners, too, had grown wealthy and made a practice of paying advance deposits on features they desired to exhibit. Hodkinson, disregarding the possibility of obtaining money from Wall Street, believed it would be possible to find several state's rights men to join in advancing the steady stream of capital to a few producers that would enable them to make a regular supply of features. By distributing the pictures on a percentage system, producers would be encouraged by larger returns to maintain a high level of production. If several other exchange owners would come into the plan, he would organize a corporation and handle the business from a central office in New York. A name could be selected for the corporation and all the pictures distributed under that one trade mark. Judicious advertising would soon familiarize the name to the public as synonymous with superior pictures.

He decided on "Paramount" as the name for such an association, and a mountain peak rearing its head aloft would be the trade mark of Paramount's product. His plan to use a trade name and trade mark was not to replace the names of stars with that of distributor or manufacturer. The star system had grown so strong by this time that to discard it would have been impossible. Besides, Hodkinson had no objection to stars. On the contrary, he enjoyed the work of most of the successful stars and constantly searched for new players who might have star quality.

With these ideas in fairly definite form, he journeyed from the west coast in the winter of 1913-14, and in New York met Raymond Pawley of Philadelphia, James Steele, associated with Rowland and Clarke, of Pittsburgh, W. L. Sherry of New York, and Walter Greene and Hiram Abrams of Boston, each of whom was a successful state's rights distributor. They formed "Paramount Pictures Corporation," electing Hodkinson as president and Pawley as treasurer. The stock in the corporation was divided in five equal parts, each group owning one part, and the board of directors consisted of five members. Wheels were set in motion to establish Paramount exchanges in each leading city.

Adolph Zukor was the principal manufacturer of features, and as the distributors who organized Paramount had handled his Famous Players output, they looked upon him as the cornerstone of their producing edifice. Paramount entered into a contract with Famous Players under the terms of which, for a period of twenty-five years, the distributor agreed to advance to the producer twenty thousand to twenty-five thousand dollars for each five-reel negative, and the producer agreed to distribute through no other medium during the life of the contract. Paramount was also to advance the cost of positives and trade-journal advertising. Gross rentals were to be divided, sixty-five percent to producer, thirty-five percent to distributor. Paramount wanted from Zukor two pictures, to increase soon to four, a month— or one a week, a very large order. The Lasky-Goldfish-DeMille combination was also brought into Paramount under a twenty-five years' contract.

Hodkinson had encouraged Hobart Bosworth, landscape painter and actor, to make features for his Progressive exchanges to distribute, and Bosworth had obtained the backing of Frank C. Garbutt, a Los Angeles capitalist with a fortune made in oil, real estate, and banking. The Bosworth-Garbutt alliance took form in Pallas Pictures and Morosco Pictures, the latter so called from its association with the well-known stage producer, Oliver Morosco, then operating theaters in Los Angeles and New York. The Garbutt-Bosworth-Morosco group, with the Pallas and Morosco Companies, made an agreement with Paramount for a period of twenty-five years.

Paramount now faced the industry with the assurance that within a short time it could deliver a steady supply of two five-reel features a week, one hundred and four a year. Hodkinson was in a position to preach his gospel of "long runs for good pictures" all over America. The leading exhibitors of the country had learned that a five-reel movie of merit could be shown for from two days to a week, and Paramount promptly began to educate theater owners everywhere to discard the daily change of program of short films and to substitute therefor a feature that would draw audiences for two or three days or an entire week.

General Film suddenly faced a competitor that could give it real battle.

CHAPTER SEVEN

THE NEW ERA

PARAMOUNT'S introduction of method and regularity in feature production and distribution marked the climax of the contest between the conservatives and the progressives that had been raging in the motion-picture world ever since the invention of Edison's peep-show. In each of the evolutionary processes that had occurred after the film was removed from the kinetoscope cabinet and thrown on the screen, the conservatives had been proved wrong. They were bewildered by the strange, unpredictable accomplishments of their own merchandise in the twelve thousand cheap amusement places in America, and the rapid, unexpected extension of its influence into foreign countries.

Something unforeseen was happening to the mind of the mob. In some mysterious manner, millions of human beings were refuting the dogma that mass mentality could not, or would not, move ahead, but that it would always mill around in circles and get nowhere in the development of anything further than the desire for additional material possessions. Perhaps this philosophy remained as true as ever; perhaps the common people had no capacity to advance to a happy, wholesome civilization; nevertheless they were making remarkable progress in creating for themselves a form of entertainment that carried with it an immeasurable quantity of stimulation, enlightenment, and education. No so-called leaders of thought or of public opinion were influencing or guiding this unprecedented movement. There was no leadership of any sort. There was merely a ceaseless, irresistible drift of millions of plain people to little ticket-windows to buy amusement—cheap, flimsy amusement that aroused the disgust or scorn of the intelligentsia. But all the time the demand was for better and better pictures, and they had to be devised and manufactured, not by intellectuals, but by mere business men whose only purpose was to make money by selling better shows to their customers.

The revolutionary desires of the movie-mad populace found concrete expression in Paramount's features, which reached the screen at precisely the right moment.

Patronage poured into the feature playhouses in astonishing numbers, giving such ready approval to the Paramount plan and pictures that the new company was assured of success from the start. Many new faces appeared at ticket-windows; millions of people who had never attended film shows now formed the habit, and others who had tried movies and not found them reliably satisfying tried them again and became screen addicts. There were so many millions of these new customers who willingly paid five or ten cents more for tickets, that the commerce of the industry surged upward in waves of millions of dollars.

Paramount's rental rates reached a scale that the trust rulers had declared impossible. General Film's charges in its best days were approximately $100 or $150 a week for the principal houses and $10 or $15 for theaters of the lowest earning-power, for a program of four to eight reels, changed daily. Paramount rented its five-reel features at $500 to $700 a week to the largest theaters —occasionally at even higher figures—charging $100 to $300 for smaller, or secondary, houses of the better class, with other rates grading down to $25 a day, or, for an old feature in a backward theater, as low as $5. Hundreds of exhibitors rented the service as promptly as it could be extended to them. The list of theaters showing Paramount films expanded within a few years to a total of five or six thousand, and many of these were new houses of large seating-capacity. Gross rentals were soon $100,000 to $125,000 per picture, and the service had to be increased from two features a week to three and four.

The short-film program system was banished very quickly from leading screens, and other houses moved into step with regularity. Within two years it was difficult for fans to remember that features had not always been their entertainment, and soon there were no short films except comedies, travelogues, news reels and novelties. Producers and exhibitors, as soon as Paramount got under way, rushed into competition for a share in this new golden field. Mutual, Fox, and Universal, well established in short-film production, became the principal contenders.

Mutual embarked on experiments of every sort, from cheap to expensive features. Universal expanded more cautiously, sticking rather closely to the less costly productions for several years, and built up a large volume of trade among the smaller houses which were reluctant to advance admittance prices beyond five and ten cents. Fox entered early into long-picture production, and was the first producer to recognize the enormous latent demand for what was later to be popularized as "sex appeal." His first noteworthy success in features was the filming of Porter Emerson Browne's stage play, "A Fool There Was," founded on Kipling's currently popular poem of the man "who made his moan" to "a rag, a bone and a hank of hair." Roy McCardell prepared the screen version of the play and Frank Powell directed it. Theda Bara, the actress to whom the leading rôle was entrusted, presented the character so effectively that she immediately became Fox's leading dramatic star. "Vampire," abbreviated to "vamp," entered the American language as synonymous with "seductive enchantress," and Theda Bara was the model by which all vamps were measured for a decade, although none ever equalled her popularity.

Fox also sensed the public yearning for "he-man" pictures of the great outdoors, and William Farnum, popular stage actor, became one of the earliest screen heroes, destroying villains for a number of years to the edification of enthusiastic audiences.

Fox promoted several players to stardom, but his biggest popular success was with Tom Mix, the Oklahoma cowboy, town marshal, and deputy sheriff who was making one-reel movies for William Selig. Fox, convinced that Mix could surpass Broncho Billy, William S. Hart, and all other western stars in popularity, offered him larger opportunities in longer pictures and Mix moved to the Fox organization. Fox was right—Tom Mix's pictures in five-reel form increased constantly in earnings until they reached gross rentals of $600,000 to $800,000 each. His feature films have appeared on more foreign screens than those of any other star except Broncho Billy and Charlie Chaplin. Fox made a fortune through his confidence in Mix's possibilities, and the actor earned for himself three or four millions of dollars in less than ten years with this astute producer.

Paramount, Mutual, Universal, Powers' companies, and several smaller units were the pioneers in regular feature production, and each prospered, although they had to meet the vigorous competition of numerous ambitious adventurers who entered the industry soon after Paramount initiated a new epoch.

THE trust was unable to adapt itself to the changed conditions. Its rulers' faith in law and lawyers had been shocked by the court's decision against their principal member, Thomas A. Edison, and although the decision was technical, permitting corrections in time, it seriously weakened General Film's industrial position. Law and lawyers, and logic and sound business practices, had not provided them with effective weapons in the warfare against "riff-raff and rabble" opponents—the independents, the outlaws, had avoided jail sentences and were rapidly absorbing all the millions of movie profits. General Film's business was decreasing at a time when the total volume of the industry was increasing by leaps and bounds.

Not alone were there such discouragements as these, but the lawsuits of independent exchange owners, alleging that General Film had wrecked their businesses and demanding treble damages under the Sherman Anti-Trust Law, were grisly specters that some day would materialize in court for final reckoning. The more than twenty million dollars demanded by these plaintiffs was a total sufficiently staggering in itself, and General Film was not sure its lawyers would not charge another twenty million for defending the cases!

These were not happy days for the men meeting in the board room to divide the profits that had made each of them wealthy within a few years. The rulers now talked of modifying their methods—to permit their exchanges to handle feature films—but their talk was too late; the tide was against them. They were too rich, too set in their ways, to adapt their minds to the demands of the new era. They had never been showmen; they had not understood the public, because they were not in tune with the public; they had stood on the side-lines and watched the procession stream by, never suspecting the longings and aspirations hidden beneath the mob's mental laziness. They were scientists, business men, and lawyers; they had been stripped of their power by men of the people.

The patents company and General Film gradually faded away. Some of its producers continued to supply General Film with short subjects until 1917 or 1918, but one after another dropped out as the volume of business shrank under the competition of features. The lawyers settled some of the Sherman lawsuits, and other cases dragged along until the trust was a hollow shell from which nothing of value could be collected, and the claims quietly vanished into oblivion.

The rise and fall of this powerful organization is without parallel in the history of business enterprise. It was created, and grew to great success—almost to complete control of a very profitable industry—and then passed out of existence without the general public ever having known enough about it to care whether it lived or died. The story of the patents company and of General Film deserves to be remembered as a perfect illustration of the futility of laws that lack the support and sympathy of the populace.

The Edison Company ventured half-heartedly into features, and presently discontinued production entirely. Kalem and Melies made no serious attempt to compete with the new demand. Biograph drifted into a few unsuccessful experiments, and retired from the industry.

The Pathé brothers, more interested in manufacturing and chemistry than in showmanship, had become important producers in France of cameras and of photographic film. The whirling development of American movies did not appeal to them. Merrill, Lynch and Company, Wall Street bankers, bought their American picture business; Pathé withdrew from General Film and opened its own exchanges. The French and American Pathé companies made an alliance with the Dupont powder and chemical interests, organizing Pathé-Dupont Film Manufacturing Company to produce raw film in competition with the Eastman Kodak Company.

J. A. Berst, who had originally come to the United States as Pathé Frères' agent, remained in charge of the new American picture corporation for a while. Merrill, Lynch and Company later advanced to the vice-presidency and general managership, Elmer Pearson, a Nebraska farmer boy, who had left the farm to become a traveling salesman, and, fascinated by the movies, got a position as salesman with a General Film exchange; he later became manager of the Pathé Omaha exchange, and finally entered the New York executive offices.

Pathé engaged in the production and distribution of features as well as short subjects, building its business on the wide popularity of its news reels, which eventually were shown on thirteen thousand screens in America alone. The corporation was a successful money-maker, with annual profits of a million to a million and a half dollars a year.

William Selig, always restless, was constantly trying out new ideas. Before other producers sensed the value of novels as screen material, Selig made contracts with Rex Beach, Zane Grey, and other popular authors. His production of Rex Beach's Alaskan novel, "The Spoilers," in eight reels, was the first "super-picture" made in the United States, and was completed in time for Mitchell Mark to use it in opening his great new Strand Theater in New York in April, 1914. The success of "The Spoilers" was tremendous. It packed the Strand, with its three thousand seats and five shows a day, for seven days, and broke theater records by showing to about forty thousand people in one week in one house. The success of the Strand itself was epochal. Mitchell Mark's dream of a great, beautiful playhouse was accepted with such enthusiasm that enterprising exhibitors in a score of cities rushed to build theaters of—it seemed then—enormous seating capacity.

Albert Smith and James Stuart Blackton of Vitagraph adhered to the policy of General Film until they saw the sinking ship could not be saved. They then embarked in the manufacture of feature films, organizing a national system of exchanges, and inducing their attorney, Walter W. Irwin, to abandon the practice of law and become its manager.

George Spoor of Essanay, Selig, and Sigmund Lubin joined Smith and Blackton in the project, and the corporation was named "V L S E," the initials representing Vitagraph, Lubin, Selig, and Essanay. Each of these companies continued to manufacture short subjects for General Film in addition to producing features for V L S E. Walter Irwin became an enthusiastic advocate of motion pictures, and under his administration V L S E for a time held a position in distribution of features second only to that of Paramount under Hodkinson.

Blackton's first important long production, "The Battle Cry of Peace," in eight reels, drew several millions of dollars to box offices and started unknown Norma Talmadge on the journey towards stardom.

The years 1914 to 1916, when movies discarded the habits of childhood and scrambled into tumultuous youth, were a fascinating panorama of business and professional achievements and failures. Hardly a week passed without a development or a movement of some sort to arouse the film industry's fever to the boiling point, and while some of the sensations were short lived, a few created conditions that continued to influence the screen for many years.

One event of outstanding importance was the production, by individuals in the Mutual Film group, of the most popular, most profitable picture in movie history. The success of this one picture might have placed Mutual at the head of the industry, but owing to lack of concord among the corporation's owners the opportunity was lost. The picture was "The Birth of a Nation," based on the Rev. Thomas Dixon's "The Clansman," a story of the south during the reconstruction period. The novel had been made into a popular play, and several companies traveled about the country presenting it. Dixon believed it would be equally popular on the screen.

D. W. Griffith was at this time producing features for Mutual in a Los Angeles studio. He and Frank Woods, manager of his editorial department, agreed with Dixon that his novel offered superb opportunities for the filming of a thrilling drama, with sweeping action in great mob scenes of men and horses.

Griffith estimated it would cost between $75,000 and $100,000 to make the super-picture he was planning. In 1914, this amount would pay the studio costs of half a dozen or ten ordinary features, and the conservative business men in Mutual Film regarded the enterprise as extremely hazardous. Harry Aitken alone agreed with Griffith, Woods, and Dixon that the public was ready for a very long, costly picture. His business associates declined to participate, and Aitken, Griffith, and Dixon organized a separate corporation, the Epoch Film Corporation, to produce "The Clansman." They obtained the necessary funds by "passing the hat," as Wall Street describes financing an operation by private subscriptions.

The photoplay upon completion was shown, in twelve reels, at Clune's Auditorium in Los Angeles, as "The Clansman." It was favorably received and distributors immediately began to buy state's rights, but Dixon, Griffith, and Aitken were not satisfied. They were confident the production had exceptional merit, and that it should be shown as a theatrical attraction, at spoken-drama prices.

After the initial showings of the picture on the west coast, Dixon changed the name to "The Birth of a Nation," a more attractive title which substantially benefited the box office, and continued to exercise his wits for ways and means to exploit the film. He was helped by the fact that the Negro race considered itself unjustly portrayed by his story, which was concerned with the reconstruction period in the south. Dixon, an ardent southerner, had represented the Ku Klux Klan as the hero, and the carpet-baggers with their Negro associates, as the villains of the piece. As a result, race feeling had run high wherever the play had been performed, and serious riots had usually occurred—with much incidental publicity and swollen box office receipts.

The company planned carefully for the Boston opening, at regular theater prices. Boston had always been the home of pro-Negro sentiment, and a week or two before the opening, colored ministers and lawyers violently denounced the film. On the opening night a vigorous riot took place in front of the theater, and firemen had to assist the police in dispersing the mob. Newspapers all over the land reported the riot, and spoken-drama theaters everywhere were eager to book this new drawing attraction. People flocked to the box offices, paying regular stage prices to see a photoplay that caused riots.

The picture itself was an astonishing revelation of camera possibilities, and it was the first film to be regarded seriously by many intellectuals and sophisticated stage patrons. The blend of melodrama, heart throbs, and romance, with the big mob scenes of armies fighting and masked horsemen rushing through the night, were acted, directed, and photographed in a manner hitherto unknown to the screen. With no star to propitiate, Griffith had been able to cast intelligently and to give each character adequate opportunity for portrayal of his part. He had assembled a company of unknown actors and actresses, and under his direction they responded so well that Mae Marsh, Robert Harron, Ralph Lewis, Henry Walthall, and other members of the cast became stars through this one picture. Griffith himself was made famous all over the world.

The financial record of "The Birth of a Nation" was in keeping with its sensational popular success. Harry Aitken is my authority for the statement that between 1914 and 1929 the picture earned about $18,000,000. The profits have been $5,000,000, and in 1931 the picture was still being shown in many theaters each year. Some time it may be remade, and a new version will probably add to its earnings record.

THE progress of Paramount, the success of "The Spoilers" and the Strand Theater, the triumph of the Epoch Film Corporation's "Birth of a Nation," and the parade of big and little companies marching along to fame and fortune, encouraged the promotion of a host of new projects and new stars during the following eight years. State's rights distributors and theater owners, soon after the establishment of Paramount, began to be curious about the earnings of Paramount and its producers. Eagerly listening to gossip, it was not long before these earnest optimists concluded that feature-producing was the richest field of the industry. Their calculations ran something like this:

Paramount, gross total rentals per picture, average,		$100,000
Paramount charge for distribution, 35 percent,		35,000
Producer's share		65,000
Producer's average costs:		
Negative	$25,000	
Positives, trade-press advertising, etc.	10,000	
Total costs,	35,000	35,000
Producer's net profits, average per picture		$30,000

Zukor was producing fifty-two pictures a year, and therefore, the optimists insisted, he must be making at least a million and a half dollars net profits a year; moreover, these calculations did not include foreign sales, which were good for $10,000 to $20,000 a picture. The Lasky Company was producing twenty-six features a year, and the optimists allotted to Lasky one-half the profits credited to Zukor. As a matter of fact, some of the guesses were not far from the truth. The Famous Players Company did make more than a million and a quarter dollars in its third year of active operation, and although other Paramount producers were not abreast of Zukor, each of them was well pleased with his own profits.

The promoters, however, did not wait until Paramount's third year to go into action. Within a year, several new combinations of exhibitors, state's rights exchanges, and producers were following the Hodkinson-Zukor-Lasky plan, more or less faithfully. Usually these organizations were inexpertly managed and passed away quickly or were merged with more substantial companies, but a few of them survived and became the foundations of later important corporations.

Al Lichtman, sales manager of Famous Players eliminated from his position by the creation of Paramount, joined with Walter Hoff Seeley, a newspaper man, in organizing Alco Films. They divided the ownership of the corporation among exchanges throughout the country. Among the Alco stockholders who later figured prominently in production were Richard Rowland of Pittsburgh and Louis B. Mayer of Boston.

Rowland, whom we met early in these pages as an exchange owner, had become associated with James B. Clarke, and the two had extended their activities to exhibition, acquiring in time a profitable chain of theaters in western Pennsylvania. When Hodkinson organized Paramount, the position of Rowland and Clarke in their district was so powerful that he invited them to become one of the five owners of Paramount. They accepted, and James Steele represented their interests on the Paramount board. When Lichtman and Seeley organized Alco, they likewise obtained the support of Rowland and Clarke.

Louis B. Mayer had been a business man in Haverhill, Massachusetts, who entered the movies through investments in a small theater and extended his interests to a partnership in an exchange. When Alco was formed he and his associates became owners of the franchise for distribution in the Boston district.

Alco started with a flourish, but following the habit prevalent in the industry, developed internal troubles and was in the hands of a receiver within a year. Richard Rowland and other stockholders gathered up the remains and reorganized them in a new corporation, known as Metro Pictures. Rowland was elected president, and Mayer secretary. Associated with them were Robert Rubin, New York attorney, Joseph Engel, formerly with Universal, Famous Players, and other companies, and Arthur James, expert newspaper man and press agent. The Metro plan differed from Paramount's in that Metro made its own pictures while Paramount contracted with producers for its supply. Max Karger was in charge of production and Metro was soon distributing twenty-four features a year.

LEWIS J. SELZNICK entered motion pictures during the chaotic era of 1912-15 and for about a dozen years remained the most sensational figure in the industry. His biography closely parallels those of many ambitious east side Jewish lads who lifted themselves from poverty and obscurity through the movies. The son of Russian immigrants, he left school at an early age to sweep out a jewelry store and run errands. He advanced to the position of salesman, and finally to ownership of a jewelry shop of his own.

A jewelry merchant, to live up to the best traditions of his trade, ought always to be careful and conservative. Selznick loved jewels, but he was seldom conservative and not always careful. Beneath the jeweler's exterior he harbored the temperament of a circus ringmaster, combined with daring and unusual shrewdness.

The kaleidoscopic whirl of the movies fascinated him and drew him away from jewelry. The film business combined all the excitement of the circus plus splendid opportunities for making barrels of money. When Selznick determined to enter the movies and looked around for an opening, Universal was the shining magnet that drew him. Just at that time, Powers and Carl Laemmle were in the heat of the most strenuous battle in Universal's career, Laemmle averring that he was in charge of the corporation, and Powers insisting that Laemmle, Cochrane, and their adherents were usurpers and must abdicate in his favor.

Selznick called at Universal headquarters, seeking an interview, but found the offices in a state of siege. The Laemmle-Cochrane forces had withdrawn to the heart of the fortress, there barricading themselves against process-servers and strong-arm men in the hire of Powers. Each visitor to the reception room was cross-examined to determine his status. Selznick hastily disguised himself as a jewel salesman, and got past the outposts by displaying gems cut and uncut, which he offered at low prices. He dazzled the office force with diamonds and rare stones, all the while making himself acquainted with the situation. In relating the incident he assured me solemnly, and I believe him, that the minds of the several owners were so absorbed in their private fight that no one was definitely in charge of the establishment.

"This was duck soup for me," Selznick reports. "If they didn't know what they wanted, I knew what I was after, so I appointed myself to a job, picked out a nice office, and went in and took it. This got by with bells on. People came in and talked to me about everything that was going on, and pretty soon I knew all about it."

Within a few weeks, being a mere underling palled on the new employe, and deciding that Universal needed a general manager to look after the film business while the owners were fighting with one another, he promoted himself to the post, ordered letterheads bearing his name and title, and settled down to work. Each of the dozen or more producers and distributors interested in Universal at this time, some allied with Powers and some with Laemmle, assumed that another had appointed Selznick to his position, and each was so busy with warfare that none made inquiry. He soon became a figure of importance in the organization, and volunteered to act as mediator between Powers and Laemmle, but succeeded only in arousing the latter's suspicion that he was a henchman of the former, with the result that when Laemmle came into control, as he did within a few months, he cut the ligament that bound the self-appointed general manager to Universal and set him adrift. Selznick was not down-hearted. During that brief term of officialdom he had learned how films were made and sold, and had become acquainted with many of the personalities of the industry.

About this time, in the winter of 1914-15, Arthur Spiegel, of Spiegel, May and Stern, mail-order merchants in Chicago, had organized a picture-making company, the Equitable, and through Moritz Rosenthal had obtained a connection with the old, conservative Wall Street banking house of Ladenburg, Thalman and Company. Selznick met Spiegel, and presently one or two small companies were gathered together under the name of World Films Corporation, with Spiegel as president and Selznick as vice-president and general manager.

World engaged as its director of productions William A. Brady, a theatrical manager and all-around showman, whose experiences had covered a wide variety of entertainment, from the management of James J. Corbett, pugilist, through early living pictures in vaudeville theaters and arcade halls, to production of feature photoplays and stage shows. Spiegel's Equitable organization distributed its films through World, and Selznick obtained also the photoplays of Peerless Pictures, a company owned by Jules Brulatour, who had made a fortune as selling agent of movie film for Eastman Kodak Company.

For more than a year World Film was a promising factor in the industry. Selznick meanwhile used his position to beat his bass drum and cry his personal wares in the market place so effectively that he became more famous than World. Then World's owners and financial backers, yearning for quiet, eased

him out of the corporation, and the flaming ex-jeweler was free
again.

Arthur Spiegel died. Moritz Rosenthal brought Ricord Gradwell, well known in business and financial circles because of his
success in managing the Oliver Typewriter Company, to direct
the company. William A. Brady continued with World for a
while and then returned to the tranquillity of stage production.
Despite Gradwell's careful management, World Film faded
away within a few years.

When he left World, Selznick's money assets were small, but
he had become expert in publicity and had made his name well
known in the industry. He now organized the Lewis J. Selznick
Pictures Company. Clara Kimball Young, a Vitagraph star, had
been acquired by World and advertised as its leading attraction.
Selznick abstracted Miss Young from World and formed the
Clara Kimball Young Pictures Company. He proposed to finance
the Selznick and Young corporations by selling a franchise to
distribute the pictures to a state's rights exchange in each key
city. The franchise owners were to advance the money to make
the pictures. A daring plan—and it worked. His sensationalism
and showmanship had attracted the attention of many exhibitors,
among them Aaron Jones of Jones, Linick and Schaeffer, and
Nathan Ascher of Ascher Brothers, owners of important chains
of theaters in Chicago, and Sol Lesser, a young, able operator
of independent exchanges in California. These men were among
the first to subscribe to his new ventures, and their prominence
in the industry was of value to Selznick in inducing others to
endorse his plan. Before the summer had ended all of the
franchises were taken and production of Clara Kimball Young
pictures was under way.

Among other friends of value to the dynamic Selznick were
Nicholas and Joseph Schenck, associated with the Marcus Loew
theater operations. Nicholas held a position in administration
second only to Loew, and Joseph was in charge of film bookings
and the selection of vaudeville performers. The brothers had been
Russian Jewish immigrants, accepting any employment they

could obtain in New York until each had saved some money. Nicholas inclined to the amusement industry, and Joseph thought it would be well to acquire an education before deciding on a business career. One day, when a few hundred dollars had been accumulated, his attention was attracted to the advertisement of a school of pharmacy which offered a complete education for three hundred dollars. To a youth with desire to advance, and with no one to guide him, "education" was education, whether it happened to be in pharmacy or what not. Joseph had never thought of being a druggist, but he had the necessary money to buy this particular education. He bought it, and became a pharmacist. Nicholas engaged in various small entertainment enterprises, which led him into connection with Loew. Presently Joseph left drug retailing to join his brother in the Loew corporations, and also in establishing an amusement park at Palisades, New Jersey, across the Hudson River from Grant's Tomb.

Selznick knew that Joseph Schenck was thinking seriously of stepping into the movie stream, when there came to the Selznick offices a player's agent trying to promote Norma Talmadge to stardom. Selznick had seen her in Vitagraph and Triangle pictures, and did not need to be told about her ability, but he knew nothing of her personally. He pumped the promoter and got the story of the little flat in Brooklyn, where Mother Talmadge, with sound Jewish sense, tried to overcome the deficits in the family budget created by the inability of her easy-going Irish husband to make money.

Norma, the eldest of three sisters, became a breadwinner in school days by posing for photographic slides used in illustrated songs on nickelodeon screens, thus partially satisfying her desire to be an actress until mother would say she was old enough to go to a movie studio. When that day arrived, she went to Vitagraph, not far away in Flatbush, and J. Stuart Blackton gave her work as an extra. Soon she persuaded her mother to let her become a member of the Vitagraph stock company; her sisters Constance and Natalie became extras when school duties permitted. Norma appeared in many Vitagraph pictures, and from

Vitagraph had gone to Los Angeles, where she and Constance were at this time working in Griffith and Ince studios.

Before completion of the promoter's story, Selznick had thought out his plans to elevate Norma and Constance Talmadge to stardom by means of Joseph Schenck. Norma Talmadge and Schenck met, and the hard-headed business man agreed with such alacrity to Selznick's schemes that the latter became almost suspicious. For weeks, Schenck saw nothing but stars, all named Norma Talmadge. They were finally married, much to Selznick's relief, and the company settled down to business again.

Joseph Schenck soon became one of the important figures in the industry. Norma Talmadge's drawing-power exceeded even Selznick's appraisal, and she has for years been one of the screen's most popular players. Her sister Constance also achieved stardom.

Selznick, equipped with money, with popular players, and with such individual productions as Rex Beach's "The Barrier," Nazimova's "War Brides," and Herbert Brenon's "Fall of the Romanoffs," was well started on his remarkable rise to power.

No ONE can say precisely when the movies became fashionable, but "Quo Vadis," Zukor's Famous Players, the Lasky Company, Hodkinson's Paramount, the Strand Theater, "The Spoilers," "The Birth of a Nation," Albert Smith's V L S E, Richard Rowland and Metro, Lewis Selznick and his fireworks—these events, as we look back, show that in a few years the movies ceased to be merely "a cheap show for cheap people" and began to attract ever-widening circles of the entire population. "The Birth of a Nation" was a powerful influence in this development. Its presentation in regular theaters at high admission prices brought it to the notice of thousands who had hitherto scornfully avoided motion pictures. As so often happens in other fields of endeavor, the worth of the movies was now measured by their cost. When theater-goers paid two dollars to see a motion picture, they accorded it far more respectful attention than they had hitherto granted the lurid melodramas of the nickelodeons and other photoplay houses.

Picture theaters had commenced to advertise regularly in newspapers, and to encourage this new source of revenue, publishers instructed dramatic editors to review the new films as well as new plays. Professional critics, with no knowledge of camera technique and no sympathy with the nickelodeon patronage which had nurtured the screen through its pioneer years, were adrift on an uncharted sea whenever they dealt with movies. To them, the playwrights of the London and New York stage represented the final word in dramaturgy, and stage players encompassed all there might be in the art of acting; naturally enough, they attempted to apply to the movies the rules of the spoken drama. The intellectuals had no conception of the great movement of the populace that had brought motion pictures from non-existence to an entertainment reaching forty or fifty millions of people in the United States as against the two or three millions who habitually visited the theater, and they were a decade behind the general public in realizing that play-acting on celluloid was a new form of expression, differing in many essentials from play-acting on a platform behind footlights.

Ignoring the important fact that nickelodeon audiences themselves had brought about most of the vital improvements in films, these new patrons of the screen decided, somewhat loftily, that something might be made of the movies if proper steps were taken. Their advice to the studios was to borrow from the stage its leading celebrities and use them in improving motion pictures.

These volunteer uplifters were for the most part ignorant of film history, and they knew nothing of the democratic forces operating behind the screen as well as in front of it. The stage had already made important contributions to the films. Motion pictures could hardly have attained their present level so quickly had not the stage already existed. Camera acting had been built on the foundations of stage art, but the movies, often unsuccessful in attempts to transfer stage celebrities to the screen, had recruited obscure players from stock companies and "ten-twent'-thirt'" traveling troupes.

In the early years of the films, while metropolitan actors regarded the new amusement as a shoddy, vulgar imitation of their art, the poorly paid actors in traveling stock companies who competed daily with the ever-increasing popularity of the movies came to understand the future importance of the screen. The harsh exigencies of their own profession—the necessity for a ready versatility and a quality of conviction in the numerous rôles they were called upon to play—had given these unknowns a grip on the realities of audience psychology of which their metropolitan brothers were largely innocent. They were not finished artists—but they knew the unsophisticated people who attended their performances and had learned, by hard experience, that they must please them or starve. The old wheeze about the stranded Thespian tramping the railroad ties back home was no joke to these players. Too many of them had done it.

While the commercial departments of the movies, the theaters and exchanges, were being absorbed by all sorts of men inexperienced in business affairs, the professional side found much of its personnel in the humble road shows and stock theaters. Some of the players became directors—D. W. Griffith, C. B. DeMille, Thomas H. Ince, George Loane Tucker, James Cruze, to name a few—and others became leading players of the screen.

What all players had to learn was that film technique and stage technique, although derived from the same source, are two very different things. The more obscure actors learned more rapidly than the head-liners who had been lured to the screen by fat contracts. They were more flexible and closer to the audiences who formed the bulk of screen patronage. But movies were not yet old enough to stand on their own merits and declare boldly that the art of the stage had little to contribute to the screen, and many more years were to pass before the fact became obvious. The movies were too new a phenomenon for anyone, within or without the industry, to have any clear comprehension of the elements with which they were dealing. Producers were as much at a loss as the newspaper critics and theater-goers who had recently joined the army of movie fans.

Zukor, pioneering with his Famous Players company, learned several years earlier than his competitors that stage fame did not extend very far. Broadway's matinée idols were unknown to the many millions of people whose support was essential to movie theaters. Each of the important producing companies made its own experiments with stage stars, and each in turn was bewildered by the results. Vitagraph, upon entering feature production, engaged Edward Sothern, then at the height of his career, but his pictures could hardly be sold to the exhibitors and the public stayed away from the theaters, even in cities where his stage appearances had attracted large audiences. The explanation was really not complicated. Movie audiences simply declined to have their stars foisted upon them. Their verdict was, and is now, final. But the film industry did not realize this fact in 1914-17, and many expensive experiments had to be made before the ruthless autocracy of the box office was fully realized and accepted.

THE most spectacular attempt to capitalize stage fame was that of the Triangle Film Corporation and its associated companies, which were the outgrowth of the disagreements in Mutual Film started by "The Birth of a Nation." The story of Mutual and Triangle is, in some ways, as significant as the history of Motion Pictures Patents Company and General Film. These four corporations, with their associates and subsidiaries, were so strong and well organized that they might reasonably have been expected to continue permanently in the industry. All of them forfeited their great opportunities and disappeared. Their death was caused by "internal dissension," the disease that proved fatal to dozens of other temporarily promising enterprises.

The principal cause of internal dissension in the industry was the difficulty of bringing about a workable understanding between experienced business men and financiers on the one hand and showmen on the other. The nature of the movie "game" demands of its followers extreme sensitiveness to public whims and exceptional agility in modifying practices to meet changing tastes. The showman wants to impress and compel the public with lavish, magnificent displays; the cautious business man is interested only in an assured return on his investment, and invariably looks thrice before leaping once. The experienced business men in General Film were successful to a certain point, but beyond that point they could not proceed because their minds were trained against the intuitive methods of showmanship. Mutual Film was brilliant, daring, and successful until its business men and financiers could no longer follow the "wild ideas" of their showmen associates. Then the business temperament and the showman temperament separated, only to discover that neither could prosper without the other. In the few movie groups which have endured since 1914-15, these divergent attitudes have been harmonized by one strong man—Zukor in his group, Loew in Loew-Metro-Goldwyn-Mayer, William Fox in the Fox companies, Laemmle in Universal, Harry Warner in the partnership with his brothers.

When Harry Aitken, the brilliant promoter and enthusiastic mainspring of Mutual, emboldened by the success of his company and by the triumphal progress of "The Birth of a Nation," conceived the plan of capturing the spoken drama and binding it to his chariot wheels, his conservative business associates wanted to "let well enough alone." Mutual was booming, and they prudently had no inclination to follow Aitken into any wild experiments with costly stage stars.

Kessel and Bauman aligned themselves with Aitken, and the three suddenly withdrew from Mutual and organized the Triangle corporation, the "triangle" consisting of the "three master directors of the screen," Griffith, Ince, and Sennett, who, Aitken announced, would take the greatest stars of the stage in their greatest plays and translate them to the screen in productions that would establish new standards. Nearly all the outstanding celebrities of spoken drama, vaudeville, and musical comedy were engaged by Triangle—Sir Herbert Beerbohm Tree, Mary Anderson de Navarro, Weber and Fields, DeWolf Hopper, Willie Collier, Billie Burke, Marie Doro, Texas Guinan, Frank Keenan, Elliott Dexter, Willard Mack, Catherine Calvert, Orrin Johnson, Helen Ware, Jane Grey, Henry Woodruff, Dustin Farnum, Taylor Holmes, George Fawcett, Crane Wilbur, Joe Jackson, Charles Murray, and other players, numbering in all nearly sixty.

Very few of the stars on Triangle's long list were known to screen audiences, one of the exceptions being Marie Dressler, a music hall artist, who had appeared in Sennett's "Tillie's Punctured Romance," supported by the then unknown Charlie Chaplin. Another less celebrated stage player engaged by Aitken was Douglas Fairbanks, who had attracted favorable attention on Broadway and had played in a few pictures. Still another little-known actor, William S. Hart, had left the stage for the Ince studios, and had won a place on the screen prior to the formation of Triangle.

Plans of this magnitude demanded large capital. Soon it became known that Smithers and Company, a Wall Street banking house reputed to be the brokerage connection of the Standard Oil Company, was prominently identified with Triangle, and through Wall Street rushed the sensational rumor that the greatest financiers of the day were behind Triangle with unlimited resources. Advertisements of Aitken's plans and gossip concerning his rumored financial backing fairly rocked the industry, and the other well-established companies suddenly shrank into insignificance before the colossal promise of Triangle. The announcement aroused much enthusiasm among the intelligent upper classes, their opinion being that the movies were now about to be raised from their low estate by the entrance of experienced stage stars to the film studios.

The Knickerbocker Theatre, then one of New York's principal houses, was taken by Aitken for the metropolitan home of

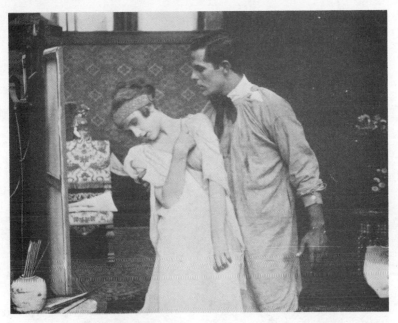

31A. *In the Lutin Quarter*, WITH ANTONIO MORENO AND CONSTANCE
TALMADGE. PRODUCED BY VITAGRAPH, ABOUT 1914.

31B. MACK SENNETT AND FRED MACE IN ONE OF A SERIES OF DETECTIVE
COMEDIES. PRODUCED BY KEYSTONE IN 1913.

32. PEARL WHITE IN AN EPISODE FROM THE FAMOUS SERIAL, *The Perils of Pauline.*
PRODUCED BY PATHÉ, 1913.

33A. *The Birth of a Nation*, D. W. GRIFFITH'S FIRST FEATURE PICTURE. PRODUCED BY THE EPOCH FILM CORP. IN 1914.

33B. WALLACE REID IN A SCENE FROM *The Birth of a Nation*.

34A. *Cinderella*, WITH MARY PICKFORD AND OWEN MOORE. PRODUCED BY
FAMOUS PLAYERS IN 1914.

34B. *In Wolf's Clothing*, WITH ALICE JOYCE. PRODUCED BY KALEM,
AROUND 1914.

35A. *The Battle Cry of Peace,* J. STUART BLACKTON'S FEATURE PRODUCTION
WHICH MADE NORMA TALMADGE A STAR. VITAGRAPH, 1915.

35B. ANOTHER SCENE FROM *The Battle Cry of Peace.*

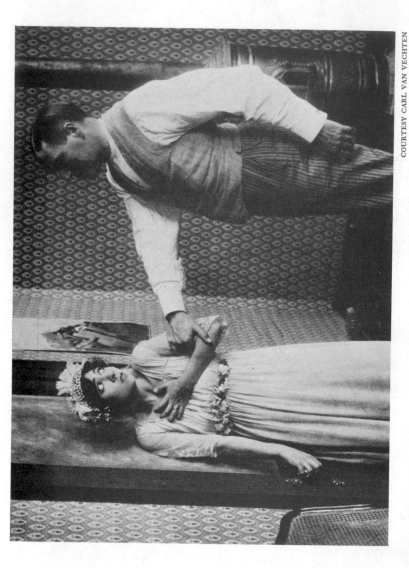

36. *Life's Whirlpool*, WITH FANIA MARINOFF AND HOLBROOK BLINN. THIS WAS THE FIRST VERSION OF FRANK NORRIS' NOVEL, *McTeague*. DIRECTED BY BARRY O'NEIL AND PRODUCED BY WORLD FILMS CORP. AT FORT LEE, NEW JERSEY, IN 1915.

37. THE THREE ESSANAY STARS OF 1915: CHARLIE CHAPLIN, FRANCIS X. BUSHMAN, AND BRONCHO BILLY.

38. *A Night Out*, WITH CHARLIE CHAPLIN, BEN TURPIN, AND LEO WHITE. PRODUCED BY ESSANAY, 1915.

39A. LILLIAN WALKER IN AN EPISODE FROM *The Blue Envelope Mystery*. PRODUCED BY VITAGRAPH IN 1915.

39B. *His Wife Knew About It*, A ONE-REEL COMEDY, WITH MR. AND MRS. SIDNEY DREW. PRODUCED BY VITAGRAPH, 1916.

40A. *The Immigrant,* WITH CHARLIE CHAPLIN, EDNA PURVIANCE, MACK SWAIN, AND HENRY BERGMAN. PRODUCED BY MUTUAL, 1916.

40B. CHARLIE CHAPLIN AND JOHN R. FREULER ON THE SET WHILE *The Cure* WAS BEING MADE FOR MUTUAL, IN 1917.

41. ADOLPH ZUKOR WITH MARY PICKFORD AND HER MOTHER, MRS. CHARLOTTE SMITH. 1916.

42A. *The Apostle of Vengeance*, WITH WILLIAM S. HART AND JOHN
GILBERT. PRODUCED BY TRIANGLE IN 1916.

42B. *Fighting Blood*, WITH WILLIAM FARNUM. PRODUCED BY FOX IN 1916.

43. *A Daughter of the Gods*, WITH ANNETTE KELLERMANN AND HAL DE FOREST. DIRECTED BY HERBERT BRENON FOR FOX IN 1916.

44A. *War Brides*, WITH ALLA NAZIMOVA. DIRECTED BY HERBERT BRENON
FOR SELZNICK IN 1916.

44B. *The Fall of the Romanoffs*, WITH EDWARD CONNELLY, ALFRED
HICKMAN AND CONWAY TEARLE. DIRECTED BY HERBERT BRENON. PRODUCED
BY A. H. WOODS FOR SELZNICK IN 1917.

45A. *The Clodhopper*, WITH CHARLES RAY. DIRECTED BY VICTOR SCHERT-ZINGER. PRODUCED BY TRIANGLE-INCE-KAY BEE IN 1917.

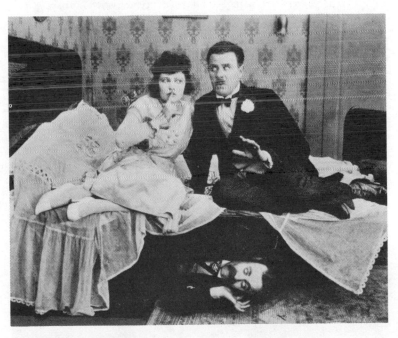

45B. *Beware of Boarders*, WITH CHESTER CONKLIN. A MACK SENNETT COMEDY PRODUCED BY PARAMOUNT IN 1918.

46A. *Within the Law*, WITH ALICE JOYCE, ANDERS RANDOLF, JOE DONOHUE
AND WALTER MCGRAIL. PRODUCED BY VITAGRAPH IN 1917.

46B. *The Poor Little Rich Girl*, WITH MARY PICKFORD. DIRECTED BY
MAURICE TOURNEUR. PRODUCED BY ARTCRAFT IN 1917.

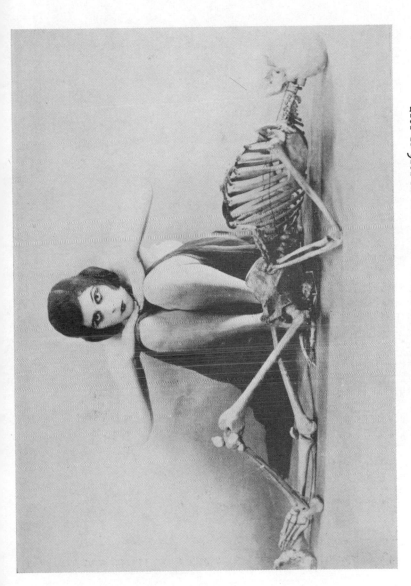

47. A PUBLICITY PORTRAIT USED BY FOX FOR THEDA BARA IN 1916 OR 1917.

48. *Cleopatra*, WITH THEDA BARA AND FRITZ LEIBER. DIRECTED BY J. GORDON EDWARDS FOR FOX IN 1917.

49A. INCEVILLE AT SANTA MONICA, CALIFORNIA, AS IT WAS FROM 1910 TO 1918. THIS PLANT WAS USED FOR THOMAS H. INCE PICTURES AND ALSO FOR KESSEL AND BAUMAN, ROBERTSON-COLE, AND OTHER COMPANIES.

49B. *The Gun Fighter*, WITH WILLIAM S. HART. PRODUCED BY TRIANGLE-INCE-KAY BEE IN 1917.

50A. *The Woman God Forgot,* WITH GERALDINE FARRAR, RAYMOND HATTON, AND THEODORE KOSLOFF. DIRECTED BY CECIL B. DEMILLE FOR ARTCRAFT IN 1917.

50B. *The End of the Tour,* WITH HAROLD LOCKWOOD AND MAY ALLISON. PRODUCED BY METRO IN 1917.

51A. *The Adopted Son*, WITH FRANCIS X. BUSHMAN AND BEVERLY BAYNE.
DIRECTED BY CHARLES BRABIN. PRODUCED BY METRO IN 1917.

51B. *The Man Who Wouldn't Tell*, WITH EARLE WILLIAMS AND GRACE
DARMOND. DIRECTED BY JAMES YOUNG FOR VITAGRAPH IN 1918.

52. *Fatty in Coney Island,* WITH FATTY ARBUCKLE AND BUSTER KEATON.
PRODUCED BY PARAMOUNT IN 1918.

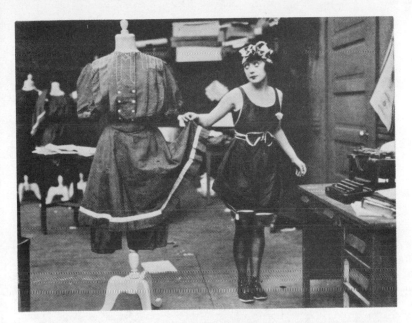

53A. *The Venus Model*, WITH MABEL NORMAND. DIRECTED BY CLARENCE BADGER. PRODUCED BY GOLDWYN IN 1918.

53B. *Girls*, WITH MARGUERITE CLARK AND HARRISON FORD. DIRECTED BY WALTER EDWARDS. PRODUCED BY PARAMOUNT IN 1919.

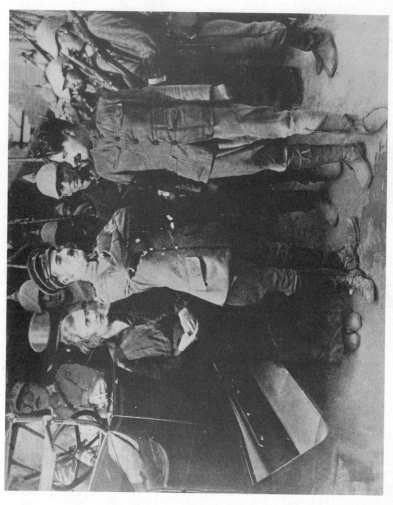

54. *Shoulder Arms*, WITH CHARLIE CHAPLIN, EDNA PURVIANCE AND SYD CHAPLIN. PRODUCED BY CHARLES CHAPLIN FOR FIRST NATIONAL IN 1918.

55. *The Miracle Man*, WITH THOMAS MEIGHAN, BETTY COMPSON, LON CHANEY AND JOSEPH DOWLING. DIRECTED BY GEORGE LOANE TUCKER. PRODUCED BY MAYFLOWER FOR PARAMOUNT IN 1919.

56. *Male and Female*, WITH GLORIA SWANSON AND THOMAS MEIGHAN. DIRECTED BY CECIL B. DEMILLE. PRODUCED BY ARTCRAFT IN 1919.

57. *Passion (Du Barry)*, WITH POLA NEGRI. DIRECTED BY ERNST LUBITSCH. IMPORTED BY FIRST NATIONAL IN 1920.

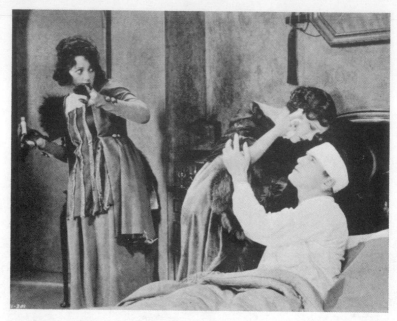

58A. *Why Change Your Wife?* WITH GLORIA SWANSON, BEBE DANIELS, AND THOMAS MEIGHAN. WRITTEN BY WILLIAM C. DEMILLE. DIRECTED BY CECIL B. DEMILLE. PRODUCED BY PARAMOUNT IN 1920.

58B. GLORIA SWANSON IN ANOTHER SCENE FROM *Why Change Your Wife?*

59A. *Judy of Rogues' Harbor*, WITH MARY MILES MINTER AND THEODORE ROBERTS. DIRECTED BY WILLIAM D. TAYLOR. PRODUCED BY REALART IN 1920.

59D. *Madame X*, WITH PAULINE FREDERICK. DIRECTED BY FRANK LLOYD. PRODUCED BY GOLDWYN IN 1920.

60. *The Kid,* WITH CHARLIE CHAPLIN AND JACKIE COOGAN. PRODUCED BY
CHARLES CHAPLIN FOR FIRST NATIONAL IN 1920.

61A. *Dr. Jekyll and Mr. Hyde,* WITH JOHN BARRYMORE. DIRECTED BY
JOHN ROBERTSON, FROM THE NOVEL BY ROBERT LOUIS STEVENSON.
PRODUCED BY PARAMOUNT-ARTCRAFT IN 1920.

61B. *The Penalty,* WITH LON CHANEY. DIRECTED BY WALLACE WORSLEY.
PRODUCED BY GOLDWYN IN 1920.

62A. *Sowing the Wind*, WITH ANITA STEWART, MYRTLE STEDMAN, AND JOSEF SWICKARD. DIRECTED BY JOHN M. STAHL. PRODUCED BY LOUIS B. MAYER FOR FIRST NATIONAL IN 1920.

COURTESY CLAIRE ADAMS

62B. *A Certain Rich Man*, WITH CLAIRE ADAMS, JEAN HERSHOLT AND ROBERT MCKIM. PRODUCED BY BENJAMIN B. HAMPTON FROM THE NOVEL BY WILLIAM ALLEN WHITE IN 1921. DISTRIBUTED BY W. W. HODKINSON CO.

Triangle pictures, and there on September 23, 1915, the first Triangle program was presented at regular Broadway prices, two dollars then being the standard top price for successful plays. The opening program consisted of three pictures: Ince's "The Iron Strain," with Dustin Farnum, Enid Markey, Louise Glaum, Fred Mace and Mabel Normand; Griffith's "The Lamb," with Douglas Fairbanks and Seena Owen; Sennett's "My Valet," with Raymond Hitchcock.

Movie theater owners throughout the country contracted for Triangle pictures at figures in excess of their customary feature rentals, and, encouraged by the success of the Knickerbocker in charging high prices, advanced their own rates from ten to fifteen cents, or from fifteen to twenty-five.

Aitken, a man of unusual imagination and ability, was a sincere motion picture enthusiast. He had no doubt of the commercial success of Triangle, believing it would follow the path of "The Birth of a Nation." He was equally confident that achievement of his great dream would bring the art of the stage within reach of the masses. He knew he had undertaken a tremendous task in transferring *en bloc* to the screen nearly all the famous personnel of the stage, but he understood the film business and had organized his studios with the best talent in the industry. Griffith, Ince, and Sennett at that time had no superiors and few equals. He understood, too, promotion, corporation organization, and finance, and in obtaining the support of high-class Wall Street bankers, had apparently fortified his project with sufficient financial backing. He anticipated most of the events that would follow his great adventure, and had prepared in advance to meet them.

Aitken and his associates expected a prompt, favorable response from exhibitors and public, and both lived up to expectations; Triangle pictures were demanded everywhere and became instantly popular. However, there were other events that were not anticipated, and a dozen years later the screen world was still trying to solve the problems they brought with them. The first of these was the attitude of stars and leading players of the movies who had worked their way up from obscurity in store shows and were advancing to wider popularity in the new ten- and fifteen-cent theaters that were now replacing the nickelodeons everywhere. When Aitken's famous troupers flocked to the Triangle studios at Culver City, near Los Angeles, and began to talk about the salaries they were receiving, the experienced camera players did not like it a little bit.... Sir Beerbohm Tree at $100,000 for six months.... Lew Fields and Joe Weber at $2,500 a week each.... DeWolf Hopper at $1,500 a week on a year's contract.... Actors accustomed to receiving $250 to $500 a week on the stage for thirty or forty weeks a year when their plays were successful and much less time when unsuccessful, were so fearful that screen appearance would injure their stage prestige that Aitken had had to double, treble, and quadruple their salaries and give them contracts for a year or more.

Successful screen stars, actors and actresses trained to the camera, who felt that they were making fortunes for their producers—and some of them were—were very unhappy when they compared their pittances of $100 to $500 a week with the princely wages of the stage favorites. The studio folk were rather awed for a little while by the presence of their wealthy, self-possessed brethren from Broadway. For a very little while. Then Monte Blue was called to double for Sir Herbert Beerbohm Tree, after the discovery had been made that Sir Herbert's technique, though admirable back of the footlights, was much less admirable when registered through a lens; and that Sir Herbert was drawing about $4,000 a week and Blue's pay envelope contained exactly thirty dollars.... And when one day it was revealed that one of the most charming girls of the stage had ankles so large that she could not be photographed walking upstairs.... And another's neckbones were so prominent that she looked like a skeleton in close-ups....

Within a few months, screen players were convinced that they had little to fear from the competition of theatrical stars, and the judgment of the studios was soon endorsed by motion-picture audiences everywhere. Theater owners who had contracted for Triangle pictures at high rates began to shriek with dismay that the famous stars of Broadway were inglorious failures on the screen. Patrons stayed at home when their pictures were announced. Exhibitors everywhere refused to pay the high rentals necessitated by the salaries of the stage celebrities and additional costs created by their unfamiliarity with camera technique. Aitken, burdened with expenses of production far greater than the average costs of his competitors, had to meet an avalanche of canceled contracts. He struggled vigorously to save Triangle from collapse, settling with the many celebrities and sending them back to the Broadway footlights. A few of the galaxy, the less celebrated, had shown indications of developing into screen stars. These Aitken retained, and around them attempted to build a new Triangle business.

Douglas Fairbanks had a set of athletic stunts that appealed to audiences and his personality was pleasing. Frank Keenan, a seasoned stage star, became successful in character rôles and for years had a large screen following. Charlie Chaplin was made a star by Mack Sennett. Others of the Aitken ensemble buckled down to the serious business of learning a new technique and won success on the screen; but their success came too late to benefit Aitken. His financial resources were weakened by the failure of the expensive pictures that failed to bring back their costs. Many of Triangle's players and directors, with appetites whetted by the large compensation of stage celebrities, demanded more and more money, and Aitken, unable to meet their demands, lost them to his competitors. There were rows and bickerings among Triangle officers and stockholders. Triangle stock, which once had sold above par, slid down and down until it faded from view, and the support of the bankers faded with it. Aitken's great dream went to smash.

CHAPTER EIGHT

THE PICKFORD REVOLUTION

AITKEN'S experiment accelerated the movement toward better pictures, although several years were to pass before the industry realized that any good had proceeded from the events following Triangle's rise and fall. Those events led to a complete revolution of motion-picture production and distribution. Business practices and studio methods were revised, executives were toppled from their thrones, and a wholly new order of things was created. Movie actors, as soon as they recovered from their astonishment at the salaries paid by Triangle to the Broadway stars, were not slow to demand higher wages for themselves. However, as they were unorganized, their individual efforts were unsuccessful until Mary Pickford and her mother created the precedents that soon altered the entire industry.

As a matter of fact, Mary Pickford can hardly be called the only factor in producing the new order, but as she had already been a focal point in so many previous events, it is convenient to trace this period of screen history through an outline of her career. Shortly after her entrance into the Biograph studio, Carl Laemmle's offer of higher wages lured her from Biograph to Imp. This was the first of a series of battles over this young actress that were to continue for a decade.

Miss Pickford remained with Imp for several months, then

played on the stage for a while, and then returned to Biograph. When Paramount was formed, she was in Adolph Zukor's Famous Players' studio at the then high salary of $1,000 a week. She had steadily progressed in popularity and was undoubtedly the most reliably effective box-office attraction the screen possessed. The Paramount service supplied one feature or two features a week to the theaters. The theater was charged a stipulated sum for the Paramount program in which the Pickford pictures were included, the exhibitor paying the same rental for Pickfords as for other less popular films. This system was the general practice of the industry.

Paramount had not been long in existence when Charlotte Pickford heard that film salesmen were saying, "as long as we have Mary on the program we can wrap everything around her neck," a phrase meaning that exhibitors could be induced to buy the entire Paramount output in order to obtain the Pickfords. Mrs. Pickford reasoned that if Mary's neck was strong enough to support the entire Paramount program, she was entitled to greater compensation, and so informed Mr. Zukor, who passed the problem on to Mr. Hodkinson. Hodkinson began to give it careful consideration.

Films, as we know, had always been sold by General Film on the flat-price, daily program system, and other distributors had followed this method, basing their charge on the size and the location of the playhouse. Under this system many theaters in a single city might show a film on the first day of its release. When Hodkinson, still with General Film, began to select better-grade movies from the program and charge a higher price for them, he also gave the exhibitor priority in showing the picture. This priority was known as the "first run," and the first-run exhibitor was protected for a week or so against the exhibition of the picture in other houses in his district.

When features began to appear in the market, owners of the larger and better theaters were willing to pay premium rentals for them, but insisted on definite protection against simultaneous showings elsewhere. After organizing Paramount, Hodkinson codified random practices, and definitely graded all houses as first-, second-, and subsequent-run theaters, giving each exhibitor protection for a certain period against competitors. First-run houses were nearly always located downtown, in the center of the amusement district, and paid the highest rental. Second runs were the smaller theaters in residential districts, "neighborhood houses," as they are known in the trade; and there were similar gradings down to fifth runs in villages and poorer sections. This arrangement was accepted by all distributors and promptly became the prevailing method of the trade. It was natural and businesslike, and seemed to be nothing more than merely a step forward in sound commercial practice. Fundamentally, however, it was much more—it marked the beginnings of power in the first-run houses.

But the development of that power was hidden in the future when Mrs. Pickford decided that her daughter was entitled to more money. Although Mrs. Pickford did not realize it, she was registering the first important protest against the program system of film rental which, in various forms, had been in existence since the organization of screen shows. Unconsciously, she was inaugurating a movement toward new methods of distribution and exhibition.

Hodkinson was fully aware of Mary Pickford's value, and he decided that Mrs. Pickford's demands would have to be met. To do so, Paramount would have to increase its advances to Famous Players on Pickford negatives, and would have to charge exhibitors higher prices for her pictures. His proposal was to sell the Pickford pictures as a "series," charging more for them than for the regular Paramount program. Apparently this was but a slight departure from the program system, but it unexpectedly broadened within a few years into a complete new method of distribution. It made possible the high salaries that were to come to actors, the increase in admittance prices to the great theaters that were to be built, and the enthusiastic endorsement of both by the public.

Some of the exhibitors demurred at the new "series" prices,

but their audiences had to have Mary Pickford and soon the theaters agreed to pay the increased rentals. Miss Pickford received a new contract with Famous Players, dated January 15, 1915, under which she was to make ten pictures a year, for $2,000 a week salary and half the profits of her productions.

Within a year, rumors of Triangle's payments to stage stars were startling the studios, and Mrs. Pickford again revised her opinions upward. She knew that Mr. Hodkinson's new plan had been successful, and she had heard that some theaters had even paid rentals in excess of Paramount's for the most prominent Triangle pictures. If these rumors were true (and she believed they were), obviously it was possible for Paramount further to advance prices on Pickford films, and to pay her more money. Mrs. Pickford announced that Mary's salary would have to be raised to $1,000 a day, $7,000 a week!

A salary of anything near this figure would so greatly increase production costs that exhibitors would have to pay double or treble the highest prices ever paid for feature film service. Theaters had raised admittance rates five or ten cents, some of the better houses advancing to fifteen and even to twenty-five cents, and many exhibitors doubted the public's ability and willingness to pay such high prices. Expensively built new theaters might succeed for a while at such rates, but films were still essentially an entertainment for people of limited means, and there was always the chance that these new theaters would be forced back to lower prices.

Mr. Hodkinson and Mr. Zukor carefully explained to Mrs. Pickford the practical impossibility of getting higher prices from exhibitors and public. Mrs. Pickford cared nothing for their explanations, sound and reasonable as they might be. She was interested only in getting more money for her daughter and she believed both that Mary was worth it and that the industry was able to pay it. She left it to Hodkinson and Zukor to work out the details, meanwhile continuing to search for means to accomplish her desire.

I MUST here digress for a moment into autobiography. Various stories of Mary Pickford's transactions with me and the events that followed them have been printed; some of these tales have been highly entertaining, but I feel that the actual facts should be recorded, as they demonstrate quite clearly the influence Mrs. Pickford unwittingly exerted over the future of a large industry. I was at the time one of the vice-presidents of the American Tobacco Company, of which Percival S. Hill was president. The movies had interested me for several years, and I had become convinced that once the films found themselves, they would attain very high importance socially and commercially. The experiments of the pioneer producers of features seemed to me to mark definite progress, and Hodkinson's creation of Paramount appeared as the forerunner of a new era. I began to study the corporations and personnel of the industry very carefully.

Aitken's experiment with Triangle was a valuable factor in my education in that it portrayed clearly the extravagance and waste in the business. Each producer, or each small group of small producers, was operating a distributing system of thirty to thirty-five branch offices, costing $500,000 to $600,000 a year; and each producing group had its own studio, each involving unnecessary costs of $250,000 to $500,000 annually. One distributing organization could easily do the work now spread over several, and consolidation of several studios ought to create efficiency, render better service to theaters and audiences, improve quality, and reduce waste.

In spite of the World War, the volume of film commerce was growing rapidly each year. I believed that as soon as the war ended there would be many new theaters and that admittance prices would continue to rise. American motion picture commerce in 1915-16 was five or six hundred millions of dollars a year. In 1925-26 the figures were a billion and a quarter. I do not assume that Zukor, Hodkinson, Aitken or any other movie enthusiast of 1915-16 could have predicted an increase of a hundred percent within ten years. These men were confident that interest in motion pictures would continue to expand, but none of them anticipated the later titanic developments.

Two hundred or more producing and distributing companies were actively engaged in business in 1915. As I surveyed the situation it seemed to me that a merger of a few of them would create a strong unit, one that could eliminate wastes of perhaps a million and a half dollars a year by the consolidation of branch offices and studios. Two of the youngest corporations in the industry appealed to me as possessing the qualities necessary to such an undertaking: Paramount, with its producers, Zukor, Lasky-Goldfish-DeMille, Pallas and Morosco; and V L S E, composed of ex-General Film producers, Vitagraph, Lubin, Selig, and Essanay.

At this time, very few big business men and financiers could be induced to regard the movies seriously. A few capitalists, Crawford Livingston, Otto Kahn, Smithers & Co., Moritz Rosenthal, and one or two others, believed in their money-making possibilities, but several years were yet to pass before movies became a recognized department of Wall Street operations.

Percival S. Hill was a man of imagination and courage. When I presented my ideas, plans and guesses as to the future of the movies, he analyzed them carefully and concluded that the industry would become one of the greatest in America. He was convinced that a merger of Paramount and V L S E would create a powerful, profitable corporation. I had calculated that the undertaking would require capitalization of fifteen to twenty million dollars, and Mr. Hill's approval assured the necessary financial backing.

Each of these corporations had built a profitable business. Zukor's Famous Players and Vitagraph each had records of net earnings of a million dollars a year or more. The Lasky-Goldfish-DeMille company, although young, was striding rapidly toward profits of a million a year. The distributing companies, Paramount and V L S E, were about two years old and each was increasing its profits steadily. The remarkable growth of movies in these early years is revealed by the fact that all of these companies had developed out of their own resources. No outside capital had been required, and their officers were unfamiliar with Wall Street methods. My proposal was to bring all these companies together into a single unit, obtain financing in Wall Street, and to list the shares on the Stock Exchange.

There were nine presidents of nine separate companies; in the proposed merged corporation there would be one president; obviously eight presidents would cease to function as the "big boss"; and if one president should presently grow where nine had been flourishing, there was a small host of vice-presidents, secretaries, treasurers, general managers, department heads, and other officers whose lustre would be dimmed. Ira M. Lowry, manager of the Lubin company, was the diplomat who worked for several months in smoothing out the human kinks in the V L S E group, while I undertook the task of convincing members of the Paramount family of the practicability of my idea. William Wadsworth Hodkinson was the reef on which my beautiful plan was wrecked.

Hodkinson sincerely believed that the three branches of motion pictures should be kept separate: the producer should concentrate on making pictures, the distributor on distribution, and the exhibitor on the ownership and management of theaters. He argued that such independence maintained interest and enthusiasm, and resulted in better pictures, better distribution, and better theater management than would be possible if all elements should be merged under one head. In accordance with Hodkinson's ideas, Paramount had made contracts with its producers for a term of twenty-five years, during which the producers could not supply pictures to other distributors. He believed that the plan of merging Paramount and V L S E was sound and desirable; he could see the economies possible under such an arrangement, and welcomed the idea of a corporation of this size which would create stability in the industry. He would not, however, agree to Paramount's producers becoming stockholders in the new company. He steadfastly refused to sanction a union of producer and exhibitor, and maintained that his producers were abundantly protected by their twenty-five-year contracts.

ADOLPH ZUKOR had risen from obscurity in 1912 to the position of leading producer in 1915. He was steadily making the best program of features of all manufacturers, and was making more money than any other producer. When I outlined my idea of a merger, he made his position perfectly clear: proper plans of consolidation were sound and would accomplish beneficial results; he would be glad to travel along with the general ideas advanced, but the Famous Players corporation and the Lasky corporation would have to be included as stockholders in the new company, and he personally must have a definite voice in the selection of officers and the determination of the new corporation's policies.

During the several weeks of our negotiations, I became deeply interested in studying this man who had done much to create a new era in entertainment. Aitken, a brilliant promoter, had blazed a trail to Wall Street, and Zukor was scrutinizing that trail carefully. He quickly got the outline of my merger plan, and then questioned me thoroughly about Wall Street, high finance, anti-trust laws, and related subjects. Within a month he had obtained and absorbed information that I had spent a dozen years in acquiring. I began to compare him with the many industrial and financial magnates whom I had met in following my trades of reporter, editor, and business man, and I soon decided that nothing like Zukor had yet appeared in America.

While pumping me about Wall Street, he was modest, restrained, quietly dignified. As time went on, and I would advise him occasionally of my lack of progress in obtaining concessions from Hodkinson, Zukor would register disappointment with drooping shoulders, a low voice that seemed to be struggling with suppressed sobs, and eyes depicting deepest sorrow. His humble manners were, of course, a mask, merely a part of a marvelous method of encouraging others to reveal themselves to him. I got the impression that he was a better actor than any of his stars, and that impression has never left me.

Back of this humility, modesty, and acting was a very shrewd and able brain. His knowledge of motion pictures was more comprehensive than that of anyone I had met. He understood the business of producing the five-reel features which had brought him success, and knew how to select writers, directors, technicians, and players, and how to organize his studio. Above all, he was an incomparable showman, with an amazing flair for sensing audience reactions long before the movie audiences themselves knew what they wanted.

When I conveyed these opinions to Hodkinson, he commented briefly that perhaps I was right: Zukor certainly was making good pictures, and he certainly had been clever enough to make Paramount pay him a good deal of money for them. Then he turned in his revolving chair, and gazed at the pigeons wheeling above the marble portico of the Astor Library. Silence settled on the room. He could not change his point of view. All my efforts to modify it so that Zukor and the Lasky group could be included as stockholders were of absolutely no avail.

During these negotiations, while we hoped for a miracle to reconcile the divergent views of Hodkinson and Zukor, it was important that members of Paramount and V L S E groups keep their own counsel. If gossip concerning the proposed consolidation should reach the industry, many producers and distributors not included in the merger plans would clamor for admittance or condemn the project as a trust. Although Paramount and V L S E controlled less than twenty percent of the total film rentals and could not have been legally declared an octopus, the federal government was actively prosecuting all corporations suspected of trust tendencies and Wall Street looked with disfavor on mergers that might have to face the Sherman law.

However advisable silence may be, secrets in the movie world are short-lived. One day a V L S E producer told a friend, in strictest confidence, the outline of our plans, and a few days later the newspapers spread the story under scareheads. The wide publicity produced several results, one of which had to do with a comedian. But producers and distributors saw nothing funny in what happened. Charles S. Chaplin, the comedian in the situation, was the first funny man to be taken seriously by his employers. Comedies had long been a staple of the program system, and comedians were so abundant and the technique of comedies so well defined, that no one player was regarded as very important. If a studio lost a funny man, the producer promptly replaced him with another. Several comedies were ground out of the studios every week, pretty much in the manner of sausage-making. The comedians threw custard pies and smacked each other with barrel staves. The films sold readily, and that was that.

Chaplin was born in England of a family of pantomimists and strolling players. His boyhood was spent in poverty, work with provincial shows alternating with employment in factories and shops. In time he reached the position of a minor music-hall acrobat-pantomimist-clown. He came to America in 1913 with an English company, Fred Karno's "A Night in a Music Hall" and his work attracted the attention of Adam Kessel, who engaged him for Kessel and Bauman's Keystone comedies, directed by Mack Sennett. Chaplin went to Los Angeles in 1914 at $150 a week.

From his first picture, Chaplin's work was distinctive and he acquired popularity so quickly that before the close of his year with Keystone, G. M. Anderson (Broncho Billy), partner of George K. Spoor in Essanay, invited him to join their company. Chaplin asked Anderson for a salary of $1,250 a week and when the industry learned that Essanay had agreed to this demand, it suddenly realized that comedians could be very serious when talking about money. Essanay advertised Chaplin vigorously, and his pictures became very successful during his year with Spoor and Anderson.

Mary Pickford's success in obtaining $2,000 a week and half the profits of her pictures in her new Famous Players contract, and Triangle's high-salaried stage stars, encouraged Chaplin, at the expiration of his agreement with Essanay, to journey to New York and see what he could do for himself. He and his brother left Los Angeles about the time that stories of the proposed Paramount-V L S E merger and the rumors of heavy Wall Street support appeared in the newspapers.

Ira Lowry, an enthusiastic Chaplin fan, was scouting for elements of value to the proposed new corporation. He heard of the arrival of Charlie and Syd Chaplin in New York, and rushed into their bedroom at the Hotel Astor before they had time to unpack their suit-cases. Chaplin was in the bathtub, and while Lowry and his brother tramped around the bedroom, the comedian conducted business negotiations between splashes.

"I want $10,000 a week salary," Charlie presently announced.

There was no precedent in the industry for such a figure, and it is probable that he merely selected $10,000 as a nice, round sum. Lowry breathed deep for a moment, and finally replied that Ben Hampton would persuade the Paramount-V L S E corporation—which he was confident would be created—to pay this price. He wrote a brief memorandum agreement on hotel note-paper, and Chaplin climbed out of the bathtub to sign it.

ALMOST simultaneously with Ira Lowry's announcement that he had secured Chaplin at $520,000 a year, Cora C. Wilkenning, broker in plays and manager of actors, read the merger story in newspapers. She called on me to declare that Mary Pickford's contract with Famous Players was ended and that Miss Pickford was about to negotiate with another producer. She advised me that if Mary Pickford was to be retained, prompt action was in order.

My examinations of Paramount and V L S E earnings had revealed Miss Pickford's power over audiences. It required no great perspicacity to realize that Mutual, Triangle, Universal,

World, or any other company not included in the merger plan, would leap at the chance to weaken the projected corporation by acquiring this pre-eminent player. I conveyed the bad news to Hodkinson and to Zukor. Hodkinson was anxious to retain this highly valuable asset, but, determined to commit no act that might permit Paramount producers to enter the merger as stockholders, he refrained from definite comment on the Pickford situation, merely passing the problem to Zukor as one for the producer to solve.

Zukor insisted that Miss Pickford's contract had been renewed by agreement, that it was in full force and effect, and he would resist any movement of another producer to take her away. He might consider an increase of Miss Pickford's salary, but the limitations of the program-and-series system tied his hands completely so that no higher compensation was possible without complete modification of the system, and such action might drive theater owners into riot.

I presented these points to Mrs. Wilkenning and tried to convince her that the entire business of motion pictures could not be upset because of the demands of one young lady. Mrs. Wilkenning replied that her object was to get more money for Mary Pickford, and if Paramount-Zukor-V L S E would not pay the price she could get it from Mutual. Shrewdly appraising the importance of this artist to my project, she suggested that I make a contract with Miss Pickford immediately, before Mutual acquired her, and work out the details with my associates later.

Meanwhile, I had passed the Chaplin proposition to the V L S E group. Vitagraph had been the producer of John Bunny's comedies and Essanay had just ended a successful year with Chaplin. It was a fair assumption that these producers had complete knowledge of the market possibilities of comedies. The conservative business men composing this organization, although staggered by the thought of paying anyone $520,000 a year, considered the proposition carefully. While they were discussing it, John R. Freuler of Mutual, whose scouts had been flirting with Chaplin in Los Angeles, heard of the Lowry agreement, and raised the bid to $10,000 a week salary, plus a bonus of $150,000, a total of $670,000 for one year. Chaplin accepted Freuler's offer, and Lowry's memorandum, which was in effect an option for a short period, became valueless.

Since the withdrawal of Aitken to Triangle, Freuler had been vigorously fighting to keep Mutual in a prominent position in the industry, and his quick action with Chaplin proved that he would take long chances. Roy McCardell, at this time writing plays for Mutual producers, came to me with confirmation of Mrs. Wilkenning's statement that Mutual was keen to acquire Mary Pickford. Accompanied by McCardell, I visited Freuler and frankly asked if he was bidding for the star. He cheerfully responded that he was, adding that he would meet her demand of $7,000 a week and half the net profits of her pictures. He offered to relieve me of a contract with her if I had one or could get one. Evidently Mrs. Wilkenning was right; if Mary Pickford was to be saved for the proposed merger someone must act quickly.

Through Mrs. Wilkenning I met Mary Pickford and her mother and began the first of a series of conversations that were not to terminate for several months. I discovered that Miss Pickford's principal interest was a desire to advance in her profession. She had been making "little girl" movies from the start, and now that she was "grown up" she wanted to play more mature rôles. Charlotte Pickford was frank, simple, and direct. She and her daughter knew what they wanted: The Mary Pickford Pictures Corporation was to be formed, Miss Pickford to receive one-half of its shares in addition to the salary of a thousand dollars each calendar day. Charlotte Pickford was to become treasurer of the company and no obligations were to be incurred nor money expended without her consent. The number of pictures was to be reduced from ten a year to eight or six in order to improve their quality by less hasty production. They were to be sold separate from other pictures—that is, outside the program system; if new methods had to be introduced into the industry in order to accomplish these results, they would have to be introduced. Miss Pickford wrote a letter embodying these points, and the letter constituted a perfectly good contract.

I told them that Mr. Zukor insisted that his contract was still in force. Mrs. Pickford disagreed, but they added to Miss Pickford's letter a provision that if Mr. Zukor's contention should be upheld, either she or I would be free to terminate our agreement.

Thus, due to the actions of three women, the most valuable actress of the day was saved for the proposed new corporation. Success was in sight if I could round up a few straggling items. Among them were these:

Hodkinson must be persuaded to admit Paramount producers as stockholders in the merger, and to give Zukor a voice in the selection of officers and the determination of policies;

Members of the V L S E group must be induced to permit Hodkinson and Zukor to occupy high positions—perhaps the highest positions—in the consolidation. The V L S E producers had been members of the patents trust. Only a few years before Hodkinson had been one of their employees, and Zukor was an upstart sitting for hours in General Film's reception room, pleading for a franchise to distribute his pictures. It was not easy for them to forget these things;

Valuations must be placed on each corporation, and this meant a hard fight to convince each owner that his property and good will were not being underestimated;

And there still remained the matter of reorganizing the existing machinery of distribution and exhibition to meet the demands of Charlotte and Mary Pickford. The question of Mary Pickford's situation with Famous Players called for prompt attention. Was or was not her contract with Famous Players in force? Had or had it not been broken? Charlotte and Mary Pickford were positively affirmative, Adolph Zukor and Elek John Ludvigh, legal counsel of Famous Players, were positively negative.

Before the appearance of the newspaper stories regarding the proposed merger, and the consternation created by the threatened loss of Mary Pickford, there had been much tension in the negotiations. Now it increased rapidly to the breaking point. Mary Pickford's demands fanned into flames the smoldering discontent between Hodkinson and Zukor. Hodkinson would not consider allowing Paramount to become directly interested in production. He suggested that some day such demands as Mary Pickford's could be met by introducing a percentage system of paying for important film rentals, but while this might have been possible in a few theaters in 1916, it was utterly impossible to induce five to ten thousand exhibitors to install the necessary accounting methods—and the necessary honesty. Discussion of the percentage system to meet the Pickford emergency was therefore purely academic; Hodkinson disliked losing her but was unwilling, nevertheless, to depart from the Paramount system. Zukor wanted freedom to move in any direction that seemed desirable, and fretted under the restraints of Paramount's inelastic system. He was becoming definitely annoyed with Hodkinson's immobility, and his mask of humility was used less frequently as the days passed slowly and we came no nearer to a solution.

He and Elek John Ludvigh soon convinced me of their sincerity in asserting that the Pickford-Famous Players contract had been extended beyond its one-year term by oral agreements and letters. Charlotte and Mary Pickford were equally sincere in their belief that Miss Pickford was free, but were willing to compose the difference if an equitable plan could be devised. Mr. Zukor did not insist that Miss Pickford continue to work at her old salary; he was ready to revise his methods to meet her demands, but to do so his hands must be untied from his Paramount contract. Miss Pickford and I quietly released each other from our agreement, so that she was free to negotiate a new arrangement.

Zukor's mind was now working on a way out of the Paramount impasse. Obviously he did not intend to lose Mary Pickford nor to permit anything to retard his progress in any way. He warned me that unless Hodkinson agreed to the inclusion of Paramount producers as stockholders and to give him a place of authority in the councils of the new corporation, the merger would not be formed. Having watched the expansion of his ambitions and the operations of his mind for several months I was convinced that he was preparing to place himself at the head of the procession.

In vain I shuttled back and forth between these two men, succeeding only in irritating Hodkinson and arousing his suspicion that I was being hypnotized by Zukor. I said bluntly that the owners of Paramount were in business to make money and that his adherence to what he called "Paramount ideals" would come to nothing if Zukor offered Steele, Abrams and Greene, and Sherry a high price for their stock.

"Zukor will buy out all your partners except Pawley," I predicted, "and you and Pawley soon will follow the others and sell to him. Our proposed merger will collapse, and Zukor will work out one of his own. I believe that Albert Smith and all the V L S E group will agree to Zukor's demands that he and Lasky be taken in as stockholders, and I think they will accept Zukor as chairman of the board. By yielding these points, our project is assured of success; otherwise it fails, and soon you will be out of Paramount."

To all of which Hodkinson replied: "I am right, and if I'm put out of Paramount for being right, there will be another place for me in the industry. If necessary, I'll start again at the bottom and work my way up." Soon he informed me that other capitalists were prepared to proceed with a merger plan in accordance with his own specifications.

I then attempted to consolidate Paramount and V L S E, trusting that once this action was completed, the V L S E officers would persuade Hodkinson to accede to Zukor's demands. The Paramount directors met in the board room and invited me to enter and submit my plan. I did so. Three votes—Greene and Abrams, Sherry, and Steele—were promptly cast against it. Zukor had acted, and three-fifths of Paramount were now voting as he instructed.

Zukor did not advertise his achievement. Famous Players, Lasky, Pallas and Morosco were yet to be consolidated. Mary Pickford's demands must be taken care of; Triangle was an uncertain element that might fade away or might develop into a serious competitor; Mutual, Universal, Selznick, Fox, World, Metro, V L S E, and many other organizations were healthy and full of fight. Until future developments should have determined their position, Zukor preferred to keep his operations in the background instead of in the center of the stage.

Hiram Abrams replaced Hodkinson as president of Paramount, Hodkinson and Pawley remaining on the board of directors for a few months until they sold their shares to Zukor's associates and resigned from the corporation. Benjamin P. Schulberg became Abrams' right-hand man in Paramount. Zukor abandoned my plan of merging V L S E with Paramount, and in its stead he created, after some months had passed, the Famous Players-Lasky Corporation, a consolidation of the four Paramount producing companies, presently electing himself president and Jesse L. Lasky vice-president. Samuel Goldfish withdrew from the Lasky company, receiving $1,000,000 for his interest. Frank C. Garbutt, Los Angeles capitalist interested in the Pallas and Morosco producing companies, remained with the new corporation. Cecil B. DeMille continued as principal director of the Lasky studio in Los Angeles.

Zukor's ideas about industrial expansion developed rapidly during these months. The common method of building the large corporations known as trusts, from approximately 1890 to 1910, when the Supreme Court became active in enforcing the Sherman Anti-Trust Law, was by consolidation of competing companies. Oil, steel, sugar, tobacco, railroads, and other industrial trusts had grown by mergers of many companies into one. Zukor did not merge other producing and distributing companies with Famous Players-Lasky, but followed a system introduced by himself, of absorbing the strength of his competitors. The power of film corporations could be measured only by the popularity of their stars. Investments in studios, equipment, and branch offices might present an imposing set of figures, but such assets were of little value without box-office attractions.

Triangle, although seriously crippled, still controlled Griffith, Ince, Sennett, Douglas Fairbanks, William S. Hart, and several minor players who were winning public favor, among the latter an actress from Mack Sennett comedies, Gloria Swanson, a comedian named Fatty Arbuckle, and a bright little girl, Anita Loos, who had grown up in the studios, writing lively stories and titles that made audiences laugh. Zukor patiently went through motions of negotiating a merger with Triangle, and no one but he could tell whether he was considering a consolidation or was merely analyzing Aitken's methods of finance and learning the value of the various properties in Triangle's possession.

Not all the distributors shared Hodkinson's faith in the program system. Walter W. Irwin, the lawyer who had become general manager of V L S E, advocated the rental of meritorious pictures individually. Lewis J. Selznick was selling his product in series, each star representing a unit, and occasionally rented an important picture separately; and other distributors were considering methods more elastic than the program-series idea.

In the autumn of 1916, a few months after the election of Abrams as president of Paramount and the consolidation of Famous Players-Lasky-Pallas-Morosco, the movie world was startled by the announcement that Mary Pickford had formed her own producing company and that her pictures would be distributed by a new corporation named "Artcraft," the ownership of which was not made public. Walter Greene was president of Artcraft, with Al Lichtman in charge of operations. Each Artcraft production was to be sold separately, and theater owners began to inquire if this revolutionary departure from the program system meant an increase in rentals.

Zukor's radical ideas had made him an object of suspicion during the earliest days of his movie career, and the continuous success of his undertakings spread the feeling that no one could guess what he would do next. Although he tried to obscure himself in the background, the gossips of the movie trade thoroughly advertised his acquisition of Paramount control and his conferences with Triangle, and these events and the Famous Players-Lasky merger intensified the feeling that he was a dangerous fellow who might attempt anything. In spite of its camouflage, the Pickford-Artcraft innovation was charged to him, and created the belief that his ambitions were moving toward domination of production and distribution.

Public enjoyment of features had doubled, or more than doubled, film commerce in three or four years. In the United States, $100,000,000 to $150,000,000 of annual income had been added to theater receipts, and the rate of increase was growing rapidly. With scores of producers and distributors competing for screen showings, the exhibitors were buying service at prices that made intelligent theater operation extremely profitable; net returns of twenty-five to fifty percent per annum on the capital invested in movie houses was assumed to be the prevailing rate, but some theaters ran this up to a hundred percent. The exhibitors had played an important part in the busting of one trust, and they insisted that no combination or individual should ever again dictate to them. At the time of Charlotte Pickford's $1,000-per-day demand, Zukor knew that advanced rental rates would arouse the anger of theater owners, and events proved his anticipations to have been well founded.

Under the Paramount system, Mary Pickford's pictures had earned in the United States rentals of approximately $100,000 to $125,000 each. Under the Artcraft system the prices were, broadly stated, trebled at the start, so that her films would yield $300,000 or more each in this country alone. As soon as information regarding these rental scales reached the exhibitors, they loudly condemned Zukor, alleging intent to monopolize stars, annihilate competition, treble picture prices, and swallow the industry. Apparently nothing would satisfy them but a general movement of theater owners to discipline Zukor rigorously before he could become more powerful. Such action was not practicable. Zukor was saved by the inability of exhibitors to get together among themselves and decide on anything. Twelve to fourteen thousand active, aggressive retailers, each an ardent individualist, could not instantly abandon life-long habits of independent thought and action and join in a co-operative movement. There was a great deal of excoriation of Zukor, but Al Lichtman and Walter Greene soon convinced the leading theaters that Mary's prices were justified, and the smaller exhibitors grumblingly fell into line.

As a matter of fact, the many better pictures now coming from several studios—including Artcraft—marked another definite step forward on the screen. Movie audiences were ahead of the producers—they were ready for better pictures before film makers realized their readiness. Owners of first-run theaters, who had been cautiously advancing their admittance rates, learned that their patrons would pay twenty-five cents, or in a few cities as high as thirty-five cents, to see the best pictures; and at these prices the profits were larger than ever before, even though the exhibitor had to pay somewhat higher rentals.

Charlotte Pickford's confidence that her daughter ought to get higher wages was justified by the approval of the box office.

ACTING, historically one of the most precarious of all professions, suddenly found itself among the best paid on earth. When the millions of American movie fans learned to identify their favorites of the screen, they changed the status of an entire craft, transferring the balance of power from the employer to the employe group.

This movement had started only in 1909-10 but it spread so quickly that almost at once any producer who discovered a popular actor or actress was assured of large profits. By 1912-13, nearly all manufacturers had abandoned efforts to sell any films that did not feature a star. All the newcomers in movie making —Zukor, Lasky, Pallas, Morosco, Selznick, Metro, World, and many others—and all the progressive pioneers—Fox, Universal, V L S E, Mutual—rushed along with the tidal wave of star popularity. By 1915-17, the demand for stars was so great that there were not enough to go around, and producers were combing the stage and the studios for more players who might develop into good box-office attractions.

During this period, fifty or more favorites arose to prominence, among them Marguerite Clark, Blanche Sweet, and Pauline Frederick of Paramount; Theda Bara and William Farnum of Fox; Tom Mix of Selig and later of Fox; Anita Stewart, Alice Joyce, and Earle Williams of Vitagraph; William S. Hart of Triangle; Norma and Constance Talmadge of Selznick; Lillian and Dorothy Gish and Mae Marsh of Griffith-Triangle; Harold Lockwood and May Allison of Metro. Mary Pickford became so peculiarly pre-eminent that her position at the very top was subject to little question or jealousy. Charlie Chaplin rose to fame like a comet, but, like Mary Pickford, he held his place with the approval of his fellow players as well as the public.

Chaplin's success in getting $10,000 a week and a bonus of $150,000 from John R. Freuler was widely publicized, and although the exact terms of Mary Pickford's arrangement with Artcraft were not announced, it was soon generally known that her salary was $10,000 a week and half the profits of her pictures, so that her total compensation might reach a million a year. The youthful industry suddenly realized that it had among its members the two highest-salaried human beings on the globe. The army of fans, not in the least suspecting that its own influence had created the situation, declared it altogether incredible that any girl or any little funny man could find ten thousand dollars apiece in their pay envelopes each Saturday night. Nevertheless, these millions of skeptics were so excited by the reports, that whenever Pickford or Chaplin appeared on the screen they crowded the theaters to see anyone who earned so much money. The theaters prospered, and the producers got their share of the extra profits.

The player group, too, contained skeptics—for a little while. But before long they were convinced that they were not dreaming, that Pickford and Chaplin were actually receiving these fantastic sums. They lacked organization, and had no conception of the peculiar conditions in the industry that made this the psychological moment to obtain their demands. Individually, but by the hundreds, they began to clamor for more money—increases ranging from one hundred to five hundred percent—together with additional privileges that seriously increased production costs.

When Artcraft was organized, representative feature negatives had been costing $10,000 to $30,000 each. After adding the cost of positives, trade-press advertising, and incidentals, the complete cost of average features could be placed at $20,000 to $40,000 each. Gross earnings of such pictures were between $50,000 and $100,000, a few of them reaching $125,000. After deducting the thirty-five percent usually charged by the distributor, there remained a gross profit of $20,000 to $50,000 a picture. The average net profits of a well-managed company were $10,000 to $20,000 a picture.

While all costs had advanced with the progress of pictures from short films to five-reel features, extravagance in studios and exchanges was not customary. Incompetent manufacturers frequently produced poor films which discerning exhibitors refused to accept, but the leading producers ran their plants in a business-like manner, avoiding excessive expense and waste as far as possible.

Competitive bidding for stars, or for players who might become stars, had been vigorous, and, although careful producers condemned the practice as insane, everyone had been forced into it by the large demand for features and the inadequate supply of experienced actors and actresses. However, up to this time, the competition had kept within the limitations of business possibilities. Stars were receiving $300, $500, or $1,000 a week; lead players (those playing opposite the star) were available at $150 to $500; character actors, "heavies" or villains, and comedians, $75 to $250. Directors were getting $150 to $500; camera men $75 to $250.

Hitherto when a star "stolen" from a competitor entered the new employer's studio, all other salaries on his list had not been upset. Now the situation was taking on a very different, and very menacing, aspect. The Pickford and Chaplin contracts had convinced all players that there was no limit to the money that could be obtained. The only fear of each was that he might not ask enough. And the fear of the successful employers, when suddenly confronted by avalanches of high-salary demands, was that all their profits would be wiped out. No longer was it possible to advance the wages of one or a few actresses or actors in a studio without advancing all; within an hour after a star received the promise of a raise, the secret was known on every stage and in every dressing room, and the next day a dozen more cases had to be settled, or the players walked out to find employment with a competitor.

The matter of wage increase was bound up with an indefinable demand for better and better pictures that seemed to have no ending. Better stories were wanted, and this meant more money for plays, novels, continuities and scenarios. Better sets, better dressing of stages and more expensive costumes; fewer pictures per star unit per year. In every section of production, manufacturers could see expenses mounting higher and higher. Negatives that had been costing $10,000 to $30,000 were now requiring outlays of $30,000 to $75,000, rising to $100,000 to $125,000 if they included first-rank stars.

Most of the established producers and distributors, and the few financiers who had become interested in the industry, did not believe that such expensive pictures could earn a profit. They were convinced that movie commerce had been pushed to the limit in the short time since features came in, and they saw little possibility of extending its boundaries for several years to come.

Even during war years, foreign audiences were eagerly accepting the new American feature films, and by 1917 exports had reached a point at which American producers could count on $10,000 to $20,000 earnings per feature from foreign sales. But it seemed hardly possible to increase either the sales or prices while the war lasted. In the spring of 1917, the United

States entered the war, just when the campaign of the players against their employers was beginning to assume serious proportions, and as no one could guess the effect of the war on any business, financiers were moving very cautiously in all industries not connected with war supplies.

In every other business than motion pictures, caution contributes to success, but in the movies the conservative has almost invariably disappeared from the industry. History had repeated itself each time radicals and conservatives came into conflict. In 1917, while prudent manufacturers, unable to adjust their minds quickly to the high-pressure methods necessitated by the new conditions, were thoughtfully analyzing wage demands, venturesome competitors rushed in and took their celebrities away from them, agreeing to salaries that generally were declared "impossible."

A few of these daring showmen got possession of stars that the public loved, and, although the prices paid seemed very high, they were able to pass the additional costs—through the theaters —to audiences, who paid the bill cheerfully. These producers made money, but others, more reckless than wise in the bidding contest, found themselves saddled with players who failed as box-office attractions. Such producers sustained severe losses in 1917-18, and some of them soon succumbed and joined the ultra-conservative producers in fading from the screen.

CHAPTER NINE
THE RISE OF FIRST NATIONAL

THAT the movies are a unique and peculiar institution is nowhere better illustrated than in the relation of its several branches to one another. All American industries are composed of six elements: Raw material, labor, manufacturing, distribution (wholesale, jobbing or brokerage), retailing, and consumption. Almost without exception, manufacturers and distributors hold the reins of power. The producers of raw material and natural resources contend that manufacturers and distributors obtain more than a just share of the wealth created by their fabrication and sale. Labor protests against the power of factory and jobbing house, and insists on higher wages and insurance against physical injuries, unemployment, and old age. Small retailers continually agitate for special legislation to protect them against the encroachments of chain stores and mail-order houses, which are in essence a vast, modern extension of the distributor's power over many forms of manufacturing. The consumers, the public, express their discontent by a constant search for "bargains" at "cut prices," the result of over-production, error, or some weakness in one of the other elements.

Motion pictures, from their inception, cast aside industrial traditions and customs, and never since then have business men and financiers succeeded in bringing them into line. When films left the organized variety theaters and entered the rabble of small, cheap store shows, they passed to the control of the consumers, the American populace, and the power then acquired has never been relinquished. This unusual condition has made the movies a phenomenon that industrial leaders, bankers, and students have been unable to appreciate. Capitalists and investors, through this lack of understanding, have lost millions of dollars in vain efforts to make films conform to the business habits that prevail in other industries; and well-intentioned intellectuals have been sadly bewildered by the screen's refusal to accept the standards of other methods of drama and story-telling.

The power of the public enabled the raw material of motion pictures—players, directors, writers, and other human elements are substantially the only raw material used in films, the actual celluloid being merely a chemical incident—to gain ascendancy over manufacturers and distributors when the star system entered the screen in 1909-10, and made possible the revolution of 1916-17, which placed the employers definitely in the hands of their player-employes. Another phase of the revolution created by the popularity of the stars proceeded from the retailing branch of the industry, and continued to grow until manufacturing and distributing were stripped of their last remnants of authority and relegated to subsidiary positions, where they have since remained. This unexpected change was all the more startling because of its complete reversal of the current trend toward separation of production and distribution and exhibition. Manufacturers who had been interested in theaters, and exhibitors owning shares in small producing companies, were concentrating their capital and energies in one or the other branch of the business. The general drift was apparently against consolidation of the three when the great transformation suddenly occurred.

After the patents-film trust had lost its grip, improvement in theaters and in pictures had advanced simultaneously. Neither the makers nor the retailers could have succeeded unless both had progressed together, but both branches ignored this fact in hard-fought squabbles over rental rates and terms. There was abundant competition. Forty to sixty producers were turning out twelve hundred to fifteen hundred films a year, and, as in each city several principal exhibitors were fighting each other, if one theater refused to pay the producer's price, another could usually be induced to do so.

Everyone was so busy with his own efforts to gather his share —and possibly his neighbor's—of the industry's increasing profits that no one had time to realize the growing influence of a few first-run theaters. No one knew that the public had concentrated, in less than two hundred houses, sufficient power to dominate all theaters in the United States—a total then of fourteen thousand or more—and eventually to dominate the screens of the world and to eliminate from the business all manufacturers and exchanges except those favored with its patronage.

The growth of first-run theater power was natural, steady, and persistent, and was merely a result of the public's increasing enjoyment of better quality in pictures and in theaters. Nickelodeons had sprung into existence by the thousands in response to the people's welcome of the living picture novelty, but the discomforts and low seating-capacity of these early houses, as well as of the larger remodeled store-rooms that succeeded them, necessitated a more attractive type of theater. In 1914-17, following the advent of the Strand Theater in New York, many new theaters were built on plans differing from anything previously known. Standard theater design called for three floors—orchestra, balcony, and gallery—and the seating capacity was usually 600 to 1,000; the new movie palaces had only two floors, dispensing with the humiliating gallery, and their seating capacities ran from 1,800 to 3,000. The public welcomed the superior comfort and beauty of these theaters, and cheerfully paid higher prices to enjoy the better music and the selected films usually shown in them. Thus their greater earning power enabled them to outbid smaller, less modern houses for desirable pictures.

The new palace theaters became liberal advertisers in newspapers and publishers responded by giving their shows publicity in news columns and reviews. The newspapers in thirty to fifty metropolitan centers throughout the country—key cities—circulate in all neighboring cities and towns, and the advertising and publicity of a first run in a key city create a demand for the picture in the surrounding district. Theaters in Long Island or New Jersey, for example, learned that a photoplay first shown at the Strand or the Rialto, in New York, would draw large audiences, while a film with no first run in the metropolis would attract little attention. Soon exhibitors everywhere in the United States followed the line of least resistance, giving preference to pictures with the prestige of key-city first runs, ignoring all others or renting them only at very low rates. Within a few years photoplays without first runs were not regarded by theater-goers as first class, and unless a producer could obtain first runs his chance of making money grew very slim.

Several years had to pass before the industry recognized the deep significance of the first-run situation. Producers and distributors were unable to believe that a time would ever come when enough first-class screens would not be available. There always had been plenty of houses, and the industry was confident that there always would be plenty.

One of the principal reasons for the inability of manufacturers to get a clear view of first-run power was the time required to make and distribute a film. Three to six months might elapse between the start of production and the release date, and about a year passed before earnings were completed. Therefore, for a year or more the producer did not have the full truth about rentals, and all that time would harbor hopes that his output would be successful. The producer could not reduce his costs to conform to earnings. The principal expense of pictures consists of the negative, and this investment is not changed by the success or failure of a picture. "The Birth of a Nation" negative cost $100,000 and earned profits of several millions; the "Ben Hur" negative many years later cost four or five million dollars, but failed to equal the earnings of "The Birth of a Nation." This principle applies to all photoplays, whatever their cost may be.

In 1915-17, representative features, if shown on first-run screens, earned in the United States from $60,000 to $100,000 gross, or about $40,000 to $60,000 after deducting the distributor's charge. These earnings, as analyzed in a previous chapter, assured well-organized producers of satisfactory profits. But if, however, adequate first runs were lacking, the earnings in second and subsequent run houses would drop to $30,000 to $40,000, which was not enough to repay producers' costs. Consequently, at the time of the revolutionary advance in players' salaries, the prestige of first-run presentation had become essential to profitable production and distribution, and when the cost of features now increased twenty-five to one hundred percent, although very few men in the industry could at that time foresee the approaching crisis, the producer who was not assured of adequate first runs was definitely headed for failure.

By HIS consolidations and acquisitions, Zukor had made himself the largest producer and distributor of features in the world. More than half of the most popular stars were on the Paramount list, and Artcraft had Mary Pickford, the magnet that drew more money to ticket windows than several other favorites combined. When theaters accepted the Artcraft increase in Pickford picture prices and advanced their admittance rates, Zukor was in a position to dominate studios and exchanges. The Paramount group of companies did not constitute a trust—at least not in the common acceptance of the term; they exercised no monopoly and controlled no more than twenty or twenty-five percent of the total volume of rentals. But Zukor had something more effective than a monopolistic corporation—he had the stars that controlled the audiences, and he believed audiences would permanently control the theaters.

He began quietly and persistently to increase Paramount and Artcraft rental rates, and presently representatives of these companies were giving preference to theaters that would use Paramount-Artcraft films to the exclusion of features made by other producers. Theater owners such as Robert Leiber of Indianapolis, Thomas Tally of Los Angeles, Jones, Linnick and Schaeffer of Chicago, Eugene Roth and Turner and Dankin of San Francisco, had followed a practice of using part of the Paramount output, supplying the remainder of their needs with pictures of Selznick, Goldwyn, Hodkinson, Fox, Metro, V L S E, Universal, and other producers. Such theaters, usually showing fifty-two pictures a year, might buy twelve, twenty-four, or thirty-six features from Paramount, dividing the other weeks between other manufacturers. In this manner, leading producers were assured of first runs, and the practice served exhibitors by maintaining competition and restraining the prices charged by producers.

Selznick and other manufacturers were not slow to follow Zukor, keeping their charges as close to his as possible without losing business. Some theaters could pay the advanced prices, and some thought they could not; however, looking beyond a consideration of prices, intelligent exhibitors foresaw that, as the logical result of Zukor's new method of giving preference to theaters showing nothing but his features, mere "preference" might soon be followed by insistence. If theaters should accede to his demands, other producers would starve to death, and Paramount-Artcraft could enforce whatever prices Zukor should elect to charge.

Only two or three years earlier, important first-run theaters would have met such a situation by throwing out the impudent manufacturer's product and showing none but pictures made by his competitors. Some exhibitors now followed this impulse and discarded Zukor's pictures, only to learn to their sorrow that control of their own houses had passed out of their hands— audiences definitely dominated the screen, the stars controlled the audiences, and many of the popular stars were employed by Zukor. Theater owners who discarded Paramount or Artcraft saw the pictures eagerly accepted by competitors at Zukor's prices and in accordance with his demand for preferential exhibition of his product. Good pictures could be obtained from other producers; about half the favorite stars were independent of Zukor; new stars were arising; but there was, nevertheless, definite box-office value connected with Mary Pickford, and the prestige of Paramount and Artcraft was steadily increasing. Even though clever exhibitors replaced Zukor's product promptly, they feared that competing theaters would woo away their customers with Zukor's glamorous celebrities. Then, presently, when the best pictures of all producers had been obtained by two or three theaters in each large city, some houses faced a struggle to find fifty-two good features a year to replace the favorites lost when they refused to accede to Zukor's terms.

Leading exhibitors, often owning a chain of several theaters, had acquired wealth and influence in their home cities. The pride and business sense of such men urged them to find means of repressing Zukor before he could acquire dictatorial power. Thomas L. Tally, of Los Angeles, now rich and prominent, but still filled with his old fighting spirit, found the way out. His idea was to create an organization of exhibitors, one member in each principal key city, which would buy, or make, and distribute pictures of its own. Such an association would be profitable in itself and would restrain all producers from asking exorbitant prices. John D. Williams, a West Virginian who had been selling and exhibiting American films in various parts of the world for a number of years, was in Los Angeles. Tally outlined his plan and Williams liked it so well that they united to put it into effect.

"First National Exhibitors Circuit" was the title given to the project, and it was to have twenty-five or thirty members, each owning the franchise for his district, and each paying his share of the cost of production. Tally's neighbors, Turner and Dankin at San Francisco, and Jensen and Von Herburg at Seattle, joined promptly, and as quickly as Tally and Williams could travel to the east the plan was approved by owners of theaters in almost every key city. Jones, Linick and Schaeffer of Chicago, Finkelstein and Rubin of Minneapolis, Stanley and Jules Mastbaum of the Stanley Company of Philadelphia, the Hulse chain in Texas, the Sanger-Jordan circuit in New Orleans, Abe Blank in Iowa, Rowland and Clarke in Pittsburgh, John Kunsky in Detroit, thé Nate Gordon interests in Boston, the Fabian circuit in New Jersey, all joined Tally's organization. The first meeting was held in New York in April, 1917. Robert Leiber of Indianapolis was elected president, Harry Schwalbe, of the Stanley group of Philadelphia, secretary, and John D. Williams, manager.

First National exhibitors owned about a hundred theaters, and in each of thirty or thirty-five key cities at least one of their houses was a leading first run that was an important customer of Paramount pictures. The association issued sub-franchises to theaters in neighborhoods and outlying cities, and within a few months several hundred important exhibitors had joined the movement. In time five or six thousand theaters were in its organization. Ownership and control of the corporation, however, remained with the two dozen original stockholders.

The Tally-Williams creation brought Zukor face to face with something new in movie affairs. As long as exhibitors merely chanted hymns of hate there was no real danger, but here were important theater owners, principal buyers of his merchandise, banded together for the purpose of disciplining him. The weapon in the hands of First National was the boycott, and although cautious lawyers restrained buoyant press agents from use of the word itself, restraint in language was no comfort to Zukor when he faced the menace of losing many of Paramount's first runs, without which Paramount's profits of several millions a year would not be possible.

When First National made its threats of regulation and hints of boycott, Zukor was not yearning for new worlds to conquer. Perhaps in a little while he would have been seeking additions to his kingdom, but at the moment his hands were full of troublesome matters. Getting exhibitors to agree to his increased prices and exclusion terms required careful, shrewd management. All producers and distributors, now aroused to the belief that he was planning to dominate the industry, were fighting fiercely to injure him whenever and however possible. Inside his own companies, jealousies were blazing, and wage demands were growing like weeds. Zukor had plenty of things to keep him busy.

Samuel Goldfish, with the proceeds of the sale of his Lasky stock, had formed an alliance with Edgar and Archie Selwyn and Crosby Gaige, successful stage producers, and Margaret Mayo, Robert W. Chambers, Rex Beach, and other well-known authors. "Goldwyn," a word coined from syllables of Goldfish and Selwyn, was the title of this corporation, and Goldfish liked it so well that he presented his old name to the state of New York and received "Goldwyn" in exchange. Goldwyn and his associates created an imposing organization of executives, including Gabriel L. Hess, legal counsel; Frederick Blount Warren in charge of advertising and publicity; and Adolph Klauber, husband of Jane Cowl, at the head of the casting department. Unconvinced by Aitken's disastrous experience, they acquired several famous stage stars, Maxine Elliott, Madge Kennedy, Geraldine Farrar and others, and from the screen took Mae Marsh, heroine of Griffith's "The Birth of a Nation."

Hodkinson and Pawley, withdrawing from Paramount, joined Frederick Collins, author and magazine editor, in creating a new producing corporation, "Super-pictures." They arranged with Triangle for the use of its exchanges until Hodkinson could form his own distributing system. Collins took Olga Petrova, stage artist, as one of his stars, and made stars of two young sisters named Flugrath, afterwards famous as Viola Dana and Shirley Mason. Hodkinson obtained other pictures from several individual producers.

William Fox, disregarding the trend toward separation of production and exhibition, had steadily acquired more houses, and when the events of 1916-17 turned the industry topsy-turvy, was in a strong position, with studios in New York and Los Angeles, exchanges in all key cities, and a chain of profitable theaters in New York and adjacent cities. Selznick seemed to be progressing daily. Universal was very active and was growing stronger. V L S E, under the management of Walter W. Irwin, Metro, managed by Richard Rowland, Robertson-Cole, Pathé, and others were important factors in feature distribution.

Hodkinson and Goldwyn, too proud to admit that Zukor was a menace to their welfare, nevertheless yearned to annihilate him. Selznick constantly advertised his plans to remove Zukor's hide and nail it to the Selznick barn door. Fox, Universal, Metro, Patrick Powers' companies, and others transferred their ancient hatred of General Film to Paramount-Artcraft, and directed their heaviest blasts at these companies.

While these storms were raging on the outside, there was constant trouble inside the Paramount-Artcraft organization. All producers were struggling with salary demands, but Zukor had a special burden to carry as author of the Artcraft plan, by which class distinctions had been introduced in the studios. All actors regarded Artcraft as the swanky member of the screen family, and Mary Pickford's huge salary had become the standard by which all players evaluated their services. Stars, advanced from $250 to $1,000 or $1,500 a week within two or three years, and lead players with proportionate increases, were far from satisfied, and their unremitting efforts to obtain more money and transference from the Paramount program to the glory of Artcraft production, added wrinkles to Zukor's brow. He might have been willing to promote some of the Paramount actresses to Artcraft, but he had to proceed gently to overcome the reluctance of Mary Pickford to admit any other feminine stars into her playground.

NOTHING like the storm that arose when First National was organized had previously been known in the industry. Tally, Williams, and Schwalbe wasted no time in buying or building studios or studio organizations, but directed their efforts solely to bidding for the big box-office names of leading producers. As noisily as possible, they announced that First National would obtain the greatest stars, and the plain inference was that First National would pay the greatest salaries. This was indeed a startling shift in the attitude of exhibitors. In 1916 they had threatened to scalp Zukor for having raised Mary Pickford's compensation and thereby increasing the burden of the exhibitor. Now, in 1917, suddenly becoming producers, they manifested their intention to boost actors' earnings far above the figures they themselves had declared to be outrageous. The industry, by now long inured to the extravagant boasts of producers, took these announcements at something less than their face value, but it was genuinely aroused when First National took Charlie Chaplin from Freuler at a salary announced as "more than a million a year."

Soon it became known that the new organization had adopted a plan calculated to be more attractive to stars than that of Artcraft. First National was not, at the beginning, an employer of players or an operator of studios. Under its contract with Chaplin, the comedian became his own producer, agreeing to make for First National eight two-reel comedies a year. First National was to advance $125,000 to make each negative, and in this sum was included the star's salary. Chaplin was free to make pictures longer than two reels, and First National would advance $15,000 for each additional reel of negative. First National also provided the money to pay for positives, trade-paper advertising, and incidentals. The cost of distribution was set at thirty percent of the total rentals, and after all costs had been recouped, First National and Chaplin were to divide net profits equally. For several years, this was First National's standard system with stars and with producers who later joined the organization.

All prominent producers were menaced by First National, but most of them were still making short films or cheap features as well as quality or star features, and if their quality business was affected they might continue to sell shorts and other low-cost product. But Zukor, Selznick, Goldwyn, Metro, Hodkinson, and a few others produced nothing but quality features. Selznick seemed to be at least partly protected by having several of the First National stockholders associated with him in the ownership of Selznick exchanges. Hodkinson had many friends among exhibitors who were encouraging him with promises of enthusiastic support. Goldwyn, too, was encouraged by alliances with important theaters in various cities, and believed that exhibitors would always buy his product in order to restrain Zukor. In general, although producers and distributors were annoyed and exasperated by First National's threats of increased salaries to stars, they could not believe that a few theaters could ever keep them from getting first runs.

Zukor, almost alone, was not in the least deceived. He correctly appraised the Tally-Williams organization for what it was, and needed no clairvoyant to tell him that First National, rapidly acquiring famous stars and able directors, would some day have enough pictures of its own to enable the theaters to "forget" Paramount. Recourse to the boycott, a weapon that might prove to be a legal boomerang, would not be needed. Exhibitors could quietly substitute First National photoplays for Paramount's, and this perfectly legal procedure would be entirely effective in amputating Paramount's profits.

Not only was Paramount menaced, but Artcraft was soon disturbed by rumors that Mary Pickford was growing restless again. Tally and Williams had acquired Chaplin first because his contract with Freuler expired before the end of Miss Pickford's agreement with Artcraft, and neither she nor First National managers denied that they had made her an offer which she was seriously considering. Zukor had not yet succeeded in adding to Artcraft any other strong elements. George M. Cohan, very popular on the stage, had not been accepted by audiences when Artcraft put him on the screen. A special picture by Geraldine Farrar, prima donna, had been handled by Artcraft, but this artist soon went to the new Goldwyn company. Elsie Ferguson, stage star, was still an experiment in Artcraft, and Douglas Fairbanks, C. B. DeMille, and others were only fairly started on their careers. If Mary Pickford deserted the company for First National, Zukor faced a severe loss of prestige and profits.

His glorious vision of domination of the screen through ownership of stars began to grow dim. Exhibitor-producers, if determined to do so, could raise wages beyond the limits of producers who hoped for large profits. Theater owners would not have to make one feature a week to accomplish this purpose; two a month with principal stars would insure the popularity of their screens. Features for other weeks could be obtained from producers hungering for first runs and willing to accept small profits if by so doing they could remain in business. The pictures could be rented at low prices, and on them the exhibitor-producers could make enough money to offset any lack of profits on films produced by their own stars.

Zukor could not attempt to safeguard his companies by entering the field of cheap film-making. He had become a producer because he sensed the public's demand for quality, and had risen to power through constant willingness to risk money and smash traditions in the process of supplying it. He believed that audiences would soon accept nothing but costly productions and manufacturers of cheap films would fade from the screen. He had to continue with nothing but expensive pictures—and no expensive picture could get back its cost without first runs.

First National now controlled many first runs. It had bought Charlie Chaplin. It was bidding very high for Mary Pickford. With Pickford and Chaplin in its possession it would own the two greatest first-run attractions in existence, and many high-class exhibitors would protect their theaters by using First National pictures. Inasmuch as Paramount and Artcraft were the principal distributors of first-run product, they would be the chief sufferers.

ZUKOR was so agile, resourceful, and unexpected in meeting emergencies that a horde of legends regarding him have sprung up. In accordance with our standard American practice of describing our national figures as noble heroes upon whom the Almighty has bestowed miraculous gifts, or as demons intimately leagued with Hades, Zukor has been portrayed as a modern combination of Napoleon and Machiavelli with dashes of oriental subtlety; or as an inspired genius, who, while selling furs in New York and Chicago shops, shrewdly planned to make himself dictator of the entertainment world and ruthlessly forced his way to the top.

His father, a merchant in a village in Hungary, and his mother, of a family in which rabbis and doctors predominated, planned to educate the older son, Arthur, and Adolph as rabbis. Father and mother died and the boys were raised by relatives. Arthur, adopting the name of his uncle, Leiberman, completed his education and became a rabbi in Hungary, but Adolph turned to business and worked in small retail shops until the lure of America possessed him. He persuaded his guardians to permit him to seek his fortune in the new country beyond the sea.

He reached New York in 1888, aged about seventeen, and found employment at low wages in various East Side factories, among them a small fur shop. Relatives and neighbors from Hungary had prospered in the fur trade in Chicago, and to that city went Zukor. Within a few years, he became a partner in the firm of Morris Kohn and Company, fur manufacturers. There, too, he met and married Lottie Kaufmann, the daughter of sturdy Hungarians who had battled their way through farming in North Dakota to a mercantile position in Chicago.

The fur business carried him back to New York. When he was about thirty years old, he invested with friends in a penny arcade in Union Square. The entertainment field pleased him, and presently he left the fur business to his partners and gave his time to the new venture. He joined William A. Brady, producer of stage plays and owner of "Hale's Tours," in early showing of travel films, and this was followed by association with Marcus Loew in nickelodeons and popular-priced film and vaudeville shows.

The truth about Zukor is far more interesting—and significant, as a lesson in the ways of our civilization—than the far-fetched legends concerning him. The decade in which Zukor was learning what makes the wheels go round was the famous "trust era" and trusts were the most popular subject of contemporary discussion. Trust-busting politicians raged at Rockefeller, Duke, Ryan, Havemeyer, Harriman, and other "malefactors of great wealth," calling on the Federal government to send them to prison. The muckraking magazines and the newspapers regularly attacked and exposed the iniquitous monopolies of illegal combinations. The government responded with a series of anti-trust lawsuits that acquired the popularity of sporting events, but a mind much less keen than Zukor's could not fail to observe that the prosecutions invariably came slowly to a common termination in the courts; the trusts were torn apart, "the eggs were unscrambled," "the octopus was cut to pieces," but no "malefactor of great wealth" ever got near a jail door.

The public was satisfied. The game had been played and ended. But Zukor, noting that each fragment of a dismembered trust promptly became a healthy and profitable octopus on its own hook, was convinced that America loves its industrial and financial magnates, its Big Business Men, much as the English love their nobility. Wealth, honor, and glory were waiting for any young man who would play the game of business in accordance with the somewhat nebulous rules of the Supreme Court, which seemed to be that one could dominate to one's heart's content if one didn't make the mistake of too blatantly piling corporation on corporation.

Zukor's industrial philosophy is the result of his youthful observations. He was able to appraise accurately the American attitude towards wealth, but even more important was his willingness to work terrifically at any task he undertook, and his eagerness to learn from other men and to expand his mind to absorb whatever they could teach him. He had no detailed plan that led from a penny arcade to a skyscraper in Times Square. The secret of his rise to the top of the motion picture industry may be found in his uncanny flexibility in meeting emergencies as they arose. While others were debating the wisdom of departure from established customs, Zukor would quietly change his opinions and move swiftly along new and apparently dangerous lines to deal with crises.

Zukor, Loew, Selznick, Nicholas and Joseph Schenck, Rowland, Fox, Laemmle, Patrick Powers, Walter Irwin, Goldwyn, John D. Williams, and other film men prominent in the revolutionary period of 1914-18, played the business game with the ardor of sportsmen and gamblers. Lewis Selznick used to say that each fellow thought he was "smarter" than the others, and he describes his own victories as triumphs in "outsmarting" his competitors. It was a time of clever, cunning, daring operations. The plain, undecorated truth about Zukor is that he persistently "outsmarted" all other players of the game.

WHEN First National began to hammer at Paramount and Artcraft, there was no indication that Zukor might attempt to save himself by the acquisition of theaters. Perhaps it was inevitable that ambition and the pressure of changing conditions should have carried him later into this large addition to his operations, but up to 1917 his plans and policies all tended toward domination through control of the popular stars.

Just then, in addition to problems inside his own corporations —and one of the most troublesome was Mary Pickford's restless leanings toward First National—Zukor was being harried by his old foe, Lewis Selznick, with whom, in a mixture of exasperation and shrewdness, he had formed a secret alliance. Selznick, constantly threatening to acquire every outstanding star, player, director, and writer in every studio, with special gestures toward Zukor's collection, had made himself the noisiest, if not the most dangerous, factor in the industry. He had financed the Selznick projects by selling shares in his exchanges to principal exhibitors in key cities, and, therefore, had as partners (in the exchanges) many important theater owners. Although he owned no stock in any of the theater corporations associated with

Selznick exchanges, his contacts with his exhibitor-associates afforded frequent opportunities to advise them regarding contracts for picture series or programs, bookings of special pictures made by various producers, rental prices and terms, and similar trade matters. As he was keen, thoroughly posted on the news and gossip of the industry, his trade suggestions were often of value to exhibitors, and his influence with them was constantly exerted to annoy Zukor and retard the progress of Paramount-Artcraft pictures in the houses of his associates.

While no competitor was safe from his attacks, his principal effort was to equal and surpass Zukor. Paramount had 208 features a year; Artcraft perhaps a dozen; Selznick, starting with two dozen, was progressing toward fifty-two. As long as Zukor was ahead of him Selznick was restless and made Zukor his constant target, working overtime to devise schemes to annoy him. Zukor began to suspect that Selznick might become a successful competitor. The Selznick enterprises, started about a year previous with total assets of Clara Kimball Young, a shoe-string, boundless ingenuity, and unlimited self-assurance, were growing rapidly, but Zukor knew that Selznick needed more capital, and Zukor had plenty of capital.

Little business men fight each other; big business men put their pride away and compromise with antagonists. Zukor had no intention of merging the Selznick companies with the Paramount group. He would not depart from his technique of absorption of living assets as distinguished from consolidation of corporation assets. Quietly he met Selznick and, convincing him that peace and prosperity would result from alliance, the Selznick enterprises became "Select Pictures." Zukor paid half a million dollars for a half interest and Selznick remained as president. Zukor's connection was secret and no one was to know of the association.

Within a few weeks, Selznick felt that he had parted with his birthright. He had accepted Zukor's gold only to learn that gold without glory is as tasteless as sawdust. Selznick pictures had become Select pictures, and he was unable now to tell the hundred million Americans about himself. His plottings to wriggle around the restrictions of the deal and replace the word "Selznick" in the movie sky gave Zukor plenty to think of when his mind could be removed for a moment from the stew-pot of Pickford-Artcraft and Paramount.

WILLY-NILLY, no matter how many kettles were on his fire, Zukor had to nullify First National's ambitious project. Openly his press agents and advertising men conducted vigorous propaganda against mergers of producer and exhibitor. Hodkinson's philosophy of the desirability of maintaining sharp distinction between picture makers and theater owners was exploited thoroughly in arguments against First National, but Hodkinson was not mentioned as its author.

Hodkinson's Paramount plan, under which the distributor supplied producers with money to manufacture pictures, adopted by various distributors, had become a common practice in the industry and remained in force for a dozen years. As a rule, the distributor financed the independent producer, in some cases by sending him weekly the money needed for expenses, in other cases by payment of a stipulated sum upon completion of the negative; the distributor charging twenty-five to forty percent of the gross receipts for his services in distribution and finance.

Fox seldom or never distributed a picture not made under his orders. Universal manufactured nearly all its own releases, but occasionally arranged for a special from an independent. Metro manufactured nearly all of its own output. Selznick, Goldwyn and others made pictures themselves and also had contracts with producers. Hodkinson never made any pictures, following his own system of financing producers as long as he remained in business. First National, Robertson-Cole, Pathé, and so many other distributors followed the same general system that in 1916-18, a third or more of each year's features came from individual producers financed by distributors.

Zukor, after obtaining control of Paramount and organizing

Artcraft, had not been distributing any pictures but those of his own corporations, but when he bestirred himself to give battle to First National, he opened the doors of Paramount and Artcraft for a few years and admitted several independent producers. He strengthened his own companies and weakened the remnant of Triangle by absorbing Griffith, Ince, and Sennett, and making independent producers of them. Douglas Fairbanks, William S. Hart, Roscoe (Fatty) Arbuckle and other players, John Emerson and other directors, and Anita Loos and other writers, joined his companies. From Vitagraph he took James Stuart Blackton, its principal director; and here and there in other studios he selected valuable people and added them to the Paramount-Artcraft staffs. William Randolph Hearst's producing company, Cosmopolitan Pictures, and Mayflower, of which George Loane Tucker was the principal director, became important contributors to Zukor distribution.

Considering John D. Williams as the driving power of the exhibitors' combine, Zukor and Lewis Selznick met him, without publicity, and offered him a position in Select Pictures Company. Williams declined the offer, believing he had greater opportunities with First National.

In such ways as these, Zukor fought against the collapse of his dream of domination through ownership of star players and successful directors and writers. His plan to control retailers without having to own and operate the retail outlets was too valuable to abandon as long as there was any hope of making it a success. Unquestionably Zukor's plan was a simple and logical scheme of industrial conquest. The oil trust, to maintain its control, had to acquire oil fields and competing refineries. Steel had to buy mines and mills. Tobacco had to pay liberally for factories owning popular brands. In the Zukor formula nothing was important except the ultimate consumer; the millions of movie ticket buyers were his if he could control the stars they worshipped;—the machinery of manufacture, distribution, and consumption became nothing but details. It was what Theodore Roosevelt would have termed "a bully idea."

One of Zukor's most ambitious efforts was the attempt to create a national "booking organization." The Stanley Company, of Philadelphia, served as the model and the basis for this project. Sigmund Lubin had owned a chain of penny arcades, nickelodeons and theaters in eastern Pennsylvania. When he collapsed with General Film, these houses and others had been acquired by Stanley and Jules E. Mastbaum and used as the foundation of the Stanley Company, which by 1917 had grown into a large, profitable group of theaters and a "booking combine" of dozens of independently owned houses in eastern and central Pennsylvania. The booking combine selected pictures for the theaters, determining the rental prices to be paid, and charged the exhibitors five to ten percent above rentals for this service.

Stanley Mastbaum was, at this time, the active head of the company, Jules, a lawyer, acting as general adviser while Stanley held the firing line. The brothers had created the most powerful single element then in existence in the theater branch of the movie industry, and in doing so they had made many friends and many enemies. Some of the latter were exhibitors who declared that the Stanley Company forced them into the booking combine with threats of building opposition theaters; others were producers who alleged that the Stanley Company was an oppressive monopoly, autocratically deciding what pictures could be shown in its territory and insisting on prices so low that manufacturers could not make profits.

Zukor's idea was to extend the booking system of the Stanley Company to all sections of the United States. He proposed that he and the Mastbaum group should organize The Stanley Booking Company of America, he to supply the capital necessary, and to issue stock to the amount of $5,000,000, one-half of which would go to the Zukor interests and one-half to First National stockholders. All First National exhibitors were to authorize the booking association to book all pictures to be used in their houses. This would include not only the houses of the two dozen or so stockholders of First National, but the thousands of theaters which held exhibition sub-franchises of the circuit. Had this extensive plan been successful Zukor would have remained in position to dominate the movies without ownership of theaters. Through Paramount, Artcraft and Select, as direct producers and distributors, he would have been able to control the supply of features and the rentals of several thousand houses; through the national booking company he would have had ascendency over nearly all remaining theaters.

When the plan was presented to First National's board of directors (composed of all of the company's stockholders), some of the members approved it as a method of protecting their personal theater investments by a connection with Zukor, but so many of the exhibitor-owners objected on the ground that it would eliminate their power to select pictures for their own houses that the proposal was rejected.

ALTHOUGH theaters, studios, and exchanges in 1917-18 represented investments of several hundred million dollars, and gave employment to a hundred thousand people, Mary Pickford remained the industry's most valuable asset. Women's place in business has grown enormously in importance in the last three decades, but Mary Pickford is the only member of her sex who ever became the focal point in an entire industry. Her position was unique; probably no woman, or man, will ever again win so extensive a following. When short films constituted the program, players appeared in two dozen or more pictures each year. As the store shows had no exclusive rights to any particular pictures, and the first-run system was not in effective operation until 1914-15, it was possible for all, or nearly all, nickelodeons to exhibit the films of the most popular players. Broncho Billy, John Bunny, Mary Pickford and Charlie Chaplin were in such demand that they appeared on nearly every screen in America, and audiences could see their favorite players several times a month. The many who learned to worship "Little Mary" had to wait only a week or two before she appeared again, and thus their interest in the star was constantly kept alive.

John Bunny died. Bill Hart, Tox Mix and other western heroes
appeared and gradually won the following of Broncho Billy.
Other favorites of short films failed to progress into features;
but Mary Pickford moved steadily forward, and when features
became popular she was the leading star. While she did not make
as many features each year as she had made short films, there
was still a new picture nearly every month, and thousands of
theaters continued to repeat her short films for several years. She
was shown on more American screens during this period than was
any other player, and not even Broncho Billy, Charlie Chaplin nor
Tom Mix has been more widely known. Year after year her
popularity increased. When a press agent declared her "the
sweetheart of America" he stated a fact. Perhaps thirty, forty, or
fifty million men, women, and children then were ticket buyers,
and while this vast audience divided its affections among
fifty to a hundred players, Mary Pickford was the outstanding
favorite of very close to one hundred percent of the fans.

When Miss Pickford moved to Artcraft and reduced the number of her productions from twelve or ten a year to four, a new
era was inaugurated. Between 1917 and 1921, it worked such
changes in the manufacture and exhibition of pictures that no
player thereafter could possibly become known to so many people, or be seen so frequently on the screen. The expensive pictures of the years following the Armistice required several weeks,
and often months, to manufacture, so that stars appeared only
half a dozen times a year. Many wealthy players in later years
found so much fun in playing with their productions that one
or two pictures a year satisfied them.

The first-run system of exhibition prevents the appearance of
a picture in more than a small portion of the total number of
theaters. Each large city has from three to eight first-run houses,
none of which will show a feature after it has appeared in a
competitive theater. Neighborhood and rural houses follow practically the same system. Thus, while Mary Pickford pictures
were seen monthly, or more often, in twelve to fifteen thousand
theaters in 1910-17, in recent years the most popular stars may

produce a picture every three or twelve months that will run in four thousand to seven thousand houses.

THE Artcraft contract with Mary Pickford was to expire in the autumn of 1918. First National began its negotiations with her in 1917, so Zukor knew long in advance that he would have to increase her compensation or lose her. Artcraft was paying her half a million a year and half the profits of her pictures. First National offered her $225,000 apiece for three negatives, with allowances for stories and other items that brought the price to about $250,000; Charlotte Pickford was to receive $50,000; and profits were to be divided equally between Miss Pickford and First National. Her Artcraft negatives, including her salary, about $125,000, were costing about $165,000 to $170,000. If First National would pay her $250,000, and if costs remained at the Artcraft figure, she would have $50,000 more to add to her salary on each picture. If she should make four pictures a year this salary increase would amount to about $200,000, or forty percent more than she was getting from Artcraft. Williams, Schwalbe and Tally assured her that First National would earn her far greater profits than Artcraft, so that her total net revenue ought to be more than a million dollars a year—perhaps two millions.

In brief, in order to retain Mary Pickford, Zukor would have to increase her compensation fifty to one hundred percent; he would have to assume an obligation to pay her fifteen to twenty thousand dollars a week. In order to pay a salary above $10,000, gross rentals would have to be increased to somewhere between $450,000 and $600,000, or else the producer-distributor could not show a profit. Theater owners had rebelled at Artcraft prices and First National was the outgrowth of that rebellion. Zukor wondered what would happen if prices on Pickford pictures were advanced from the Artcraft scale of, say, $360,000 to a new scale of, say, $500,000! If he paid the price and kept her, what would happen? If he did not pay the price, she would go to First National. Would that aid First National to circumvent Paramount-Artcraft?

A hard problem. Zukor solved it characteristically—by listening carefully to another man, and modifying his own point of view.

AUDIENCES seemed to be hopelessly riveted to their adoration of stars, and exhibitors, producers and distributors were convinced that profits could be maintained only by the use of celebrities. Behind the screen, however, in the studios, the directors, the men who really made the pictures, disagreed violently with this view. Nearly all directors had been actors, and they resented the caprice of fate that brought wide-spread popularity and high awards to the players in front of the camera while they remained in obscurity and received salaries that seemed to them disproportionate. A director might be an able artist—several of them were then, and others developed in later years—but audiences were not yet educated to realize that direction is usually as important as acting. Movie patrons admired the players they saw on the screen, but the man responsible for the production was generally not even a name to them.

Stars, receiving five to ten times the salaries of directors, had also acquired large discretionary powers in the selection of story material, supporting players, sets, etc., and the director, who had been the autocrat of the studios before the rise of stars, had lost influence as they advanced. Writers, also (their craft had not yet acquired standing in the studios), were regarded as hacks whose business it was to shape and distort feeble stories to fit the limitations of the stars.

A few directors and writers, thoroughly disgusted with the ineptitudes of the star system, insisted that a good story, written into an effective "shooting script," with a cast of players selected for individual fitness instead of for existing box-office fame, and directed by a skilful director, would produce a picture of high quality and greater appeal. Ten years later these ideas were commonplace, but in 1917-18, although "The Spoilers," "The Birth of a Nation," "The Battle Cry of Peace," and a few other non-star photoplays had been very successful, the industry as a whole was so thoroughly obsessed by star frenzy that only a handful of people believed the public would ever accept anything different. The extent of the star craze is demonstrated by the fact that of the six hundred or more features then produced in America each year, not more than five percent dared to seek a market unless bolstered by a real or alleged "box-office name."

Cecil B. DeMille was one of the first directors to insist that a good motion picture is based on a good story. Associated with him was Jeanie MacPherson, author of screen stories and an expert continuity writer. In 1918, DeMille, with Jesse Lasky's approval and cooperation, made an experiment to prove the soundness of his theories, producing a new negative of "The Squaw Man" with an "all star" (which is, of course, non-star) cast at a cost of $40,000. "The Squaw Man" was rented as a single picture, that is, distributed on the Artcraft system instead of the Paramount program or series method. It earned $350,000 gross. DeMille followed this with "Old Wives for New"; the negative cost was $66,000, gross earnings $380,000.

The making of Mary Pickford pictures had been transferred from New York to Los Angeles, so that discussions of a new contract between the actress and Zukor in 1918 were held in Hollywood.

DeMille pointed out to Zukor that, in a period of unlimited competition, with hundreds of men eager to break into the movies and with capitalists at last aroused to the commercial possibilities of the industry and equally eager to supply the money, the steadily mounting star salaries would sooner or later bankrupt anyone who played the game to the finish. He offered to select obscure players, and by good direction to make box-office names for them in two or three pictures. Famous Players would be sure of continual profits instead of facing the constant gamble of whether or not a star would earn his keep. To support his argument he used the figures of "The Squaw Man" and "Old Wives for New" in comparison with the costs and earnings of

Mary Pickford's pictures: "Squaw Man," cost $40,000; "Old Wives," cost $66,000; Mary Pickford's average costs $165,000 to $170,000 with gross earnings about equal, $350,000 to $380,000 each.

DeMille's point of view seemed unassailable, but Lasky and Zukor had to consider as well the problem of whether or not Paramount-Artcraft could maintain its ascendency if the star system was weakened or destroyed. Twice in the history of the movies, the industry had been dominated by a single group. Motion Pictures Patents Company and General Film had in theory, and practically in fact, enjoyed a monopoly by virtue of the patent laws. Zukor and his associates were now trying to dominate the business by employing most of the leading stars. The patents monopoly had been smashed and exterminated. If the star system should break down, and if, in accordance with the argument advanced by DeMille, the public should form the habit of swinging quickly to new favorites, control of the industry through stars would no longer be possible. Any producer at any time might develop a player who would suddenly displace existing favorites. Producers with fading stars under long-term contracts might easily lose all their profits before the contract periods ended. Also, if the all-star system should come into vogue, many new producers and distributors might enter the industry; no one would be able to bring them into an effective association, and competition would run wild.

Zukor pondered for several weeks, and then followed the course so often successful with masters of opportunism—he evolved a compromise plan: Mary Pickford could go, and DeMille could proceed to put his theories into practice. If the public approved the results, Famous Players-Lasky could extend the all-star method indefinitely. Meanwhile he and Lasky would maintain the star system and let time decide which of the two was the best business practice.

Still reluctant to allow First National to acquire Miss Pickford, Zukor tried one more plan.

"You've worked very hard for years," he told her. "Why don't you take a vacation? If you will stop making pictures for five years, I will give you $250,000."

"Oh, I couldn't do that, Mr. Zukor," she answered. "I love pictures, and I'm just a girl. I couldn't quit now."

They said good-by, and Mary Pickford went to First National.

CHAPTER TEN

THE POST-WAR BOOM

IN 1918, while the pall of the World War hung over everything, forces within the movie industry were obscurely but inexorably assembling for a bitter, intensive struggle. The protagonists of the drama saw only the dim outlines of the forthcoming contest, and minimized its importance. Fighting had always been the daily diet of the film trade; a new battle could hardly differ materially from its predecessors.

The World War compelled the industry to give it a place in its thoughts ahead of internal dissensions. How long would it last? What would be the effect of its prolonged duration on motion pictures? How long could theaters and studios endure the strain of war conditions?

The problems arising from internal conflicts had been accumulating since 1916, at the beginning of Charlotte Pickford's revolution. The increased costs of production had been passed on to the exhibitors, and in 1917 nearly all theaters had added five to fifteen cents to admittance prices. The best first-run houses in New York now charged twenty-five and thirty-five cents, and were experimenting carefully to see if forty and fifty cents could be obtained. All over the country the better houses now charged anywhere from fifteen to thirty-five cents, although the small neighborhood theaters still remained at ten and five. The successive increases in admittance prices were absorbed by patrons without apparent injury to the industry until 1917, when the removal of several million young men from homes to training camps struck a blow at theater receipts. General business conditions were bad—except in the production of war supplies—and fewer persons were visiting the movie houses.

The exhibitors who in 1909 had blessed the star system for the millions of patrons it attracted were now struggling under the terrific load of star salaries. In 1918, a fresh burden was placed on their shoulders—the federal government levied a war tax of ten percent on tickets selling at ten cents or more. The larger, more prosperous theaters were not seriously affected by the tax. In most of them, the patrons accepted increases in ticket prices; in a few instances, exhibitors paid part of the tax out of their profits. But the smaller or older houses, or theaters in districts in which general business conditions were bad, had already been struggling against decreasing attendance, and many of them were unable to advance prices or to pay the tax out of profits that were largely non-existent. Such theaters closed their doors, and the speed of the industry was materially reduced for the first time since screen pictures made their appearance in 1896.

With the transfer of hundreds of thousands of boys to France, leaving scarcely a family in America untouched, the thoughts and desires of ordinary life were superseded by serious considerations of the tragic drama in progress "over there." The spontaneous, enthusiastic, light-hearted adoration of movies gave way to acceptance of the screen as a means of relief from the worries and the horrors of the day. Movies heretofore had been an entertainment; now they became an emotional safety valve. People looked to the film theaters as to an old friend who would give them relief from heartaches, and the screen, always sensitive to public feeling and opinion, responded with plays glorifying the participation of American soldiers and their allies in the struggle. The families of soldiers were comforted and sustained by romantic portrayals of the heroism of their loved ones in the trenches, and they fairly clung to the screen in the dark days of 1918, when the lists of dead, wounded, and missing brought their quota of pain into an increasing number of homes.

By early autumn the programs of the theaters contained many war plays, news reels of domestic and foreign events concerning the war, with riotous comedies as a foil to the tense emotionalism of war themes. But audiences were responding too quickly to stories producing tears and sobs, and too hysterically to the laugh-getting recipes of slap-stick comedians. The industry was in a serious dilemma, and no one knew what the ultimate effect of the war might be, whether it lasted for years or suddenly ended, as some authorities predicted.

THE studios marked time. With domestic business moving sluggishly and with export trade severely restricted by war conditions, producers were compelled to exercise caution in their operations. Los Angeles had grown to be an important producing center, but New York was still the principal seat of manufacture. The simultaneous growth of features and of star salaries had broken down much of the ancient antagonism between stage and screen, and many actors now divided their time between Broadway and the studios. There were still not enough experienced players in Los Angeles to meet the severe requirements of the long photoplays, and players were shuttled back and forth across the continent.

Los Angeles, then a city of about half a million population (somewhat less than half its size ten years later), had been greatly elated by the development of the industry in 1915-17. Triangle had built a large studio at Culver City; Carl Laemmle had moved Universal to a site of a hundred acres or more in San Fernando Valley; the Lasky Company bought a ranch near Universal; the Metro plant in Hollywood was expanding; in East Hollywood was Vitagraph; W. W. Hodkinson had contracted for pictures for his own new distributing company whose most important producer, Paralta Plays, had built a new studio, under Robert Brunton's supervision, on Melrose Avenue, Hollywood;

Fox had purchased a studio on Sunset Boulevard, Hollywood, and was beginning to make his pictures in the west; Mary Pickford and Charlie Chaplin had announced that they would remain in Los Angeles, and there was general belief that First National's expansion would bring more famous stars to the city. Two dozen smaller companies were regularly grinding out one- and two-reel serials, comedies, and other short subjects.

Puritanical mid-westerners—retired farmers and merchants from small communities in the central states, whose immigration to Los Angeles had increased its population four-fold in three decades—were perplexed and disturbed by the movie people, by their bright motor-cars, sports clothes, jewels, their free and easy scattering of money in hotels, restaurants, dancing places, bathing beaches, and mountain resorts. Puritans might be annoyed, but Los Angeles merchants, bankers, and real estate dealers welcomed the flow of three or four hundred thousand dollars of eastern money into its business channels each week from studio pay-rolls and expenses. The "interesting and amusing" film folk of a dozen years earlier had developed into a factor of paramount importance in the city's economic affairs, and when the annual tourist influx was decreased by the war in the winter of 1917-18, the value of movie dollars was materially magnified.

The momentum of the industry slackened in the spring of 1918. The Los Angeles studios began to quiet down; by mid-summer many of the smaller plants were closed and the large lots were operating with reduced staffs. Not so many motor cars were purchased; the jewelers' shops had few customers; eastern picture executives were besieged in the Alexandria Hotel by actors and actresses, directors, camera men and technicians seeking work. A few great stars were secure in their positions, but for the lesser stars and the several hundred actors and actresses—all of whom, only a year or so before, had been carried away by salary increases that seemed to insure permanent riches—there was doubt and uncertainty. A fog of fear and discouragement settled on the gay young movie colony.

But all of these evils were as nothing compared with the twin calamities of the autumn of 1918 which shook the industry to its very foundations. In the late summer an epidemic of influenza entered the United States and spread rapidly through the country, and by October it was adding an appalling list of deaths to the daily casualty reports from France. Doctors and hospitals were unable to check the fury of the disease, and health officials closed schools, theaters, and other places of public congregation in all seriously affected cities and towns in America. The motion picture industry, already made uncertain and nervous by its various problems, now faced darkened playhouses all over the land. Studios closed entirely, or operated on part time, and pessimists croaked that this was the beginning of the end.

There remained, however, another ordeal for the young industry to meet, and it followed hard on the heels of the influenza epidemic. On November 11, 1918, the Armistice was signed. A wave of joy flooded the country and everywhere men and women left their work and joined their fellows in spontaneous celebration of the end of the war horror. All day great throngs milled about the streets of the cities, throwing ticker tape and confetti, laughing, shouting, singing. By evening many of the millions turned their steps to the movie theaters. Yesterday, last week, for months back, war pictures had been the most reliable box office asset, and nearly all theaters were exhibiting war plays on Armistice Day. A cluster of three boys and three girls pushing slowly through the mob that packed Longacre Square, stopped at the entrance of a movie palace, and read the title of the play.

"Oh! It's a war picture!" said one of the girls. "We're fed up on war—and it's over anyway. Let's go somewhere and see a *real* picture."

The great American public voted with the girl. On November 10th war pictures were saleable merchandise; on the night of November 11th they became unmarketable. During the dull months of 1918, while the studios were marking time, the principal item of production had been war pictures. On Armistice Day, distributors and producers had almost nothing else in their warerooms; they faced the loss of many millions of dollars in property now worthless through this sudden twist in the taste of their customers, as well as an additional loss, of no one could guess how many millions, until audiences could be enticed back by films that were remote from war subjects.

November and December were indeed dark months for manufacturers and distributors. Conservative business men and financiers again cautioned the showmen to go slow, to wait to see what effect the influenza epidemic had had on theater attendance; to be sure that the public would return; to discover if the war had not, perhaps, worked such changes that a new form of entertainment would rise to popularity. Again history repeated itself. As in 1909-11, when Carl Laemmle, William Fox, Harry Aitken and other independents created the star system in pictures and broke the grip of the patents trust; as in 1912-14, when Zukor, Hodkinson, Lasky, Goldfish, DeMille, Bosworth, Griffith, Aitken and other pioneers organized long pictures and led the industry into new fields of success; as in 1916, when daring showmen bid ridiculously high prices for celebrated stars and made fortunes by exploiting the public's worship of personalities; so again in 1918, the producers who hesitated lost ground in the struggle that was shaping its lines for the final test of industrial survival, and those who disregarded common business prudence and rushed ahead on a showman's hunch saved their skins.

The reckless producers mercilessly consigned their war stories to the scrap heap, or rented them to cheap theaters at any prices obtainable; and poured their available capital, plus all the money they could borrow, into the feverish filming of new plays dealing with nothing but romance and adventure, the old recipes that were so successful before America's entrance into the war dislocated the audience mind. Cautious producers and distributors waited—only a few weeks—but during those few weeks they lost ground that never was recovered.

Early in 1919, devastated Europe began to buy vast quantities of food, manufactured products, and raw materials in America. All European countries had to have wheat, corn, meat, clothing, shoes, materials for homes, factories, farms, ships—all the things that had been used up in war time now had to be replaced quickly in order that civilized life might be restored to its normal courses. South America, Asia, and Africa, too, each had its pressing needs; and buyers from all the continents hurried to America, arranged credits with bankers, and furiously bid against each other for the things they must have for their peoples back home.

America itself needed many things that it had not been able to manufacture or build during the years that its factories, mines, and farms were devoted to the business of war. Houses, factories, office buildings, schools, roads—these and other things had been neglected under the pressure of war conditions, and now they had to be built or rebuilt, and new implements, tools, and machines in vast quantities were required in the process.

The necessities of the entire globe concentrated for awhile on the United States, and the people of this country soon found themselves in the whirl of a gigantic business boom. More wealth was in circulation than anyone had ever dreamed could exist, and it was money more widely distributed than ever before. The whole nation, down to the lowliest laborer, was suddenly prosperous.

For a dozen or more years, the movies had been educating the American public to better homes and furnishings, the use of labor-saving apparatus, the enjoyment of motor cars, and many other articles generally classed as luxuries. The new-found wealth now flooding the country quickly transformed the luxuries of yesterday into the necessities of today. Motor cars, expensive clothes, phonographs, furniture, new homes, tractors and farm machinery, all sorts of costly things, were freely bought by millions of people. Under the impetus of great prosperity and great spending, the movie-educated American people, in two or three years, paved the way for more widespread changes in our social and economic patterns than had been accomplished during several preceding decades.

The mercurial movies, the most sensitive instrument yet created by democracy to minister to its needs, quickly sensed and promptly responded to the new mood, the unformulated demands, of the public. In 1917-18 the people sought the theaters for relief from depression; in 1919-20 they packed the playhouses because they had plenty of money to spend for pleasures. New, expensive theaters arising in the downtown districts of American cities were not sufficient to accommodate the enormous patronage surging nightly to ticket windows. The building of neighborhood houses in residential districts started in Chicago and Los Angeles and soon spread over the country. The neighborhood theater brought movies close to home. Well-built and attractively decorated, with a capacity of 600 to 1,000, hundreds of neighborhood houses arose in all cities. Even in the smaller cities, new theaters were built or old ones remodeled, and within a few years store shows had practically disappeared from the scene.

Between 1914 and 1922, perhaps 4,000 new theaters were built, but these figures tell only a part of the story, since the new houses seated many times the number of patrons than those they displaced. It is probable that 16,000 theaters of 1922 could accommodate as many people as 40,000 houses of the types existent in 1912-14.

The prices of admittance paid by movie-goers in the boom days of 1919-20 and in the years following astonished the theater owners. Marcus Loew voiced the opinion of many exhibitors when in 1919 he declared that fifty cents was the limit that the public would pay for screen entertainment. But within four years, many downtown houses had advanced to sixty-five and seventy-five cents—some as high as a dollar—and second-run and neighborhood houses were charging twenty-five, thirty-five, and fifty cents. To see the movies for ten or fifteen cents one had to go to fifth-run theaters in side streets. Either films had ceased to be a "poor man's show" or there were no poor men left in the United States. The movie habit now encompassed nearly all city and town dwellers, and the millions of motor cars being purchased by farmers and villagers made the screen easily accessible to the rural population.

AGAIN the studios began to hum with activity. All the players in Los Angeles were quickly absorbed and New York was combed for material. Wages rose dizzily, and the salaries of 1916-17 seemed like "chicken feed." A character actor who was glad to get $200 a week in 1916, and satisfied if he had thirty weeks' work a year, was paid $600 in 1919, and toward the end of that year was so startled when a producer offered him a contract at $1,000 a week, with a guarantee of fifty weeks during the year, that he was left literally speechless. The producer interpreted his silence as dissent, and increased his offer to $1,250 a week.

His experience was typical. Salaries were raised all along the line. The costs of production doubled and trebled in one year. In 1918, several of the large companies were making five-reel features for $12,000 to $20,000, negative cost, each. By the close of 1919, ordinary program features (negatives only) were costing $40,000 to $80,000. Specials of six to nine reels, the making of which became a practice in 1919-20, cost from $100,000 to $200,000.

Los Angeles, quiet and depressed in October, 1918, was alive with energy and optimism in January, 1919. The Lasky and the Universal studios, then the largest movie employers in California, were working at top speed; Samuel Goldwyn bought the Triangle plant and announced that he had abandoned the east and would make all his pictures in Culver City; Fox bought more land, built more stages, and moved several more of his companies from New York. By April, the Paralta studios, which had been acquired by the Robert Brunton Company, and were rented to various independent producers and directors, had twenty-five companies at work, in place of two in October.

First National was in an exceptionally strong position. Organized in 1917, it had made no committments involving large financing except to Charlie Chaplin and Mary Pickford, and these stars were so popular with audiences that every film they produced was an assured success before it was made. Chaplin's first attempt at long pictures was a story of the trenches, "Shoulder Arms," a classic in three reels. "The Kid," in six reels, (in which Jackie Coogan was made famous), followed about two years later. Mary Pickford adhered closely to the poor little, or rich little, but always good little girl formula that she had used for years in building up her following.

Williams, Schwalbe and Tally strengthened First National's list of productions by adding several popular stars and producers to their list. D. W. Griffith transferred his productions to First National. Louis B. Mayer, entering the producing field, brought with him Anita Stewart, popular Vitagraph star. B. P. Schulberg contributed a series of pictures of Katherine MacDonald, a beautiful young woman with a large screen following. Joseph Schenck transferred Constance Talmadge from Selznick, and shortly after brought Norma Talmadge to First National. Jack Pickford, Mary's brother, Lionel Barrymore and several other prominent players, and Marshall D. Neilan, Frank Lloyd, Fred Niblo, Whitman Bennett and other well-known directors soon joined the exhibitor-producer organization. Theater owners, confident that the cooperative policy of First National assured them a permanent curb on Zukor's immeasurable ambitions, almost fought for the privilege of signing contracts giving them the right to exhibit First National pictures—and binding them to do so.

Paramount, however, was many lengths ahead of the procession. Neither war, nor influenza epidemic, nor reconstruction booms, found the Zukor companies unequal to the emergencies. The well-organized Paramount studios—Famous Players in New York, and Lasky and Garbutt-Morosco in Los Angeles—supplied with abundant capital, expanded rapidly to meet the increasing demand. The loss of Mary Pickford to First National, which seemed, a few months before, to have been a very serious matter, had no effect on the fortunes of Artcraft-Paramount. Douglas Fairbanks, Wallace Reid and other stars in the Zukor-Lasky family were acquiring large followings, and DeMille's adoption of the non-star method used successfully by Griffith, Selig, and several other producers at various times, was proving enormously profitable. Zukor and Lasky later restricted their distributing facilities to the output of their own studios, but in 1919-20 the list of their own productions was considerably augmented by the pictures of the several independents then associated with them, chief among whom were Thomas H. Ince, William S. Hart, Mack Sennett, Maurice Tourneur, D. W. Griffith, William Randolph Hearst's Cosmopolitan, and the Mayflower.

THROUGH the years of short films and nickelodeons, while movies were "the poor man's show," the varied fascinations and allurements of the screen were enjoyed and experienced principally by those in the humbler walks of life, and from their ranks came most of the candidates for fame and fortune. When features and fine theaters extended the movie habit into all classes, making it the universal American entertainment, the infection spread everywhere. Newspaper and magazine editors discovered that stories and articles about the characters of Hollywood were eagerly devoured by large numbers of readers. Newspapers established departments devoted to personal gossip about the movie idols, and nothing seemed too silly to please the millions of fans whose appetite for intimate details taxed the ability of the country's most efficient press agents, half a hundred of whom were drawn to Los Angeles by the high salaries that came after Armistice Day. Other writers located in Hollywood to supply the demand of Sunday newspapers and magazines for special articles concerning the private lives and daily habits of celluloid celebrities.

Between 1912 and 1920, a dozen weekly and monthly publications, devoted solely to motion pictures, sprang into existence. These "fan magazines" reached an aggregate circulation of several million copies, and one or two of them developed into well-edited publications, dealing intelligently with the varied subjects of the screen. Within a few years Hollywood became one of the most famous spots on the globe.

The wave of prosperity that swept into the movie world in 1919-20, and the saccharine adulation accorded screen personalities by newspapers and magazines, released such floods of ambition that for five years harassed executives in Los Angeles studios feared that nearly the entire population of the United States was resolutely determined to "break into the movies." Thousands—tens of thousands—of men and women, boys and girls, sincerely believed that somewhere in this fascinating business they would find the path to fame or wealth.

Hundreds of manuscripts poured into the studios each week. They came from famous authors and playwrights, judges and lawyers, college presidents, newspaper men, policemen, milliners, society women, farmers' wives, and occasionally from inmates of penitentiaries and insane asylums. For several years the studios, keen to discover talent in unsuspected places, maintained extensive editorial departments and carefully examined each manuscript submitted. Of a hundred thousand stories reviewed by studio staffs in five years, perhaps a hundred themes or suggestions from non-professional writers were found acceptable. The rejected offerings were old or impracticable plots, or plain plagiarism thinly disguised. In some instances the disguise was very thin. A gentleman in Nashville merely removed the binding and title-page from Zane Grey's novel, "Desert Gold," labeled it with a new title, and sent it to a producer, explaining that he could supply other stories of equal quality.

Difficulties arose. The amateur scenarists, later seeing films which they thought resembled their rejected manuscripts, assumed that the movie companies had swindled them. Others, less innocent, brought suit for plagiarism against producers, and to avoid litigation and unpleasant publicity, the producers fell into the evil habit of settling such cases as cheaply as possible. This was, in effect, submission to blackmail, and as nothing thrives so well on submission, the producers soon found themselves involved in cases which could not be settled so simply. A woman in the south brought the situation to a head by declaring that C. B. DeMille and Jeanie MacPherson had stolen from her the plot of the "Ten Commandments," and she demanded damages of several hundred thousand dollars. DeMille's attorney, Neil McCarthy, determined to submit to no more thrifty golddiggers, cast himself in the rôle of Sherlock Holmes, and eventually exposed the lady and her accomplices so completely that the case was thrown out of court. However, DeMille's expenses in clearing himself of the unjust charge, amounting to about $20,000, were not repaid by the plaintiff, nor were she and her associates punished in any way by the courts.

Finally, in self-protection, the studios built a stone wall between themselves and the amateur writing tribe. Manuscripts were received by reliable clerks, registered to provide evidence that they had not been read, and returned to the senders. The producers turned to professional novelists, playwrights, and screen writers for their stories, and Hollywood became the Mecca toward which most authors turned their hopes. Prior to 1919-20, the screen rights of novels and plays had been purchasable at a thousand to ten thousand dollars. In later years, producers have paid a thousand, five thousand, and ten thousand dollars for the right to adapt a magazine story, and novelists have received $25,000 to $100,000 for popular books. Successful plays have brought as high as $225,000.

The volunteer scenario writers were annoyance enough, but a more serious problem was presented by the movement of movie-mad girls to Los Angeles after the boom of 1919 got under way. From east, west, north, south—from cities, villages and farms, from every social class and intellectual level—the fascination of the screen drew flocks of young women to the studios. Their minds were filled with the glamorous stories of success that appeared constantly in newspapers and magazines, and they were so completely unable to differentiate between fact and fiction that Hollywood took form in their imaginations as the complete answer to a young girl's dreams.

The complexities of this situation were further intensified by the three business booms operating simultaneously in Los Angeles and advertising southern California as a land of exceptional opportunity. The first of these was the expansion in motion picture studios. The reliable climate and lower living costs made Hollywood production less expensive than in the east, and the availability of hundreds of craftsmen, technicians, and writers were further advantages. Players were less numerous, but this lack was soon remedied by moving several scores of stage and screen actors and actresses from the east. Within a few years, Hollywood became the capital of motion picture production, and eighty-five or ninety percent of the world's films are manufactured there.

The boom in picture production was followed closely by the discovery of oil at Signal Hill, Long Beach, Sante Fe Springs and a dozen other new fields near Los Angeles. Scores of thousands of people rushed to southern California and created a real estate boom that made fortunes for many people who had not profited directly through movies or oil.

The three booms working together soon made Los Angeles famous throughout America as a place in which anyone might grow famous or rich very quickly. Thousands of girls were lured to Los Angeles, and most of them were bitterly disillusioned. No one will ever know how many girls journeyed there in the ten years beginning in 1919, nor what became of most of them. Perhaps 20,000, perhaps 50,000—the latter figure is more likely to be correct—were drawn to the city by movie ambition and the hope of romance. A few of them found the way to success. Perhaps a thousand of the pilgrims, in ten years, obtained employment in small parts; perhaps a hundred realized their aspiration to become stars or leading women. Some of the disillusioned seekers of fame and fortune found employment in offices, retail stores, and restaurants, but by 1922-23, when the oil and realty booms had lost their initial force, there were so many applicants for every job that any sort of work became hard to get, and the matrons at the police stations had to find lodgings and food for many young women whose visions of stardom had faded into a harsh reality.

The producers, after hoping in vain for several years that the madness would exhaust itself and the stream of girls would cease to flow, organized an educational campaign to keep them at home. Newspapers and magazines published articles calculated to reduce the movie fever, and Paramount produced a delightfully humorous and satirical picture entitled "Hollywood," in which fifty or more stars appeared in a laudable effort to tell girls to "keep away from Hollywood." This stay-at-home propaganda was fairly successful, and reduced the annual pilgrimage from thousands to hundreds. Most of those who made the journey in later years took with them enough money to pay boarding-house bills until the gods of good luck might give them a chance to pass the doors of casting offices.

THE promotion of new movie companies, which had been a striking characteristic of the industry from its earliest days, declined almost to the vanishing point in 1918, but was renewed with great vigor in 1919-20. The promotions following Armistice Day required much larger investments of capital than those that took place during the preceding decade. The cost of standard negatives had advanced from $1,000 in 1909, to between $25,000 and $100,000 in 1919, and the maintenance of a national system of exchanges cost $10,000 to $15,000 a week. New producing or distributing ventures needed abundant financing if they hoped to survive. Business men and bankers, noting the rapid recovery of the industry from the war depression, the influenza epidemic, and the peculiar conditions following Armistice Day, were finally convinced that, in spite of its puzzling defiance of sane business practices, it offered opportunities for profitable investment. Such capitalists poured millions of dollars into the two or three dozen larger companies which seemed to be firmly established and reasonably well managed.

Dozens of small units were promoted by enthusiasts to exploit a small group of stars, or a single star,—undertakings which required, generally, an investment of $100,000 to $1,000,000. Wall Street, and bankers in other cities, engaged to some extent in this class of financing, but the promoters got most of their funds from individuals willing to "take a flier in the films." Most of the new companies were located in Los Angeles and New York, but movie madness was so widespread that studios appeared in more than a dozen cities throughout the United States and Canada.

There were, all told, several hundred ventures of one sort and another, nearly all of them inspired by men or women with but slight experience in the management of picture companies. Ambitious directors, camera men, actors, or film salesmen, related so many stories of the prodigious profits of the producers for whom they had worked—although the yarns were fantastic most of them had some foundation in fact—that even hard-headed business men were induced to take a chance in the glittering game. Vanity nearly always entered into such ventures—they generally included a financier whose wife or daughter or son or sweetheart was confident of achieving stardom once he or she appeared on the screen.

Although nearly all these projects resulted in failures, with losses of millions of dollars, comparatively few of the promotions were of the sinister wild-cat type. The danger of picture ventures came not so much from the few rascals who organized companies to sell stock to gullible investors, but from incompetent enthusiasts or egotists, each of whom genuinely believed himself to be a master producer or a world-beating distributor and could not be convinced to the contrary except by experience.

The losses of investors in many small companies were, however, only a small part of the final total of financial failures following this period of expansion. The heaviest blows—amounting to millions—fell on established distributors and producers and the capitalists allied with them who refused to believe that Paramount, or First National, or any other competitor could interfere with their success. Since the collapse of General Film, owners of great, first-run theaters had become too rich and too proud to submit to the domination of Zukor or any other man; the general belief of the industry was that another movie trust was impossible. The theaters were free, and anyone with ability to produce good pictures could be sure that plenty of screens would welcome his product. The temper of the industry ran counter to monopoly; the nature of movie-making was such that its product could never be completely standardized but must remain an operation basically dependent on individual talent, and no trust could capture all the available talent. And, ran the final argument, the day of trusts in the United States had passed; the government, acting through the Federal Trade Commission, now prevented not only monopoly but even unfair business practices. This was the mode of reasoning with which the overwhelming majority of the industry's leaders comforted itself. They were convinced that nothing within or without the industry could ever restrain trade in motion pictures.

For a number of years the popularity of the star system had practically safeguarded skilful manufacturers and distributors against losses. The worship of movie personalities was so intense and so reliable that the producer-distributor's only problem had been to find actors and actresses able to attract and build up a box-office following. The star system seemed to constitute a solid foundation of bed rock under the industry, and on its continuance most film people in 1919-20 were building their hopes for the future.

But audiences were already beginning to drift away. Here and there were appearing slight indications of inconstancy. Star worship was less feverish than it had been, although the fervor was still so general that very few producers gave heed to the changing public temper. The industry as a whole failed to realize that the children of a decade earlier were now men and women—they had been through school, they had experienced war and the wide distribution of wealth in the post-war boom; they had "grown up" with the movies, and in the process of growing up had unconsciously formed habits of differentiation and selection.

Young people, who constitute the most influential section of screen audiences, continued to love their stars, but appreciation of the superior quality of many non-star pictures was undermining their former sheep-like idolatry. Non-star versions of successful stage plays and novels were becoming as popular as the productions of high-priced stars, while the films of C. B. DeMille and occasional offerings of other directors were earning more profits that the pictures of much-advertised celebrities.

Within two years after Armistice Day, defections in star adoration were definitely reflected in many box offices, and the changing condition began to worry the more acute showmen. If the star system should lose its grip on the public, what would take its place? Each clue that might lead to a solution of the problem was followed frantically by the producers, and many experiments were made. Some were very interesting, some very valuable, many of them very foolish, and nearly all of them very expensive. Much harsh criticism has been directed at the movies for the extravagance and waste of the studios, but while much of the criticism has been justified, it is necessary to take a glance at studio organization to understand the entire picture.

First is the important matter of geography: the executive offices of producing and distributing companies are located in New York, and in Los Angeles, three thousand miles away, are the studios in which the merchandise is manufactured. Does the dog wag the tail, or the tail the dog? Is New York the dog or the tail? Or Los Angeles? This question was difficult, but not unanswerable, prior to the 1919-20 boom: New York was the head, and Los Angeles took its instructions from eastern executives. The practice of the big bosses was to journey to Los Angeles a few times a year for purposes of inspection and conference. These events were important occasions, for during the presence of the High Hat, honors and rewards were bestowed, salaries were increased, players were advanced to higher positions, and unlucky wights were demoted or decapitated.

A throng of studio officials and stars would meet the great one at the railroad station, sometimes with a brass band. One of the companies introduced the quaint custom of building a triumphal arch from curb to curb in front of the studio gate, on which was inscribed, "Welcome to John Doe, King of the Movies." As the chubby, smiling little king descended from his gasoline chariot, a band played "Lo! the Conquering Hero Comes," and gladsome actresses strewed flowers in his path. All that was needed to complete this charming ceremonial in the springtime of the movies was the barbecue of one or two fat comedians, and I shall always wonder why press agents failed to include that colorful touch.

The big bosses, on their flying visits from New York, followed a common routine: first, the welcome at the railroad station, and another at the studio; a quick talk with the studio manager; visits of conciliation to temperamental stars; then conferences on various items of administration, production, finance, labor, and such. Sessions in projection rooms to inspect completed or partially completed pictures and tests of new players, and conferences in regard to new stories and casts would be sprinkled through the discussions of business matters. The visits of serious-minded owners and executives to their studios were a steady grind of hard work, and most of them were too keen, too ambitious, to fritter away much time. Evenings given to social matters were arranged to include stars of the studio, or from other studios; and almost as much business was transacted in these hours as during working periods in the offices.

It was not possible for the president or another official, rushing from New York to Los Angeles for a visit of a week or two, to become acquainted with very many of the people on his pay roll. Stars were his greatest asset, and, therefore, he had to know the stars, and the players who might be developed into stars. He had to know directors, for, from the beginning of film-making, the director had always been the owner's connecting link with studio operations. Originally the director had executed or supervised all the details of movie making, writing the simple scenarios required for short films, selecting and directing the players, devising the settings, editing and titling the film. "The mysteries of the movies" were locked up in his brain, and the producer had to rely on his craftsmanship.

Continuity or scenario writers were used at first merely to submit brief story ideas to the directors, and were paid five to twenty-five dollars for each accepted suggestion, the director usually taking the idea and reshaping it to suit himself. When five-reel features came in, and longer and more complete scenarios were needed, the writer received more employment, to save the time of the director, but the director continued to revise manuscripts and looked upon the writer as more or less of a hack. Some of the writers were hacks, but others, as time was to prove, possessed ability of high order. Members of the scenario craft were galled by their inferior position, but as long as the manufacturer vested all power in the director, the penman had to worry along with his fairly adequate pay, but meager glory and no authority.

The stars gnawed into the power of the director, and made him unhappy; but there never was a moment when the directors, as a group, did not reciprocate by regarding all players, as a group, as so many puppets, brought to life by the man behind the megaphone.

The producer had only two principal sources of advice in the studios, the stars and the directors, when the star system showed its early signs of weakening. The continuity and scenario writers were well-paid and were moving upward toward a voice in management, but in 1919-20 very few of them carried any great weight in the councils of owners or chiefs. The directors were willing to accept all the responsibility for picture-making, but for a while the producers could not agree that to the director should be given the power and the glory. The production, in 1919, of "The Miracle Man," exercised a profound influence in raising the status of directors.

"The Miracle Man," a story of a faith healer who brought regeneration to a group of crooks, written as a novel by Frank L. Packard, had been made into a stage play by George M. Cohan, without particular success. Isaac M. Wolper, a retail merchant in a Boston suburb, inspired by the progress of Louis B. Mayer, invested in the stock of a New England motion picture studio that proved to be a failure. Wolper, persisting in his desire to break into the movies, promoted a company called "Mayflower." He met and engaged as director, George Loane Tucker, an actor and director who had been making pictures in London and later in New York for Universal, Goldwyn, and other companies. Tucker went to the Robert Brunton studio in Los Angeles and there met Thomas Meighan, a character actor, who had been dreaming that some day someone might give him the chance to do the rôle of the principal crook in "The Miracle Man." Tucker obtained the screen rights to the story, and assembled a cast consisting entirely of able but non-star players.

Meighan got his part, Betty Compson, earning $125 a week as a free lance in Christie Comedies and Jesse Durham Hampton's dramas, was cast as the girl crook; Elinor Fair was the heroine; Lon Chaney, then unknown except in the studios, was selected as the cripple because of his talent for contortion and make-up; Joseph Dowling, an old character actor receiving $75 a week in the Brunton stock company, was the Miracle Man. The negative, produced as a special of eight reels, cost $120,000, a moderate figure as expenses were running then. Wolper had made arrangements for distribution with Paramount, and the picture was a sweeping success. The story was well told; the direction was convincing; the acting was excellent. Audiences everywhere gave their heartiest approval to the production, and the powerful Christian Science Church welcomed it as propaganda for Mrs. Eddy's teachings.

"The Miracle Man" made stars of its hitherto unknown actors and immediately increased their earning power 500 to 1,000 percent. It placed Tucker in the front rank of directors, although he did not live to do any other important work. He was ill with an incurable disease when he made "The Miracle Man," and died about two years later.

"The Miracle Man" earned all told about $3,000,000, and its

success seriously shook the faith of producers in the star system. Perhaps, many of the big bosses inquired of themselves, would it be wise to take directors at their word and accord them equal importance with the stars? They pondered the risks involved in placing authority in the hands of men unaccustomed to executive responsibility and without experience in the handling of large sums of money. The experiment might prove disastrous,—directors, as a group, were autocratic, headstrong, scornful of their employers, considering themselves artists and their employers mere dollar-chasers—if these wild men should get control of the studios there might be many bad smashes!

The puzzled producers were not permitted to ponder long. The increasing popularity of all-star pictures was arousing audiences to more discriminating demands, and each month the inroads on the star system became more apparent. Practically all principal manufacturers concluded to adopt Zukor's compromise—pay large prices, if need be, to directors, novelists, dramatists and continuity writers, hoping thereby to find something novel and startling to attract the crowds to their own photoplays.

Thus dawned the day of opportunity for the directors. Their salaries were raised until they reached the standards of all but the most highly paid stars. In a few years, DeMille was earning more than any player except Mary Pickford, Chaplin, and Fairbanks. The publicity resources of studios were concentrated on elevating directors to stardom, and they were given the power to spend money as they thought best in the selection of story material, writers, players, camera men, settings, film editors. Although most directors eagerly accepted the enlarged powers and increased rewards, and a score or more of them were given the most extravagant opportunities to make stars of themselves, Cecil Blount DeMille was the only one who succeeded in building a box-office name comparable to that of David Wark Griffith. A dozen other men were equally able, and several of them have produced pictures that are landmarks in the history of the screen, but the public, the last court of appeal, never permanently accepted as stars any directors except Griffith and DeMille.

Griffith, unable to repeat the success of "The Birth of a Nation," had turned to the lavish use of money to recapture the public's favor. He seemed to believe that great mob scenes, titanic settings, mere extravagance of money and materials, might serve as a huge battering ram to break down the wall of public indifference and afford him another great triumph. "Intolerance," which he produced in 1916-17, at a cost of a million and a half dollars, was conceived on a grand scale. It contained four stories in one, seventy-five or eighty reels—about twenty hours of screen time! Griffith finally reduced his picture to a dozen reels; all of the hundreds of thousands of dollars represented in the discarded hours of unused film found their home in the furnace.

The power of massed dollars failed to function in "Intolerance." The public declined to be impressed by its extravagance, and the picture was eventually divided into four parts, each of its stories being distributed separately. Griffith later turned to an artistic effort to win the applause of the intelligentsia, "Broken Blossoms," adapted from Thomas Burke's gruesome story of a white girl amid the Chinese of London's Limehouse slums. It obtained praise from the critics and indifference from the general public, and left Griffith's reputation just about where it had been placed by "The Birth of a Nation."

DeMille had been carefully studying the mind of the populace to find the perfect box-office formula. Eclectic and practical, willing to provide whatever was wanted so long as it made for entertainment, DeMille developed his box-office sense to a degree hitherto unknown. To his own idea of the non-star photoplay, he added an important discovery of Jeanie MacPherson—that the one thing in which people are always interested is "sex appeal." With Miss MacPherson's discovery, a whole new era, embracing a variety of possible subjects and treatments, suddenly opened.

The principal exponent of sex appeal, until this time, had

been Theda Bara, whose interpretations of the vampire type had been very popular and widely imitated. Miss MacPherson's idea was to avoid the vampire and siren types—perhaps because they were so completely monopolized by Miss Bara—and to broaden the scope of this ingredient to include all the subtle manifestations of feminine charm which had come into vogue after the war.

To test the soundness of Miss MacPherson's theory, DeMille purchased the screen rights of "The Admirable Crichton," James M. Barrie's delightful play about the astonishingly re- sourceful butler who proved equal to all the emergencies of shipwreck on a desert isle, to the amazement of his aristocratic but useless employers. Jeanie MacPherson and Cecil DeMille renamed the play "Male and Female," and expanded it until it was an almost perfect recipe for box-office success, filled with comedy, romance, thrills and sex appeal, the latter element being supplied principally by Gloria Swanson, a girl who had begun as a bathing beauty in Mack Sennett comedies, later playing important parts in Triangle films. In "Male and Fe- male," a retrospect, fading from the present time to the dim past, revealed the charming Gloria costumed almost à la Eve in a Garden of Eden setting, with Thomas Meighan in the Adam rôle. Another fade-out and fade-in, and the retrospect carried the story forward to scenes of oriental splendor in an ancient land, with Meighan as the king and Gloria as the humble maid beloved by his majesty.

The public's joyous reception of "Male and Female" con- vinced DeMille that the new formula was very positively in tune with the times. New longings were stirring in people's minds; events following the war were producing great economic and social changes, and to many Americans the prevailing movie methods had become "old-fashioned." A large section of screen patronage was waiting for interpretations of the new order of life. Many new fortunes had been made in America during the war, and a great many more were being made in this period of titanic money-freedom after the war. Hundreds of thousands of families were enjoying a prosperity that had never been dreamed of. Everyone was buying fashionable, expensive clothing; women had almost stopped wearing cotton underwear; sales-girls, factory workers, domestic servants, everyone was wearing the silk lingerie and stockings heretofore monopolized by the rich; motor cars were being bought by millions of families; hundreds of thousands of new dwellings were being built and decorated and furnished; luxuries of every sort were rapidly spreading to the common folk.

New hotels and restaurants, country clubs, golf courses, night clubs, summer and winter resorts, all sorts of places where people could mingle with their fellows, were springing up everywhere. The old social order, rigid, exclusive, aristocratic, was breaking up; society, symbolized by the Four Hundred in New York and miniature Four Hundreds in every other city in the land, was rapidly disappearing and the citadel of social preferment was being stormed by thousands of eager newcomers whose wealth bought them admittance. There was an intense curiosity about wealth, about the manner of life of the rich, about the things that money can buy, clothes, houses, decorations, cars, the thousand and one appurtenances of modern American life. A world had been wiped out during the war years. A new world was coming of age with the widespread prosperity of the post-war period. A new generation of moviegoers, not in sympathy with the way of life of its elders, was demanding pictures in harmony with the life it was leading or, at least, hoped soon to lead. Class distinctions had broken down. The way of the rich was becoming the way of the land, and people were suddenly interested in etiquette, in social forms, in behavior, in the standards and clothes and beauty lotions and habits that would help them to be like the people they admired.

Accurately appraising the new civilization that was emerging, DeMille decided that the majority of theater patrons were fundamentally curious about only money and sex. Magazines and books were trying desperately to satisfy both interests, but the screen was so obviously a more effective medium that De-Mille was in no further doubt about the kind of picture he would make. The age of jazz, prohibition, and flaming youth had dawned, and a new kind of photoplay was needed.

DeMille combined money and its by-products with sex appeal, in a series of American society comedy-dramas that were admirably designed to meet the demands of the moment. He withdrew the curtains that had veiled the rich and the fashionable, and exhibited them in all the intimate and lavish details of their private lives. He did it cleverly and with such superb showmanship that he quickly rose to a commanding position in his profession.

For the making of these films, DeMille assembled at the Paramount studio in Hollywood the finest staff of artists, craftsmen, and technicians he could find. Architects and decorators were encouraged to exercise their imaginations in designing huge, lavish interiors. The public wanted to see how the rich lived and whether the furnishings they read about were actually real, and DeMille showed them the objects of their dreams in actual use. With his acutely developed sense of showmanship, he knew to a hair the value of over-emphasis and over-elaboration, and where to draw the line; his interiors, exaggerated as they often were, were nevertheless convincing; anyone of them might have been in the home of a multi-millionaire, and many of them undoubtedly were after DeMille pointed the way.

If the DeMille era materially influenced the design of American homes, his services in this field aroused less attention than his contribution to the art of dress. The great fashion shows of Paris and New York, from which the styles for the entire world were promulgated, had been as a sacred temple to which only the elect—that is, the wealthy—were admitted. Smart clothes were the last exclusive privilege of position, and the system of control, simple but extremely effective, operated to keep the latest fashions from widespread popularity until their first fine flush had dimmed. The women's magazines and the department stores attempted to satisfy the universal hunger for fashion news, but necessarily their influence was limited and, moreover, might be three to six months behind the latest edicts of the Rue de la Paix or Fifty-seventh Street.

From time to time, a few movie producers had made tentative attempts to invade this field, by allowing a star an extra budget for clothes which she usually selected to please herself, assisted by the counsels of dressmakers. But the efforts of a single actress, however beautiful or fashionable the clothes she wore, could hardly fill the need for a complete fashion show that could be viewed by millions as well as by the fortunate few. These attempts were, therefore, interesting but inadequate, until De-Mille assembled his forces to level the walls of Fashion.

He accomplished his victory by a combination of simplicity and strategy. He transferred the fashion show to his photoplays, and lured from the sacred temples the most celebrated priests and priestesses of the Sacred Art of Dress, and thereafter the actresses in his plays were outfitted literally from head to foot by artists. Hair-dressers from New York and Paris came to Hollywood to sculpture their tresses; wig makers produced elaborate wigs; shoes were ordered from the smartest manufacturers or were made to order to meet the requirements of particular situations; lingerie, gowns, hats, furs, accessories of all sorts, were designed and made by the DeMille staff of style experts.

Thus DeMille made it possible for every girl with the price of a theater ticket to feast her eyes on fashion shows more elaborate than the esoteric ceremonies of New York and Paris, and equally authentic. Hollywood came to rank as a new center of fashion, and, with the advantage of the screen as a medium of popularizing its modes quickly, widely, and most effectively, soon began to exert a profound influence on the clothes of women throughout the world.

DeMille had discovered no new principles of screen dramaturgy. He had found only a new formula, but so efficiently did it work that his pictures thronged the box offices. His fame soon equalled and presently surpassed that of Griffith. Pickford, Chaplin, De-Mille, were stars whose names in the lobby assured exhibitors of theaters filled to capacity.

When DeMille blazed a new trail with "Male and Female," astute competitors followed him immediately into the field of lighter, merrier films with an admixture of drama and sex appeal; and as soon as the first of his modern American pictures, "Why Change Your Wife?" written by William C. DeMille, appeared in January, 1920, many producers turned their studios into fashion shops, and the screen was flooded with imitations of the DeMille discovery. Wise wives, foolish wives, clever and stupid wives, any kind of wives, were portrayed in every variety of domestic situation that gave an opportunity for display of wealth, money-getting and money-spending, smart clothes, and romance.

In dealing with sex themes, movie writers, in deference to the family patronage of the theaters, usually elided the franker infidelities of husband or wife, carefully selecting for screen presentation only minor infractions of the seventh commandment. One director, who achieved great fame as the master in sex interpretation, would make two versions of his films, one for use in America, in which sex scenes were presented in accordance with American notions of propriety; another for presentation abroad, in which greater latitude was possible.

That old stand-by, the western, was also refurbished to meet modern demands. The simple ranch house of the earlier days became a beautifully reconstructed Mexican hacienda, and the cowboy hero blossomed forth in expensive *chaparreras, sombreros,* decorated saddles and boots, and silver-mounted equipment. In the evening scenes, he might even appear in the latest fashions of Bond Street and Saville Row.

But glorified westerns and the exploitations of sex appeal and wealth did not affect the popularity of the Cinderella motif, which continued through this period to occupy a prominent position among box-office attractions. The Cinderella theme was brought up to date. Cinderella no longer swept the kitchen floor

and scoured the pots and pans. The modern version discovered
her as a snappy, chic stenographer, or a sales-girl in a gown
shop. The prince was a wealthy business man, rather fed up
on a wife mad about clothes, and more clothes, and still more
clothes; to satisfy curiosity on this point, the screen revealed
the wife witnessing a parade of pretty manikins, displaying
extravagantly expensive gowns and furs and lingerie. The wife
often complemented the exhibition by trying on various frocks
herself, revealing, in the process, charms that caused male members of the audience to wonder why her husband allowed his
thoughts to wander from his own fireside. Thus two birds were
thriftily killed with one stone: feminine curiosity regarding
clothes, and masculine curiosity regarding sex, were both pleas-
antly titillated, with no shock to the family patronage of the
theater, for the display of semi-frocked damsels was in the sacred
cause of dress, and, therefore, could give no offense.

Dress and its by-product of sex having been attended to, the
principal chapters of the modernized Cinderella story were out
of the way. Cinderella found the glass slipper, now, invariably,
a string of pearls. Always a string of pearls; never by any chance
a diamond necklace, or a motor car, or a block of stock in
Umadilla Copper that would rise and rise and rise in value.
The novelists and dramatists might use such properties, but the
string of pearls was as essential to the screen as the film on the
celluloid. When Prince Charming offered the pearls to Cinderella, she might decline them, or accept them platonically,
either way maintaining her spotless virtue, although often it
seemed in peril; and in the end she persuaded her prince that
his own fireside was best, and if he would increase his wife's
dress allowance to $10,000 a month, she would become a loving
and devoted ornament to a happy home.

Husband and wife, reunited, leave for the Rue de la Paix.
Cinderella accepts the proposal of honorable marriage from the
proprietor of the lingerie shop, or from the poor but honest
young man in the law office who has just made a million dollars
by promoting a new gadget for an electric ironing-board. Every-

one is happy,—and not a stone has been removed from the sacred foundation of Family Entertainment, so zealously guarded by censors in Philadelphia, Detroit, Topeka, and other centers of indubitable righteousness.

CHAPTER ELEVEN

UNITED ARTISTS AND OTHER DEVELOPMENTS

MARY PICKFORD had no sooner signed her contract with First National than an astute young man realized that this young woman, who had been a prime influence in movie economics on several important occasions, could be used effectively in creating still another method of collecting greater tribute from film fans.

Benjamin Percival Schulberg was born in Bridgeport, Connecticut, in 1892. The family moved to New York when he was a few years old and there Benjamin was educated, later attending City College where he made an excellent record as a student. He had literary ambitions, but realized that he would need some technical training by which to earn his living, and studied stenography at night. He left college at the age of sixteen, a friendly member of the faculty assisting him to obtain a position as stenographer with Henry Stoddard, publisher of the *Evening Mail*. Joseph Edward Chamberlin was literary editor of the newspaper, and soon the lad induced Chamberlin to permit him to assist in reviewing books. There was no monetary compensation for this extra work, but it enabled him to write and kept him in the way of a literary career.

At this time, in 1909-10, the independent producers and distributors were in the thick of their great battle with the Motion Pictures Patents Company, and their association was publishing a weekly trade journal which carried the independents' arguments and advertisements to the exhibitors. Schulberg, searching for opportunities to write, made a connection with this small publication and soon was its editor and publisher. From this position he went to Rex Pictures, a company owned by Joseph Engel and Ed Porter, producing one-reel films for distribution through Universal. He was in charge of the scenario department of Rex, writing stories for directors, writing advertisements, buying stories from players and reporters, editing film, and doing any other jobs that came his way. Jeanie MacPherson, a young actress, was one of his regular authors, to whom he paid $15 a story, or two for $25.

When Adolph Zukor organized Famous Players in 1912, taking Ed Porter as his chief of production staff, Schulberg went to the Zukor studio as head of the scenario department, progressing in time to the distributing branch of the business. After Zukor obtained control of Paramount, Schulberg was made general manager of the company.

Zukor merged Paramount, Artcraft and the Paramount-Artcraft producing companies into the larger Famous Players-Lasky Corporation in December, 1918. Hiram Abrams (elected president of Paramount when Hodkinson was released in 1917) and Zukor had not been happy in their relations, and after the several corporations were consolidated, Abrams resigned and Zukor became president. Schulberg and Abrams had worked closely together, and the younger man was so intensely loyal to his superior that upon the latter's withdrawal from Paramount, he impulsively, and contrary to Zukor's advice, left the company.

As sales manager of Paramount and Artcraft he was thoroughly familiar with the prices paid by all classes of theaters for all pictures, and realized more acutely than was practically possible to any other person the extreme popularity of Mary Pickford. He knew that Pickford-Artcraft prices had been obtained during the two most difficult business years of the screen's existence and that, moreover, since Armistice Day the theaters had been making more money than ever. He believed that if Pickford pictures were removed entirely from association with any company distributing-program or series of films, the exhibitors would have to pay almost any price set upon them.

As the Pickford output of three or four films a year would not alone support the expense of a distributing organization, Schulberg directed his thoughts toward other items that might be included. Douglas Fairbanks had risen to great popularity, and Schulberg was confident that his box-office value would soon equal that of Mary Pickford. Charlie Chaplin was at the height of his glory. Griffith was still the most famous director. Schulberg concluded that Pickford, Fairbanks, Chaplin, and Griffith ought to withdraw from association with all other companies, form one of their own, and make and sell their own pictures. "United Artists" would be a fitting name for such a group; Hiram Abrams should be the president of the distributing company and he—Schulberg—its general manager. Abrams warmly endorsed his young friend's plan, and together they went to Los Angeles and submitted it to Charlotte and Mary Pickford and Douglas Fairbanks, all of whom were pleased with the idea. Fairbanks suggested that it would be well to get a man of national prominence to head the company, someone whose name associated with motion pictures would be of benefit to them and to the entire industry.

The leading movie stars had given their services to Liberty Loan campaigns during the war, and many of them had come to know and admire William Gibbs McAdoo, secretary of the treasury, head of the Federal Railroad Board during the war, and son-in-law of President Wilson. Fairbanks suggested McAdoo as the ideal head of the proposed United Artists Company, and the nomination was promptly ratified by all the parties.

McAdoo welcomed the offer, but modified it to the extent that Oscar F. Price, his principal associate in the Federal Railroad administration, be made president of the company. McAdoo, resigning from his governmental positions, became its counsel. The corporation was organized as a distributor, each of the four artists retaining entire control of his or her respective producing activities, delivering to United Artists the completed pictures for distribution on the same general plan that they would have followed with a distributing organization which they did not own. The stock of United Artists was equally divided between the four players and McAdoo.

This arrangement introduced a new method into the industry. Heretofore producers and distributors had been the employers, (with the exception of First National), paying salaries and sometimes a share of the profits to the stars. Under the United Artists system, the stars became their own employers. They had to do their own financing, but they received the producer profits that had heretofore gone to their employers, and each received his share of the profits of the distributing organization.

At the time of the United Artists organization, any one of several manufacturers would have paid Mary Pickford a million dollars in salary for making four pictures. Douglas Fairbanks could have obtained $500,000 a year in salary and a share of profits that would have brought his earnings to at least a million a year. Chaplin could easily have earned a million a year had he produced steadily. Fairbanks and Charlotte and Mary Pickford believed they could exceed these figures by operating under the United Artists plan, and events in the ten years that elapsed after their corporation got under way justified their confidence.

They bought a modern studio, built by Jesse Durham Hampton, on Santa Monica Boulevard in West Hollywood, and within a few months—when Fairbanks' contract with Paramount had ended and Miss Pickford had completed her year's engagement with First National—they began to make their own pictures and distribute them through United Artists.

Charlie Chaplin established his own studio at Sunset and La Brea, in West Hollywood, which he has since used exclusively for his own productions.

Mrs. Pickford's single-track philosophy had always been that the public was willing and able to pay whatever admittance prices were necessary to obtain the pictures it wanted; Mary Pickford and Fairbanks, subscribing heartily to this theory, spent money lavishly in their efforts to produce the finest photoplays possible. Miss Pickford continued to select stories of the same general nature as those in which she had previously appeared. Fairbanks remained for a while in the romantic melodramas which afforded opportunities to use the athletic stunts so much enjoyed by his audiences, but in 1920 he turned to the old tale of "Robin Hood," and so began a series of films in a wholly new genre.

"Robin Hood" cost $700,000 but earned more than $3,000,000, and Fairbanks was encouraged to spend nearly $2,000,000 in making "The Thief of Bagdad," a fantastic Oriental conception that appeared in 1922. Fairbanks spared no pains to create exquisite settings and costumes, and "The Thief of Bagdad" established a high-water mark in elaborate entertainment. The film was beautifully mounted and evoked a series of marvelous scenes that might have come from the "Arabian Nights." But beautiful as it was, "The Thief of Bagdad" suffered from the same weakness as Griffith's "Intolerance": it was too much entertainment for an audience to assimilate. Too many superb settings, too many great mobs, too many chapters shifting rapidly from one to another. The ordinary brain could not absorb in one evening all the glories that Fairbanks offered, and the average patron left the theater rather bewildered by the amazing spectacle.

"The Thief of Bagdad" was commercially successful, but its gross earnings did not equal those of "Robin Hood" and its cost was nearly three times as great. In after years, Fairbanks made no further efforts at extravagant fantasy, nor did other producers; the day of extremely elaborate, highly expensive productions seemed to have passed within a few years after its initiation. Audiences apparently exhausted all the thrills that could be extracted from such entertainments, and the public mind became more interested in the development of plot and characterization than in mere bigness and elaboration.

Mary Pickford was not as successful in her new productions as was her partner-husband. (She had married Douglas Fairbanks soon after the forming of United Artists.) In attempting to depart from her little girl rôles, she made a screen version of Charles Major's novel, "Dorothy Vernon of Haddon Hall." It was an adequate story, and she made it into an excellent picture; her own work was splendid and she proved her ability to play an adult rôle well. But unfortunately, in the language of the trade, "the picture didn't click"—her audiences were not satisfied, and "Dorothy Vernon" was not an outstanding success.

The reactions of motion picture audiences offer a fertile field of investigation to the psychologist. Mary Pickford's millions of adorers refused to permit her to "grow up" on the screen. Apparently she had so definitely made herself a symbol of youth that her admirers instinctively felt that they too were advancing in years when they saw her portraying more mature rôles, and resented the implication to the extent of remaining away from the theater rather than see their idol in a mature part. Her problem paralleled in many ways that of Charlie Chaplin, the "little funny man with the big shoes," who burned with ambition to portray other rôles than that of the wistful, lonesome little tramp. Unquestionably Chaplin is one of the finest actors the world has ever known, a master of pantomime—perhaps the greatest living master of this art which has now almost disappeared—and understands the camera and the screen as few men understand them. But the public, which elevated him to the heights of popularity, would never permit him to move beyond the limitations of a battered derby hat, floppy trousers and over-sized shoes. Audiences had definitely decided that all heroes must be tall, and Chaplin is too short to be a lover; all villains must be sinister—Chaplin, they are sure, cannot be anything but comical. Should he essay another characterization, his public would laugh heartily at the burlesque, or else condemn him unmercifully for obtaining money under false pretenses.

His one attempt to break through the restrictions imposed by his millions of masters occurred in the closing scenes of "The Gold Rush," in 1927, in which, after the tramp had obtained a fortune, he appeared as a well-dressed, prosperous gentleman, a hero who accomplished the standard happy ending by "getting the girl." "The Gold Rush" was such hilarious comedy that audiences had to like it, but so many people wagged dolorous heads at the sight of a smartly dressed Chaplin that he never repeated the experiment.

Another effort to give vent to his repressions took the form of a photoplay which he wrote and directed in 1923, "A Woman of Paris," with Edna Purviance as the star and Adolphe Menjou, then unknown, as her leading man. The picture was an uncannily beautiful piece of work; Chaplin's direction was a masterpiece of characterization. "A Woman of Paris" won high praise from intellectuals, but the moment the lover committed suicide, Chaplin killed all chances of box-office success;—without a happy ending, pictures cannot hope to win wide approval, and no ending can be happy unless the final fade-out shows hero and heroine in a tight "clinch." The laws of the Medes and Persians are as wax in comparison with this adamantine statute of the American motion-picture audience.

Chaplin's name did not appear in the cast of characters of "The Woman of Paris," but he slipped into the film as the porter in a French provincial railroad station—a tiny fragment of a rôle, but it gave the comedian one chance to escape from the dented derby and the No. 12 shoes, if only for a moment.

DURING the first few years of United Artists, Fairbanks contributed two or three pictures a year to its exchanges, and Mary Pickford was not far behind. Chaplin played along with his productions so slowly that one film a year or two came to be his rule. Griffith, the other member of the team, was committed to the completion of contracts with capitalists who had financed a corporation for him, so that some time had to elapse before he was in position to deliver photoplays to United Artists. His most noteworthy production in this period was "Orphans of the Storm," founded on an old French story, with Lillian and Dorothy Gish in the leading rôles.

In order to occupy the distributing facilities of the United Artists, franchises were granted to various producers under the name of "Allied Artists," and in this manner a number of pictures were brought into the exchanges and assisted in swelling the profits of the corporation, which was soon pouring fortunes into the pockets of its stockholders. A brief review of Mary Pickford's approximate earnings per picture shows clearly the accuracy of Schulberg's conclusion that star worshippers were willing to pay for their entertainment:

1912-14: $40,000 to $60,000;

1914-17 (Paramount): $125,000 to $150,000;

1917-19 (Artcraft and First National): $300,000 to $500,000;

1919-24 (United Artists): $600,000 to $1,200,000.

As already noted, Fairbanks' films reached larger sales than Mary Pickford's—"Robin Hood," "The Thief of Bagdad," and "The Black Pirate" each went into the millions, and almost anyone of his productions reached a million and a half to two millions. Chaplin's occasional offerings earned two or three million dollars each.

Benjamin P. Schulberg, who had conceived the project, did not participate in its profits to any appreciable extent. The conferences necessary to organize United Artists and to bring McAdoo into the undertaking, extended over a period of several months, too long a time for Schulberg to remain idle. George Beban and Mack Sennett had completed a picture and were casting about for a distributor. Schulberg saw the picture, liked it, and decided that he could make some money by distributing it through state's rights exchanges while waiting for the United Artists' kettle to boil. He and Abrams had an oral agreement under which Schulberg believed themselves to be equal partners in film projects, and so, leaving Abrams in Los Angeles to handle the United Artists matter, he took the Beban-Sennett picture in charge and sold it to independent distributors. Mc-Adoo and Abrams concluded an arrangement making Abrams general manager of the United Artists company, his compensation to be two percent of the gross earnings of the pictures. "Two percent" seems a small amount, but when applied to five, ten, or twenty millions of dollars annually it becomes a considerable sum, even though it be divided with a partner. After the transaction was completed, Abrams neglected to include Schulberg in the arrangement. Months passed by, and Schulberg brought suit against his erstwhile partner. He won the case and made a settlement, and passed out of the United Artists situation. Abrams remained with the corporation until his death in 1928.

Schulberg now embarked on the production of pictures for himself, organizing a company for Katherine MacDonald, and later forming Preferred Pictures, Inc., and B. P. Schulberg Productions, Inc. But his capital was insufficient for these projects and they passed into other hands. Schulberg associated himself with Louis B. Mayer for a while, and in November, 1925, returned to Paramount Famous-Lasky as "associate producer" with Zukor and Lasky and general manager of their Los Angeles studios, where he has since remained, the active head of the largest producing organization in the industry.

Schulberg was not, of course, the only individual who, in 1918-20, believed that motion-picture rental prices could be advanced to very high levels. Zukor, Charlotte Pickford, Aitken and Hodkinson, in the earlier years of features, Williams, Tally and Schwalbe in First National, Cecil DeMille in his experiments, and other individuals, had all believed that no one could accurately forecast the limits the public would pay for its entertainment.

Schulberg's conception of the United Artists idea, and its practical application by Fairbanks, McAdoo, and Abrams, dramatized this belief, making it a concrete, active business principle instead of a vague generalization. The cycle of thought and its corollary cycle of action were very simple: millions of individuals, finding enjoyment in the appearance of a star, insisted on seeing that star; the star insisted on higher and higher wages; the employer had to accede to the demands or lose the box-office asset to a competitor; then the employer had to raise the price of the pictures to the theater; and the theater had to increase the price of tickets. Now the cycle had been completed by several of the most popular artists organizing their own machinery of production and distribution, and raising prices to levels heretofore unknown in the business.

In order to swell the earnings of a single photoplay to a million to four million dollars, methods of exhibition were modified materially. Kleine had shown "Quo Vadis" in spoken-drama theaters at spoken-drama admittance prices; "The Birth of a Nation" and a few other important pictures from time to time had been successfully presented in this way. In such showings the film was given in its longest form, usually about ten to twelve reels, or two and one quarter to two and one-half hours of screen time.

After a play had had its run at the one- to two-dollar admittance rate, its length was reduced to eight, seven, or six reels— the reduction in screen time being necessary to fit the picture into a program of two hours—and was rented to first-run houses. The road shows (exhibitions in spoken-drama theaters), created prestige so that when the film reached movie theaters, it was sure of large, profitable attendance.

When expensive methods of production became general, in 1919-22, numerous pictures too costly and too valuable for distribution as features, but not powerful enough to be sold as road shows, became classified as "specials." Their length was six, seven, or occasionally eight reels, in comparison with the standard four and one-half or five reels of features. One or more leading theaters in each large city formed the practice of showing a special for two to six weeks, the duration of the run depending on the picture's popularity; and producers gave such exhibitors one month to three months' priority before releasing the picture to week-run theaters. These pre-release houses might advance their regular admittance rates when exceptionally attractive specials appeared, but the long run in itself yielded much greater returns to the producer than he would have received from a regular release to a week-run house.

Thus, through road shows and pre-releases in long-run theaters, and through the increase in admittance prices in thousands of new first-run neighborhood houses, there was created the machinery for enormously increasing the revenues of the industry. If a photoplay was sufficiently popular to employ all of the methods, its earnings could mount up to staggering totals. "The Birth of a Nation," first as a road show, then as a long-run special, then as a feature, totalled more than $15,000,000 of gross intake; "Ben Hur" will reach eight or ten million; forty or more films in the ten years from 1919 to 1928 reached gross earnings of a million and a half to four million—and among these I do not include any talking pictures.

After the industry entered into the era of expensive specials and road shows in 1919-20, Cecil DeMille, Douglas Fairbanks, and other very popular producers discontinued the making of features, concentrating on the production of specials. If, when a special was completed, it seemed to be especially meritorious, it would be presented in New York or Los Angeles as a road show, and if audiences accepted it as such it would be exhibited throughout the country at the highest scale of admittance rates. If it fell short of the highest prices it could be successfully pre-released for long runs.

THE SCREEN had now definitely moved forward to a still higher level of entertainment, and, as had invariably happened in the past, audiences enthusiastically welcomed the improvement and expected the better films to become the rule, rather than the exception. More backward sections of box-office patronage lingered for a year or two with old-fashioned films, but most theater-goers, once they had seen specials costing $150,000 to $400,000, and a few road shows involving a million or more, soon began to regard ordinary features, costing $60,000, $80,000 or $100,000, as rather poor offerings; preference drifted steadily toward the high-priced productions.

The new first-run and neighborhood houses, with large seating capacities and consequent ability to pay well for pictures, were the principal beneficiaries of this condition. First National, with the greatest number of quality theaters included in its list of franchise and sub-franchise holders, moved forward like a giant in the battle for supremacy. When, at the end of a year, Mary Pickford moved to United Artists, Joseph Schenck transferred Norma and Constance Talmadge from Selznick to First National, and enabled the latter company to continue its progress without the slightest difficulty. Although the public's frenzied idolatry of stars was now quieting down, Norma Talmadge rose to great popularity. Within a year or two her films were drawing more patronage than Mary Pickford's, and Constance, too, acquired a box-office following of great value.

Charlie Chaplin's first long picture, "The Kid," in six reels, and "Passion," an elaborate German-made photoplay portraying the French Revolution, were very successful and added substantially to the prestige and profits of First National. Williams paid only $30,000 for the American rights of the German picture, and it earned more than a million. "The Kid" brought such fame to Jackie Coogan, the six-year-old lad around whose rôle Chaplin built the story, that Sol Lesser made a star of him and Jackie Coogan—with the exception of a few years spent in schoolrooms—continued into young manhood as a box-office personality. Pola Negri, unknown in America, played Du Barry in "Passion," a type of cocotte new to American audiences. Movie-goers liked her work in this rôle and Negri was brought to Los Angeles. She was not, however, a First National attraction after "Passion"; Paramount obtained her soon after the German picture appeared in this country.

63. MARY PICKFORD, DOUGLAS FAIRBANKS, CHARLES CHAPLIN, AND DAVID WARK GRIFFITH. THE UNITED ARTISTS OF 1920.

64A. *The Four Horsemen of the Apocalypse*, WITH RUDOLPH VALENTINO
AND ALICE TERRY. ADAPTED BY JUNE MATHIS FROM THE NOVEL BY
VICENTE BLASCO IBÁÑEZ. DIRECTED BY REX INGRAM.
PRODUCED BY METRO IN 1921.

64B. ANOTHER SCENE FROM *The Four Horsemen*.

65A. *Way Down East*, WITH LILLIAN GISH, MARY HAY, LOWELL
SHERMAN, CREIGHTON HALE, AND RICHARD BARTHELMESS. PRODUCED BY
D. W. GRIFFITH FOR UNITED ARTISTS IN 1920.

65B. *Tol'able David*, WITH RICHARD BARTHELMESS. DIRECTED BY HENRY
KING FROM THE STORY BY JOSEPH HERGESHEIMER. PRODUCED BY FIRST
NATIONAL IN 1921.

66. A DIRECTORS' MEETING OF THE UNITED ARTISTS CORPORATION IN 1921. FROM LEFT TO RIGHT: DENNIS F. O'BRIEN, HIRAM ABRAMS, H. T. BANZHOF, MARY PICKFORD, W. G. MCADOO, SYD CHAPLIN, D. W. GRIFFITH, DOUGLAS FAIRBANKS, OSCAR A. PRICE, JOHN FAIRBANKS, AND NATHAN BURKAN.

67A. *Among Those Present*, WITH HAROLD LLOYD AND MILDRED DAVIS. DIRECTED BY FRED NEWMEYER. PRODUCED BY HAL ROACH FOR PATHÉ IN 1921.

67B. *Movie Fans*, WITH PHYLLIS HAVER. A PARAMOUNT-MACK SENNETT COMEDY. 1923.

68A. *Disraeli*, WITH GEORGE ARLISS. DIRECTED BY HENRY KOLKER.
PRODUCED BY UNITED ARTISTS IN 1921.

68B. *The Sheik*, WITH RUDOLPH VALENTINO AND AGNES AYRES. DIRECTED
BY GEORGE MELFORD. PRODUCED BY PARAMOUNT IN 1921.

69A. *Idols of the North*, WITH DOROTHY DALTON. DIRECTED BY R. WILLIAM NEILL. PRODUCED BY PARAMOUNT IN 1921.

69B. *On the High Seas*, WITH DOROTHY DALTON, JACK HOLT AND MITCHELL LEWIS. DIRECTED BY IRVIN WILLAT. PRODUCED BY PARAMOUNT IN 1922.

70A. *Foolish Wives*, WITH ERICH VON STROHEIM. DIRECTED BY ERICH VON STROHEIM FOR UNIVERSAL IN 1922.

70B. *Orphans of the Storm*, WITH DOROTHY AND LILLIAN GISH. PRODUCED BY D. W. GRIFFITH FOR UNITED ARTISTS IN 1922.

71A. *The Eternal Flame*, WITH NORMA TALMADGE AND CONWAY TEARLE. DIRECTED BY FRANK LLOYD. PRODUCED BY JOSEPH SCHENCK FOR FIRST NATIONAL IN 1922.

71B. *When Knighthood Was in Flower*, WITH MARION DAVIES AND FORREST STANLEY. DIRECTED BY ROBERT G. VIGNOLA FROM THE NOVEL BY CHARLES MAJOR. PRODUCED BY COSMOPOLITAN FOR PARAMOUNT IN 1922.

72. *Nanook of the North*. PRODUCED BY ROBERT J. FLAHERTY FOR REVILLON FRÈRES AND RELEASED BY PATHÉ IN 1922.

73. *Robin Hood*, WITH DOUGLAS FAIRBANKS AND WALLACE BEERY. DIRECTED BY ALLAN DWAN. PRODUCED BY DOUGLAS FAIRBANKS FOR UNITED ARTISTS IN 1922.

74A. *The Prisoner of Zenda*, WITH RAMON NOVARRO AND LEWIS STONE. DIRECTED BY REX INGRAM FROM THE NOVEL BY ANTHONY HOPE. PRODUCED BY METRO IN 1922.

74B. *The Spoilers*, WITH ANNA Q. NILSSON AND MILTON SILLS. DIRECTED BY LAMBERT HILLYER. PRODUCED BY JESSE DURHAM HAMPTON FOR GOLDWYN IN 1923. THIS WAS THE SECOND FILM VERSION OF REX BEACH'S NOVEL; THE FIRST WAS MADE BY SELIG IN 1914.

75. THE MEETING WHICH ELECTED WILL H. HAYS PRESIDENT OF THE MOTION PICTURE PRODUCERS AND DISTRIBUTORS OF AMERICA, INC, IN 1922.

BOTTOM ROW: LEWIS J. SELZNICK, E. V. HAMMONS, J. D. WILLIAMS, WILL H. HAYS, ADOLPH ZUKOR, MARCUS LOEW, CARL LAEMMLE; TOP ROW: W. F. SHEEHAN, MYRON SELZNICK, COLONEL COLE, COURTLAND SMITH, WILLIAM FOX, SAMUEL GOLDWYN, J. J. ATKINSOM, R. H. COCHRANE.

76. *The Ten Commandments*. DIRECTED BY CECIL B. DEMILLE. PRODUCED BY PARAMOUNT IN 1923.

77. *A Woman of Paris*, WITH EDNA PURVIANCE AND ADOLPHE MENJOU.
WRITTEN AND DIRECTED BY CHARLES CHAPLIN. PRODUCED FOR
UNITED ARTISTS IN 1923.

78A. *Flaming Youth*, WITH COLLEEN MOORE AND ELLIOTT DEXTER. DIRECTED BY JOHN FRANCIS DILLON. PRODUCED BY FIRST NATIONAL IN 1923.

78B. *The Navigator*, WITH BUSTER KEATON. DIRECTED BY BUSTER KEATON AND DONALD CRISP. PRODUCED BY M-G-M IN 1924.

79. *The Thief of Bagdad.* DIRECTED BY RAOUL WALSH. PRODUCED BY DOUGLAS FAIRBANKS FOR UNITED ARTISTS IN 1923.

80A. *Anna Christie*, WITH BLANCHE SWEET AND GEORGE MARION. DIRECTED BY JOHN GRIFFITH WRAY, FROM THE PLAY BY EUGENE O'NEILL. PRODUCED BY FIRST NATIONAL IN 1923.

80B. *Rosita*, WITH MARY PICKFORD, GEORGE WALSH, AND FRANK LEIGH. DIRECTED BY ERNST LUBITSCH. PRODUCED BY MARY PICKFORD FOR UNITED ARTISTS IN 1923.

81. *The Covered Wagon.* DIRECTED BY JAMES CRUZE FROM THE NOVEL BY EMERSON HOUGH. PRODUCED BY PARAMOUNT IN 1923.

82. *The Red Lily*, WITH ENID BENNETT. DIRECTED BY FRED NIBLO.
PRODUCED BY M-G-M IN 1924.

83. *Greed*, WITH JEAN HERSHOLT, ZASU PITTS, GIBSON GOWLAND, AND JOAN STANDING. DIRECTED BY ERICH VON STROHEIM FROM FRANK NORRIS' NOVEL, *McTeague*. PRODUCED BY GOLDWYN IN 1924.

84A. *The Marriage Circle*, WITH MARIE PREVOST AND MONTE BLUE. DIRECTED BY ERNST LUBITSCH. PRODUCED BY WARNER BROTHERS IN 1924.

84B. *The Deadwood Coach*, WITH TOM MIX. DIRECTED BY LYNN REYNOLDS. PRODUCED BY WILLIAM FOX IN 1925.

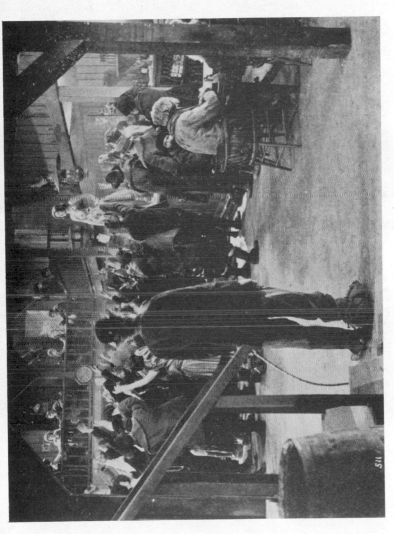

85. *The Gold Rush*, WITH CHARLIE CHAPLIN AND GEORGIA HALE. PRODUCED BY CHARLES CHAPLIN FOR UNITED ARTISTS IN 1925.

86. *The Big Parade*, WITH JOHN GILBERT AND RENÉE ADORÉE. DIRECTED BY KING VIDOR FROM THE NOVEL, *Plumes*, BY LAURENCE STALLINGS. PRODUCED BY M-G-M IN 1925.

87A. *Hands Up,* WITH RAYMOND GRIFFITH. DIRECTED BY CLARENCE BADGER. PRODUCED BY PARAMOUNT IN 1926.

87B. *La Bohème,* WITH LILLIAN GISH, JOHN GILBERT, RENÉE ADORÉE, AND EDWARD EVERETT HORTON. DIRECTED BY KING VIDOR. PRODUCED BY M-G-M IN 1926.

88A. *Moana.* ROBERT J. FLAHERTY'S PRODUCTION MADE IN SAMOA WITH AN ALL-NATIVE CAST. RELEASED THROUGH PARAMOUNT IN 1926.

88B. ANOTHER STILL FROM *Moana.*

89A. *Ben Hur*, WITH RAMON NOVARRO AND CARMEL MYERS. DIRECTED BY FRED NIBLO FROM THE NOVEL BY GENERAL LEW WALLACE. PRODUCED BY M-G-M IN 1926.

89B. *Ben Hur*. A STILL SHOWING THE INTERIOR OF ONE OF THE GALLEYS.

90A. *Ben Hur.* THE CHARIOT RACE IN THE ANTIOCH CIRCUS.

90B. *Ben Hur.* PHOTOGRAPHING THE CHARIOT RACE. (FRANCIS X. BUSHMAN
AS MESSALA.)

91A. *Behind the Front*, WITH WALLACE BEERY AND RAYMOND HATTON. DIRECTED BY EDWARD SUTHERLAND. PRODUCED BY PARAMOUNT IN 1926.

91B. *The Cohens and the Kellys*, WITH GEORGE SIDNEY, CHARLES MURRAY, VERA GORDON, AND KATE PRICE. DIRECTED BY HARRY POLLARD. PRODUCED BY UNIVERSAL IN 1926.

92. *What Price Glory?*, WITH DOLORES DEL RIO, VICTOR MCLAGLEN, AND EDMUND LOWE. DIRECTED BY RAOUL WALSH FROM THE PLAY BY LAURENCE STALLINGS AND MAXWELL ANDERSON. PRODUCED BY FOX IN 1926.

93A. *Beau Geste*, WITH WILLIAM POWELL, RONALD COLMAN, NOAH BEERY, NEIL HAMILTON AND RALPH FORBES. DIRECTED BY HERBERT BRENON FROM THE NOVEL BY PERCIVAL C. WREN. PRODUCED BY PARAMOUNT IN 1926.

93B. *The Magic Flame*, WITH RONALD COLMAN AND VILMA BANKY. DIRECTED BY HENRY KING. PRODUCED FOR UNITED ARTISTS IN 1927.

94A. *Resurrection,* WITH DOLORES DEL RIO AND ROD LA ROCQUE. DIRECTED BY EDWIN CAREWE FROM THE NOVEL BY LEO TOLSTOY. PRODUCED FOR UNITED ARTISTS IN 1927.

94B. *Underworld,* WITH GEORGE BANCROFT, EVELYN BRENT, AND CLIVE BROOK. DIRECTED BY JOSEF VON STERNBERG FROM A STORY BY BEN HECHT. PRODUCED BY PARAMOUNT IN 1927.

WHILE other manufacturers and distributors were engaged in small business battles and when the boom of 1919 aroused them to frantic efforts to make enough pictures to supply the demand and to avoid disaster in the sharp rise of studio costs, Zukor was keenly analyzing the new conditions in the industry, and preparing another series of those effective maneuvers which Lewis Selznick described as "out-smarting the other fellow."

The Paramount-Artcraft system of exchanges was the largest in existence. The manager and salesmen of each office kept tab on the rentals of all competitors, and through their reports Zukor could calculate accurately the volume of business and the net earnings of every important corporation. Keeping himself free from the delusions of grandeur that obsessed some of the movie magnates, he studied the facts and was not in the least deceived by the extravagant boasts of Goldwyn, Metro, Hodkinson, Selznick, Fox, Universal, Robertson-Cole, Vitagraph, and the troop of minor contenders. Knowing thoroughly the real strength and weakness of each, he dismissed them as factors that could be left to take care of themselves. But First National, as he had anticipated from its start, had become a dangerous rival.

The increasing popularity of all-star plays, and the success of First National, convinced Zukor that the theaters were replacing the star system as the dominant factor of the screen, and that control of the industry would soon rest solely in first-run houses. A producer might make splendid pictures, and his distributor might be a very able business man, but without constant access to high-class screens, they could not earn the studio cost of the expensive negatives now demanded by audiences. If the right man should happen to appear in First National and weld the loosely knit, semi-cooperative institution into compact form, it would be so powerful that it would tower above the whole entertainment industry. Who might be cast for this Napoleonic rôle?

In studying the menace of First National, Zukor made a careful analysis of the structure of the industry, and obtained a comprehensive knowledge of the relations of each of its three branches to the other. I do not know of any other man in motion pictures who appreciated so fully the status of producers, distributors, and exhibitors. The vital point of his study is revealed by this statement which he made in 1919 to investment bankers:

"The Famous Players-Lasky Corporation sales department estimates that the gross annual return of the 15,000 American theaters during 1919 will be $800,000,000 and that the total amount the producers will receive in the form of sales and leases of film and accessories will not be over $90,000,000. It is apparent to anyone who has had theatrical experience that this is not an equitable division. Producers claim that even when full consideration is given to the extra cost of large orchestras and other attractions required of picture houses, they should receive from twenty-two to twenty-five percent of the gross theater income."

A literal construction of this statement would include all the 15,000 theaters then operating in the United States, but Zukor applied his analysis only to first-run and larger second-run houses. His argument to bankers was that through the ownership of quality theaters in about fifty cities, the producer (including of course the distributor), would receive a much larger share of box-office receipts in these specific houses, and that the advertising and prestige thus acquired by his pictures would enable the manufacturer to increase rental rates in other theaters.

Zukor sampled the benefits to be derived through control of retail outlets by acquiring in the spring of 1919 the Rialto and the Rivoli theaters in New York and the Grauman Million Dollar and the Rialto in Los Angeles. These houses enabled him to deal effectively with First National competition in these cities, and at the same time to increase Paramount's share of theater receipts.

In New York City the Strand, then the only high-class first-run house in the Longacre Square district except the Rialto and the Rivoli, was affiliated with First National; in Los Angeles, the only large house aside from Grauman's Million Dollar was the Kinema (afterwards named the Criterion), then owned by Tally.

Thus Paramount and First National were supreme in the two principal motion-picture cities of the world, and in these two centers the producer who failed to obtain a booking for his special films was given a foretaste of the bitter fate that awaited him in the near future.

After a few months' experience with these four houses, Zukor decided that Paramount could deal effectively with First National by buying or building first-run theaters in principal cities. Such a program would require many millions of dollars, but he was confident that Paramount could obtain abundant capital in Wall Street. But other points must be carefully considered. Would he run afoul of some of the vague provisions of the Sherman Anti-Trust Act? Might it not some day close in on him? And what of the newer law, the Clayton Act, passed by Congress to punish business men who kept inside the nebulous boundaries of the Sherman law, but laid themselves open to the Federal Trade Commission on charges of "unfair practices"?

Rockefeller, in building the oil trust, had employed several effective methods, one of them the obtaining of secret rebates from railroads on shipments of his own oil, but the government had stopped such practices. Duke's domination of tobacco was based on his acquisition of cigarette-making machinery patents, enabling him to undersell his competitors. Havemeyer's sugar trust was a consolidation of numerous competing factories and the acquisition of important sources of raw material. All the old trusts, the ones that had been prosecuted under the Sherman Act, had been ruthless in underselling their products when such a course was necessary to crush or to frighten rivals. But secret rebates were not available to Zukor; he had no patents that gave him any advantage over competitors; and if he attempted the use of any of the "rough stuff" of earlier industrial magnates, the Sherman and the Clayton acts would stop him quickly. Obviously, if he was to become the ruler of the movies, he would have to employ more subtle methods than had been developed by any of his predecessors in the art of trust building.

Pondering over these problems, he observed that Walter W.

Irwin, general manager of V L S E, was aggressively boosting the rental prices of Vitagraph features to the limit that Vitagraph traffic would bear. Irwin was well known to all exhibitors and many of them were very friendly to him. And, as Irwin was a lawyer, it was a fair assumption that he would know how to avoid business methods denounced by the Sherman and the Clayton statutes. Irwin was offered and accepted a vice-presidency in the Zukor corporation.

He "suggested to Zukor"—I am quoting from Irwin's testimony on the witness stand several years later—"that Paramount could destroy First National if it would go into each one of the First National cities and build, or threaten to build, the finest and largest theater in the city, as the industry had been through the influenza period, in which all exhibitors had lost money and many of the houses entirely closed for many weeks; and that the First National franchise holders had to pay considerable sums of money on contracts with stars to make pictures for them. Some of the First National stockholders were considerably extended financially in their banks, and if Zukor's representative went to these cities and threatened to build theaters the banker would be very likely to call the First National member in and ask that man why he was engaging in a fight with a very large and very strong corporation. A banker would naturally consider such a fight to be poor policy, and no matter how apparently satisfactory the explanation of the First National exhibitor might be I thought it very likely that the banker would tell the depositor that he had better make a substantial reduction in his loan the next time it became due. Such action by bankers would cause disruption in the First National organization. In any event it would not be necessary for Zukor to build more than a few theaters to frighten the First National members."

In his investigations of Triangle, when the collapse of that company occurred in 1917, Zukor had come into contact with Kuhn, Loeb and Company, a principal member of which, Otto Kahn, had been associated with Crawford Livingston in the financing of Mutual. Through one of their affiliated companies,

American International Corporation, Kuhn, Loeb and Company had made an extensive examination of the motion-picture industry in 1919, and A. G. Connick, vice-president of American International, confirmed Zukor's analysis of the profits of movie theaters. The essential part of Connick's findings is summarized in this quotation from a report to his corporation:

"From an examination of such records of theater operation as are available, and assuming that the sum required to amortize the building will not exceed two percent of its cost, and that the amount of the ground rent per annum does not exceed thirty dollars per seat, and with prices of admission ranging upward to sixty cents, a preliminary guess has been made that a theater with 3,100 seats will return at least twenty-five percent on the investment in addition to the usual first run rental charge in their district for the use of the films. That the twenty-five percent is conservative is indicated by the fact that the Grauman Theater of Los Angeles is now earning profits of one hundred percent a year; the Rialto in New York at the rate of about eighty percent a year; the Stillman in Cleveland at the rate of over one hundred percent a year."

In the autumn of 1919, Kuhn, Loeb and Company and associated bankers sold a $10,000,000 issue of preferred stock of Famous Players-Lasky Corporation, and both preferred and common shares of the company were listed on the stock exchange. Investors bought the preferred readily, and trading in both issues became active. The successful floating of this issue placed Zukor in position to obtain by public financing any sums necessary for the expansion of Paramount in the theater field.

In keeping with the almost invariable practice of the industry, Zukor's companies heretofore had been financed with his own money and that of his associates. Their large profits had been reinvested in the business, until at this time the Paramount corporations were worth twenty-five or thirty million dollars. Practically no public financing had been sought by picture projects in the past, the only exceptions being Triangle and World Film, both of whose flotations had resulted in loss to the investors. Zukor's entrance into Wall Street marked a new era in movie finance, and within a few years the shares of Loew's, Inc., Pathé, and Fox were listed in stock exchanges, and five years after Famous Players-Lasky was introduced to investors, Wall Street bankers were handling the shares of a dozen movie corporations.

The popularity of larger, expensive pictures forced producers into capital investments of such magnitude that private financing became a thing of the past. Film companies had to fall in line with older industries in admitting "high financiers" into their councils and giving them a voice in the administration of affairs. Samuel Goldwyn enlisted in his projects Frank Joseph Godsol, an American-born citizen of France, who had made a fortune in buying and selling war supplies to France; Godsol interested the Duponts and other capitalists in the Goldwyn companies. Hodkinson acquired the backing of Jeremiah Milbank, a Wall Street multi-millionaire allied with Borden Milk, Southern Railway, Chase National Bank, Blair and Co., and other powerful interests. Fox's alliance was with the John F. Dryden-Prudential Life Insurance group of Newark, New Jersey.

ZUKOR continued as Selznick's silent partner in Select Pictures, Inc., until the latter's struggles to obtain publicity for the Selznick name became rather more of a nuisance than Zukor cared to tolerate. Selznick, too shrewd to be deceived by the flattery of sycophants, nevertheless lived on glory; the booming of publicity's big bass drum acted as a force that aroused his ego to action. For a couple of years he remained in retirement behind the Select trade name, in accordance with the understanding when Zukor bought a half-interest in the company. Then Myron Selznick, Lewis' son, bloomed forth as a producer, with Olive Thomas, a pretty girl from the Ziegfeld Follies, as his first star, and "Selznick" was restored to the motion-picture cosmos. Zukor regarded this revival of the Selznick name a definite breach of good faith. It is to be surmised, too, that Zukor no longer considered Selznick the menace he had been three years before. The success of First National and the increased costs of studio operation had altered the entire aspect of things. Now, without first-run houses of his own and lacking adequate financial resources, Selznick's ability to make mischief had become a thing of the past. There was a stormy, dramatic session, and Selznick purchased Zukor's interest in Select Pictures for $1,000,000.

Select, making good features with popular but inexpensive stars, and keeping its production costs below the high averages of Paramount, had filled a definite place in Zukor's plan. Theaters that could not afford to pay, or were unwilling to pay, Paramount prices could obtain a steady supply of good medium-priced pictures from Select. With the specials of C. B. DeMille and stars such as Douglas Fairbanks, Elsie Ferguson, and William S. Hart, the high-priced program features of Paramount, and the medium-priced programs of Select, Zukor was in position to deal with all grades of competition except that of the cheapest features, a field which did not impress him as having sufficient permanance to make it worthy of attention. Select was a profitable enterprise, and its profits the first year, according to Selznick, were $1,800,000. A million dollars seemed to be a modest valuation of a half interest in such an enterprise, and Selznick, quite sure he had out-smarted Zukor in the trade, and elated by freedom, entered enthusiastically into a program of expansion. His success in building the Selznick corporations from a shoestring to a large business, and the record of profits in Select, were a picture very attractive to capitalists, and a group of financiers in central New York agreed to supply $2,000,000 to the new Selznick corporation which absorbed Select and its subsidiaries.

Selznick bought the exchanges of the World Film Company, and renamed them "Republic Pictures," using this organization for the distribution of medium- and low-priced features. The Select trade name, changed to "Selznick Select," was applied to costlier features and specials, distributed through Selznick exchanges. Clara Kimball Young had left Selznick to go under the management of Harry Garson, and Norma and Constance Talmadge had moved to First National. Lewis and his son, Myron, assembled a new set of stars, among them being Olive Thomas, Eugene O'Brien, Elsie Janis, Owen Moore, Marie Doro, and Elaine Hammerstein. Myron Selznick embarked in the making of specials, costing from $300,000 to $600,000 each, typical among them being a new edition of Robert W. Chambers' "The Common Law" with Corinne Griffith in the leading rôle, and Anthony Hope's "Rupert of Hentzau" with an all-star cast.

Soon after Zukor's withdrawal from Select, a new company, "Realart Pictures," appeared, with Arthur S. Kane, former general manager of Select, at its head, and with other former Select officers on its staff. Realart took over the Morosco-Pallas studio in Los Angeles, and began the production of medium-priced features of substantially the same quality and box-office value (excepting those of Norma Talmadge), that had been supplied to theaters by Select. Mary Miles Minter, Constance Binney, Bebe Daniels, and other stars were the attractions offered by Realart. Its pictures were well made and effectively distributed at moderate prices, and the company had no difficulty in establishing itself.

Realart was ostensibly an independent, and although Selznick and other producers vehemently declared it to be a Zukor vassal, Zukor did not take the trouble to deny or affirm the charge. While it drew business from various sources, Selznick exchanges were the principal sufferers from Realart competition, and since the large profits previously enjoyed by Select were now falling to Realart, Zukor's acceptance of Selznick's offer turned out to be not ill-advised. For two years, Realart served the purpose of supplying plenty of competition in the field of medium-priced features, and when it was no longer needed Zukor closed its studios and exchanges and the Famous Players-Lasky Corporation absorbed its assets.

THE increasing power of first runs and Zukor's entrance into theater ownership, inspired several producers to attempt to acquire exhibition affiliations to protect themselves. The Goldwyn-Godsol interests started to buy stock in theaters in a few cities, and even Hodkinson, philosophically opposed to combination of the three branches of the industry, wavered for a few months and made tentative arrangements to include theater owners as stockholders in his corporation, but abandoned the idea when he obtained the financial support of Jeremiah Milbank. Several organizations of producers and exhibitors were formed in 1918-20, in imitation of First National. The theory of these projects was that through such unions the theaters could obtain pictures at lower rentals, but their organization was less sound than First National's with its two dozen stockholders, all theater owners. These new so-called cooperatives had an unlimited membership, each association striving to obtain as many franchise-holders as possible. The ownership of stock, however, usually remained in the hands of the promoters.

J. A. Berst, general manager of Pathé, C. R. Seelye, sales manager of the same company, and Lee Ochs, owner of neighborhood theaters in New York, were the founders and principal officers of "United Theaters, Inc.," which engaged Kitty Gordon, Frank Keenan, and other stars. Pathé organized "Associated Exhibitors," and one of its stars, Harold Lloyd, became so popular that his pictures eventually earned $1,000,000 to $3,000,000 each.

Lewis Selznick engaged Charles Pettijohn, an Indiana lawyer and politician who had become interested in motion pictures, to organize "National Picture Theaters, Inc.," to insure the Selznick-Republic exchanges of steady access to screens.

Several other ostensibly or partially mutual associations sprang up, but none of them lived long. The exhibitor members had no real interest beyond hammering down rental prices, and the producers, of course, resisted reductions as destructive of profits. Mere affiliation of producers and exhibitors, or participation in mutual associations, proved to be flimsy makeshifts which could be broken or dissolved whenever inducement or provocation became sufficiently great. First National continued as the only exhibitor group to obtain and retain a strong position in manufacturing and distribution.

In 1921 all business in the United States was compelled to face the agonies of "deflation" that followed as a natural consequence of the expansion and inflation which came after Armistice Day. Under the abnormal demands of reconstruction, industry and commerce had been extended to unhealthy proportions—too many goods were being produced, wages and prices were soaring to impossible levels. The inevitable readjustment crippled or wrecked many companies in all industries. In the movies, while the theaters endured the strain without very serious dislocations (patronage fell away for a few months, but in general attendance maintained fairly normal levels), the producing and distributing branches of the business did not escape so lightly. Most of the smaller companies hastily promoted in 1919-20 now suspended operations, never to resume, and many of the larger corporations suffered severely.

Gross earnings of pictures had grown steadily during the two boom years, but studio costs had become enormously swollen. Film producing had changed from a business of dependable profits to one of great hazards. Briefly recapitulating the situation, the manufacturers' expenses may be placed thus:

In 1918 and through the summer of 1919, feature negatives cost $30,000 to $60,000 each;

In 1920-21, features, of approximately the same quality, $70,000 to $100,000 each;

In 1918-19, specials, $100,000 to $200,000 (very few costing more than the latter figure);

In 1920-21, specials, $150,000 to $350,000 (omitting those of Douglas Fairbanks and an occasional production of D. W. Griffith).

Fairbanks' costs and earnings, indicated in the story of United Artists, were so much more than representative averages of this period that the record of typical C. B. DeMille specials affords a better illustration of the upward movement. When, in 1918, he was convincing Zukor and Lasky that all-star pictures would be more profitable than Mary Pickford's films, DeMille produced negatives for $60,000 and $70,000 which earned $300,000 and $400,000. (Earnings are "gross," from which must be deducted the cost of distribution and finance, which may be placed at twenty to twenty-five percent.)

"Male and Female" cost $170,000 and earned $1,250,000.

The introduction of fashion shows, expensive costuming and elaborate sets, even with no stars at fancy prices, brought his cost totals to $250,000 to $400,000, and rentals did not always increase in proportion to studio expenses, as these figures will reveal:

"Don't Change Your Husband," cost $74,000; earned $300,000;
"Why Change Your Wife?" cost $130,000; earned $1,000,000;
"Forbidden Fruit," cost $340,000; earned $850,000;
"Adam's Rib," cost $400,000; earned $880,000;
"Manslaughter," cost $385,000; earned $1,200,000;
"Golden Bed," cost $440,000; earned $800,000.

While the DeMille and the United Artists figures portray the advance in production costs that took place in a short time in all studios, they are not representative of the earnings of average photoplays. The pre-eminent popularity of Fairbanks, Chaplin, and Pickford placed them so far above all other stars that the returns of their pictures could not be used as a basis of reasonable expectation by other producers, and no other director enjoyed repeated box-office success equal to DeMille's.

The enthusiastic promotion of new companies and expansion of established corporations in the boom of 1919-20 had brought about, in addition to increased costs, very serious over-production of films. Six hundred to eight hundred features were being made each year, and as all screens could have been supplied with about seventy-five percent of the output, the industry was over-producing to the extent of one hundred and fifty to two hundred negatives annually. With so many more features coming from the studios than the theaters needed, competition became intense, and exhibitors could easily beat down rental prices on all pictures except those imperatively demanded by their patrons.

Paramount, with its efficient distributing machinery and its increasing number of alliances with first-run houses; First National, with its long list of important theaters; and Fox, with his own houses and several players who had been popular for years, were in the strongest positions. These three companies had acquired most of the successful stars and many of the directors and writers who were beginning to have box-office value, and "around the necks" of their popular products they could "wrap" less popular films, thus safeguarding themselves against the unbridled competition created by over-production.

The cream of the rentals of features and specials went to these three companies, leaving the remainder for Hodkinson, Goldwyn, Selznick, Metro, Robertson-Cole, Vitagraph, and other corporations specializing in productions of five reels and longer. These feature-making companies had to compete with the elaborate, expensive specials and road-shows of United Artists, De-Mille and other Paramount productions, and many of First National's offerings, or fall behind in the race for public favor.

Occasionally a picture distributed by these smaller producers would earn gross rentals of $400,000 to $800,000, serving as a will-o'-the-wisp to lead the producers hopefully into further investments; but ordinarily the earnings of their program features ran, let us say, $75,000, $150,000, or $200,000 each, sometimes higher. As competition grew more intense, the tendency definitely was toward lower levels. After deducting twenty to thirty-five percent for the cost of operating exchanges, there remained approximately $60,000 to $125,000 apiece on program features, and often the producers' costs began to amount to more than net receipts.

There were, besides, another thirty or forty producing-distributing corporations known as the inhabitants of "Poverty Row," the makers of "quickies," or features manufactured quickly and at small expense. These studios, by employing the less costly

stars and avoiding every form of extravagance, produced negatives at five to fifteen thousand dollars each, and looked to the
smaller theaters in poorer districts and villages for their patronage. This branch of the industry would have been prosperous, except that here, too, as in the field of medium prices,
over-production kept rentals at the minimum. Universal, Pathé,
and Fox were well organized in the lower-cost field, and divided
among them the lion's share of this class of business.

Although Goldwyn, Hodkinson, Selznick and all other producers of medium- and high-priced pictures could not realize it,
the fact was that, with Poverty Row pushing them on one side
and Paramount and First National advancing rapidly from
the other, their lack of assured first-run connections was placing
them between the devil and the deep sea.

CHAPTER TWELVE

THE BATTLE FOR THE THEATERS

THE MOST powerful exhibiting organizations were the Stanley Company of Philadelphia and the Saenger Amusement Company of New Orleans. Each of these companies had succeeded by employing the "booking-office system" under which theater owners paid them a fee for selecting the pictures to be shown on their screens. Stanley and Saenger collected five or ten percent from the exhibitor and an equal amount from the distributor. Their argument was that consolidation of the purchasing power of many houses enabled them to obtain better prices from the manufacturers, and that a well-trained agent at the central office could select better pictures than an individual exhibitor could choose for himself. During the early years of features, when good pictures were rare and hard to get, Stanley and Saenger were in position to obtain the best for their large theaters, and exhibitors in small cities often welcomed an alliance that could assure them a steady flow of product for their screens. The Stanley company owned or controlled nearly all important theaters in Philadelphia and eastern Pennsylvania, and the Saenger company held a similar position in Louisiana and the portions of other states served from New Orleans. Each owned the valuable First National franchise for its own territory.

The value of theater control was demonstrated perfectly by

these two corporations: in the Philadelphia and the New Orleans exchange districts, no manufacturer could hope to obtain living prices for his product unless he obtained the good will of Stanley and Saenger. By 1919-20, when over-production was sending more pictures to market than screens could absorb, manufacturers who had not induced Stanley and Saenger to represent them were compelled to subsist on very slim pickings in the Philadelphia and New Orleans territories or forget that these sections existed. There were many bitter protests from producers, and several lawsuits were threatened or started, but litigation dragged slowly through the courts, and protesting producers feared they would be out of business before judges and juries acted on their complaints.

The Stanley method was followed by Alfred S. Black, operating in New England as Black's New England Theaters, Inc., Exhibitors Film Booking Office, and under other corporate titles. Black, starting with large ideas and small capital, wisely selected the theaters in small cities and villages as his initial field of endeavor. He calculated that, in 1919, there were 6,500 theaters in towns of less than 5,000 population, and his plan was to bring 4,000 of them under his control. In a statement to financiers whom he tried to interest in his project he made these noteworthy comments:

"Past efforts to secure control of the moving picture business have been through control of the big stars. This principle is fundamentally wrong. Control of this great industry is coincident with the control of its source of revenue, namely, the theater.... It is only fair to assume that, at the present time, the destinies of the United States—social, commercial and political—lie largely within the power of the motion picture theater."

Although unsuccessful in his efforts to interest Wall Street capitalists, Black proceeded with the funds at his disposal and was so successful in persuading or frightening exhibitors that he soon had thirty or forty houses in New England, some of them located in important places such as New Haven, Pawtucket, Quincy, and Malden, Mass., and Dover, N. H. Presently he advanced to alliances with William P. Gray, Nate Gordon, and their associates, who owned or controlled several important theaters in New England, embracing forty or more houses in Boston and other large cities. The Gordon group owned the First National franchise for New England.

Another exhibitor operating along lines somewhat similar to the Stanley method was Stephen E. Lynch, of Asheville, North Carolina, who controlled twenty-five or thirty houses in the principal cities of North Carolina, South Carolina, Georgia, Alabama, Florida and adjoining states. At the formation of the Paramount company, Hodkinson had appointed Lynch as distributor of Paramount pictures in eleven southern states, and when Hodkinson retired from Paramount, Lynch purchased his stock in this company. Through the valuable Paramount distributing franchise and his ownership of theaters, Lynch had become a formidable figure in the south, a hint from one of his salesmen that an exhibitor was not paying high enough prices for Paramount products usually being interpreted as a warning that soon a Lynch corporation would buy or build a competing theater in the recalcitrant's city.

WHEN Zukor, after two years of analysis and study, set his plan of theater conquest into motion in 1919-20, he moved rapidly and surely to accomplish his purpose. He quietly purchased a foothold in the Stanley Company, the Saenger Amusement Company, and the Black-Gray-Gordon corporations in New England, thus acquiring not only theaters and booking-offices, but interests in corporations owning three memberships in First National. Now that he was in position to obtain information and to study the operations of his principal competitor from the inside of its organization, it is fair to assume that nothing took place at meetings of First National directors without a report traveling quickly to the executive offices of Paramount.

Through the movie world rumors soon spread that Zukor had started to buy all the leading theaters in America, that he had penetrated First National and soon would absorb it, and that any theater owner whose house Zukor coveted would either have to sell or face the competition of a larger and more beautiful theater in his district. Following his custom of silence when speech is unwise, Zukor neither affirmed nor denied these rumors, merely declaring that Paramount "had no desire to enter into the exhibition business unless forced to do so because of a lack of proper theaters in a particular community, or because of our inability to obtain proper representation for its product."

Lynch suggested that Paramount should try to secure control of theaters throughout the entire south, and this suggestion meeting with Zukor's approval, several corporations—Southern Enterprises, Inc., Georgia Enterprises, Inc., S. A. Lynch Enterprises, Inc., Amusement Finance Corporation, and others—were organized and equipped with capital to execute the plan.

The methods of the energetic Lynch in dealing with theater owners were hardly gentle. His emissaries soon became known by such names as the "wrecking crew" and the "dynamite gang." Some times the "dynamiters" or "wreckers" gave an exhibitor the opportunity to remain in business if he would sign a contract to use Paramount pictures exclusively, or to give them preference. Sometimes Lynch's representatives merely bought theaters or built new ones without warning the exhibitors, who struggled against the competition for awhile and then closed their doors.

Although the Lynch operations started in the eastern southern states, their principal objective was Hulsey, the most prominent exhibitor in Texas and Oklahoma, owner of four theaters in Dallas, two in Houston, two in Galveston, one in Waco, and affiliated with other theater owners throughout the two states. Hulsey owned the First National franchise for Texas and Oklahoma, and because of his personality and vigor was one of the most important members of the First National organization. Zukor was already represented in three seats at the First National table, and if he could bring Hulsey into line he would gain not merely an additional seat, but the prestige of Hulsey's reputation.

The noise of Lynch's dynamiters and wreckers as they traveled through the southeast reached Texas in advance of Lynch's entrance into the Lone Star state, thoroughly advertising to Hulsey and all other exhibitors the treatment they could expect when Lynch came to their cities. Lynch, personally leading a crew of twelve men into the southwest, organized Southern Enterprises of Texas, Inc., and began to buy theaters in Texas, Oklahoma, and Arkansas, giving widespread publicity to the purchase and declaring openly his determination to buy or build enough theaters to give him control of Texas and neighboring states.

Hulsey, in common with all exhibitors of his standing and character, had made a comfortable fortune, but had reinvested it in building new theaters. He had borrowed of his bank several hundred thousand dollars, which he was paying off regularly with the profits of his houses. He was in excellent standing with his bank until the Lynch crew invaded Texas and began operations. One day his bank received a telegram from the Federal Reserve Bank in New York placing one million dollars to the credit of Southern Enterprises of Texas, Inc. Money talks, and a million dollars in Dallas is not a whisper. As Walter W. Irwin had predicted to Zukor, the banker was frightened. He sent for Hulsey, Hulsey sought out Lynch, and Southern Enterprises bought the Hulsey theaters.

This transaction was not advertised, as had been Lynch's other conquests in all southern states. Hulsey's theaters quietly "went into the bag" of Paramount, and Hulsey remained in charge of the properties. Zukor was not ready to dramatize this acquisition, preferring to permit the rumor to sift through the industry and spread its poison of doubt and uncertainty in the ranks of First National. This master-stroke of business strategy accomplished its purpose. Thomas Tally told me (several years after the event) that months passed before he and his associates really believed that Hulsey had been acquired by Zukor, and during that period the nerves of all First National members were constantly shaken by the thought that "if Hulsey has been licked and is keeping quiet about it, how many more of our stockholders are really Zukor's representatives at our board meetings?"

Tally finally asked Hulsey, at a meeting in New York, and the latter answered so indefinitely that Tally, convinced of Zukor's control of Hulsey properties, returned to Los Angeles and sold his Kinema Theater and First National franchise to Gore Brothers and Lesser. Tally retained the house bearing his name, and turned his energies toward playing with his ranches. Gore Brothers and Lesser formed West Coast Theaters, Inc., absorbing Turner and Dahnken, owners of a circuit of theaters in and about San Francisco, and other exhibitors, until the West Coast corporation got control of most of the important houses in California.

Tally, Hulsey, and Turner and Dahnken had been enthusiastic, aggressive members of First National, zealots who regarded their organization as the leader of a great battle to save theater owners from domination by any individual. Turner and Dahnken's enthusiasm was so great that they bought not only the membership for San Francisco, but when Williams and Tally had some difficulty in selling the New York franchise, took that membership also. Zukor's strategy in obtaining Hulsey caused the votes of these zealots to pass to men who were not imbued with the spirit of crusaders. While First National was an important asset in the affairs of Gore Brothers and Sol Lesser, it was merely an asset, not a matter of principle, as it had been with the former owners.

While Lynch was working in the south, and Black, Gray and Gordon were extending their power in New England, Walter W. Irwin was conducting a campaign in the larger cities of northern and central states. Irwin employed no rough methods, but his results were as effective as the sledge-hammer tactics of Black and Lynch.

Irwin's knowledge of exhibition conditions in each district and his experience as a lawyer enabled him to work swiftly and effectively. He would drop into a city and promptly select the best site for a new Paramount theater, and with equal promptness obtain an option on the property. Local bankers everywhere were acquainted with the high commercial standing of Paramount and often after an interview with Irwin they offered to finance in part or entire the building of Paramount theaters in their cities. Zukor accepted some of these offers, and local capitalists and Paramount each eventually profited largely by such arrangements.

Robert Lieber, owner of the Circle Theater, in Indianapolis, was a prominent member of First National. In St. Louis, William Sievers owned the First National franchise and aggressively exploited the company and its pictures. Irwin's earliest visits were to Indianapolis and St. Louis. In Lieber's city a large house was erected across the way from the Circle Theater; in St. Louis, a plot across the street from Sievers' principal house was acquired, and the American and the Missouri, the latter with 3,800 seats, soon gave Paramount a strong position in the city.

In San Francisco, a prominent firm of attorneys, Rothschild, Golden and Rothschild, and a well known exhibitor, Eugene Roth, were associated in the ownership of important theaters, the California, with 2,300 seats, being one of the largest and most beautiful houses in the city. The California and half a dozen other theaters in the city by the Golden Gate were soon members of the Paramount family.

By purchase of all or part of the stock of existing houses or by building new ones Zukor acquired theaters in Chicago, Cleveland, Denver, Baltimore and a dozen other cities in the United States. The Famous Players Canadian Corporation was organized and through purchase of the Nathanson circuit of a dozen or more houses placed itself in position to dominate Canada. At the end of 1921 Paramount was in control of four or five hundred theaters (large and small) and was adding desirable houses and circuits to this formidable list.

WHILE Zukor was executing this coup de force, his partner of early years in penny arcades and nickelodeons, Marcus Loew, was expanding rapidly in the field of exhibition. Loew's Inc., and its subsidiary corporations, owned about forty theaters in the New York metropolitan district and a hundred more in other American and Canadian cities, and had stock holdings in and affiliations with others not classified directly as Loew houses. Loew and Zukor were not associated in the ownership of Loew's Inc., or Famous Players-Lasky Company, but until Loew's death in 1926 the two men were close friends. Zukor's daughter had married Arthur, the elder son of the Loews. The "business tie-up" between Adolph Zukor and Marcus Loew rested not on a foundation of stock holdings or legal contracts, but on the more substantial basis of long friendship and family connections.

Loew theaters were consistent customers of Paramount and there was no occasion for Zukor to invade any Loew territory. In some cities in which each desired representation the two friends worked closely together, as in Cleveland, Ohio, where Emanuel Mandelbaum invited Zukor to become his partner in the new Stillman Theater, and Zukor responded by buying thirty percent of the stock for Famous Players-Lasky and bringing into the company Marcus Loew, who bought another thirty percent. Mandelbaum was the owner of the First National franchise for the Cleveland district.

In 1920, Loew concluded that he ought to be a producer as well as an exhibitor. Metro Pictures, already feeling the pinch of Zukor on one side and First National on the other, and harassed by the necessity of obtaining large capital to meet increased studio costs, was seeking a haven. Richard Rowland convinced Marcus Loew that he needed the Metro corporation, and Loew's, Inc. bought it. As Marcus Loew said in a speech a year and a half later, he was "surprised to learn how many things about picture making an exhibitor did not know!" In the same speech, Loew declared that $2,000,000 of his theater profits "had been fed into the Metro studio" to make good its losses.

Rowland, however, changed this situation by the production of Blasco Ibáñez's novel, "The Four Horsemen of the Apocalypse" which appeared in 1921. It was the first post-war photoplay of the World War to be accepted by the public, and its success was titanic. June Mathis, the screen writer who made the adaptation of the novel and to whom Rowland entrusted the production of the picture, selected an unknown player, Rudolph Valentino, for the lead, and Rex Ingram, an ambitious young Irish sculptor-actor, as director. Ingram's wife, Alice Terry, played the girl rôle. Mathis, Valentino, Ingram, and Terry were all elevated to stardom by the enormous popularity of "The Four Horsemen," and its large profits repaid much of the money Loew had invested in the Metro corporation.

THE trade mark selected for Paramount by Hodkinson at its inception was a lofty mountain peak, rising high above its neighbors. In 1921, in the eighth year of its existence, Paramount Famous Players-Lasky was the tallest peak in the industry, the only neighbors approaching it being Loew's, Inc. and First National.

Month after month, as Zukor added new theaters to his list, as First National's output of pictures increased, as Loew acquired new theater affiliations and increased the business of Metro, and as Sol Lesser and Abe and Mike Gore gathered in more members or houses for their West Coast Corporation, fewer and fewer screens were left open to independent producers. Goldwyn, Selznick, Hodkinson, Vitagraph, and others, weakened by deflation and high production costs, had difficulties in holding fast to the old faith that "there have always been plenty of theaters, and there always will be."

A new theater, the Capitol, with 4,000 seats, had been built in the Longacre district of New York, and as Frank Joseph Godsol and Edward Bowes of the Goldwyn Company acquired control of it, the Capitol gave preference to Goldwyn pictures. The only other first-run houses in New York were the Rialto and the Rivoli, owned by Paramount, and the Strand, which was used by First National. Fox and Loew showed their pictures in several of their large movie-vaudeville houses, thus giving them the prestige needed for out-of-town and neighborhood bookings.

Hodkinson, Selznick, Vitagraph, and other producers found themselves unable to obtain first runs in New York, Philadelphia, New Orleans, San Francisco, Chicago, and steadily the list of cities in which the best theaters were closed to their product grew longer. Goldwyn had made "tie-ins" with a few exhibitors throughout the country, but with the exception of the Capitol in New York, these tie-ins often represented stockholdings of insufficient size to protect Goldwyn, and Zukor, Loew, Fox, or West Coast acquired control of the houses by buying the majority stock.

EXHIBITORS in the southern states which had been swept by Lynch's crews organized an association of protest and protection and soon obtained several hundred members. The movement spread rapidly throughout the country, local associations springing up in various states, and uniting in 1920 in a national body, Motion Pictures Theater Owners of America, with Sydney S. Cohen, owner of a circuit of neighborhood houses in New York, as president. By 1921, Cohen claimed a membership of ten or twelve thousand for the association, and many enthusiastic meetings of protest and condemnation were held in all sections of the country.

Most of the alleged acts of "oppression' and "bulldozing" had occurred in the states in which Black and Lynch were operating, but everywhere exhibitors testified to Paramount increases in rental rates which they believed they must accept or be prepared for the visitation of a Lynch or Black wrecking crew or the quiet call of Irwin. These meetings were reported in newspapers, and trade journals bristled with resolutions passed by the angry exhibitors in one section after another, declaring that emergency conditions existed and prompt and thorough action must be taken. One trade journal became the organ of the M P T O and devoted itself to fiery denunciations of Zukor and his methods of conquest and absorption.

Independent producers and distributors were heartened by these events, and began to hope that out of the intense agitation would come a program to restore the prosperity they had enjoyed before Zukor began to acquire first-run theaters. It was apparent to everyone that independent producers, distributors, and exhibitors must get together on a common platform if they were to save themselves from extinction. But how were they to accomplish this miracle of cooperation?

There had always been natural business hostility between sellers and buyers. The rental terms of films had never been perfectly standardized; perhaps standard prices for merchandise affected by so many conditions were not possible; at any rate, sales were accomplished by dickering and arguing, and disagreements and conflicts over terms, booking dates, cancellations, damages to films and so forth were so common that exchanges and theaters were in constant battle. Now it seemed imperative that these hostilities should cease, and distributors and exhibitors unite in a brotherhood to annihilate Zukor.

The relationship between exhibitors themselves was not much more friendly than the feeling between distributors and exhibitors. Competing theater owners quarreled over the booking of pictures, the rights to prior showings, the extent of the territory to be covered by their showings, and a dozen other matters. Exhibitors frequently invaded or threatened to invade the territory of others, and suspicion and turmoil were the regular routine of every theater owner. Large exhibitors and small ones had almost no points of contact. The owners of a metropolitan first-run house playing to audiences of 25,000 to 50,000 a week had no problems in common with the fifth-run exhibitor in a small town. Each of them used film as merchandise, and at that point their common interest ended.

The metropolitan theaters, with an investment of a million to five million dollars each, necessitated the corporate form of ownership, with stock distributed among several or many shareholders, and under these conditions the intense individualism of nickelodeon and store-show days was disappearing from the large city houses. The owners were interested more in dividends than in personal aggrandizement, and were willing to join with First National or Loew or Zukor or Goldwyn or any other company that promised safety for their investments.

In the smaller cities and villages a different situation existed. Here the theaters—many of them new and well built—were still family affairs. These theaters were just as fiercely individualistic as if they had been the old store shows; the owning family was proud of its playhouse, the theater was emphatically not for sale. Any attempt to dictate to such exhibitors was resented as bitterly as nickelodeon owners had resented the rules of the patents trust.

The task ahead of Sydney Cohen and the Motion Picture Theaters Owners Association was to harmonize all these discordant elements, reduce the inflammatory speeches of convention days to a set of principles that would work in all days, and put the independent majority of the industry into a position of safety against the machinations of the ambitious, resourceful Zukor.

James J. Walker, then member of the New York senate and later mayor of New York City, had become known to motion picture people in the years in which they had journeyed frequently to Albany to protect their interests against the attacks of freak legislation. Walker was a friend of the movies, and now, in the emergency that demanded all the assistance available, the exhibitors invited him to become their counsel and advisor. Walker accepted the position, and for a year or two was the spokesman of the association. Cohen and Walker buckled down to the hard job of devising a policy that would unite all independent factors and factions.

Producers and distributors pointed out that although Zukor had obtained four or five hundred theaters, ten or twelve thousand independent houses were united now in the M P T O, and if these exhibitors would give their wholehearted preference to independent studios, Paramount's loss of business would soon bring Zukor to terms. The weakness in this plan was the popularity of Paramount pictures and Paramount stars. Exhibitors needed Paramount productions, or else competitors would absorb their audiences.

In reality the theater owners wanted only one plank in their platform, and that was a pledge from *all* producers and distributors that they would remain out of the field of exhibition. After all the denunciatory oratory and harmony speeches were boiled down to their essence this was the residue, and Cohen and Walker accepted it as the policy of the association and set about obtaining such a pledge from the manufacturers. The inclusion of *all* producers and distributors was merely a gesture. Fox had always been producer, distributor, and exhibitor. Loew had recently bought Metro. First National was a combination of exhibitors operating in the producing field. The Goldwyn Company, or Frank Joseph Godsol, owned an interest in the Capitol in New York, the Roosevelt, and other Ascher Brothers' theaters in Chicago, Miller's houses in Los Angeles, and perhaps other holdings throughout the country. Selznick and Pathé had semi-mutual associations with exhibitors. Only Hodkinson, Vitagraph, and a score of smaller producers had no theater holdings. The exhibitors had no real expectation or intention of changing any of these arrangements. Their fear and animosity were inspired solely by Zukor, and he was the target at which they were shooting. They had no hostility toward Marcus Loew or Fox or Godsol, none of whom had ever shown any inclination to enter the small town field of theater ownership; they were big city operators, and the small fellows believed they would never invade their cities and villages. Zukor's agents, Black and Lynch, were harvesting in small communities, and thousands of independent exhibitors were fearful that they might be the next to fall.

All producers who were not owners of theaters cheerfully

agreed with Cohen and Walker to refrain from theater acquisition. Loew, Fox, and Godsol were not pushed very hard for pledges, and the assurances they gave were regarded as satisfactory to the association. A committee of M P T O officials interviewed Zukor and upbraided him for the practices of his agents, demanding assurance that Paramount withdraw from the theater field or at least agree to buy no more houses. Zukor frankly declared his opposition to oppressive methods, and guaranteed that no action of the sort would occur again. Withdrawal from the exhibition field was impossible, as Paramount had to have theaters to protect itself from First National, but, he declared, Paramount had no intention of entering any city in which its pictures had proper representation.

This statement was merely a repetition of previous declarations, but, right or wrong, the exhibitors felt that they had wrung concessions from Zukor. Some of them expected that he would severely discipline Black and Lynch, and would buy no more theaters. Black was presently superseded in his position by Gray, and Lynch, having obtained about everything needed in his states, laid the big stick aside and used quieter methods. But Paramount continued to absorb theaters, principally in the larger cities, and when a few months had passed and the exhibitors had been unable to discern any cessation of Zukor's activities, they became very bitter.

The annual convention of the M P T O was to be held at Minneapolis in the last days of June, 1921. For several months Cohen and Walker went the rounds of the principal cities, addressing meetings of exhibitors, lashing them into a frenzy against Zukor. By the middle of June, public feeling in the industry was boiling hot. Readers of the trade press and men listening to conversations in theaters, exchanges, and studios, could easily believe the time for discussion had passed,—at Minneapolis there would be *action,* and the only action satisfactory to the infuriated theater owners was the annihilation of this dangerous man who was trying to dominate the entire industry.

Two or three thousand men journeyed to the M P T O convention at Minneapolis in one of the hottest weeks of the summer. The night before the opening session the air was surcharged with a heat greater than that of weather—the anger of theater owners who had come from all parts of America to unite solidly against Zukor and force him to refrain from theater acquisition. Every independent producing and distributing company was represented by its principal officials and sales managers, and these men roamed the hotel lobbies adding fuel to the anti-Zukor flames. All of them knew that the situation of the independents was precarious, but each nurtured the hope that in some way he would save himself even though his competitors might go down to destruction.

Into a group of producers and exhibitors edged Monte Sohn, a young journalist who had been conducting the most vigorous trade-paper campaign against Zukor.

"What do you think?" he exclaimed excitedly and answered the question himself, "Zukor had the nerve to climb on the special train that brought the eastern delegation from New York, and rode all the way out here with them! I'll say that takes nerve—to ride 1,500 miles with a gang of tigers that are ready to tear you to pieces! He talked all the way out, and cried, and swore he was sorry, and if the boys would give him another chance he'd be a good Indian. He's got just about everyone on that train believing he's all right."

"What do you think, Monte?" inquired the owner of a prosperous theater, and his voice was so earnest that I was not surprised when, less than a year later, he sold his house to Paramount.

"Well, I don't know," replied the editor thoughtfully, "I'm just wondering if we haven't been misjudging Zukor. Maybe we've been too harsh with him. I'm on the fence. I wouldn't be a bit surprised if he means to do the right thing. The directors are going to have him at a special meeting upstairs tonight and put him on the pan. If he comes clean and swears on a stack of Bibles to leave the exhibitors alone, I'll believe him."

A messenger came and drew me aside. "The directors are going to roll Zukor over a barrel, and Sydney Cohen wants you to wait around until they're through with him and then come upstairs and talk to the board."

I waited. The crowd thinned out as the hours slipped by, and about half past one in the morning a small man came quietly down the broad stairway from the parlor floor and vanished through the dim light of a side corridor and out the street entrance. With bowed head and drooping shoulders, the unobtrusive, humble chap might have been a suburban school teacher called before the board of education to give his reasons for requesting ten dollars a month more wages. I seemed to be the only loiterer in the lobby who recognized him as Adolph Zukor, drifting back to his hotel after several hours on the M P T O griddle.

The messenger reappeared and took me to the conference room. Sydney Cohen was in the chair, and Senator Walker sat beside him. The chairman and the senator described the session with Zukor, which had left the entire group shaken. Zukor, able actor, had entered the presence of his enemies alone, to meet a bombardment of hostile accusations and charges. In their eagerness to attack their arch foe, several speakers were often shouting at once.

When they were somewhat exhausted, Zukor answered them, and tears rolled down his cheeks as he declared his lack of personal responsibility for the acts of oppression committed by the Black and the Lynch crews, and assured the directors he would seek out the injured exhibitors and make proper reparations. He repeated the statements often made that he had no desire to own theaters in any city in which Paramount pictures were properly exhibited, and declared that his business record proved him innocent of any double dealing or a desire to injure any one.

I could not see that any new promise had been wrung from the president of Paramount, but his courage, emotionalism, and apparent frankness during the long, hot hours of grilling had affected many of the board members deeply. The optimistic ones believed they had won a great victory; the pessimistic were suspicious that Zukor had merely hypnotized them.

Prior to the convention, Senator Walker, visiting Los Angeles to confer with exhibitors and producers, had asked me, "Where do you stand on this invasion of the exhibition field by producers?"

To reply to this question required several long conversations, the digest of which was that "Zukor could not protect himself and his associates except by owning theaters; Loew has protected his theaters by acquiring a producing company; Fox from the start has been both producer and exhibitor and his business is on a firm foundation because of his assured retail outlets; all other producers will have to acquire first-run houses, or they will dry up and blow away.

"The leaders and many of the rank and file of the M P T O believe that First National will prove itself a permanent bulwark against the aggressions of trust builders, but on this point I disagree, my opinion being that no mutual organization can withstand an ambitious individual like Zukor. First National," I predicted, "will be absorbed piece by piece by Zukor or interests friendly to him.

"The principal weakness of the exhibitors' movement is that the M P T O is merely fighting *against* something; it is not fighting *for* anything, and such a negative attack is nearly always foredoomed to failure. If the theater owners would forget their fear of Zukor, and unite in a constructive, cooperative movement to form a picture-making and distributing corporation of their own, they could keep the industry free from trusts."

President Cohen and Senator Walker now asked me to repeat to the M P T O board the conversations Walker and I had had in Los Angeles. I did so, adding that in my judgment, all attacks on Zukor were futile, as he had evolved methods of operation that would enable him to dominate the industry without creating a trust, and I believed that neither the Sherman nor the Clayton acts could be effectively invoked against him.

On the following day, the first open meeting of the convention was held. Walker thrilled the exhibitors with his defense of their independence, and many exhibitors exhorted their fellows to fight to the bitter end to retain their freedom. Along in the middle of the afternoon, when the heat and humidity had reduced the delegates almost to pulp, Sydney Cohen put me on the platform and I talked for an hour. At the hall door leading into the assembly room, I noticed Zukor, standing quietly by the wall. He listened to my address, and disappeared.

When later I returned to my hotel, Zukor was sitting in the lobby. He arose, came forward and shook hands, and said, "I understand you said some nice things about me in your speech today, and I want to thank you for them."

I laughed, and answered, "Yes, I said many nice things about you, and I pleaded with the convention to get together on a program that will really clip your claws. You heard every word I said as you stood back there in the doorway, so we'll not have to repeat the speech. Tell me how you hypnotized the board meeting last night. You came out here to Minneapolis like a sad shadow and now you've simply tucked the convention away in your pocket. How do you do it?"

Not a muscle of his face betrayed his interest as his voice sank to a whisper and he asked eagerly, "Did I really do what you say I did?"

"Certainly, and then some," I responded, "and now I'd like to have you tell me what you're going to do with this industry."

Zukor and I talked for nearly two days and most of three nights. We talked in his hotel suite; we walked the streets of Minneapolis during the hot nights, and talked, twice, until the dawn appeared. We talked frankly and fully, with no reservations. I had deep respect for this man who had come to this country an immigrant and by his own power had placed himself in his present high position. Also I was confident that unless his ambitions were modified not many years would pass until the whole industry would be in his power. But knowing his ability to change his mind freely if convinced of a better course,

I thought this might be a propitious time for him to develop a new set of ideas under which independent producers could be permitted to live.

Hodkinson, John D. Williams, and others in the industry believed that the screen would progress more rapidly and soundly if production could be kept independent of theater control or any form of trust methods. Undoubtedly there were too many small units; there was too much waste in studios and exchanges; some consolidations were necessary, but I agreed with the Hodkinson-Williams viewpoint that production ought always to be kept free. I deplored the tendency toward concentration of picture making in a few studios; I wanted to see conditions under which a constant stream of new directors and new writers could be given opportunity to express themselves. Literature, music, and the plastic arts thrive because of the freedom with which youth can have its try at them, and I believed that the movies should be equally accessible.

Zukor agreed with these ideas, but asked how such results could be accomplished. No distributor could depend on a flow of pictures from independent sources; many had tried it, and everyone had failed. Book publishers, music publishers, and dealers in paintings are not compelled to issue a specific number of volumes or compositions or canvases each week; they sell as many as they can get, or at least as many as their trades will consume. The movies must encourage new picture makers all the time, but release dates must be met regularly.

I finally suggested the consolidation of all distributors into one corporation, the elimination of all exchanges except one in each city, this centralized company to handle pictures made by any producer in a manner as neutral, as impersonal, as the post-office department carries the mail. The producer would grade his own pictures, naming whatever rental prices he desired, and could do his own advertising and employ his own salesmen to push his product with exhibitors. The neutrality of the corporation could be maintained by placing the stock in a voting trust for five or seven years, thus insuring the permanence of the original board of directors during that period. A man from outside the industry, one in whose high character distributors and exhibitors would have confidence, should be selected as president or chairman of the corporation, and I suggested Senator Walker as a good man for the position.

The organization of such a distributing machine would permit independent producers to operate and good pictures to succeed; the others would fail. No producer would have to own theaters to protect himself, and exhibitors who wanted to retain their houses could be sure of obtaining pictures from the neutral distributor. Anyone with a grievance could present his case to the head of the organization and obtain justice.

Zukor considered these suggestions carefully. Although the Hays association was not formed until the following year, evidently the thought of a strong, central organization, with an outsider of high repute serving as umpire, had already been receiving his attention, and my proposal of Walker for such a position interested him so deeply that we brought the senator into one of our night sessions.

Walker scrutinized the proposed plan thoroughly, turning it inside and out to see how his exhibitors would fare under such an arrangement; concluding that they would be benefited, he declared himself as favoring it, if Sydney Cohen and the directors of the M P T O would approve. Zukor did not commit himself further than to express his willingness to meet producers and distributors on their return to New York and go into the subject thoroughly. If the principal corporations in the industry should approve the proposal he believed that Famous Players-Lasky would join the movement.

So many men had come to the convention that its sessions had to be transferred from a hotel to a theater, and there for several days angry theater owners inveighed against Zukor's invasion of what they regarded as their rights. One of the most interesting and dramatic events of these meetings was Marcus Loew's defense of his friend, Zukor.

"Go up on the stage, Marcus," called a score of voices when

Loew arose from his seat in the theater and good-naturedly but firmly disagreed with the bitter attacks on Zukor. The assemblage gave him a rousing ovation that proved him to be the idol of exhibitors. Although his corporation and the Paramount group, as far as an impartial observer could see, were engaged in identical business operations, the theater owners were not afraid of Loew, while they were intensely suspicious of every move Zukor made.

Loew talked plainly and definitely, telling the exhibitors they had been needlessly aroused to hysteria, and insisting that no one could create a trust in motion pictures. He resolutely defended Zukor, as an individual and as a business man, and his magnetism and arguments were effective in swinging many wavering delegates to a position of neutrality. The convention listened to many speeches, passed resolutions declaring eternal loyalty to the cause of independence, and the delegates went home.

For some weeks M P T O officials discussed with independent producers the subject of an alliance under which pictures would be made for exhibition in M P T O theaters, and early in 1922 the announcement was made that cooperative studio operations would be started, but nothing ever took definite form. My suggestion of the formation of a central, non-partisan distributing corporation received some attention after the Minneapolis convention, but was allowed to die as an idealistic, impractical scheme that could not be worked out in fact. I record it here merely because I was convinced that Zukor at that time would have joined in such a movement had other distributors given evidence of their willingness to cooperate to preserve the freedom of production.

ZUKOR purchased no more small city or village theaters after the Minneapolis meeting, unless they happened to be units in chains acquired by Paramount. The rough-shod methods of Black and Lynch crews were not extended into any additional communities.

The small exhibitors, the backbone of anti-Paramount agitation, were perhaps convinced that the M P T O had been of service to them, but that it was no longer needed, and the association began to lose the crusading enthusiasm that had kept it active for two years. Soon the speeches and resolutions of the Minneapolis convention were merely recollections, with no power to inspire action.

As a matter of practical fact, Zukor had no desire for a string of little theaters scattered over the country. He had taken the Black and Lynch collections as he found them, some large, profitable houses and some of moderate size and moderate desirability, and quite a number of little ones which Black and Lynch had hastily gobbled up in their lust for acquisition. The operation of small houses, or houses in small towns, proved to be such a burden of administration that within a few years Paramount was glad to sell or rent them to individual operators. The chain-store theory could be applied successfully to grocery stores in villages, but not to motion-picture theaters, experience demonstrating that personal, or family, operation of a small theater was the only system that could be made to pay.

With the removal of the menace to about fifteen thousand small exhibitors, the emotional, or publicity, value of the fight against Zukor lost its force. As long as many family or personal units were imperiled by a prospective movie octopus, orators and press writers could arouse a measure of interest, but when the struggle narrowed down to a few hundred large, wealthy exhibitors the human quality of the contest was greatly decreased, and anti-Zukor agitation gradually faded away.

Owners of important first-run houses lost confidence in the effectiveness of a national exhibitors' association and bestirred themselves to organize circuits of their own, or to merge their houses with one of the many circuits that were rapidly forming in various sections. Within a short time very few important houses were operated individually; nearly all of them had been purchased by a circuit, or had started one of its own.

The drama of individual operation in the screen world was

drawing to a close. The movie business was no longer an infant industry in which anyone might find fame and fortune. It had passed the middle period in which men with moderate capital might establish themselves. Within a few years it had grown to maturity and had become one of America's greatest industries, subject to the large capital necessities and the financing rules and regulations of big business and Wall Street. Twilight was descending on independent control of theaters, studios, and exchanges.

Gore Brothers and Sol Lesser expanded their West Coast corporation, taking in as stockholders William Fox and other theater owners and several California capitalists. Jensen and Von Herburg extended their Seattle circuit until they controlled the northwest. Several smaller groups operating in the Rocky Mountain states allied themselves with Jensen-Von Herburg or West Coast or Paramount. Finkelstein and Rubin, operating originally in Minneapolis and St. Paul, expanded until pictures could not be shown profitably in Minnesota and the Dakotas without their cooperation. Abe Blank in Iowa and Thomas Saxe in Milwaukee became powerful in their respective sections. Kunsky was branching out in Detroit and Michigan, Levy in Louisville and Kentucky, and other exhibitors everywhere were drawing more and more houses under unified control. Paramount and First National dominated Missouri, and Lynch and Saenger had brought Texas, Oklahoma, and the southeastern states into their hands.

Scores, eventually hundreds, of exhibitors, some of whom had been in the industry since nickelodeon days, disappeared as the circuits proceeded on their forward march. Notable eliminations of well-known names from the theater field occurred in Chicago. Two boys, Barney Balaban and Sam Katz, starting as ushers and piano players in store shows, had risen to ascendency. Their remarkable progress began with a little house, purchased with their own savings, but they soon extended to a larger. By and by, John Hertz, the taxicab king, Albert Loeb, and other capitalists, joined the young men in building large palace theaters in various districts of Chicago—the Central Park, the Riviera, the Oriental. Jones, Linnick and Schaeffer, and Ascher Brothers were owners of important chains, and with the rise of Balaban and Katz both of these older firms faded from the industry, some of their houses going to Balaban and Katz, one to Laemmle, and another to the Goldwyn interests. Balaban and Katz acquired the First National franchise, and Sam Katz became a very active, influential member of the First National directorate.

Soon the Pacific slope, the Rocky Mountain states, most of the Central states, Texas, the southwest and the southeast, were closed to independents; eastern Pennsylvania and Delaware were controlled by the Stanley Company; Paramount shared New England with Loew and Poli; Loew, Fox, Paramount, and First National controlled New York. Loew and Paramount had already penetrated Ohio and were strong in Cleveland and Cincinnati; they were making alliances in Michigan. There remained New Jersey, Maryland, the District of Columbia, and a few sections scattered throughout other states, that had not come under the domination of Zukor, Loew, First National, and their allies.

For a while the merging of theaters into powerful circuits worked to the advantage of Zukor, without compelling him to invest in the ownership of their stocks. Each circuit had to protect itself by obtaining contracts for the regular delivery of good pictures, and Paramount was the largest supplier of good pictures. Each circuit had to safeguard itself, at least insofar as possible, against the invasion of its cities by strong, new theater competitors; and Paramount and Loew were the largest, most powerful theater owners in the world. Consequently, men controlling the circuits were willing to be friendly with Zukor and Loew, and friendliness took the practical form of arrangements to exhibit Paramount and Metro pictures.

Each of the first-class circuits owned a First National franchise, so that First National's position was in reality improved by the growth of the chains, but the reverse of this condition applied to other producers and distributors of high-grade and medium-grade pictures. As more and more first-run houses fell into line with the circuit movement, all producers and distributors except Paramount, Loew-Metro, and First National felt the tightening of the lines. One city after another closed its first-run screens to independent photoplays except rare ones of outstanding box-office quality, and for these they paid only the minimum price possible.

ZUKOR's penetration into First National, which was progressing skilfully and might have led to eventual absorption of the exhibitor-owned company, was halted by the action of the Federal Trade Commission in 1922, in bringing suit against the Paramount corporations and their principal officers, on the charge that they "have conspired and confederated together to unduly hinder competition in the production, distribution and exhibition of motion picture films in interstate and foreign commerce, and to control, dominate and monopolize the motion picture industry."

The attorneys for the government declared that Zukor's acquisition of four or five hundred theaters (of various classes and sizes) had placed Paramount in a monopolistic position. "It is absolutely necessary, for financial and exploitation reasons," stated the attorneys in their brief to the commission, "that a good feature picture must have first-class first-run showing. It is very obvious that all of the producers of pictures cannot own theaters in the key cities, nor can all the distributors of pictures own such theaters; so that if it is not an unfair method of competition for producers and/or distributors to own such theaters it means the practical elimination of all small producers of pictures and distributors from the business, and that the entire picture industry will shortly be controlled and monopolized by those companies which have the financial power to own and control the first-run motion picture theaters."

To correct the situation, to destroy the monopoly alleged to have been created by Zukor, and to restore conditions under which all producers, distributors and exhibitors could engage in competition, the attorneys for the government asked the commission to issue an order directing the Paramount group of corporations and individuals "to divest themselves of all interests, either direct or indirect, which they may have in theatrical properties which exhibit motion picture films, or divest themselves of the interests which they may have in producing and/or distributing companies, in the United States."

In short, the attorneys insisted that Zukor and his associates should become either producers and distributors, or theater owners and operators, but that they should not be permitted to continue in all three branches of the industry. The great growth of Paramount in a few years was evidenced by the statement of government counsel that "we realize the far-reaching results of such an order, and that it contemplates the disposal of property of a probable value of more than one hundred million dollars."

An action to dissolve a trust through decision of the Federal Trade Commission follows a course not similar to action under the Sherman law. In Sherman law proceedings witnesses are summoned to a federal court, testimony is taken before judge and jury, and a decision is rendered, from which either side may appeal to the Supreme Court. In Federal Trade Commission actions, attorneys and investigators for the commission travel to any parts of the country where evidence may be obtained, and summon witnesses to hearings at which they give their testimony, counsel for the commission and respondents being present and engaging in examination and cross-examination. Trade Commission investigations and hearings may stretch over a period of several years. It is not the intention of the commission summarily to drag business men into court, but rather to attempt to bring about modification of practices by conciliation, arbitration, and agreements that will avoid the disruptions of industry produced by sharp, decisive court orders.

The Paramount case, following the custom of the commission,

entered into several years of investigations and hearing of testimony from producers, distributors, and exhibitors in various parts of the country. Meanwhile, the action of the government deterred Zukor from acquiring additional influence in First National's affairs and encouraged the stockholder-members who desired to strengthen and expand the organization and thereby retain control of their own chains.

Their first step was to invite Senator Walker to become general counsel of the company. Walker resigned his position with the M P T O to ally himself with First National, remaining with the company until he entered the political activities that resulted in his election as mayor of New York City.

A difference of opinion regarding the process of obtaining pictures brought about important changes in First National's administration personnel. John D. Williams had organized the company not as a direct manufacturer but as a buyer of pictures made by independent producers, reasoning that better quality was obtainable in this manner. As the company increased its list of sub-franchise holders, including thousands of smaller theaters requiring two or three features a week, the officers encountered difficulties in obtaining a regular, dependable supply of independent product sufficient to meet the demand of the exchanges, and many of the members swung away from Williams' viewpoint and advocated the erection of a studio and the employment of a staff of producers, writers, directors, and actors. Williams resigned as general manager in October, 1922, and Richard Rowland, former president of Metro, was elected in his place. The following year First National embarked in the production of its own pictures. A large, modern studio, eventually representing an investment of several million dollars, was built at Burbank, a suburb of Los Angeles, and the company produced approximately as many pictures annually as Paramount.

First National's studio expansion was financed in part by an issue of preferred stock, amounting to two or three million dollars, Richard Hoyt, of Hayden, Stone and Company, Wall Street bankers, handling the issue and thereafter participating actively in the company's affairs. Within a year or two Hoyt and Sam Katz were dreaming of a great First National corporation, in which all the theaters owned by common stockholders should be merged with the studios and the exchanges. A truly great vision! If all First National owners should put their circuits into one company, it would own fifteen hundred to two thousand theaters, and if only half of the score of director-members should accept the plan, a thousand or more of the best houses in America would be joined together. This would indeed constitute a combination of great size and almost unlimited power. Paramount would drop to second place, and even if Zukor should try to merge all remaining available theaters, he could never get enough to place Paramount on a parity with the Katz-Hoyt vision of First National.

Katz and Hoyt enthusiastically advocated the merger plan to members of the association, and the idea made headway. Zukor, with his usual foresight, accurately measured the menace to Paramount, but what could he do? At one time he had served his purpose well by obtaining "seats at the First National table" through interests in Stanley, Saenger, Hulsey and Gordon; but the holding of First National interests no longer had a dramatic effect, and, indeed, as such holdings might provide the Federal Trade Commission with ammunition in the anti-trust suit, Paramount had grown chary of them. Paramount's connection with the Stanley Company had been in the form of bonds, convertible into stock, but Paramount did not convert them, and Stanley paid them off. Paramount disposed of First National common stock that had been acquired, or was later acquired, in the purchase of theaters.

Nothing as simple as mere "influence" obtained by alliances with First National members would be effective against a plan as powerful as the Katz-Hoyt merger idea. Nothing but actual, outright ownership of a majority of First National theaters could combat this scheme—if First National members should look with favor on it. With the Federal Trade Commission camping on his trail, could Zukor even attempt to bring about a titanic merger of theaters? Because Paramount had acquired a few score of large houses and several hundred smaller ones, the commission had already charged him with violation of anti-trust laws. What would happen if he multiplied these figures by five or ten or twenty? Zukor's solution of the problem must be left to a later chapter, while we review the intervening events which seriously affected the character of American motion pictures.

CHAPTER THIRTEEN

HOLLYWOOD SCANDALS AND CENSORSHIP

IN ADDITION to the painful economics of deflation, the movie industry had specific problems of its own that threatened to wreck many of the corporations and most of the individuals then prominent in the industry. Zukor's progress toward building a new type of trust was an internal, industrial problem that meant business life or death to many men and women; but aside from that there existed a grave public situation, and for a time it seemed that professional reformers and fanatics were determined to lynch the entire movie business.

In the liberalizing drift of the post-war period, the new phrase, "sex appeal," became very popular. Producers of newspapers, magazines and plays were not the only exploiters of the theme; manufacturers of wearing apparel, motor cars, furniture and other commodities, all advertised their wares as possessing the desirable quality of sex appeal. Movie producers, realizing that their bread and butter depended on maintenance of the screen as a family institution, approached the subject cautiously, leaving advanced pioneering in this new medium to publishers and the stage. Photoplays did not attempt to acquire the freedom of any other form of entertainment in dealing with sex situations.

Novels with doubtful sex themes were greatly modified when translated to celluloid; and many stage plays that enjoyed long runs and high praise were never made into pictures because of sex presentations that would have been condemned by tens of millions of movie patrons who never saw any of the plays current in metropolitan centers, or read any of the popular novels depicting the problems of matrimony or the urges of flaming youth. The widest horizon of the overwhelming majority was bounded by the movies, daily and weekly newspapers, farm journals and the church.

With the limited intellectual bounds of family patronage constantly before their eyes, movie producers usually followed the beaten path of conservative themes and treatments until cautious experiments in 1919-20 were welcomed so eagerly by audiences that bolder souls in the studios began to push back the barriers and attempt to supply the screen with the flavor of current magazines, novels, and the spoken stage. Not one in fifty of these offerings contained more than a few "sexy" situations, but photographs of such scenes could be displayed in lobbies, and seductive sentences and drawings could appear in newspaper advertisements. Ticket buyers, led by occasional spicy advertisements to believe that the screen would present situations and dialogue as "naughty" as the spoken stage, were usually disappointed; movie sex appeal was reduced to a faint whisper of the lusty frankness of the theater.

No censorship, except that of the police power and trial by jury, was operating against the printed word or the theater until after the advent of movies. When short films, picturing chases, fairy and magical stories, and themes assumed to benefit juvenile and retarded minds, were replaced by one- and two-reel plays of romance and adventure, professional reformers, sniffing an opportunity to extend the areas of their occupations, declared that screen cowboys and imperiled heroines were debauching the childhood of the nation. They demanded the organization of state or municipal censorship bureaus, and politicians, always willing to create more jobs at the taxpayers' expense, harkened to the demand.

Although a dozen states created censorship boards—solely for motion pictures, not for newspapers, magazines, books, stage, lecture platform, circus, county fair, or any other form of entertainment—efforts to extend this expression of bureaucracy did not make headway until after the war. Under the inspiration of "making the world safe for democracy," Americans had surrendered nearly all their rights of personal liberty. The Federal government, through various espionage laws, the Volstead Act, and other repressive measures, had supplied the most delightful opportunities to professional reformers and fanatics that these gentry had known since their ancestors gave up the pleasant sport of burning witches. After the excitements of war days died down, these patriots had to find new fields of endeavor, or lose the emoluments and glory of their positions. Some of them noticed the lobby displays and newspaper advertisements of sex-appeal pictures, and fervently rushed to the rescue of the American family. Neglecting to observe the constant publication in all magazines and newspapers of sex-appealing advertising and illustrations, and generally ignoring the frankness of the stage and printed novels, professional reformers insisted that movies everywhere be submitted to rigorous censorship.

About this time the high salaries of screen stars began to arouse wide public interest. For several years the stories of huge wages were regarded as showman exaggerations, merely the reckless boasting of inspired press agents. People thought it preposterous that a girl, unknown a year or two earlier, should be receiving $2,000 a week, or that a plumber's assistant should have become a comedian worth a quarter of a million a year. But gradually theater patrons came to realize that these stories were true, and realization was accompanied by mixed emotions that in many instances turned to bitterness and hostility. Admiration and adoration of movie celebrities had developed without any very sound basis, and now many people who had formed the habit of idolizing their favorites as superior beings were shocked to discover that their divinities were money-grubbers of the most ordinary variety. Merchants and professional men, struggling to earn five or ten thousand dollars a year, began to curse the "pretty boys" of the screen who received as much in a month or a week, and their wives grew caustic in commenting on the "dough-faced girls who hadn't brains enough to act, but were lucky enough to get a fortune for being clothes-horses."

While reformers were pushing their demands for censorship, and jealousy and bitterness over movie salaries were stirring in many minds, an unfortunate series of events fanned all latent hostilities into a consolidated conflagration that threatened to destroy the entire movie edifice. The incidents were in no way related to one another but anti-movie agitators lumped them together as material for sensational attacks on picture personnel and the industry as a whole.

Mary Pickford purchased a home in Nevada and declared her intention of becoming a resident of the state. After the time specified by law to establish a residence she applied for and obtained a divorce from Owen Moore, and soon thereafter she and Douglas Fairbanks were married in California.

Roscoe "Fatty" Arbuckle, a young man starting business life as a plumber's helper, had risen to great popularity as a screen comedian, holding for a time a position inferior to none except Charlie Chaplin and Harold Lloyd. He was under the management of Joseph Schenck, who was paying him a salary of several thousand dollars a week.

Arbuckle spent his money rather flamboyantly, and between periods of work he was accustomed to visit San Francisco and, free from the Puritanical atmosphere of Los Angeles, make merry for a few days. On one of these holidays, he was entertaining friends in his suite at the St. Francis Hotel, and a young woman named Virginia Rappe, who had appeared occasionally in unimportant screen rôles, accompanied by another girl, joined the party. While the group of several men and women were chatting and drinking, Miss Rappe had an attack of a chronic pelvic illness, and died.

William Deane Taylor, an English director in the Lasky studios, was murdered one night in his bungalow in Los Angeles.

Olive Thomas while on a visit to Paris with her husband, Jack Pickford, committed suicide. Although no scandalous details could be wrung from the event, other than that the girl was in a temporary fit of despondency, the fact that husband and wife were movie stars was enough to justify columns of notoriety and much innuendo.

The Pickford-Moore divorce and Miss Pickford's marriage to Douglas Fairbanks had created some murmurs of criticism, but these had nearly died away when a Nevada official declared his intention to institute proceedings against Miss Pickford and her husband on the charge that she had not been a bona fide resident of Nevada. Thousands of Americans had established residences in the state, had obtained divorces, and had not been attacked. It seemed strange that Nevada reformers had seen fit to ignore other cases and to focus on that of two wealthy motion picture stars, whose popularity might be seriously injured by the charges. It was peculiar, too, that the attack was not made while Mrs. Moore's divorce action was pending in the courts, and that nothing had been done until after she had re-married. Whatever the reason for the delay, the charge against the world's most popular actress was well timed. Movie haters joined professional reformers all over America in throwing mud at two stars whose personal lives could bear comparison with the manners and morals of husbands and wives in any other sphere of activity. The turmoil added fuel to the anti-movie flames for several months, and then the Nevada charges disappeared. They were so absurd that apparently they perished in the light of publicity.

The Arbuckle incident was more serious. The foulest stories imaginable were circulated, their essence being that Virginia Rappe was a noble, beautiful girl done to death by Arbuckle during an orgy. All the details that could be printed, and columns of almost unprintable filth, filled the newspapers for weeks.

The Taylor murder combined the lure of a mystery novel and a story of sex appeal. Evidence before the coroner's jury and gossip in the newspapers produced no scandal concerning the dead man. He had changed his name from Tanner to Taylor, apparently as players often adopt a stage name. His thoughtfulness, kindness, and courtesy to actresses had won for him the respect and affection of all women who had worked under his direction. The names of two stars, Mabel Normand and Mary Miles Minter, were featured prominently in the case. Newspaper gossip intimated that Miss Minter was in love with the director, and the evidence seemed to indicate that he had been in love with Miss Normand for several years. It was charged that a dope-peddler had been warned by Taylor to keep away from the studio and to refrain from selling narcotics to any actresses, and had been thrashed by Taylor for failure to heed the warning. A jealous girl, or one of her relatives, or the dope-peddler, or someone else, might have shot the director.

The newspapers found the mystery a tremendous stimulus to circulation and kept it alive for months. One editor, several years later, told me that the Taylor stories sold more newspapers everywhere in America than were ever sold by any item of news, not excepting war news, before or since. After a lapse of a decade the mystery is still unsolved; Taylor's murderer has never been arrested.

Arbuckle was indicted on the charge of manslaughter by a San Francisco grand jury and the case was placed on the court calendar for trial several weeks later. After the indictment the affair lost its news value until the time for the trial, and regular reporters and newspaper correspondents had returned to other work. They were succeeded by a flock of "special writers," most of whom had no regular journalistic connections but followed the precarious trade of free-lancing. They descended upon Los Angeles and industriously dug into the lives of Arbuckle and Taylor for dirt that could be peddled profitably to the press.

Every wild or silly escapade that could be linked, however thinly, with the comedian, was pictured as a Bacchanalian orgy. Beautiful maidens were ruined; oceans of alcohol were consumed, and hints of the most horrible forms of debauchery were indicated, the hinters stopping only at the point at which their publications would have been barred from the mails.

The legitimate facts of the Taylor mystery were soon exhausted but the dirt writers had found the "dope" trail, and this enabled them to produce lurid tales of dope fiends to add to their fabrications of drunkenness and sexual excesses. When they ran short of Arbuckle and Taylor material, they ransacked the lives of all studio people for pegs upon which to hang stories portraying Hollywood as the naughtiest spot on the globe, where beautiful lady stars and handsome heroes rioted from one orgy to another, committing murders and suicides as incidents of their frolics.

The free-lance writers were assisted in their efforts to exterminate the motion picture colony by the scarlet women who had been attracted to Los Angeles by reports of easy money during the oil and real-estate booms. Ladies of the evening, coming to California for the first time, did not know of the state's vagrancy law, under which a man or a woman unable to declare regular employment can be sent to prison as a "common vagrant." They formed the habit of registering as extras at the studios, and then, when haled into police court at midnight, they declared their occupation as "actress," and glibly reeled off the names of a few casting directors. This was enough to save them from commitment as vagrants, and also it was enough to permit sensational newspaper correspondents to announce to the world that "three beautiful film stars were arrested in a bawdy house," or "beautiful film star causes shooting affair at wild gin party." Scores of such stories were fed to the public, but in not a single instance was an actress of even moderate prominence involved.

Jealousy, anger, and disgust aroused by the enormous salaries of players, followed by this series of sensational scandals and the torrent of falsehoods, enabled professional reformers and politicians to rally to their support thousands of sincere, well-intentioned ministers, church members, club women, and school teachers. The movies, once the most ardently beloved institution in America, were made to appear as the foulest, most hideous creation ever known. Every star, every player, every executive, was under suspicion, as any day might bring an exposé of one's favorite hero or heroine as a dope addict, a drunkard, or a sex degenerate. The adulation lavished on screen celebrities had been extravagant; now, more extravagant, and more unreasoning, was the barrage of suspicion and venom directed at yesterday's idols.

THE growing animosity was consolidated into demands on many state legislatures for censorship laws and on city councils for censorship ordinances. The reformers demanded sweeping regulations concerning the portrayal of sex situations, crime, deadly weapons, the use of alcohol and narcotics, hospital and medical scenes, and almost every other element of drama, melodrama, or tragedy; had they accomplished their desires, the making of motion pictures for theater entertainment would have ceased. The screen, which was just beginning to find itself, just beginning to be effective and beautiful, could never have surmounted the barriers proposed during the dark months of the Arbuckle-Taylor horrors.

The industry was not in the slightest degree organized to deal with the situation. There was a national association of producers, distributors, and exhibitors with headquarters in New York, but because of the fiercely competitive conditions then prevailing, the association had never been effective. William A. Brady, its president, had striven earnestly to bring about good feeling in the ranks, but the members never provided him with the capital nor gave him sufficient cooperation to do more than stage little battles at Albany and other state capitals. In Los Angeles, the center of the scandal storm, the studio executives had overcome their suspicions and jealousies enough to have formed a local organization, Motion Picture Producers' Association, to deal with labor troubles and other industrial matters concerning the studios, but their coherence was not sufficient to permit them to engage in politics or other affairs concerning large policies. Frank Garbutt was the motive power behind the producers' association, with W. J. Reynolds as executive manager.

When the waves of Arbuckle-Taylor filth and vituperation began to sweep the country, Garbutt and Reynolds aroused studio officials to a realization that "they must hang together, or they would hang separately," and the producers' association stepped forth and gave battle to the anti-movie forces. Reynolds, determined to sift all charges to the bottom, employed detectives to work in the studios and when necessary to watch the movement of players and technical people under suspicion of immoralities or delinquencies. With Garbutt's assistance and the cooperation of Glenn Harper, Sol Lesser, and other southern California theater owners, a staff of speakers was organized to address audiences in theaters, club women's meetings, luncheon clubs, churches, or wherever an important group could be reached. Will Rogers, well-known humorist and actor, Rupert Hughes, the novelist, Rob Wagner, author of many books and stories regarding movies and movie people, Frank A. Woods, screen writer and then president of the Writers' Club in Hollywood, were among those who gave freely and energetically of their time to this work.

THE producers' and exhibitors' associations asked me to join in the movement. A year or two after Zukor and Hodkinson had broken off relations, and my attempts to merge the Paramount and V L S E groups had failed, I had resigned my position as vice-president of the American Tobacco Company and entered the production of motion pictures. After moving from New York to Los Angeles, my contacts with friends in magazines and newspaper offices were maintained by their visits to Los Angeles and by correspondence with editors, who frequently wrote me regarding phases of motion picture affairs that happened to interest them. In 1920 this correspondence, together with information acquired in various other ways, convinced me that the drift toward sex-appeal pictures was building up a strong pro-censorship public opinion which, unless checked, would cripple the industry.

The most criticized sex films were being made by small, fly-by-night promoters, who would rent studio space, hire a director and a cast, "shoot a story," and peddle the film to state's rights distributors. This class of temporary manufacturers, usually deficient in both capital and morals, was willing to "go the limit on sex stuff," and there were exhibitors who would screen their cheaply made stories if the lobby photographs contained suggestive scenes.

Reformers and agitators lumped all producers together in one class, the good and the bad, the decent and the indecent. No credit was given to studios that turned out wholesome product; there was no differentiation; all of us were tossed into one basket, and the standing of the respectable manufacturers was being seriously menaced by the irresponsible fly-by-nights. I attempted to arouse other producers to action, but my efforts did not get far. Most producers were too busy with the day's work to look beyond the boundaries of their own affairs, and there was no national association that could effectively move in any direction.

An editorial friend, B. A. MacKinnon, of *Pictorial Review*, stimulated me to independent action with a letter in which he declared that unless the producers and exhibitors cleaned their own house, and cleaned it thoroughly, there might not be much house left when the reformers finished the job. I wrote several articles for *Pictorial Review*. I reviewed the position of the movies in American family life, frankly faced the existence of sex-appeal pictures, and with equal frankness spoke my mind regarding professional reformers and politicians hunting for more offices for henchmen to fill. Declaring censorship to be un-American and unworkable, and insisting that parents who were relying on censors to supervise the mental habits of their children were dodging responsibilities that must rest in the home, I called on the club women of America to work with decent producers and to agitate for the use of the police power in sending indecent manufacturers, distributors, and exhibitors to jail.

I was astonished at the interest aroused by these articles and others that followed them in other magazines. For several years I had been learning something of the grip acquired by movies on American life, but when thousands of letters and newspaper clippings poured into my study I began to realize that neither I nor anyone else had an adequate conception of their deep hold on the classes as well as the masses. There were many letters from university and college presidents and professors, school teachers, lawyers, ministers, club women, bankers and members of other groups to prove convincingly that the influence of the movies had permeated every section of American society.

I was astonished, too, by the wide variety of approval and condemnation expressed by the correspondents and the commentators in newspapers, magazines and trade journals. Nearly all letters from sources not connected with stage or screen, nor professional reformers and politicians, endorsed my views, but the most effective correspondence came from intelligent club women, seeking methods by which they could cooperate with worthy producers and exhibitors to improve the screen without bureaucratic censorship.

However responsive to my opinions the general public might be, the *Pictorial Review* article on sex and censorship was a terrific shock to motion picture magnates. Producers and distributors in New York were hastily summoned to a meeting at Delmonico's to discuss the situation and the fellow whose writings were responsible for the excitement. Opinion was divided: one section of hot heads favored swift and terrible death to the producer who, "in order to advertise himself," would so much as intimate that anything short of perfection existed in motion pictures; another suggested that the large corporations should advise magazine publishers that if any more of my writings appeared, motion picture advertisers would withdraw their patronage. A few more level-headed producers briefly described the arguments I had advanced, and presently the idea spread through the assembly that perhaps there was something in my position, and that it was a clever trick to "pass the censorship buck to the parents and the club women."

Boiled down to its essence, the Delmonico meeting was not hostile to my views; the movie magnates—none but the most important executives in the industry were present—had grown so accustomed to a diet of praise from their press agents and sycophants that their anger was directed not toward the opinions expressed, but against the impudent individual who expressed them. These producers had no desire to make sex-appeal pictures or any other films that might injure the business. Their success was based on their ability to please the great public—not a small minority of any kind, but the masses and the classes between the top and the bottom of the intellectual scales. They might be called inartistic, or silly, or artistic and wise, the selection of terminology depending entirely on the point of view, but there was not the slightest justification in the reformers' allegations that they were "degraders" or "debauchers of American homes." The meeting adjourned without formal decision, but the general sense of the evening was that my opinions were sound enough, but that I myself was an undesirable person for having expressed any opinions without having submitted them to the censorship of the leaders of the industry!

This attitude of producers and distributors was not shared by the other branch of the industry, the theater owners. My suggestion that the police power be invoked to send makers, distributors, and exhibitors of indecent pictures to prison cut deep into the cuticles of theater owners who had specialized in suggestive lobby displays and spicy newspaper advertising. They clamored for the destruction of this anathematized producer, and a few of them insisted that any film bearing my name be boycotted.

Nevertheless, the motion picture press courageously approved my position and endorsed my suggestion that the police replace censorship. Arthur James, editor of the *Motion Picture World,* and James R. Quirk, editor of *Photoplay,* most emphatically gave their support, and William Allen Johnston of the *News* and Martin Quigley of the *Exhibitor's Herald* conducted in their publications campaigns to urge the three branches of the industry to abandon youthful jealousies and suspicions, and unite to deal with their common problems. *Pictorial Review* met the charge that it was permitting a producer to use its pages for self-advertising by inviting other movie people to contribute articles dealing with censorship, sex-appeal, and other subjects of general interest. Norma Talmadge, Jesse L. Lasky, Samuel Goldwyn, and others accepted the invitation, and for nearly two years *Pictorial Review* presented discussions of motion picture matters that undoubtedly had a great deal to do with bringing about a better understanding of the screen.

The most vigorous condemnations of my magazine and newspaper articles came from the professional reformers, of whom Rev. Wilbur F. Crafts, president of the International Reform Bureau, with headquarters at Washington, D. C., was the most zealous. I urged Dr. Crafts to study movie conditions for himself, and after some correspondence he came to Los Angeles. The producers did not receive him gladly. Dr. Crafts annoyed them by referring to me as the "spokesman of the industry" until I convinced him that I was a small frog in a big pond and that what I had been doing was completely voluntary and must be charged to no one but myself. I explained to him that the industry had no spokesman, and the only way he could get information was to visit the various studios and talk with executives separately, and then form his own conclusions.

Crafts was a man past middle age, but very active and vigorous. I found him narrow, of course; all reformers are narrow; but I became convinced that he was entirely sincere, and to the best of his ability was willing to understand and to help in the situation. From the producers he received varying treatment; some of them haughtily refused to talk with him; others were cool but frank; and others met him more than half way and gave him such an education in the difficulties of movie-making that before he left Los Angeles his position on censorship had changed completely. His glimpses into studio work convinced him that most of the movie makers were fundamentally decent; that they were merely servants of the box office, trying earnestly to satisfy the ticket-buying masses; and he learned to differentiate between producing companies, and indeed to criticize or approve specific pictures. Thereafter he was never able to advocate state or local censorship, but insisted on the producers censoring their own pictures before making them.

His speeches and interviews showed such a marked change in his attitude that various zealots accused him of having deserted his fellow reformers, and Crafts attempted to redeem himself by advocacy of federal "supervision of film commerce." But this was in itself tantamount to an admission that state and municipal censorships were not successful, and, coming from a reformer of Dr. Crafts' standing, had the effect of reducing the demand for regulation throughout the country.

The success of the producers in dealing with Dr. Crafts encouraged some of them to invite other reformers and members of censorship boards to visit Los Angeles, and during the next year or two several delegations studied the making of movies on the ground. Some of the censors could be quickly classified as bigots; others as plain grafters; but many of them were honest, sincere, misguided men and women led into the advocacy of censorship by genuine desire to improve conditions. Members of this latter class were distressed when they faced the facts regarding bureaucratic regulation of art and literature, and returned to their homes determined to abandon censorship and work for police control of indecent pictures. One woman from Kansas who had given several years of her life to earnest service on the state censorship board, resigned her position, frankly declaring her change in attitude, and thereafter worked with club women and parent-teacher associations to bring about specific approval of worthy pictures and condemnation of injurious ones.

WHILE the agitation was at its height, there appeared a minister with sanity enough and courage enough to step forward and give assistance to Garbutt, Reynolds, and the members of the Los Angeles producers' and exhibitors' associations. This man was Dr. Herbert Booth Smith, pastor of Emanuel Presbyterian church in Los Angeles, the third largest congregation of the denomination in America, numbering among its members several motion picture families.

Dr. Smith, in his pulpit and in addresses to the ministers' association, insisted on a fair trial for Arbuckle, and cessation of the hostile movement against pictures and picture people. His courage and sound sense marked the turn in the tide, other ministers and leaders of opinion in southern California following him in protest against the use of lynch law, and urging a return to sanity in dealing with studio problems and personnel. For several months Will Rogers, Rupert Hughes, Rob Wagner, and other speakers of the producers' and the exhibitors' associations continued their addresses, and the newspapers gave liberal space to reporting the speeches and to friendly, helpful discussions of the situation. When the smoke of battle had cleared away, Los Angeles and the studio workers understood each other better than they ever had in the past.

The charges of immorality and degeneracy sifted down to very small dimensions. The investigations of the detectives employed by the producers' association were thorough, but yielded a meager harvest. There were in Los Angeles at that time perhaps forty or fifty thousand people employed in the studios in various capacities. Perhaps two or three thousand of these could be classed as "important people," stars, leading men and women, character actors, small part players, directors, camera men, art directors, and others drawing high salaries. Back of this group was an indeterminate number of extras, men and women who received occasional employment. Very, very few of the "important people" were drunkards, dope fiends or even on the doubtful list. Good behavior, due in individual cases to moral or ethical viewpoint, was enforced in general by the merciless lens of the movie camera, which invariably records the tell-tale lines left by vice, bad habits, or even such carelessness as over-eating. Ambition and business prudence have made the Los Angeles movie colony a class of careful people who hesitate before doing anything that may reduce their earning power.

There were, during the Arbuckle furore, half a dozen gentlemen given to "wild parties." The producers caused them to disappear suddenly from the payrolls, and several of them left Los Angeles and remained in exile in the east for five years. There were about two dozen pathetic drug addicts, the most prominent of whom, Wallace Reid, a very popular star, died a few years later. Several other players not so prominent, among them a beautiful girl named Juanita Hansen, were ruined by drugs and had to retire to private life. The terror created by the Reid and Hansen cases was such that in recent years only a few other victims have been claimed by the drug habit. Studio executives inserted in their contracts with players a "morality clause," under the terms of which the employer may dismiss the employe at any time he or she is even accused of moral dereliction, but in the years following these agitations there was no occasion to enforce this rigorous provision.

Arbuckle was tried three times by San Francisco juries and each time was found not guilty, but nevertheless the notoriety given to the case was so great that he was never permitted to return to the screen. Public opinion decided that even if he was not guilty of manslaughter, or was innocent of everything in connection with Virginia Rappe except admitting her to the presence of his friends, giving her a drink, and trying to alleviate her sufferings before the doctor arrived, he had proven himself a low person, one not fit to arouse the enthusiasm of audiences. The pictures made but not released prior to the San Francisco escapade represented an investment of several hundred thousand dollars, all of which had to be sent to the scrap heap.

PRODUCERS and distributors were at last convinced that they must get together and create an effective national association. In 1922, they formed the Motion Picture Producers and Distributors of America, Inc., and elected Will H. Hays, postmaster general in President Harding's Cabinet, as president. Nearly all producers and distributors joined the association and paid into the treasury each year a small percentage of their gross receipts, thus providing ample funds for effective operation.

Will Hays soon proved himself a sound investment for the industry. He organized a staff with headquarters in New York and a branch in Los Angeles, with representatives abroad, bringing into the association a number of able men, such as ex-Governor Milliken of Maine, Charles Pettijohn, attorney, who had been connected with the Selznick enterprises, and Gabriel L. Hess, counsel for the Goldwyn Company. The several departments of the company were organized to deal with a wide variety of internal and external problems, ranging from the employment of extras in the studios and the settlement of disputes between exchanges and theaters, to the handling of demands in legislatures and in Congress and the problems of American film manufacturers in foreign lands.

The producers met the two situations that menaced their progress and prosperity—that is, censorship and the sensational charges against Hollywood's morals—by giving Will Hays almost autocratic power. The Hollywood branch of the association, managed by Fred Beetson, working closely with the studios, eliminated the conditions that made possible the perplexities and dangers of previous years. Beetson maintains a centrally located employment bureau, the costs of which are paid by the studios, at which extras must present themselves for examination by a staff of professional sociologists. If they pass the tests, they are registered and classified in accordance with the types, or characters, they can represent before the camera, and then are assigned to the various studios when their services are needed. The scientific handling of this phase of studio activity by Beetson's organization has removed the possibility of prostitutes defaming the profession by declaring themselves actresses, and scandals have thus been reduced to a minimum.

Players, writers, and directors seeking divorce must be very careful that no sensational charges appear in the testimony, and one young actor who broke into newspaper headlines merely by evading alimony payments found himself facing the heavy disapproval of Will Hays and the studio executives. Men and women who have been made notorious by divorce, murder, or other scandals, may capitalize their notoriety on the stage, but they cannot obtain employment on the screen. These illustrations are sufficient to indicate that when the producers undertook their own "house cleaning" they did it drastically and thoroughly.

The newspapers have cooperated with the studios in eliminating from Hollywood the free lances whose only desire was to dig up salable dirt. Interest in motion picture news and rumors having increased with the years, newspaper syndicates and press associations opened Hollywood offices, placing them in charge of experienced men and women writers of character and responsibility. Thereafter, when an extra woman became involved in a sensational incident, the newspapers described her as an extra and not as a beautiful film star; and if a cowboy got drunk and beat his wife he was reported in the police news as a cowboy and not as a movie hero gone wrong.

The Hays association inaugurated a campaign of education to keep movie-mad girls away from Hollywood, and the feminine tide to the studios decreased substantially. Statistics from the Beetson office were used to discourage men, women, and children from coming to Los Angeles in the hope of obtaining employment in pictures. Eleven thousand extras are registered in this largest employment agency in the world, and although forty telephones ring all day and nearly all night in the efforts of Beetson's staff to find work for this army, only a few hundred a day can be placed in the studios. So seldom do the same people obtain regular engagements that, although wages are five, seven and one-half, and ten dollars a day, very few of the extras earn even a bare living. The trend of the screen to talking pictures has decreased the use of the mob scenes prevalent in silent films, and the openings for extras have grown very limited. Two or three thousand men and women absorb all the employment for which four or five times that number are candidates.

The producers dealt with the censorship menace by creating a system of "self-censorship" with Hays as the highest court of appeal, his powers beginning with the selection of material for the screen and following through to elimination of dangerous or doubtful scenes in completed films. While none of the manufacturers are legally bound by his decisions and at times there are earnest disagreements between various producers and Hays and his staff, the studios have held to the restrictions imposed by the "Czar" in avoiding novels and stage plays, and specific situations in stories and plays, that might give offense to screen audiences.

For the most part, the screen has eschewed the increasing latitude of the stage, as a glance at the rules adopted by the studios for the guidance of their writers and directors will show. The corporations composing the Hays association, substantially all the producers and distributors in the United States, unanimously agreed to the "self-discipline and regulation" of a code, the intent of which was to insure establishment of general principles. For the further guidance of studio craftsmen and technicians the code was amplified by a series of "particular applications," as follows:

CRIMES AGAINST THE LAW:

These shall never be presented in such a way as to throw sympathy with the crime as against law and justice or to inspire others with a desire for imitation.

  1. *Murder.*
     (a) The technique of murder must be presented in a way that will not inspire imitation.
     (b) Brutal killings are not to be presented in detail.
     (c) Revenge in modern times shall not be justified.
  2. *Methods of Crime* should not be explicitly presented.
     (a) Theft, robbery, safe-cracking, and dynamiting of trains, mines, buildings, etc., should not be detailed in method.
     (b) Arson must be subject to the same safeguards.
     (c) The use of firearms should be restricted to essentials.
     (d) Methods of smuggling should not be presented.
  3. *Illegal drug traffic* must never be presented.
  4. *The use of liquor* in American life, when not required by the plot or for proper characterization, will not be shown.

SEX:

The sanctity of the institution of marriage and the home shall be upheld. Pictures shall not infer that low forms of sex relationship are the accepted or common thing.

  1. *Adultery,* sometimes necessary plot material, must not be explicitly treated or justified, or presented attractively.
  2. *Scenes of passion* should not be introduced when not essential to the plot. In general, passion should so be treated that these scenes do not stimulate the lower and baser element.
  3. *Seduction or Rape.*
     (a) They should never be more than suggested, and only when essential for the plot, and even then never shown by explicit method.
     (b) They are never the proper subject for comedy.
  4. *Sex perversion* or any inference of it is forbidden.
  5. *White slavery* shall not be treated.
  6. *Miscegenation* is forbidden.
  7. *Sex Hygiene* and venereal diseases are not subjects for motion pictures.
  8. Scenes of *actual child birth,* in fact or in silhouette, are never to be presented.
  9. *Children's sex organs* are never to be exposed.

VULGARITY:

The treatment of low, disgusting, unpleasant, though not necessarily evil subjects, should be subject always to the dictates of good taste and regard for the sensibilities of the audience.

OBSCENITY:

Obscenity in word, gesture, reference, song, joke or by suggestion, is forbidden.

DANCES:

Dances which emphasize indecent movements are to be regarded as obscene.

PROFANITY:

Pointed profanity or vulgar expressions, however used, are forbidden.

COSTUME:

1. *Complete nudity* is never permitted. This includes nudity in fact or in silhouette, or any lecherous or licentious notice thereof by other characters in the picture.

2. *Dancing costumes* intended to permit undue exposure or indecent movements in the dance are forbidden.

RELIGION:

1. No film or episode may throw ridicule on any religious faith.

2. Ministers of religion, in their character as such, should not be used as comic characters or as villains.

3. Ceremonies of any definite religion should be carefully and respectfully handled.

NATIONAL FEELINGS:

1. The use of the Flag shall be consistently respectful.

2. The history, institutions, prominent people and citizenry of other nations shall be represented fairly.

TITLES:

Salacious, indecent or obscene titles shall not be used.

REPELLENT SUBJECTS:

The following subjects must be treated within the careful limits of good taste:

1. *Actual hangings,* or electrocutions as legal punishments for crime.
2. *Third Degree* methods.
3. *Brutality* and possible gruesomeness.
4. *Branding* of people or animals.
5. *Apparent cruelty* to children or animals.
6. *Surgical operations.*

The appearance of talking pictures, in 1926-28, created new problems in applying the code's principles, and the producers and distributors association in March, 1930, established a committee in the Hays organization for the review of doubtful scenarios, or sequences or scenes in scenarios, or the review of negatives or portions of negatives, to the end that infractions of the code might be eliminated before camera work; and if any crept into the actual film they could be removed before public presentation. Provisions were made for appeal to a higher committee composed of "leading factors in the industry ... who will be called upon to arbitrate where there is any doubt about interpretation, and thus the common judgment of men with a common purpose will be the deciding influence." All studios formally agreed to submit to the code and submit their productions to the committees of review and arbitration and submit to the final decisions.

Although the activities of Rev. Wilbur F. Crafts occurred prior to the entrance of Will Hays into screen affairs, the self-censorship adopted by producers was the system earnestly advocated by the chief professional motion picture reformer. Dr. Crafts died within a few years after his visit to Los Angeles, but had he lived his pride would undoubtedly have been immeasurably gratified by the accomplishment of Will Hays in establishing industrial laws, and not even Dr. Crafts himself could have devised a sharper set of "teeth" for the enforcement of legislation than the Hays association created by its code interpretations and appeal and arbitration committees.

Needless to add, the distance between the stage and printed fiction on the one hand and the screen on the other was not lessened by the Hays code; rather it was increased. Since Armistice Day, New York stage audiences, creating the mode for American theaters in general, have grown so sophisticated and blasé that no themes or treatments can be too open and frank to please them. Nude and almost nude girls have become commonplace. Adultery is the principal theme of serious plays, and the infidelity of middle-aged husbands and wives affords material for merry farces. White slavery has become a tame subject, and houses of prostitution have been exploited often enough to reduce their novelty-value. Even homosexuality and degeneracy are losing their spice unless bolstered with a liberal assortment of bootleggers or gangsters. Profanity and the use of words and phrases classified as "obscene" a decade ago are employed as a common constituent of dialogue. Modern realistic novelists have as much latitude—perhaps more as their fellow craftsmen of the stage.

Screen producers have paid as high as $100,000 for the photoplay rights of a modern novel or $225,000 for a stage production, and almost invariably sophisticated critics have deplored the "emasculation" of the motion picture version and condemned the producer for his lack of "artistic appreciation." The movie people can make only one answer to such criticisms: "We are not manufacturing entertainment for a small minority of liberal-minded readers or stage-goers, but for the vast majority of families who are far removed from sophistication. Our transcripts of life may lack the realism of novels and the stage, but we are confident that motion pictures have contributed their share toward higher artistic standards in the last ten or twenty years. Until the great public decides that it wants us to widen the latitude of our themes and treatments we shall remain within our boundaries."

CHAPTER FOURTEEN
"BIGGER AND BETTER PICTURES"

AMERICAN industry recovered quickly from the readjustments of deflation. Theaters all over America were among the first business institutions to reap the benefits of the general revival, and the winter of 1922-23 found large patronage again appearing at the ticket windows. A great demand for new pictures arose and boom times had come again. Within a few months producers saw clearly that earnings of a million to two million dollars per picture were as surely attainable in 1923 as half a million had been in 1919-21.

Many producing and distributing companies had disintegrated under the pressure of deflation and the centralization of theaters. Only a score or so of studio groups remained, and apparently among these few the business of the renascence would be distributed. This situation seemed to the independents to have been made to order for their especial benefit, and glowing optimism dispelled the depressing doubts of the last two years. Again, as when theaters began to form in chains and circuits and first runs began to be hard to obtain, the arguments of independent producer-distributors followed such lines as these:

"It is true that nearly all leading houses have come under control of Paramount, First National, Loew-Metro and Fox, but it is equally true that in acquiring theaters these companies have made of themselves exhibitors first and producers second. The theaters now are their chief source of profits, and while the corporations make money on successful pictures and break even on all or nearly all others they have come to look to the exhibiting section of their business as the mainstay of dividends. The houses must be filled to capacity as many times a week as possible, and as nothing but pictures of outstanding box-office appeal will draw capacity patronage, all theaters, whether owned by big companies or independents, will eagerly accept a powerful picture, no matter who makes it. Therefore, if I produce even a few good box-office pictures a year, I can get them shown in a first-run house in each key city, which will create all the prestige necessary to carry them successfully into second and subsequent runs. Two or three good box-office knockouts a year will give me enough prestige to sell my entire program to neighborhood and small city exhibitors."

Box-office appeal was the one essential to insure profits. But what is box-office quality, and how can it be determined, in advance, and injected into pictures? Each manufacturer, great or small, had to find the answer to these questions; each approached the problem differently, but their conclusions were fairly identical, as their actions show. If quality was something people paid for, then quality—an intangible property in itself—could nevertheless be measured by money. Money, then, would buy quality, and all that was necessary to produce meritorious pictures that would attract large audiences was to spend as much money as possible on their manufacture.

It is a sufficiently specious chain of reasoning, but the events of the previous few years seemed to justify it. Audiences had given their greatest approval to sumptuous, costly productions; less expensive features had not usually been highly successful. Likewise, the palace theaters, splendidly designed and magnificently decorated and equipped, were drawing enormously profitable patronage, while less costly, less ornate, houses had dropped behind in the procession. Bigness—elaborateness—sumptuousness—lavishness—these seemed to constitute the elusive "quality" the public wanted. "Bigger and better" seemed to be the infallible recipe for success. These words were repeated so often in newspapers, trade journals, and fan magazines in 1922, that "bigger and better pictures" became the slogan of the studios.

"Bigger" was a measurable term. Griffith had made a bigger picture when he employed mobs of extras for scenes in "The Birth of a Nation"; DeMille's bigness had taken form in costlier settings, costumings, displays of fashion models; Erich von Stroheim, in making one or two successful specials for Universal, had built reproductions of Monte Carlo and other places and filled them with great crowds of men and women; June Mathis, in filming "The Four Horsemen," had used big sets and big mobs freely.

Griffith, DeMille, Von Stroheim and a few other directors were known to photograph a hundred thousand, or two hundred thousand, feet of film for a ten-reel picture. Apparently they shot all the scenes they and their writers could think of, regardless of expense, and in the cutting room selected those that seemed most desirable, ruthlessly throwing the residue into the scrap box. "Bigness" in the use of negative film, shooting many scenes where only one could be used, this was measurable. Perhaps through their extravagance these successful directors had captured the elusive germ of box-office appeal?

"Better" was a harder term to define. No one really knew whether or not a picture was "better" until the box offices of the large cities turned in their reports, but the faith of producers in the power of money caused them to believe that by spending money freely they would at least be sure of getting bigger pictures and they were confident that "better" would follow the other adjective; and thus the slogan of "bigger and better pictures" was translated into action in the form of "bigger and better bankrolls," and a bigger and better battle to spend them quickly. In other years, picture manufacturers had striven to "out-smart" their competitors; now the contest of nimble wits was superseded by a battle of money, a struggle to "out-spend" the other fellow. Every extravagance was condoned on the theory that quality could be bought if enough money were poured into the studios.

The fundamental necessity, of course, was the attainment of box-office appeal, and, as this essential element had been produced at various times by three classes of workers—actors, directors, and writers—the first duty of bigger and better spending was to engage the individuals in whom reposed the secret of popularity. Players, writers, directors were frantically sought. Salaries, having doubled and quadrupled in 1919-20, now in many instances doubled and quadrupled again. One studio executive received a quarter of million a year; another was reported to receive three-quarters of a million. Some directors got $20,000 to $50,000 for directing a single picture. Screen writers advanced into the "big money" classes, receiving $1,000 to $2,500 a week or $10,000 to $25,000 for a story written for the screen or a screen adaptation of a novel or a play for which the producer might already have paid $25,000 to $200,000. Title-writing became a specialized function, and title writers were sometimes paid higher salaries than continuity writers.

After individual players, directors and writers were engaged at fabulous prices, there remained the problem of determining which group, or which person in each picture-making unit, should have the authority and responsibility of selecting stories, casts, directors, writers, settings, and so forth. Each star, each director, and each writer was eager to assume the responsibility, and for a while producers compromised by increasing the authority of each faction and then by trying to divide the responsibility between them.

A complete illustration of star operation was afforded by a grand opera favorite, who selected her husband as her leading man when she went into the movies.

"My audience," madame explained to the scenario writer, "comes to the theater to see Me. Consequently the script must have me in nearly all the scenes. In perhaps half of them I should appear without my husband, and in half or more of the others my husband and I should appear together. The director will see that my face is constantly before the camera and of course there must be an abundance of my close-ups."

Madame's analysis of audience reactions represented fairly the sincere conviction of all members of the star group and applied accurately to conditions of a few years earlier, but, unfortunately, screen enthusiasts had advanced so far in a short time that treatments of yesteryear were now archaic and worse than useless. No matter how celebrated the star, patrons would stay away from a theater unless convinced that they were to see a good story, well directed and ably acted by a well-balanced cast. With three-quarters or more of each play concentrated on the heroine and her hero, the producer was unable to discover a photo-dramatist who could develop any other characters or evolve a plot that would satisfy the advanced demand of movie patrons, and madame soon faded from the screen.

The principal contributions of the director group to the wastes of these years were caused by delays and "over-shooting." Producers found themselves paying fantastic prices for negatives of which between thirty and fifty percent represented scenes that never were used in the final versions. After $800,000 had been invested in one picture, all the film was thrown away and the director made a new start, the finished negative costing about $1,500,000. Another spectacle that cost $4,000,000 could have been made for $1,500,000.

Although several directors established high records in the era of unbridled extravagance, first place should be awarded, I think, to Erich von Stroheim. One or two of his important pictures, produced for Universal at costs within commercial limits, were very successful, and brought fame to Von Stroheim and profits to his employer. Then came the man hunt that always occurred as soon as a player or a director showed signs of box-office appeal, with producers bidding against each other fiercely, and Von Stroheim found himself in the Goldwyn Company (of which Frank Joseph Godsol then was the principal owner), with an apparently unlimited supply of money and freedom to spend it.

He selected a grim story * and after months of preparation, during which the salaries of himself and his staff would have paid for a fairly expensive special, camera work started; after several months, the shooting was finished at a cost so much above a million dollars that the producer was deeply worried. More months passed, and Von Stroheim finally announced that his masterpiece was ready for the screen—in twenty-eight reels, approximately seven hours of screen time! He accompanied the announcement with a declaration that he had produced an immortal work of art and that no profane hand should touch the beauty he had wrought in celluloid. Twenty-eight reels was the length of his edited story; twenty-eight reels it must remain; not one foot could be spared from his creation.

The Goldwyn Company had been passing through two years of costly pictures, many of them unsuccessful, and, concentrating his hopes on this production as a life saver, Godsol had planned to spend $300,000 to $500,000 on the negative. The final costs were about $1,000,000 and he had twenty-eight reels and threats of dire trouble if he reduced the film to screenable length. After several weeks of indecision he faced the inevitable—Von Stroheim was allowed to go, and unemotional film editors began the task of cutting twenty-eight reels to nine. The producer paid the price of three or four pictures and got one. The film was a failure. Newspaper critics and the intellectuals found much to praise even in the cut version, but the public pronounced it dull and uninteresting. The exact earnings of the production are unknown to me, but I believe the $1,000,000 investment brought back gross receipts of three or four hundred thousand.

When writers, the third group upon which authority was bestowed, began to search for quality with the wide-open pocketbooks of the employers, the results were equally astonishing. As a class, the writers, with few exceptions, were apt to concentrate their efforts on the intelligent minority of movie audi-

* "Greed," based on "McTeague," a novel by Frank Norris.

ences, forgetting that films could not survive without the support of the great majority, to whom entertainment is basic and art incidental. Many writers sought to achieve box-office success by artistic handling of story, continuity, direction, acting, photography and titling, but, with one eye fastened on the dramatic pages of New York, Chicago, and Los Angeles newspapers, and the other on the criticisms in smart magazines, they too often spent the employer's money to win the applause of intellectuals, neglecting the populace that in the long run pays for everything.

The experience of an able, sincere writer, June Mathis, illustrates the danger of trying to provide democracy with intellectual fare to which it is not accustomed and does not enjoy. After Miss Mathis had written several successful features for Metro, Richard Rowland gave her full authority to produce a super-picture of "The Four Horsemen." She developed immediately into a competent executive and organized a staff that worked enthusiastically with her and the director to plan the details of camera work before photography began. This process of planning had been followed by Tucker and a few other directors, who called it "shooting the story on paper before shooting it on film." "Shooting on paper" is efficiency engineering applied to films. It requires highly trained technical knowledge, clear thinking, a power of visualization, and a rounded conception of the picture before camera work begins. Its advantages are low cost of production, small wastage, and a smoother, better picture than the product of ordinary manufacture. Miss Mathis' carefully and skilfully planned "Four Horsemen" came through the studio with a reasonable total cost and proved enormously popular. Because of Rowland's confidence in the girl's ability, Metro reaped a profit of several millions on this one picture.

Frank Joseph Godsol, after accumulating a large fortune in other lines of business, had been brought into motion pictures by Samuel Goldwyn, making his advent into films just when the studios were beginning the battle of unlimited expenditures. He and a syndicate of Wall Street friends put several millions into the Goldwyn corporations, and when these disappeared like magic and more millions were needed, Godsol reluctantly abandoned the comfortable life of an easy-going multi-millionaire and plunged into movie labors to protect his heavy investments. Attracted by Miss Mathis' splendid success, he offered her a large salary to take full charge of his studio's professional department, and she accepted.

It is one matter to organize a small staff, a single unit, to produce one picture in four to six months, but it is quite another to direct the operations of a large studio, which must ship one well-made picture to New York each week or two. A large output requires a dozen writers, a dozen directors, a dozen stars—each with a healthily developed ego, and each strenuously insisting on his or her rights—a small army of other players, several hundred architects, draughtsmen, decorators, costumers, photographers, chemists, electricians, and mechanics; all must be merged into a harmonious whole that functions smoothly and intelligently.

The ability to produce one good photoplay once in a while is rare enough, but to direct the activities of an entire studio requires administrative talents of a high order. Movie corporations have spent millions of dollars in searching for such ability, and not more than a dozen men have been found equal to the task. To assist the management in the selection of stories, casts, directors, and so forth, and to view the rushes (the day's camera work) of a negative after it had progressed far enough to present a part of the story, most studios made a practice of calling writers, film editors, directors and others from various departments into informal conferences. Sometimes small audiences of non-professionals are asked to the studio projection-room to view the "working print" (the rough assembling of scenes), so that the producer can listen to their comments and change the story by retaking defective scenes or adding new material.

Harry Rapf—when he was Hollywood production manager for Selznick-Select and Warner Brothers—often authorized his chauffeur to invite amateur critics to express opinions on new films and the chauffeur's committee consisted of carpenters, electricians, the studio barber, the young interne in charge of the hospital, the gate-keeper, the gymnasium masseur, and their wives and children. Harry Rapf, regarding this audience as fairly representative of average theater patronage, frequently made changes to win its approval, with gratifying box-office results.

Samuel Goldwyn, irritated by newspaper reviews of his photoplays, swung to the other extreme and brought to Los Angeles, at high salaries, half a dozen professional screen and stage critics, and assigned to them the responsibility of telling his writers and directors how to do their work effectively. His was not a gesture of sarcasm or revenge; he was desperately sincere. His critics criticized, and gave of their "expert" knowledge and advice, and whenever their employer followed it he produced nothing but failures.

When Miss Mathis assumed the duties of her Goldwyn position she organized a committee to pass on production, and made the mistake of including in it authors of smart stage plays, a professional dramatic critic, and a few writers whose principal work had been confined to essays and articles for intellectual magazines. These sophisticates strenuously and sarcastically condemned as "melodrama" and "hokum" all suggestions of widely popular themes and treatments, and Miss Mathis permitted herself to be convinced that movie audiences were ready to assimilate a higher class of ration. The studio steadily swung away from the showman ingredients of screen construction, and most of its offerings became smart, modernistic themes selected to win the approval of the intelligentsia. Many of the pictures produced under Miss Mathis' administration were technically excellent, but too many of them were almost totally lacking in entertainment value for large audiences. The costs were very high, and the burden of losses became so great that the corporation succumbed and its properties passed into a merger of several companies.

Thus, whether authority were vested in stars, directors or writers, or in a combination of the three, the mania of out-spending continued to engulf employers in enormous wastes. There seemed to be no limit to the excesses nor any method of curbing them. As all manufacturers had been swept off their feet by the tide, no one studio could bring about changes in conditions, and all were too bitterly determined to destroy their competitors to think for a moment of getting together in a concerted effort to introduce sanity and commercial prudence into their operations. Measured by the costs of excellent, successful silent pictures prior to the orgy, millions of dollars were needlessly spent between 1922 and 1927, when talking films created a new situation —no one can say how many millions, perhaps fifty, perhaps two hundred.

It is useful to compare costs in the ten-year period from 1914, when Paramount formally organized feature production and distribution, to 1924, when studio extravagance was in full blast: In 1914, feature negatives cost $10,000 to $30,000; in 1924, ordinary pictures, made for program release, had practically disappeared, audiences refusing to be pleased with anything but films the expense of which entailed $150,000 to $500,000 each. It is probably conservative to say that within this ten-year period representative program offerings had advanced from an average cost of $20,000 each to $300,000—fifteen hundred percent in a decade.

These startling extravagances increased the volume of criticism from bankers and business men acquainted with the industry. They had condemned the salary advances of 1919-20 as uneconomic and foolish; now, however, these ancient wages, in comparison with 1922-23 scales, appeared as almost too modest to have been possible.

"Why don't the egomaniacs and lunatics who are supposed to run the studios hire a few efficiency engineers to show them how to manage their affairs before they drive the entire film business into bankruptcy?" was a common query in Wall Street and Los Angeles financial circles. Unquestionably many millions of waste were due to the vanity of producer-distributors who had been successful in the years of inexpensive films, and who, living in

New York and concentrating on the business departments of their corporations, never really learned anything about actual production.

During the years of struggle from poverty to affluence they were keen, sharp showmen and shrewd traders, but prosperity surrounded them with self-seeking sycophants—"yes-men" became the movies' term for these boot-lickers—and in time many magnates, listening to the praise of fawning admirers and accepting the outpourings of press agents as gospel truth, acquired the belief that they were infallible geniuses in business, finance and art. As a matter of fact, many of them were supremely ignorant of the fundamentals of their own business. They continued their practice of rushing from New York to Los Angeles, enjoyed their comic-opera welcomes, and gave out pompous interviews, prepared by publicity writers; they "conferred" extensively with studio managers, stars, writers, and directors, and went through all the motions as of yore, but adequate results were not forthcoming; steadily rentals drifted from them to corporations headed by men who had learned the secrets of producing by actual personal labor in the studios, men who either lived in Los Angeles or spent much of their time there, and whose pictures when completed were sure of exhibition on screens owned by their own groups.

Adolph Zukor was a master producer, and Jesse Lasky moved to Los Angeles when he first entered motion pictures and remained in personal, active contact with Paramount studios until his duties became so extensive that Benjamin P. Schulberg was taken in as associate producer. Louis B. Mayer did not attempt to become a studio executive by taking flying trips from east to west coast, but in 1918 moved to Los Angeles and started to learn production from the ground up. Carl Laemmle spent several months of each year at Universal City, and during the long period of his corporation's large success much of it could be attributed to his personal supervision of production. Samuel Goldwyn, Joseph Schenck, the various administrators of First National, Mack Sennett, Hal Roach, Al and Charles Christie, and other manufacturers made their homes in Los Angeles and were constantly in touch with studio operations; but too many other owners and high officials tried to spread themselves between New York and Los Angeles; and when out-spending set the studios ablaze they soon became a sadly bewildered lot of men, hopelessly at the mercy of plausible stars, directors, and writers, whose child-like faith in the unlimited power of money to manufacture art led their employers deeper and deeper into the quicksands of extravagance.

However, the matter of applying efficiency methods to the studios was not a new suggestion. Years before, several studios had engaged experts and engineers, who installed systems which brought pictures through on time and cut out large quantities of waste, saving the employers an important portion of the cost of each film. Unfortunately, the public did not enjoy the entertainment produced by the engineering skill that had made all other American industries the envy of the world. Two of the producers who adopted scientific management went into bankruptcy; a third requested the resignation of his efficiency expert and saved his studio by returning to the non-scientific practices that produced profitable entertainment; and others retained their experts but told them to make haste very slowly, concentrating their efforts on cost-accounting, the purchase of supplies, the handling of labor and similar items, but keeping far away from anything connected with acting, directing and writing.

The basic difficulty encountered in all attempts to organize studios on factory lines was found in handling the raw material, which consists not of iron, cotton, celluloid, lumber or any other tangible thing, but is composed of ideas, dreams and emotions, fabricated into merchandise by the inspiration and temperament of writers, directors, players, architects, decorators and photographers. The first efficiency methods in the studios convinced producers that a rigidly operated system restricted spontaneity and reduced inspiration. When temperamental players, directors and writers could not play at play-acting their work often became heavy and dull; the economical, efficiently manufactured films lacked the mysterious something that aroused emotions in audiences. Employers—fearful that when their boys and girls were harnessed too closely to charts, schedules and report forms, the elusive raw material would lose its flavor—swung to the other extreme and gave them rather too much freedom.

As competition increased, and costs continued to climb crazily upward, the journeys of corporation executives between east and west became so frequent that bedevilled owners shuttled back and forth like suburban commuters in vain efforts to make their studios operate effectively and their New York offices retain their rapidly disappearing first runs. There wasn't much fun in being a magnate if you had to spend your life on railroad trains, hustling from the Atlantic to the Pacific, pursued by thoughts of competitors stealing your theater connections while you were in one place, or annexing your most valuable players or directors when you were in another; and although wealthy movie owners tried in many ways to overcome the freak of fate and climate that had caused the studios to become established in Los Angeles while the financial capital of the industry remained in New York, no system ever was successful in eliminating the annoyances and hardships.

After a time, one producer, deciding that another cog was needed in the machinery, devised the "supervisor," a new studio official to be placed in authority over writers, players, directors and others employed in each film-making unit, his duty being the coordination of all departments with the two-fold intention of insuring high quality and eliminating waste. The supervisor system seemed to be an intelligent move toward workable efficiency methods, and supervisors soon appeared in all studios. Some of the men elevated to this new position had been writers, others directors, and others small independent producers glad to abandon their own precarious companies and enlist with the big fellows, where compensation was liberal and constant.

No system functions automatically or is stronger than the individuals composing it, and, as the supervisors were not infallible and as the stars, directors and writers over whom they were placed resented any form of authority, there was much friction before the new method operated smoothly. Eventually it was established everywhere except in the studios of stars making their own pictures.

THE concentration of theater control into a few corporations was proceeding rapidly, and by 1924 nearly all of the first-run houses in the United States and Canada had been acquired by Paramount, Loew's, Inc., the Stanley Company, and large circuits affiliated with the Zukor, Loew, Mastbaum and First National groups. Fox retained his chain, Universal had several houses and the Goldwyn-Godsol group had several. The plausible theory that had aroused the optimism of independent producers and distributors in the renascence of 1922—that they would be able to produce a few pictures each year with sufficient box-office appeal to win them a place on the first-run screens—was not working out at all well. Occasionally an independent production broke through the lines of Paramount, First National and Loew to win success, but even in such instances victory was merely temporary, leading to nothing substantial or permanent.

While Pathé was distributing Harold Lloyd's productions this comedian became very popular, but Paramount presently acquired distribution of Lloyd pictures. Hodkinson distributed "Down to the Sea in Ships," by Elmer Clifton, introducing a new girl, Clara Bow, The picture won a long list of first-run showings, but B. P. Schulberg, recognizing Clara Bow's box-office appeal, placed her under contract, and soon she appeared on the Paramount list. Goldwyn got a few pictures that ran into good earnings, among them "The Spoilers," remade by Jesse Durham Hampton from Rex Beach's novel, in which Milton Sills played the lead; First National promptly made a star of Sills.

From time to time other producers and distributors, aside from the leading theater-owning groups, hit the bull's eye of popular approval with individual pictures, but these isolated successes were far from sufficient to meet the heavy costs of their exchange systems and the extravagances of studio operations. When First National became its own producer, sending one or more pictures weekly to the screens of its thousands of exhibitors, the position of independents became acute, and when Marcus Loew purchased the Metro studios, the Loew theaters naturally gave preference to Metro product. With the screens of Paramount, Loew and First National closed to independents, they were left helpless. They could spend $200,000 to $500,000 on each picture in a series of two dozen or more a year, but they could not rent them to enough houses to recover their costs. One in ten, or one in twenty, might be profitable, but the remainder of a season's output merely added large figures in red ink to their balance-sheets.

One by one, the most optimistic producer-distributors were compelled to face the fact that domination of the industry had definitely passed from manufacturers to retailers. The first-run theaters were the administrators of the movies, and the power of assured profits was concentrated in the hands of the few men who controlled a few hundred of the great houses. Before these manufacturer-exhibitors sent money to the studios, they knew that their theaters would recover the costs of a season's studio operations, and usually enough more than the costs to insure a profit on production, in addition to the theater profit. Zukor had analyzed the situation correctly in his statement to the Kuhn, Loeb banking group in 1919. With the assurance of abundant showings and a fair division of receipts between theaters and studios, the theater-owning manufacturers were in far better position to endure the extravagances of out-spending than were their non-theater-owning competitors. Theater receipts *always* rolled into the owners' pockets; very infrequently did they find their way into independent pockets.

Capitalists and investment bankers, studying the trend of the time, grew fearful of advancing money to any film enterprises except the largest and most powerful, and financiers allied with independent producers and distributors began to look for the way out. One by one, corporations and individuals heretofore famous and apparently substantially established, closed their doors or lost their identity in mergers, and passed on to join their ancient foes, the patents trust and General Film, in the Happy Hunting Ground. Although he struggled hard to avoid the inevitable, the various enterprises of the colorful Lewis Selznick went into bankruptcy, his play rights and similar assets passing to Universal, where his movie career began, for less than $100,000. Selznick entered the real-estate business, and his sons, Myron and David, continued the family name in movies as supervisors in Metro-Goldwyn-Mayer and Paramount studios.*

Reorganization of the Goldwyn company placing Frank Joseph Godsol in the president's chair, Samuel Goldwyn moved to Hollywood, and joining United Artists, embarked on a new career as personal producer of two or three fine specials a year. Godsol's health failed and early in 1924 the Goldwyn corporations, Metro, and Louis B. Mayer's producing companies were consolidated under the name of Metro-Goldwyn-Mayer, with Mayer at the head. Loew's, Inc., the owner of Metro, controlled the M-G-M corporation, which concentrated its activities in the Goldwyn studio in Culver City and soon became a producer equal in size and importance to Paramount.

Jeremiah Milbank reorganized the W. W. Hodkinson Company, changing the name to Producers Distributing Company. He appointed F. L. Munroe president, and Hodkinson retired to his books and fishing tackle on Long Island. Raymond Pawley remained with the company for several years, retiring in 1927. Cecil DeMille resigned from Paramount in January, 1925, to become one of the principal owners of Producers Distributing

---

* In 1926-27 Lewis Selznick re-entered pictures by obtaining management of Associated Exhibitors, Inc., an affiliate of Pathé. Although he summoned forth his old-time daring, shrewdness, and resourcefulness, success was denied him— talkies suddenly appeared, and, as Associated was not prepared for sound films, it passed away. Lewis Selznick moved to Los Angeles. In 1928-29, there was organized in Hollywood, under Myron Selznick's name, a corporation that soon became very successful as the agent of players, directors, and writers. It was believed that the hand of the father could be detected in the son's profitable operations. In 1931, David Selznick resigned from Paramount and organized a producing company, and the Selznick name again appeared on the screen.

Company, and took charge of all its producing. About the same time, P D C made an alliance with the Keith-Albee-Orpheum circuit of vaudeville theaters, and a little later Pathé and P D C were merged under the name of Pathé.

Vitagraph, the sole survivor of General Film, was purchased by Warner Brothers.

Robertson-Cole passed through a reorganization and was re-named "Film Booking Office of America, Inc.," shortened in trade parlance to F B O. Joseph Kennedy, a Boston banker, came into the management of F B O, and in 1928, F B O and Keith-Albee-Orpheum were consolidated by the financial group con-nected with Radio Corporation of America, the title of the new company being "Radio-Keith-Orpheum." * When Radio Cor-poration of America entered R-K-O, the officers of Keith-Albee-Orpheum retired, Radio nominating their successors, of whom Hiram C. Brown was the chief. Pathé passed to the control of R-K-O, and Cecil DeMille left the Pathé organization, joining Metro-Goldwyn-Mayer to produce one or two large pictures a year.

By adding Fox, Universal, Hearst, Columbia, Tiffany—a com-parative newcomer of the same general type as Columbia—and United Artists, this brief roll-call includes all the names of pic-ture producers or distributors of any prominence surviving after the smoke of battle had cleared away. The other members of the lusty army that had fought strenuously for three decades had disappeared. This handful remained.

In the field of short subjects, Educational Film Company, dis-tributing Kinograms (a news reel), travels, and the comedies of several manufacturers, and Amedee J. Van Beuren were almost alone; Mack Sennett, Harold Lloyd, Christie Brothers, and Hal Roach were the principal remaining comedy producers. Short subjects had never been manufactured by Paramount and Metro-Goldwyn-Mayer until 1927, when each entered this branch,

---

* As Radio Corporation of America owns National Broadcasting Company, the R-K-O merger marked the first union of movies and radio, the two modern forms of entertainment. Adolph Zukor later acquired for Paramount a half in-terest in Columbia Broadcasting Company.

Paramount organizing its own staff to gather photographic news, while M-G-M contracted with Hearst, from whom Universal also obtained its news, for this service. Paramount, already distributing Lloyd's comedies, took over the output of Christie Brothers, and M-G-M added Hal Roach's products to its list.

During the years of extravagant studio competition, Carl Laemmle steered a safe middle course with Universal. He produced one or two large specials or super-specials each year, and several features of more than ordinary quality, typified by "The Cohens and the Kellys," which cost about $150,000 and earned $2,000,000, and "Uncle Tom's Cabin," which cost nearly $2,000,000 and failed to arouse a generation that had never heard of Harriet Beecher Stowe and had forgotten the Uncle Tom troupes that had barnstormed the country before nickelodeons brought in a new form of entertainment. Otherwise, Universal's important screen plays covered a wide field of historical and modern subjects, most of which were directly profitable and indirectly valuable as "window dressing" for the rental of the company's westerns and other low-cost features and comedies, which Laemmle continued to supply to smaller theaters long after General Film, Mutual and many of his other competitors of early years had passed into history. Universal's careful cultivation of the humble exhibitor trade gave the corporation a healthy annual balance-sheet for many years. Laemmle financed his business with its own profits until 1925, when he sold an issue of $3,000,000 of preferred stock through Wall Street, retaining for himself a majority of the common or voting stock, with Cochrane as an important minority stockholder.

Universal had acquired theaters in several large cities prior to 1925, and in that year, Laemmle allied himself with Shields and Company, investment bankers, to organize Universal Theaters Corporation. Several hundred houses, principally in small cities, were purchased or built by this corporation and its subsidiaries, and these theaters, although not comparable in size or strength to those of Paramount, Loew or Fox, gave Laemmle a moderately firm trading position until talking pictures swept into popularity and wrought a drastic change in all conditions.

Producers specializing in low-cost features, the studios grouped in movie parlance as "Poverty Row," and state's rights exchanges handling this class of film, were almost wholly exterminated during the battle of bankrolls. The only noteworthy company to endure was Columbia Pictures, owned by Joe Brandt and Jack and Harry Cohn, the three lads who had started business life as office boys in my advertising agency. When the market for cheap features was destroyed, Brandt and the Cohns evolved a clever method of producing high-class photoplays at moderate prices. The principal element of their system consisted of thorough preparation in advance of camera work—"shooting on paper"; the other money-saving practice was the employment of expensive artists by the day instead of the week.

During the years of great expansion in the industry, from 1919 to 1926, and particularly after all-star photoplays became popular, favorite actors and actresses were in great demand and many of them declined to make annual contracts with producers, finding it more profitable to sell their services as free-lances by the week. Numerous players often worked in two pictures at the same time, camera schedules being arranged so that the actor or actress would appear at one studio for a few days and then go to another for a few days. In this manner, some players obtained more than fifty-two weeks of employment a year, Noah Beery establishing a record with seventy-four weeks in twelve months. In order to include a famous box-office name in each production, Columbia perfected a practice of "bunching" all scenes in which an expensive actor or actress appeared so that the shooting of these scenes could be done in a few days. Thus, they would engage for the stellar rôle Betty Compson, Claire Windsor or another star for the period needed, often paying more than their regular weekly salary on a per diem basis. The star was supported by famous leads and character players, hired on the same system, and so Columbia pictures went to the screen with attractive casts of celebrated players. Columbia stuck to its own

methods of making good pictures at moderate costs, rigidly restraining its expenses to the limit of attainable rentals in second-
run houses, with occasional showings on first-run screens. This
practical policy kept the company out of range of the heavy ar-
tillery of high-cost studios, and enabled Brandt and the Cohns
to remain in business after larger and wealthier companies had
crumbled to dust. When talkies swept the country, Columbia
arranged for licenses to use sound-recording devices and swung
their productions into line with new demands.

They had established their company with their own savings
and the profits of their pictures, and other modest financing
from private sources. Lacking the large capital to organize Columbia exchanges, they distributed through state's rights offices,
and from time to time bought an exchange of their own. In
1929, they consolidated their studios and exchanges and bought
other exchanges to complete a national distributing organization.
A Wall Street banking house refinanced the corporation, selling
an issue of its securities to the public and listing the shares on
stock exchanges.

William Randolph Hearst may be placed at the other pole of
movie operation from Columbia. At various times, Hearst owned
several producing and distributing companies, the range of his
product extending from news reels and two-reel serials to the
photoplays released as "Cosmopolitan Pictures." As changes in
public demand brought about corresponding changes in production methods, several of his companies outlived their usefulness
and were retired; his interests eventually were concentrated in
Cosmopolitan, with Marion Davies as it principal star, and in
his international camera news organization. Cosmopolitan Pictures were distributed by Paramount until the consolidation of
Metro, Goldwyn and Mayer, when they were transferred to the
latter organization. Hearst maintained a large studio in the east
for several years, but after the war he joined the general migra-
tion to Los Angeles, and in later years all his features have been
produced at the M-G-M studio in Culver City.

Despite the multiplicity and importance of his newspapers,

magazines, realty holdings, and other properties, Hearst has devoted much time to his picture business, and few producers have derived more enjoyment from the movie game. His film affairs, large or small, have always received his personal attention. When features were beginning to supersede short pictures, Hearst inaugurated the two-reel serial thrillers that became very popular, selecting as a star Irene Castle, then famous as a dancer. When five-reels became the vogue he produced a program of features with Alma Rubens and several other stars; and when the "bigger and better" movement got under way he responded with many expensive super-specials, "Humoresque," with an all-star cast, directed by Frank Borzage, and Marion Davies in "When Knighthood was in Flower," being among his first; when talkies reached a point of mechanical possibility, he produced "The Broadway Melody," a talking and singing picture generally recognized as one of the best sound productions of the early see-and-hear period.

The production of expensive pictures gave Hearst an outlet for some of the urge that had made of him one of America's foremost patrons of art. The collections that adorn his several homes in the east and the west represent an outlay of thirty or forty million dollars. In accumulating these treasures, he acquired an extensive knowledge, and he can qualify as an expert in most branches of the fine arts. When he focused his attention on movie settings, furniture, costumes, and other details, the results were interesting—and frequently very expensive. No outlay of brains, effort, or money was too great for Cosmopolitan Pictures. "Sets" and "props" involving small fortunes were made and remade until Hearst approved them as authentic. A wig worn by Marion Davies in one picture cost $1,200. The floral detail of a frieze— a detail that would never have been noticed by one in a million movie-goers—was incorrect, and a set costing $40,000 was rebuilt to satisfy the Cosmopolitan producer's taste.

On another occasion a medieval sailing ship had been built on a huge stage from drawings and designs by Joseph Urban.

The vessel was decorated with elaborate carvings, faithful to the period, but Hearst observed that it was painted in monotone.

"Weren't the carvings on royal galleons always decorated with bright paints and gold leaf?" he asked, after expressing admiration of the workmanship.

The technical experts answered in the affirmative, saying that Urban's sketches were in colors, but, as dull paint would photograph as effectively as colors and gold, they had used monotone to avoid the expense of decorations.

"Let's have it done right," suggested the chief. "I think the players will enter more enthusiastically into the spirit of the story if the ship looks as it would have looked in reality."

Hearst owns a few theaters, the Ziegfeld and the Circle in New York, and one or two others used for musical comedy and spoken drama, but these have been acquired as real-estate operations and are not connected with his motion picture business. He has never interested himself in screen houses, the reason perhaps being that he finds his fun in picture making and is willing to leave to others the more certain emoluments that arise from less exciting branches of the industry.

CHAPTER FIFTEEN

THE SILENT FILM'S APEX

ONE of the many producers unable to survive the concentration of theater ownership and the excesses of the spending era was Herbert Lubin, who one day in 1925 found himself no longer engaged in the manufacture of photoplays, without money, and shouldered with corporations that had liabilities of a million dollars or so and a few doubtful assets. He had long dreamed of building the world's largest theater, and he made the dream come true—while out of funds and heavily in debt.

The Roxy, in the Longacre Square district of New York, is the substantial evidence of his accomplishment. Representing an investment of about $12,000,000, the Roxy is the most extraordinary of the hundreds of "palaces of the people." Its auditorium seats 6,200 people, with room for an additional 2,000 in lobbies and lounge rooms; the stage is large enough for several hundred players and dancers; an orchestra platform, with three organ consoles and a hundred musicians, rises from the basement to stage level; there are dressing-rooms for two or three hundred actors, singers, and dancers, and offices for two hundred officials and employees; 8,000 people often assemble at one time under the Roxy roof.

Lubin was born in New York in 1886, and is in no way related to Sigmund Lubin, the Philadelphia film pioneer. He had

the public-school training and the odd-jobs experience of a Manhattan boyhood, and then became salesman of real estate, life
insurance, or anything else that he could sell. The movies attracted him; he sold films for state's rights exchanges, prospered,
and engaged in buying and selling pictures. Shortly after the
World War he formed a producing company with Herbert
Sawyer under the name of Sawyer-Lubin, distributing through
First National and Metro. One of their stars was Barbara LaMarr
and when costly pictures became popular, Sawyer-Lubin made a
series of expensive productions starring her, obtaining the necessary capital in New York and New England. The girl was
stricken with an incurable disease, and unfortunate gossip, much
of it unfounded, spread among movie fans and adversely affected
her popularity. After a few months of suffering, she died, and as
the death of a screen favorite means an immediate loss of audience interest in the celebrity's productions, her films were assets
of very doubtful value. All of Lubin's capital was invested in his
companies, which now had liabilities of more than a million
dollars, and practically nothing but the dubious earnings of La
Marr pictures with which to pay them. The star's illness and
death occurred at the time when First National, M-G-M, and all
other leading companies had ceased distributing independent
productions. Lubin's chance of getting another opportunity to
produce was very remote, and even if such an opportunity should
arise, the difficulty of obtaining capital was almost insurmountable.

While his prospects were at their blackest, Lubin was filling
out the details of a vision of a great theater, the largest and finest
in the world. Day after day he paced the streets in and adjacent
to Longacre Square, studying real estate, asking prices, and
building, in imagination, his titanic movie palace. One day his
wanderings brought him to the corner of Seventh Avenue and
Fiftieth Street, where Bing and Bing, real estate operators, had
bought the old street-car barns, covering a large block extending
from Sixth to Seventh Avenues, and from Fiftieth to Fifty-first
Streets. A sign announced that they were offering the land in

parcels. Lubin stopped on the corner and did some hard thinking. The location was good, save for the fact that, according to
the theater "sharps," a house must be on Broadway to draw the
crowds. But this point did not worry Lubin. He would build a
theater so attractive people would come from Broadway to see
it. The real problem was where to find the money.

Money or no money, he decided to talk to the agent, and entered the small, temporary office in one corner of the old barn
building. On the wall was a large map of the property, which
Lubin studied for a few minutes, and, marking a piece of about
an acre and a half, asked the agent, a pleasant, middle-aged man,
for the price of the parcel. A few minutes' calculation placed the
value of the marked acre at $3,000,000.

"What is your smallest down payment on it?" Lubin inquired,
and the pleasant realtor replied that $500,000 would be sufficient
to hold the purchase for a reasonable time.

"I'll take it," said Lubin, and then he introduced himself to
the surprised agent, William Guthman, who had never before
sold so much real estate in five minutes, and outlined his dream
of a great theater. Guthman believed so enthusiastically in the
idea that he agreed to execute an agreement of sale for a down
payment of $25,000, Lubin binding himself to pay $100,000 each
thirty days until the initial half-million should be covered, with
customary terms thereafter. The agreement was drawn up and
signed, and Lubin wrote his check for $25,000.

"I wish you'd hold this for a few days," he said. "I haven't
that much money now, but I'll raise it within a week."

Guthman smiled and consented.

Lubin raised the $25,000 from friends in New York, and ob-
tained the remainder of the half-million from the men to whom
his producing company was in debt. Then all he needed was a
million or so to pay the balance on the purchase price of the land,
and ten or eleven millions more to build the theater and equip it.
Raising ten or twelve million dollars was not easy. In fact it was
a task so difficult that Lubin had to perform miracles to accomplish it.

Paramount owned the Rialto and the Rivoli, and was building a magnificent 4,500-seat theater and skyscraper office building in Times Square at a cost of six or eight million dollars. Loew was completing a large, modern house just across the way on Seventh Avenue, and through Metro-Goldwyn-Mayer controlled the Capitol. First National had the Strand. Motion-picture experts, bankers, and capitalists were exceedingly dubious about a venture that proposed to compete with these powerful corporations. Even if Lubin should succeed in building his giant house, there might be no producer from whom it could obtain a steady supply of high-class pictures. Each of the big companies would use its best productions on its own screens, and as Fox, the only important producer not already represented in the Broadway district, had announced his intention of building a new theater, his films would not be available to the Roxy.

Week after week, Lubin visited one investment banker after another, only to have each of them decline his proposition, but he plugged along, following every Wall Street lead he could discover, until he reached Charles Richardson of Pope, Richardson and Company, and Harold Roberts, of Mulliken and Roberts. Richardson, before becoming a banker, had been connected with William Fox and had learned the possibilities and the psychology of the movie game. Roberts had been business manager of *Munsey's Magazine* in its youth, advertising manager of the Tobacco Trust, president of the Havana Tobacco Company, and publisher of *McClure's Magazine*. His experiences had given him a broad point of view toward the entertainment industries. These bankers listened to Lubin, and convinced of the soundness of his ideas, underwrote an issue of preferred stock with a bonus of common, in all about $5,000,000. S. W. Straus and Company, specialists in realty bonds, took the Roxy corporation's senior security, a bond issue of $4,250,000, and Lubin raised the balance of the needed money by selling stock to friends, to manufacturers of seats, carpets and other equipment, to the architects, the builders and the excavators.

IN Stillwater, Minn., Gustav Rothapfel, a shoe repairer, had an active son named Samuel, who led a gang of youngsters in keeping Stillwater in hot water until the family moved to New York in 1894. Sammie joined the U. S. Marines, and after seeing the world for a while went back to citizen's clothes and became a book agent. In a mining town in Pennsylvania he fell in love with a barkeeper's daughter, married her, and joined his father-in-law in running the saloon. When screen movies appeared he persuaded his father-in-law to open a film show in an empty room above the saloon. He developed so many ideas about the exhibition of pictures that one little show shop did not hold him long. He moved to larger and larger theaters, until Mitchell Mark made him manager of the Strand, in New York, where he remained until Crawford Livingstone and Otto Kahn built the Rialto on the site of Hammerstein's music hall, at Forty-second Street. Rothapfel became manager of the Rialto.

In the Rothapfel viewpoint there was no limit to the possibilities of popular entertainment. He wanted a great orchestra and fine music, great singers, a great ballet; if a picture was good, these additional features brought more people to the box-office, and if a picture was not good, the orchestra, the singing and the dancing, flowers and paintings in the lobby, and ushers trained to meticulous politeness, made patrons comfortable and happy and induced them to come again. Although he became a very successful assembler of larger audiences, there were times when his expenditures for constantly more gorgeous entertainment brought acute distress to the owners of theaters in which his talents were displayed. Rothapfel answered criticisms by insisting that lapse in profits was due not to his methods but to the size of the theaters; his entertainments, he declared, could draw more people than existing houses could seat. When the Capitol Theater was built it was, with its 4,000 seats, the largest movie theater in New York, and Rothapfel, engaged as manager, gloried in the largest orchestra and largest stage he had ever had; his music and spectacular choruses and ballets attracted huge audiences, even though profits were sometimes reduced by his extraordinary expenditures.

When radio became popular, and many theater owners were fighting it as a menace to the movies, Rothapfel took the opposite view, and, deciding that broadcasting could be used to advertise his playhouse and himself, organized a group of air entertainers, "Roxy's gang," with Roxy himself as announcer. His musical selections for orchestra and vocalists struck the popular fancy exactly right, and millions of sets tuned in weekly to listen to Roxy's program, which included a glowing description of the current entertainment at the Capitol Theater.

LUBIN was personally acquainted with the managers of all the important theaters, and, reviewing the list, to select the most spectacular for the most spectacular house which he hoped to build, decided on Roxy as the only man for his theater. Roxy knew New York, and New York knew Roxy. His ideas in entertainment coincided with Lubin's, and in the new house he would have the things he had been clamoring for—the biggest auditorium, the biggest orchestra, the biggest stage, the biggest radio room—everything the biggest in the world. He concluded to see Roxy, offer him a large salary, a block of stock, a percentage of the profits, and to name the house after him. Rothapfel liked the idea, and after obtaining Lubin's assurance that he would be permitted to spend any amounts to present his elaborate stage spectacles, entered into the project.

Throughout the undertaking, from inception to completion, Lubin preferred the emoluments of a promoter to the glory of an exhibitor, and remained in the background; Rothapfel was president of the company and the spotlight of publicity was centered exclusively on him. Lubin was satisfied with his fee as promoter from the investment bankers, and with his control of the common or voting stock; he took no official position of any kind in the corporation.

Erection of the Roxy started in 1925; the theater was com-

pleted and ready for opening in the spring of 1927. Building and
equipping theaters is work of such infinite and peculiar detail
that contractors will not undertake such construction for a specified sum. The Roxy was built on a cost-plus basis, and when
the opening day drew near, Lubin knew that he faced a deficit—
or an "over-run" in costs—of about $2,500,000, and an over-run
is not a pretty thing to finance. The bond bankers had protected
themselves with an underlying mortgage, and the stock bankers
had safeguarded share-holders by making their preferred stock a
lien junior only to the bond mortgage. An over-run of $2,500,000
simply meant that bondholders and preferred stockholders had
just that much more property behind their securities, while
Lubin, promoter and controlling holder of common stock, had
to raise the money to take care of the over-run, or lose his holdings in a foreclosure procedure.

Secrets in the movie world simply do not exist, and everyone
in Times Square and Longacre Square gossiped about the over-
run, the general opinion being that Lubin would not be able
to finance the additional sum. Other theater owners were sure
that the money would not be raised and that even if it were and
the theater opened, Roxy's extravagance would run it into bankruptcy. Wall Street unanimously declined to produce additional
financing, and as the huge house moved steadily toward opening
day, the specter of over-run haunted the young promoter through
waking and sleeping hours.

During the later months of construction, A. C. Blumenthal,
theater scout for William Fox, frequently visited Lubin, and
joked with him about the hard job of gauging an over-run in
advance, the difficulty of this last piece of financing, and the uncertainty of obtaining pictures when all principal producers had
their own theaters. He tried to induce him to sell his stock to
Fox and to retire on his profits. Lubin invariably replied that he
was perfectly willing to sell to Fox, but he insisted that the Roxy
would prove to be a very profitable theater and he demanded an
apparently impossible price for his holdings. Lubin's own belief
was that the Roxy's box-office receipts would average $100,000 a

week, a figure that would show a handsome profit on the total capitalization, including the common stock.

Blumenthal could not agree with this prediction of earnings. Theater receipts had increased enormously in the last few years, but, reviewing the intakes of the largest, most popular New York houses, very great optimism was needed to see the soundness of Lubin's contention. The Capitol had been remodeled and its seating capacity increased to 5,300. Its normal gross receipts were $50,000, running as high as $65,000 perhaps once a year, because of some extraordinary attraction. The Strand, with 2,900 seats and normal receipts of $25,000 to $35,000, broke all records the week that Charlie Chaplin's "Gold Rush" brought $72,000 to the box office. The Rivoli had 2,200 seats, and its normal receipts ran $20,-000 to $25,000, exceptional weeks bringing in as high as $35,000. The bankers who had underwritten the Roxy bonds and stocks had accepted the calculation of experts that the Roxy could expect normal gross receipts of $65,000 to $70,000, and in exceptional weeks, $80,000 to $85,000.

As the theater neared completion, the owners of several chains located throughout the country looked with longing eyes at this titan and negotiated for Lubin with his stock, but they backed away when they learned the price. Blumenthal persisted, scarcely a day passing in which he did not plead with Lubin to "get down to earth and name a figure that a sane man will pay."

One night, a week before the theater was to open, Blumenthal took William Fox into the Roxy. A regiment of workmen was rushing day and night to complete the interior decorations, lay the last carpet, screw down the last chair. An orchestra of one hundred and ten pieces was rehearsing. In a practice room a ballet master was training two hundred dancers. The superintendent of ushers was polishing his crew of one hundred and twenty young men to the highest lustre of courtesy. Everywhere were the sights and sounds of tense activity so that at the appointed hour six thousand two hundred selected patrons would witness the inauguration of "the cathedral of motion pictures." In the list of invited guests were high officials of federal, state, and city governments, great bankers, famous business men, notables from the world of science, literature, art, drama, music.

William Fox strolled quietly through the vast edifice, observing everything, and saying little. Perhaps memories crowded his mind. Thirty years is not a long time. His own first little show shops...a shooting gallery with kinetoscopes...a nickelodeon....The audiences of all his early theaters could have been seated in one section of this auditorium. The cost of the Roxy represented a sum larger than the total investment in all his theaters, his studios, his exchanges, only a few years ago. Once, nickels were pushed into a flimsy ticket window by workingmen and children; and now first nighters were paying speculators ten to twenty-five dollars each for seats with the distinguished audience that would fill the Roxy next week....The movies had traveled a long journey in the three decades since William Fox first knew them.

Somewhere in the turmoil and confusion of the army of artisans and workmen, Blumenthal led his chief to a small man in shirt sleeves, perspiring and dust-stained, his normally husky voice hoarsened to a croak with nervous tension and lack of sleep —somewhere they found Herbert Lubin, and in a few minutes William Fox had bought the controlling interest in the Roxy corporations for about $5,000,000. After debts were wiped out and settlements were completed, the Fox payments would deliver to Lubin more than $3,000,000 for his promotional labors.

THE success of the Roxy theater exceeded the most optimistic expectations. Its gross business one week in its first year was $135,000; its average in-take was in excess of $100,000 a week. The large attendance at the Roxy did not reduce attendance at neighboring theaters. Loew's new house and the new Paramount, opening prior to the Roxy, were filled nightly, and the Capitol, the Strand, the Rivoli, and the Rialto continued to roll up big records.

Acquisition of the Roxy was an important event, but only one

95A. *Chang*, THE ANIMAL PICTURE MADE IN THE JUNGLES OF SIAM BY
ERNEST B. SCHOEDSACK AND MERIAN C. COOPER. RELEASED BY PARAMOUNT
IN 1927.

95B. A PORTION OF THE ACTUAL FILM FROM *Chang*.

96A. *It*, WITH CLARA BOW AND ANTONIO MORENO. DIRECTED BY CLARENCE BADGER FROM A STORY BY ELINOR GLYN. PRODUCED BY PARAMOUNT IN 1927.

96B. *Seventh Heaven*, WITH JANET GAYNOR, CHARLES FARRELL, AND GLADYS BROCKWELL. DIRECTED BY FRANK BORZAGE FROM THE PLAY BY AUSTIN STRONG. PRODUCED BY FOX IN 1927.

97A. *The King of Kings*, WITH JOSEPH STRIKER, H. B. WARNER, AND JOSEPH SCHILDKRAUT. DIRECTED BY CECIL B. DEMILLE FROM THE SCREEN PLAY BY JEANIE MACPHERSON. PRODUCED BY PATHÉ IN 1927.

97B. *The King of Kings*. MONTAGU LOVE AS THE CENTURION, VICTOR VARCONI AS PILATE, AND RUDOLPH SCHILDKRAUT AS CAIAPHAS.

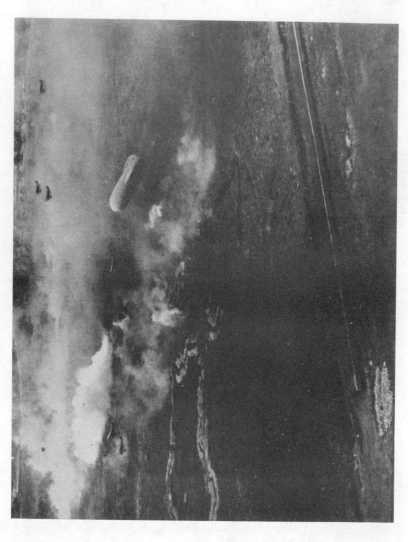

98. *Wings*. DIRECTED BY WILLIAM WELLMAN. PRODUCED BY PARAMOUNT, 1927.

99. PRESIDENT COOLIDGE PRESENTING THE CONGRESSIONAL MEDAL OF HONOR TO COL. CHARLES A. LINDBERGH. FOX MOVIETONE, 1928.

100A. *Chicago*, WITH PHYLLIS HAVER. DIRECTED BY FRANK URSON FROM THE PLAY BY MAURINE WATKINS. PRODUCED BY PATHÉ-DEMILLE IN 1928.

100B. *Sadie Thompson*, WITH GLORIA SWANSON AND RAOUL WALSH. DIRECTED BY RAOUL WALSH FROM THE STORY BY W. SOMERSET MAUGHAM. PRODUCED FOR UNITED ARTISTS IN 1928.

IOIA. *The Jazz Singer*, WITH AL JOLSON AND MAY MCAVOY. DIRECTED BY ALAN CROSLAND. PRODUCED BY WARNER BROTHERS IN 1927.

IOIB. *Lights of New York*, THE FIRST FULL-LENGTH TALKING PICTURE MADE. DIRECTED BY BRIAN FOY AND PRODUCED BY WARNER BROS. IN 1928.

102A: *The Rawhide Kid*, WITH HOOT GIBSON AND ED HENDERSHOT. DIRECTED BY DEL ANDREWS. PRODUCED BY UNIVERSAL IN 1927.

102B. *The Crowd*, WITH ELEANOR BOARDMAN AND JAMES MURRAY. DIRECTED BY KING VIDOR. PRODUCED BY M-G-M IN 1928.

103A. *The Last Command*, WITH EMIL JANNINGS. DIRECTED BY JOSEF VON STERNBERG. PRODUCED BY PARAMOUNT IN 1928.

103B. *Interference*, WITH DORIS KENYON AND WILLIAM POWELL. SILENT VERSION DIRECTED BY LOTHAR MENDES, SOUND VERSION BY JOHN J. POMEROY, FROM THE PLAY BY ROLAND PERTWEE AND HAROLD DEARDEN. PRODUCED BY PARAMOUNT IN 1928.

104A. *The Broadway Melody*, WITH BESSIE LOVE, ANITA PAGE, AND CHARLES KING. DIRECTED BY HARRY BEAUMONT. PRODUCED BY COSMOPOLITAN FOR M-G-M IN 1929.

104B. A SET FROM *Broadway*. DIRECTED BY PAUL FEJOS FROM THE PLAY BY PHILIP DUNNING AND GEORGE ABBOT. PRODUCED BY CARL LAEMMLE, JR. FOR UNIVERSAL IN 1929.

105A. *Hallelujah,* WITH DANIEL HAYNES AND NINA MAY MCKENNY. THE FIRST ALL-NEGRO PICTURE, DIRECTED BY KING VIDOR. PRODUCED BY M-G-M IN 1929.

105B. ANOTHER SCENE FROM *Hallelujah,* WITH VICTORIA SPIVEY.

106A. A DANCING SCENE FROM *Rio Rita*. DIRECTED BY LUTHER REED, FROM THE MUSICAL COMEDY BY GUY BOLTON AND FRED THOMPSON. PRODUCED BY WILLIAM LE BARON FOR R-K-O IN 1929.

106B. *Untamed*, WITH JOAN CRAWFORD. DIRECTED BY JACK CONWAY. PRODUCED BY M-G-M IN 1929.

107B. *Moby Dick*, WITH JOHN BARRYMORE AND JOAN BENNETT. DIRECTED BY LLOYD BACON. PRODUCED BY WARNER BROS. IN 1930. THIS WAS THE TALKIE VERSION OF *The Sea Beast*, ALSO BASED ON HERMAN MELVILLE'S NOVEL, AND MADE BY BARRYMORE IN 1926 AS A SILENT PICTURE.

107A. *The Phantom of the Opera*, WITH LON CHANEY AND MARY PHILBIN. DIRECTED BY RUPERT JULIAN FROM THE NOVEL BY GASTON LEROUX. PRODUCED BY UNIVERSAL. THIS PICTURE WAS FIRST MADE IN 1925 AS A SILENT FILM, AND RELEASED AGAIN IN 1930, WITH THE ADDITION OF SOUND, AS A SYNCHRONIZED PICTURE.

108A. *The Big Kick*, WITH HARRY LANGDON. DIRECTED BY HAL ROACH. PRODUCED BY M-G-M IN 1930.

108B. *Pardon Us*, WITH STAN LAUREL AND OLIVER HARDY. DIRECTED BY JAMES PARROTT. PRODUCED BY HAL ROACH FOR M-G-M IN 1931.

109A. *A Woman of Affairs*, WITH GRETA GARBO, JOHN GILBERT, AND HOBART BOSWORTH. DIRECTED BY CLARENCE BROWN FROM MICHAEL ARLEN'S NOVEL, *The Green Hat*. PRODUCED BY M-G-M IN 1929.

109B. *The Common Law*, WITH CONSTANCE BENNETT, LEW CODY, HEDDA HOPPER, AND JOEL MCCREA. DIRECTED BY PAUL STEIN FROM THE NOVEL BY ROBERT W. CHAMBERS. PRODUCED BY R-K-O-PATHÉ IN 1931.

110A. *All Quiet on the Western Front*, WITH LEW AYRES AND LOUIS WOLHEIM. DIRECTED BY LEWIS MILESTONE FROM THE NOVEL BY ERICH MARIA REMARQUE. PRODUCED BY CARL LAEMMLE, JR. FOR UNIVERSAL IN 1930.

110B. *Morocco*, WITH MARLENE DIETRICH AND GARY COOPER. DIRECTED BY JOSEF VON STERNBERG. PRODUCED BY PARAMOUNT IN 1930.

IIIA. MARIE DRESSLER IN *Anna Christie.* DIRECTED BY CLARENCE BROWN FROM THE PLAY BY EUGENE O'NEILL. PRODUCED BY M-G-M IN 1930.

IIIB. *Little Cæsar,* WITH EDWARD G. ROBINSON. DIRECTED BY MERVYN LEROY FROM THE NOVEL BY R. W. BURNETT. PRODUCED BY FIRST NATIONAL IN 1931.

112A. *Laughter*, WITH NANCY CARROLL AND FREDRIC MARCH. DIRECTED BY HARRY D'ARRAST. PRODUCED BY PARAMOUNT IN 1930.

112B. *The Royal Family of Broadway*, WITH INA CLAIRE, FREDRIC MARCH, MARY BRIAN, AND HENRIETTA CROSMAN. DIRECTED BY GEORGE ZUKOR AND CYRIL GARDNER, FROM THE PLAY BY EDNA FERBER AND GEORGE S. KAUFMAN. PRODUCED BY PARAMOUNT IN 1931.

113A. *Cimarron*, WITH RICHARD DIX AND IRENE DUNNE. DIRECTED BY WESLEY RUGGLES FROM THE NOVEL BY EDNA FERBER. PRODUCED BY WILLIAM LE BARON FOR R K O IN 1931.

113B. THE LAND-RUSH SCENE FROM *Cimarron*.

114A. *A Connecticut Yankee*, WITH WILL ROGERS, WILLIAM FARNUM, BRANDON HURST, AND MITCHELL HARRIS. DIRECTED BY DAVID BUTLER FROM THE NOVEL BY MARK TWAIN. PRODUCED BY FOX IN 1931.

114B. *The Smiling Lieutenant*, WITH MAURICE CHEVALIER AND CLAUDETTE COLBERT. DIRECTED BY ERNST LUBITSCH, FROM THE PLAY *Waltz-Dream* BY ERNST VADJA. PRODUCED BY PARAMOUNT IN 1931.

115A. *Hell's Angels*. PRODUCED BY HOWARD HUGHES FOR UNITED ARTISTS
IN 1930.

115B. *The Front Page*. DIRECTED BY LEWIS MILESTONE FROM THE PLAY BY
BEN HECHT AND CHARLES MACARTHUR. PRODUCED BY HOWARD HUGHES FOR
UNITED ARTISTS IN 1931.

116A. MICKEY MOUSE AND MINNIE MOUSE IN AN ANIMATED CARTOON BY
WALT DISNEY. 1931.

116B. *Big Game,* AN ÆSOP'S FABLES ANIMATED CARTOON PRODUCED
BY AMEDEE J. VAN BEUREN, 1931.

117A. PHOTOGRAPHING A SEQUENCE FROM *Street Scene*. DIRECTED BY KING VIDOR FROM THE PLAY BY ELMER RICE. PRODUCED BY SAMUEL GOLDWYN IN 1931.

117B. *A Free Soul*, WITH NORMA SHEARER, CLARK GABLE, AND LESLIE HOWARD. DIRECTED BY CLARENCE BROWN. PRODUCED BY M-G-M IN 1931.

118A. *The Guardsman*, WITH ALFRED LUNT AND LYNN FONTANNE. DIRECTED BY SIDNEY FRANKLIN FROM THE PLAY BY FERENC MOLNAR. PRODUCED BY M-G-M IN 1931.

118B. *Susan Lenox: Her Fall and Rise*, WITH GRETA GARBO AND CLARK GABLE. DIRECTED BY ROBERT Z. LEONARD FROM THE NOVEL BY DAVID GRAHAM PHILLIPS. PRODUCED

119. THE FOX BEVERLY HILLS STUDIOS IN HOLLYWOOD.

120. THE METRO-GOLDWYN-MAYER STUDIOS, CULVER CITY, CALIFORNIA.

121. THE PARAMOUNT STUDIOS IN HOLLYWOOD.

SOUND STAGE
7-8-9-10

THE 4 STORY
DRESSING ROOM
BUILDING WILL
RISE

WHERE STAGES 5 AND 6
WILL BE ERECTED

ELECTRIC
TRANSFORMER PLANT

NEW SCENE
DOCK

OFFICES
AND
DRESSING
POOM

STAGE 4

OFFICES
AND
DRESSING
ROOMS

STAGE 3

ELECTRIC
DEPT.

MECHANICAL
DEPT.

ADMINISTRATION
BLDG. "A"

ADMINISTRATION
BLDG "B"

MILL

PAINT SHOP

STAGE 2

PROPERTY DEPT
AND OFFICES

OLD SCENE
DOCK

PROJECTION
AND
CUTTING ROOMS

STAGE 1

CAFE

DANCE
REHEARSAL
BLDG.

CUTTING ROOM

ELECTRIC

LAMP
STORAGE

VAULTS

REHEARSAL
HALL

GATE

GARAGES

AUTO PARK

MELROSE   AVE.

122. THE R-K-O STUDIOS, LOS ANGELES.

123. THE UNITED ARTISTS STUDIOS, HOLLYWOOD.

124. UNIVERSAL CITY, CALIFORNIA.

125. WARNER BROTHERS FIRST NATIONAL STUDIOS IN HOLLYWOOD.

of many important events taking place in the affairs of William Fox. Able showman and vigorous fighter, Fox had always played a lone hand from the time he left the garment trades to become the antagonist of the patents trust and General Film. Year after year his own studios manufactured successful box-office pictures with star material discovered or developed by Fox—William Farnum, Theda Bara, Tom Mix, Gladys Brockwell, and others —and Fox made large profits by exhibiting the films in his own houses and renting them to other theaters. No stars except Mary Pickford and Charlie Chaplin ever earned more money per dollar of investment than Farnum and Theda Bara, and it is probable that Tom Mix brought more profits to his employer than any other star ever in the movies.

William Fox, Saul E. Rogers, his attorney from earliest days, and Winfield Sheehan, right-hand man and general factotum, comprised the inner cabinet, and these three were always sufficient unto themselves to cope with every emergency that arose in the turbulent trade. When large capital was needed, Fox had obtained it from financiers, but always retained control of his corporations, none of the voting power ever leaving his hands.

After that memorable milestone, Armistice Day, when a new generation suddenly asserted its power and remade the movies to suit current desires, the closely knit Fox film family began to feel the pressure of the changed order. Young people considered Fox stars out-of-date, and Fox pictures began to slip behind in public favor; his corporations continued to make money, but for a while they were dangerously near standing still, and in the film industry a lack of progress, or hesitation for a short time, had usually meant retrogression and defeat. While the changing tastes of the box office were diminishing his earnings, and the increasing costs of pictures were sending studio expense-sheets to the sky, Zukor, Loew, Mastbaum, and First National were hammering away at Fox's theater position. Fox had been expanding steadily, but not at a pace sufficient to keep abreast of Zukor and Loew, and in many cities they had gone ahead of him by acquiring or building new houses that threw his own into the second class.

Suddenly and dramatically Fox seemed to awaken to the hazard of his position, and moved forcefully to reorganize his affairs. Winfield Sheehan was dispatched to Los Angeles, to take charge of the studio, and to live there and create a new order of picture-making; Fox, bestirring himself to observation and analysis of the theater field, brought A. C. Blumenthal from the west coast to Fox headquarters to hunt out desirable existing houses to be purchased and locations upon which others could be built.

One by one, Fox celebrities faded from the firmament. Fickle youth had distributed its diluted affections among so many exotic ladies, from Barbara LaMarr to Pola Negri and Greta Garbo, that Theda Bara, most famous siren, had disappeared while her professional ability was yet at its height. Married to Charles Brabin, a director, the great Theda retired to their home in Hollywood. William Farnum, with health none too sturdy, returned to the stage; Gladys Brockwell became a free-lance character actress in Los Angeles and built a new reputation for herself; Tom Mix remained with Fox until 1928, when he transferred to F B O (Radio-Keith-Orpheum) for a year, and then "joined out" with Miller Brothers 101 Ranch and Wild West Show—which he had left years before to go with Selig. Later, when his friend John Ringling bought the Sells-Floto circus, Mix became its star.

Lee De Forest, scientist and inventor, had been experimenting for years with sound waves, trying to devise a method to record them on photographic film so that sound and pictures could be projected simultaneously. Theodore W. Case, an engineer in the Fox organization, had been tinkering away at the same problem. William Fox decided that talking pictures must arrive before long; Case was provided with funds and equipment to speed up his experiments, and Fox acquired an option to buy De Forest's patents.

Within a year Fox had made a new program and new policy

for himself, and the revolution wrought in his operations was as drastic as that of Henry Ford in sending the old model flivver to the boneyard and designing a modern, stylish car to meet the new demands of the American people. Winfield Sheehan's administration of the Hollywood studio was quiet and non-sensational, but his results were startling. Somewhere in his career as reporter, Manhattan police-department official, and general handy man for William Fox, Sheehan had acquired an uncanny understanding of the popular mind and a sure hand in devising entertainment that would please it. Fox pictures again leaped into the first rank of popularity, and his profits increased half a million to a million dollars a year.

Sheehan, arriving in Los Angeles at the time when the star system was beginning to crumble under the assaults of the all-star idea, abandoned the individual star method, concentrating on a search for good stories that could be made into effective continuities, and then selecting players who he believed could portray the rôles. The actresses and actors might be famous stars or leads, or they might be new and unknown aspirants; Sheehan cared nothing about their reputations if they were able to play the parts. Minor rôles were cast as carefully as the leads, as for example, in "What Price Glory?", in which two experienced actors, Victor McLaglen and Edmund Lowe, and an unknown girl from Mexico, Dolores Del Rio, divided the honors so evenly that none could be called the star. Another stage play, "Seventh Heaven," by Austin Strong, was adapted to the screen by Benjamin Glazer, a Philadelphia lawyer turned playwright, and made into a picture by Frank Borzage. Two unknown youngsters, Charles Farrell and Janet Gaynor, were found on the Fox lot working in small parts. Sheehan gave them the leads in "Seventh Heaven," and the public made stars of them overnight.

In the theater department of his personal revolution, Fox expanded with a rapidity that took him into Wall Street to obtain twenty-five to fifty million dollars through public financing. Halsey, Stuart and Company became his investment bankers

and shares of Fox corporations were listed on the New York
Stock Exchange and the New York Curb Market. Wherever
he needed theater representation, or where Zukor or Loew or
First National had better houses than he, Fox speedily moved
to place himself in position to cope with any competition. He
built modern houses in important cities from the Atlantic to
the Pacific, from Canada to Mexico. With a succession of splendid pictures coming from Winfield Sheehan to the screens of
fine theaters, Fox soon recovered his lost ground and in a few
years was in a position to rival Paramount.

DURING the orgy of extravagance that obsessed the studios
from 1922 until 1927, when talking pictures wrought a fresh
revolution, the broadening of tastes, noticeable after Armistice
Day, became so unpredictable that producers had nothing substantial upon which to base analyses or guesses. Although June
Mathis and other intellectuals had over-estimated the mental
development of movie audiences, and had failed because of offering themes and treatments that only small groups of theater
patrons were prepared to accept, there were definite signs that
large sections of the public had passed through the infantile
and youthful periods of screen enthusiasm and were entering
into maturity. Methods and rules that seemed, a few years earlier,
to constitute a set of permanent principles, revealed themselves
suddenly as practices subject to change without notice; on the
other hand, producers could not safely dismiss any element as
outworn as there was always the possibility that audiences might
award a million to three million dollars of theater rentals to a
competitor who had made a film out of the same out-of-date
material.

The public attitude toward players had passed through noteworthy modifications. The inevitable candy-sweet pretty girls
and collar-advertisement heroes of an earlier day were losing
their popularity. Girls with charm, or the indefinable quality
of sex appeal, could win a large following even though they did

not qualify as pretty, and heroes might be "homely" and yet satisfy the romantic longings of ticket buyers. Battling male stars now might safely present dirty faces and torn clothing; no longer was it necessary for the hero at the conclusion of a knock-down-and-drag-out encounter with two dozen villains in a western drinking hell to appear in his close-ups as though he had just left his valet. It even became possible occasionally to modify the happy ending. Nevertheless, while realism was apparently encroaching on the romantic idealism heretofore demanded by the movie public, audiences by the millions would pour into theaters to see a film based on a theme that had been pronounced hopelessly old-fashioned. A blind guess seemed to be as effective in predicting results as the most careful and intelligent analysis.

The fate of westerns illustrates the changes that were coming about in entertainment values. Cowboy thrillers had always been "sure-fire money-getters," and their manufacture was one of the principal sub-divisions of the industry. Each large studio made several important westerns every year, and some small producers specialized in features of this class, the output of several grades totaling a hundred or more each season. Broncho Billy retired in 1915-16, but a score of other heroes rose to popularity, Tom Mix and Bill Hart heading the list. With a hundred or more stories of the same type coming to the screen each year for fifteen or sixteen years, the novelty of westerns was completely exhausted. Only a few basic themes were available, and the continuities had settled down to stereotyped forms; most westerns merely repeated the same formula and producers had to employ highly skilful writers to imbue the stories with sufficient interest to carry them. Manufacturers of low-cost features could not afford to pay authors $10,000 to $50,000 for the use of their novels, and, as famous western stars believed that the interest of their followers was firmly set in personality admiration, making story-value of secondary importance, the major portion of the cowboy output persisted in retaining substantially the same production standards as had existed since the early days of features.

After audiences had seen the expensive productions of various themes, including westerns, for several years, the standardized cowboy films lost their magnetic power. Many movie-goers walked away from the "old reliables" and exhibitors became afraid of western subjects. Studios concluded that the final curtain was about to fall on this class of entertainment. And then, just when the end seemed in sight, Paramount made a large, expensive production of Emerson Hough's "The Covered Wagon," directed by James Cruze, and to the surprise of the industry, it was received eagerly by audiences and earned several million dollars. It did not, however, revive the vogue of the single-star, cowboy picture. Audiences continued to enjoy well-made, all-star plays from the novels of Zane Grey and a few other authors, but the demand for standard cowboy-star stories became so slight that within a few years Tom Mix, Bill Hart and all heroes of their type disappeared from the screen. *

This period of uncertainty prompted extensive experimentation. Costume and historical subjects, sacred and secular themes, exotic backgrounds, stories of the underworld, modern novels and plays—everything, in fact, that would pass the Hays censorship, was tested for screen possibilities. Writers became skilled at producing smooth, swift-flowing continuities; architects and artists designed beautiful and convincing sets; directors had progressed in their technique to the point where good direction was common and extraordinary direction frequent; actors and actresses had learned their trades and competent acting became the rule rather than the exception. The chemistry and engineering departments of film-making had made enormous advances. Machine makers, lens grinders, and electrical and chemical laboratories had developed tools so efficient and films so highly

---

* In the autumn of 1931, Carl Laemmle persuaded Tom Mix to return to the screen to make six pictures a year. Buck Jones, another former Fox cowboy star, appeared in Columbia westerns in 1931.

sensitized that expert camera men wrought new beauties of photography.

Cecil DeMille turned from society dramas to "The Ten Commandments" and created a spectacular photoplay that enjoyed long runs at spoken-drama prices. Roy Pomeroy, a technical genius, made the camera perform stunts that seemed like miracles. He divided the Red Sea, permitting the children of Israel to pass over on dry land, and caused the waves to engulf the pursuing host; and when Moses received the tablets of stone on which the Almighty's finger had traced the laws, the scene was one that fascinated scientists and frightened the superstitious. Under the title, "The Phantom of the Opera," Universal made a film in which Lon Chaney proved himself a master of physical and facial make-up. At the other swing of the pendulum Paramount took Herman Hagedorn, who had never been an actor, but resembled Theodore Roosevelt enough to be his double, and made an enjoyable picture of the Spanish War, "The Rough Riders."

The stage led the screen in experiments to determine whether or not the public had recovered sufficiently from the shock of the World War to witness portrayals of its scenes. A play by Lawrence Stallings and Maxwell Anderson, "What Price Glory?", achieved great success on the stage, and picture producers saw a ray of hope through the fog of uncertainties that had been surrounding them. If the public, drifting away from westerns and other melodramas, should now accept pictures of adventure, romance, and heroism in the World War, the screen could supply enough of this material to satisfy them for years. William Fox bought the screen rights of "What Price Glory?", but before he made it into a picture, King Vidor had taken "Plumes," a novel by Lawrence Stallings, and with the assistance of the author and Harry Behn, a brilliant young continuity writer, produced for Metro-Goldwyn-Mayer "The Big Parade," that ran for two years in the Astor Theater, New York, at spoken-drama prices, and was comparably successful everywhere else in America. Vidor's negative cost less than $200,000; the gross receipts of the Astor Theater alone were more than $800,000. "The Big Parade" swept away uncertainties—the World War was a safe recipe for box-office success, and war pictures flooded the screen. William Fox and Winfield Sheehan, however, took their own time to produce "What Price Glory?" and when it appeared in 1926 it proved extremely popular.

The increasing interest of the public in aerial traffic carried the movies into the air. Aeroplane stunt artists from all over the world assembled at Los Angeles and sold their services to the studios by the day, the week, or the stunt. Melodrama, once achieved by a cowboy on a pony, transferred itself to the cockpit or wings of an aeroplane, where wild aviators took chances that sometimes ended in death. Paramount consolidated thrills and heart throbs in "Wings," a massive war and air production that cost $2,000,000 but proved a profitable investment.

Will Hays put his foot down squarely when producers tried to adapt sex plays of the franker types from the stage, but Gloria Swanson defeated even the Czar of the Movies by screening Somerset Maugham's play of the South Seas, "Rain," under the title "Sadie Thompson." True, Sadie's bright crimson was toned down to a glowing pink, but the screen play eluded state and municipal censors and was eagerly received by audiences.

American movies had become a satisfying form of entertainment, but they were being created at costs that were neither profitable nor justifiable. In 1913-14, "The Birth of a Nation" cost $100,000 and made many millions for its owners and many millions for exhibitors. The change in conditions in a dozen years is revealed by such expenditures as these: "Ben Hur," $4,500,000; "The King of Kings," $2,500,000; "The Trail of '98," $2,000,000; "Wings," $2,000,000; "The Rough Riders," $1,600,000; "Old Ironsides," about $1,500,000; "Beau Geste," $900,000; approximately $1,000,000 was invested in each of many productions, such as Norma Talmadge's "Camille," "What Price Glory?", Universal's "The Phantom of the Opera," and others.

The history of "Ben Hur," the most expensive picture ever filmed, dramatized the uneconomic methods of the industry in the era of extravagance and waste. I have placed the cost of this production at four to five millions, using figures from the best sources available, but the real total may be greater; none but the high officials of Metro-Goldwyn-Mayer know the exact figures. The film was started by the Goldwyn corporation, prior to the merger of Metro, Goldwyn and Mayer; and studio officials, believing that authentic Italian backgrounds would be more convincing than sets constructed in Los Angeles, sent writers, technical men, directors, and players to Italy, where they met with political, labor and social difficulties that nearly wrecked the nervous system of every executive. Enormous sums were spent without satisfactory results. When Louis B. Mayer entered the company, he reorganized the entire undertaking, practically starting anew, and made most of the final version of the picture in California. "Ben Hur" was a massive production, but had Mayer's plan been followed from the start, the cost would probably have been somewhere around $2,000,000 and possibly as low as $1,500,000.

Cecil B. DeMille produced "The King of Kings," the life of Christ, at the next highest cost on record, $2,500,000. It is probable that no photoplay will ever excel "The King of Kings" in the authenticity and beauty of its settings, costumes, and other technical details. Historians, artists, craftsmen and skilled workers in half a hundred trades cooperated to reproduce faithfully the settings. The exteriors and interiors of buildings, the garments worn by every character from Pontius Pilate to the humblest beggar, the vehicles, the wineskins, the weapons—each item that appeared on the screen was designed by experts and specially made.

No estimate of the technical qualities of "Ben Hur" and "The King of Kings" can be too high nor too enthusiastic; they were faithful, authentic, and awe-inspiring in their conception and execution. It is probable that they will stand permanently as the highest point of film production, and, if chemists should discover a way to preserve the photographic coating on celluloid, may be considered by future historians, together with Douglas Fairbanks' superb fantasy, "The Thief of Bagdad," as noteworthy achievements of the American civilization that inspired them.

THE development of widely diversified tastes in themes and treatments had its effect on the position of the stars. They now shared their glory, not only with a large number of other stars of equal magnitude, but with directors and writers as well. Nominally, the system continued to flourish, but the day was gone when any single player could hope to capture first place in the hearts of audiences. As a result, salaries, too, became uncertain. Employers grew very timid about signing a long-term contract with any star at $10,000 to $20,000 a week. If the star made four pictures a year the salary alone would amount to $125,000 to $250,000 per picture; and most stars wanted to make only two or three pictures a year, in which event the salary item would be increased fifty to one hundred percent per picture. A play loaded with one salary of $125,000 to $500,000 would reach a total cost of $750,000 to $1,000,000, and figures such as these had become too speculative for corporations that had to pay dividends to thousands of stockholders.

Several stars had reached a position in popularity at which they believed they were justified in receiving the highest compensation paid to any player. Norma Talmadge, Gloria Swanson, John Barrymore and Harold Lloyd were very successful, and a few years earlier any one of them might have expected to receive the salaries attained only by Mary Pickford and Chaplin. Corinne Griffith and several other players had acquired large audience followings and believed that they were due for advancement to the "big money." For a year or so, stars and employers wrangled constantly over contract renewals, each side unable to recede from its position, and then Joseph Schenck contributed to the solution of the problem by forming an alliance with Douglas Fairbanks, Mary Pickford, Charlie Chaplin and D. W. Griffith in the United Artists corporation. Schenck became the administrative and business head of United Artists, and broadened the scope of the organization to include important stars who had grown too expensive for producers to employ. By using their own money, or obtaining the necessary capital from financial connections, the players could make their own pictures as long as the public wanted to see them.

United Artists obtained, by purchase or lease, theaters in principal American cities and some in Europe, so that its photoplays were insured of first runs in its own houses. In this manner, the organization expanded until it was a large, self-contained business unit, combining production, distribution, and exhibition. Norma and Constance Talmadge, Gloria Swanson, John Barrymore, William S. Hart, Corinne Griffith, Ronald Colman and other stars became members of United Artists, and Samuel Goldwyn and Howard Hughes later transferred their productions to this organization. Harold Lloyd formed his own company, distributing his pictures through Paramount.

The salaries paid to stars by employing producers settled to a basis of approximately $7,000 a week at the top although Thomas Meighan, Pola Negri, Tom Mix, Colleen Moore, and a few others exceeded this figure—and ranging downward; $2,000 to $5,000 a week representing the average in 1926-27. The employers were helped in the adjustment of salary matters during this period by the acceptance of American theater-goers of actors and actresses from Latin, Teutonic, Scandinavian, and Slavic countries. The entrance of non-English speaking players to American studios in any considerable numbers was in itself an interesting evolution. From the beginning of film-making, although there never was any prejudice against foreign actors, the difficulty of directors and other staff members in making themselves understood to those with limited knowledge of English caused delays and expense that were avoided by employing Americans or players of British derivation. The exceptions were a few Europeans who knew English. Able artists, such as Jean Hersholt, a finely trained Danish actor, and others who drifted into Hollywood, had difficulty in getting their feet on the ladder of success until they had become workably conversant with the language.

When Pola Negri, Rudolph Valentino, and other foreign actors began to appear in important pictures, their films were warmly welcomed by audiences in their own countries. Attendance at theaters in the native lands of the foreign players, and in nations of affiliated racial stocks, was greatly increased and as distributors were able to charge much higher rentals for their pictures, foreign artists began to have value in Los Angeles. Producers scoured the studios and stages of Germany and Central European states, the Scandinavian peninsula, Mexico and South America for talent that could be transported to Los Angeles and fabricated into profitable export merchandise. Many of their discoveries pleased not only foreign screen audiences, but American movie-goers as well.

Wages in the United States seemed fabulous to the foreign players—at first. Many of them came to Los Angeles without contracts, and started the round of the studios as free-lances. Whenever the opportunity for a rôle appeared they promptly bid for it at lower salaries than established players were asking. The foreigners would accept $250, for example, for a part for which an American actor would insist on getting $500 to $750, and for a while there were bitter comments in the film colony on the "foreign invasion" and "price cutting." Producers or their scouts drumming up talent in Europe found artists very happy to accept contracts at wages that seemed like bargain day to the studio executives in Los Angeles, and while this cheery condition lasted the employers were very proud of the boys and girls they had brought across the seas. But as soon as the foreigners got their feet firmly planted on Los Angeles soil, they began to display an unfortunate familiarity with Los Angeles values. One European actress discovered by an American producer traveling in Europe, was offered a contract with $300 a week the first year and $500 the second. Such sums were beyond the dreams of most players anywhere except in America, and she could not sign quickly enough. In her first few American pictures she made a hit, and when soon a competing producer offered her thousands instead of hundreds she began to display extreme unrest. Her employer offered to revise the contract upward, but not far enough to meet his competitor's offer. His star hesitated, and he threatened deportation if the contract were broken. She earnestly assured him she would not break the contract, but soon thereafter her ability to understand English departed from her, causing many expensive delays in production. Surely there is nothing illegal in that? Certainly not! The producer compromised and raised her salary to a satisfactory figure,—and her knowledge of English suddenly returned.

Even after the adjustment of star salary levels had been more or less ironed out, the employers had to carry a heavy and hazardous economic burden in unexpired contracts with actors who were passing out of public favor. A producer paying $5,000 to $10,000 a week to a player over a period of five years, might find himself at the end of the third or fourth year with a star whom audiences had quietly abandoned, and before the termination of the contract the employer might lose more than all the profits he had made on the star during the period of his or her ascendency. This condition continued until 1927-28, when producers adopted a system of short-term contracts, usually for a year. Often the producer took an option on the player's service for additional years with compensation increasing annually. This system removed some of the hazards, but in 1928-9, when talking pictures had swept the silent film into the background, producers found themselves paying wages throughout a year to successful silent players who were not useable in the talkies.

CHAPTER SIXTEEN
IN FOREIGN LANDS

BEFORE the World War, movies had become firmly established in all countries, and everywhere American films were the leading items of screen entertainment. When the production of features in America became organized (about 1914), these longer Yankee movies were successfully introduced in foreign lands, and audiences increased rapidly until war conditions restricted exports and closed many theaters and exhibition halls. After Armistice Day, screen shows everywhere became even more popular, attracting larger audiences in all cities in which they had been established and spreading into communities in which they had been shown infrequently or not at all. Thousands of new playhouses, halls, or gardens were opened all over the world, and in the leading countries, especially England, Germany, and France, large motion picture theaters were built.

Many houses have arisen in the British Isles, some of them financed or leased or purchased by American producers, and others built and managed by English groups awakened to the money-making possibilities of supplying amusement to the populace. These theaters follow American methods closely, and some of them have imported American managers to supervise operation. Popular prices of admittance are charged, and audiences increase steadily. Unquestionably the British Isles are ready for a large development in movie attendance if theaters can be built more rapidly, but unless construction costs are reduced and taxation becomes less onerous, expansion cannot progress at American and Canadian speed. In Germany, France, and other European countries, the movie habit steadily increases. American conquest of the screens of the world, started in nickelodeon days, has been complete, but the popularity of American films has been maintained against the most serious industrial and political opposition in nearly all countries.

After the war, German, English, and French producers resumed activities. The Italians, who were leading in 1910-14, made a few attempts at large productions, but seemed unable to catch the drift of popular taste. The Russian Soviet seized upon the screen as a very effective method of propaganda, and the government subsidized several studios. Occasional attempts at producing were made in Spain, Scandinavia, South America, Japan, China, India. For several years there seemed to be a chance that German producers might find a definite place on the screens of the world. Important bankers, newspaper owners and industrialists, following the modern practice of all German business, merged small companies into a few large ones and equipped them with adequate capital. A few pictures of outstanding merit appeared, some of which (notably "Passion," with Pola Negri, and "Variety" and "The Last Laugh," with Emil Jannings), were popular in this country.

Carl Laemmle, Adolph Zukor, and Marcus Loew made alliances with German producers, to develop production in Germany and use the pictures in American distribution. By reciprocal arrangement, these American manufacturers could make use of the distributing and exhibiting facilities of their German associates for their own product. Zukor and Loew joined in a loan of $4,000,000 to Ufa, the leading German corporation; but none of these experiments resulted to the satisfaction of the Americans and within a few years they withdrew from financial participation in German production. The finest actors and directors of the German studios finally came to America, where they established themselves as stars. Among them were Emil Jannings, F. W. Murnau, Ernst Lubitsch, Josef von Sternberg, and, most recently, Marlene Dietrich, the latest sensation among foreign actors in this country. When talking pictures came in, Jannings returned to Germany.

In England, extensive promotion of motion picture companies was supported by appeals to national pride, and $40,000,000 or more were subscribed by the public for shares in corporations that promised to make, distribute, and exhibit English films equal to the American, with comparable profits to stockholders. The success of "The Four Horsemen," "The Big Parade," "What Price Glory?", and other war pictures in the United States encouraged English producers to make films glorifying British soldiers and sailors, and productions of this type were popular in the British Isles for a year or two, but did not arouse enthusiasm in other parts of the world.

Aside from the success in Britain of a few war pictures, after millions of pounds had been invested in studios and picture production, the English had made no perceptible progress in the art or the business of motion picture production. English studios sent a score of pictures to America each year, some of which ranked with second-grade silent film productions of Los Angeles, but most of them were of poor quality. None reached the highest American quality nor equalled the German-made "Passion" in box-office popularity or "The Last Laugh" in artistry.

A few Russian pictures have been very successful in New York and other American cities with large foreign populations, but most of them have been heavily laden with Soviet propaganda and, apart from specialized assemblies, Americans have not found them entertaining. Several Russian films, such as "Potemkin," "The End of St. Petersburg," and "October," have exhibited unusual ability in direction and camera work.

The Scandinavians, despite fine actors and directors, lean so frequently toward gloomy, sophisticated stories that they have been negligible factors in production, as far as wide distribution is concerned. The French, the Italians, and all other Europeans have not succeeded in establishing successful film producing activities of their own. The Japanese have become enthusiastic movie-makers and their films are popular in sections of the Far East.

While foreign producers have exported comparatively few pictures that have been popular in America in the five years ending in 1931, Scandinavia, France, and England have supplied Hollywood with several actors who have acquired premier positions. Greta Garbo, a Scandinavian player popular throughout Continental Europe, was brought to the United States by Metro-Goldwyn Mayer, and won an extensive following. The English Ronald Colman, in Samuel Goldwyn pictures, established a firm position for himself. Maurice Chevalier, imported from Paris by Jesse Lasky, became a very popular favorite in the United States.

For many years the upper classes of England and other European nations paid even less attention to the cinema than similar classes here had accorded nickelodeons. The solid, responsible leaders of society, politics, finance, and industry, finding their entertainment in the opera and the stage, had no knowledge of the spread of the movie habit until about 1912, when English and German traders noted that American merchandise was beginning to supersede theirs in markets formerly under their control. Investigation proved that American films were responsible for the change in conditions. They began to complain to their governments that audiences saw American sewing-machines, typewriters, furniture, clothing, shoes, steam shovels, saddles, automobiles, and all sorts of things in the cinema shows, and soon began to want these things and insist on buying them in preference to similar articles made in England, Germany, France, or elsewhere.

These complaints were increasing in volume and intensity when the World War upset all affairs. After the war, German manufacturers and exporters brought the subject to the attention of their government and the English again tried to arouse their bankers, newspapers, and politicians to this serious Yankee menace, but the rulers in both countries knew so little about the cinema that for a while they could not believe that these cheap shows could be exercising an influence so insidious and extensive. Politicians and financiers persisted in ascribing the expansion of American foreign trade to Wall Street's active support of our manufacturers and exporters, and did not abandon this opinion until their boards of trade and chambers of commerce presented facts and figures that left no room for doubting the potency of Yankee films in creating commerce for all Yankee industries.

Countless thousands of words on the subject have appeared in the reports of consuls and commercial agents and in the newspapers and periodicals of all countries at interest. A fair, impartial summary of the situation would indicate that trade inevitably followed the film and that wherever American films penetrated, American trade shortly established a foot-hold. More than ninety percent of the pictures shown in most foreign countries were American, and they wielded a large influence.

When Europeans finally awakened to the danger, they encouraged the organization of studios to produce pictures that would drive the Yankees out of their home and foreign markets. Unfortunately their films fell flat, and business men, moviemakers, and politicians were left bewildered by the continued preference of audiences everywhere for American screen shows. A stream of propaganda against American pictures and picture makers poured forth from commercial and governmental press bureaus and secret agencies. Every possible charge was made, from attacks on the manners and morals of the Hollywood studio colony, to allegations that American industrialists and financiers had combined with film makers to control international commerce through the subtle advertising of merchandise in our motion pictures.

German and French propaganda was as extensive and as bitter

as their film producers, business men, politicians, and publicity agents could make it. *Le Matin* of Paris declared editorially:

"The truth is that the Americans are trying to make Europe give way to their ideas and rightly believe that the propaganda in motion pictures which permits the American influence to be placed before the eyes of the public of all countries is the best and least costly method of spreading the national influence. It has been said in the United States that since American films have been scattered to all parts of the globe the country's commercial exportations have increased extraordinarily and that the sale of American goods follows closely everywhere upon the track of the motion picture."

This European attitude was, on the whole, somewhat naïve. The fact is that American films have always been made for entertainment only and for no other purpose; if incidentally they have aided the world-wide distribution of American goods, such aid has been incidental and not deliberate. American ticket-buyers would have resented any attempts at direct advertising in pictures sold them as entertainment, and any producer who attempted such methods would quickly have come to grief. The simple truth is that foreign audiences, seeing in American films articles of wear, household appliances, automobiles, machinery, and other commodities not readily obtainable in their own countries, straightway gave their patronage to firms that imported these American goods. But to suppose that there existed a deep-laid conspiracy between American film producers and the other American industries to capture the world's markets through film propaganda, is to believe in a fantastic fable.

THE propaganda, pleadings, and threats of European politicians, business men, and journalists had little effect on the people of their own countries or on those in their colonies. Everywhere American films retained their popularity, and, indeed, many nationals, resenting the efforts of their ruling classes to make them favor the productions of domestic studios, followed the

American habit of staying away from theaters unless their favorite American pictures were shown.

European journalists and industrial investigators visited Los Angeles to uncover the mysteries of Yankee cinema supremacy, and made lengthy reports on studio conditions and technical operations. An Englishman, Henry King, writing in the *Adelphi,* a London publication, revealed the secret by telling his readers that Hollywood popularity had been acquired by "giving the public what it wants. The movie is the art of the millions of American citizens who are picturesquely called Hicks—the mighty stream of standardized humanity that flows through Main Street." This English writer also made the discovery that democracy was responsible for this Hick art:

"As though we had no Hicks at home, in this free and enlightened country. Dear old Hicks! Why it is even possible that our own home-grown Hicks may be a little more Hickory than the originals, inasmuch as they stubbornly prefer the American film to the home-product. And if we do not call them Hicks, a rose by any other name may smell as sweet.

"Not the Hicks, therefore, are responsible for the conditions of the cinema, but something altogether less distinctively American—democracy. Does any one seriously imagine that if the great American producers were to aim at giving the English public what it wanted, the films would be better than those which satisfy and delight the dwellers in Main Street? Have the indigenous British films ever shown themselves to be better by a single caption than the imported Americans? They are on the same level as far as subject and treatment are concerned, and infinitely inferior technically.

"The cinema is, through and through, a democratic art; the only one. . . . Nothing will ever come of 'educating the public'! Educating the public is, indeed, pure humbug. No amount of public education will bring the public to like better films, or better books. And what, anyhow, is the good of its liking better films, or better books? There is no such distinction in the world of art; there are good films and bad ones, good books and bad ones. The public cannot be brought by easy stages from liking bad to liking good. That only leads to the worst condition of all: pretending to like that which is neither bad nor good, but simply rotten.

"Let us away with the pious humbug of 'educating the public' to like anything: and above all with the particular humbug of educating the public outside the cinema to like better things in the cinema. It can't be done; and if it could, the result would be merely nasty—the singularly putrescent hypocrisy that masquerades as 'artistic culture.' If the cinema public is to be educated it must be educated by the cinema."

In France, the association of motion picture theater owners entered into open conflict with the French producers and distributors, the exhibitors bluntly stating they would have to close their theaters unless they could show American pictures.

When German propagandists charged German players and directors with lack of patriotism for having accepted large salaries in Los Angeles, a writer in a Berlin newspaper presented these uncomfortable facts for the consideration of his countrymen:

"The 112 recognized directors in Germany turned out only 225 screen productions in 1928. One lucky director guided the fortunes of seven pictures, while sixty-two had to be content with just one apiece. Of the 179 film actresses of standing who had engagements last year, 100 took part in only a single production, forty-two played twice, twenty-one three times and only five managed to face the camera in four productions. The male actors had about the same luck.

"One result of the lack of jobs is naturally a limited income. . . . If a well known actress is highly paid and succeeds in getting two pictures a year she has an income of ten thousand to twenty thousand marks ($2,400 to $4,800) a year, but out of this sum she has to meet the cost of costumes in modern society films, which, as I have been able to convince myself by personal investigation, is not much less than the amount of her honorarium. . . . Incomparably worse situated are all those who have to be satisfied with much smaller pay or who are employed in only one film in a year. Under no circumstances can they live on their acting income alone. But the worst fate is reserved for those who—despite a good name and reputation—have to run day in and day out from one film office to another in order to get at least a minor part. They get about 100 marks ($2.40) a day, and they are lucky if they work from twenty to thirty days in a year."

All else having failed, the Europeans passed laws "with teeth in them." Business men and politicians would have welcomed legislation that completely barred American pictures from their countries, but action as drastic as this might have aroused disturbances from theatergoers, and laws had to assume the guise of benefits to their domestic film industries. Germany created a "kontingent," and France adopted a similar method, under the terms of which nearly all pictures shown in the theaters of these countries were to be made at home. Hungary placed a tariff on foreign films, the proceeds to be used for the benefit of the domestic picture industry, and other European states followed the general movement with legislation along similar lines.

England carefully considered the subject and after extensive hearings by the Board of Trade and thorough agitation in the press, Parliament passed a "quota" bill in 1927, under the provisions of which films are not calculated as separate pictures but by length. In the first year of the quota's operation (1928), each distributor was required to rent seven and one-half percent of British-made films, and each year thereafter the quota was to be increased at the rate of two and one-half percent per annum until a maximum of twenty-five percent should be reached. The law provided that British-made pictures must be made by British subjects or a British-controlled company and that not less than seventy-five percent of the salaries and wages must be paid to British citizens or to persons domiciled in the British Empire. Films of news events, or national scenery, or educational, scientific, commercial, or industrial pictures are not subject to the operations of the law.

Advocates of these measures assured their countrymen that several benefits would derive from such protective legislation: first, their own home studios would prosper, through the enforced exhibition of domestic pictures; second, American producers would be compelled to buy their "kontingent" or quota of German, French, or English movies in order to obtain licenses to distribute their own productions in these countries; these European pictures when shown on American screens would spread the ideas of the various countries in the United States, and advertise the merchandise manufactured in these countries;

third, the "kontingent" and quota systems, by placing what practically amounted to a tariff on foreign films, would make the cost of export too high for poor pictures, and European audiences thus would be assured of seeing none but the best product of American studios.

The foreign market had been an important part of the American industry's business for many years. During the era of Hollywood's extravagant "out-spending" it was entirely possible for a picture costing, say, $300,000, to barely earn its cost, or even less than its cost, in the United States, and yet close its books with a profit through good foreign sales or rentals. In 1926-28, the foreign sales of American pictures represented twenty-five to forty percent of their total earnings, or, stated in another way, a picture that would earn rentals of $500,000 in the United States could be expected to obtain $125,000 or $150,000 in foreign countries; perhaps an exceptional production might go to $200,000. These figures are approximate and illustrative, and from the gross earnings must be deducted the costs of distribution. England—or, rather, the United Kingdom—is, next to the United States, the principal film consumer of the world, the English section of the foreign field representing by far the largest single item in American movie exports. Broadly speaking, the average picture made in America received about half of its foreign revenue from England, allowing always for exceptions in which a popular German, French, Latin, or Scandinavian star in a Los Angeles production brought large returns from his native country.

In 1925-27, American producers enjoyed almost a monopoly of the English field. The London correspondent of *Variety* gave these statistics concerning distribution:

"In 1926 there were released in the United Kingdom 625 feature films. Out of this total 577 were American, 25 Continental European, and 23 British product. In percentages: America, 92-8/25; Continental, 4; home product, 3-17/25."

In 1927, he placed the distribution as follows: American, 74¼ percent; Continental European, 24¼ percent; British, four and one-half percent. The "decrease in popularity" of American product in 1927 he ascribed to carelessness in the preparation of films for English screens and to the objections of British exhibitors "who are getting sick of prices being pushed up and up, and of being blackjacked in a million other ways by high-powered salesmen."

"You are registering a fall in your film sales here," he warned the American producers, because "you are not studying this market, nursing it, and keeping it nursed, being concerned for stuff from our angle.... Think what your own fans would say —and do—if they had a long-sustained diet of English films featuring cricket matches, or our part in the war, all titled in our conception of the American idiom! You shouldn't put your pictures out that way here, but you do, just because you distribute your own stuff on this side and you take the 'this is how it comes to you' attitude towards our public, secure in the belief that you control this market."

American producers bought their kontingent or quota of movies made in foreign countries, and brought some of them to the United States and put them on exhibition. Very few of them were successful, and the European hope that Americans would learn European habits and customs and merchandise through their films soon faded. The disappointed European producers bitterly alleged that American producers, controlling the leading theaters, did not give their pictures a fair chance on the screens of the United States. I do not believe that the facts warrant this charge. Paramount, Loew, First National, Universal, and other large theater owners each extensively exploited certain foreign-made photoplays. First National's success with "Passion" was one of the high-water marks of the company's career. Paramount gave "Variety" a long run at the Rialto Theater in New York and pushed it vigorously throughout the country. Paramount tried to make a success of the German picture "Metropolis," spending a large sum in editing the film to meet American box-office standards and advertising it lavishly, but the story did not appeal to Americans as entertainment. Carl Laemmle featured "The Last Laugh," "Michael Strogoff," and other foreign productions as earnestly as if they had been made at Universal City. And so on, through a long list of foreign movies that were tried and in the main found wanting as first-run material for large houses.

The American movie magnates are business men, with whatever virtues and defects business men anywhere in the world may have. They are the survivors of an industrial battle that has raged for two decades, and the fact that they have survived proves them too shrewd to overlook any opportunities to advance the interests of their own corporations. Their principal source of profit is the theaters, and their attitude toward all pictures— American, European, South American, Asiatic—is determined solely by box-office response, which rests in the hands of the ticket buyers. And that in turn rests solely on the point of view regarding *entertainment*. Nationalism or internationalism enters into the subject not one mite—American audiences are as indifferent to the place of origin of a photoplay as they were to the struggle of the General Film-Patents Trust to exist, or to the Federal Trade Commission's suit against Adolph Zukor, or to what has become of last year's favorite stars. When an individual in the army of fifty or sixty million ticket buyers in the United States leaves the theater he has either been entertained, or he has not, and that is the court of last appeal. Americans enjoy and give large patronage to dozens of pictures of foreign subjects, with foreign settings—but made in Los Angeles. They have found entertainment in very few of the foreign-made films, and the reasons are simply that Europeans have not learned how to make pictures that appeal to the general public, the democracy that must be "catered to" if mass production is to be successful.

In 1928-29, after their legislatively nurtured movie industries had rocked along in the doldrums for several years, the leaders of the business in Germany and France inaugurated movements to impose heavier burdens on American pictures. German producers and distributors called conventions of the motion picture interests of all European countries, and organized a European *bloc* against American films. The intent, and no effort was made to conceal it, was to harass and hamper Yankee producers by tariff regulations and restrictions of every sort that could be devised. English, French, German, Scandinavian, and Italian distributors agreed to distribute each other's product and to cooperate in every possible manner to build up the film industries of the nationals in the *bloc.*

Soon after this *bloc,* or association, had been formed, France became the center of the war against American producers, through the demand of French producers that the government increase the quota. Under the French system, licenses for the distribution of foreign films were given to the domestic producers, who sold them to the American producers. The quota and the license-purchases only slightly reduced the distribution of American movies in France and increased the business of the English and the Germans, without accomplishing any noteworthy increase in the consumption of French films at home or abroad. The principal demand of French film manufacturers thereupon took form in demands that the Americans establish a "film bank" with a capital of $10,000,000 and lend money at low rates of interest to French producers; or, that the Americans make outright loans, aggregating a million or a million and a half dollars, to French producers. The American producers, speaking through the Hays organization, declined to accept the proposition, saying they could not afford to "establish the dangerous precedent of paying for the privilege of doing business" in European countries. The French producers persisted in their demands, and the Americans closed their exchanges in France, dismissed their several thousand French employes, and ceased to ship pictures into the country.

French theater owners, knowing that without American films their audiences would stay at home, made clamorous protests to their government, saying that their producing and distributing brethren were killing the goose that laid the golden eggs.

After some months of oratory and agitation the French film commission abandoned the program of French producers and restored American films to approximately their previous position.

THE European countries have all the elements needed for the production of motion pictures. They have, as has been seen, been very successful in making certain films which have established high-water marks in artistry and camera craft. But precisely therein lies the reason for their lack of commercial success. From the earliest days of the film, European movie-makers have directed their efforts not at the populace but at the cultured classes. Instead of tapping the vast audiences already waiting for entertainment, they placed themselves in direct competition with the stage for the patronage of classes who instinctively, by birth and training, preferred the stage to the screen. The populace, that might have supported the infant art, was never given a chance to do so; no such movement as America witnessed during the nickelodeon era ever transpired in Europe. The movies, like all other entertainment, looked for their support from the cultured classes.

The result was that when cheap American films invaded the field, providing an entertainment the common man could understand, they achieved a complete conquest from which it has since been impossible to dislodge them. And until foreign producers realize that the way to capture the interest of Demos is to communicate with him on his own terms, they will continue to search for the "mystery" of American films. The mystery is nothing but a willingness to give the public what it is willing to pay for instead of a desire to "educate" the public against its will.

CHAPTER SEVENTEEN

TALKIES

1926. . . . Accepting George Kleine's statement that "1896 marked the beginning of all things in motion picture commerce," the industry had reached the age of thirty years. Story-telling in movies started about ten years later, so the art developed by the industry was not more than twenty years old. Famous Players, the first of feature-film companies, was organized by Zukor in 1912, and Paramount was organized by Hodkinson in 1914; the larger growth of the industry and the more extensive developments of the art had taken place during the dozen years after 1914. Whether one allows an age of twelve, or twenty, or thirty years, the American movie industry had accomplished an astonishing growth by 1926. Wall Street bankers calculated the investment in studios, theaters, exchanges, and merchandise at $1,500,000,000; *Variety* made a careful compilation of figures that placed the total at more than $2,000,000,000; 20,000 theaters claimed an attendance of 100,000,000 a week, and the annual commerce of the American industry was placed at $1,000,000,000 to $1,250,000,000. The movies had grown from nothing in 1896 to a position among the half-dozen largest industries in the United States in 1926.

At the head of this business was Adolph Zukor. Whether or not he had built a new kind of trust that crushed competition is a question that may never be answered by the courts, but his Paramount Famous-Lasky Corporation, worth $150,000,000, with theaters and theater affiliations in all countries, was the most powerful factor in motion pictures, and Zukor was the foremost individual in the studios and the screens of the world. The product of the industry of which he had made himself the dominant individual was reaching into the lives of more men, women, and children in more places, and coloring their thoughts and affecting their habits and customs more effectively than newspapers and books, religious institutions, and political governments. An immeasurable, invisible world power rested on the desk of the Emperor of Entertainment in the lofty Paramount Building in Times Square.

Marcus Loew and William Fox were important personages in movie matters, standing next to Zukor, but Loew had been relaxing his driving urge for several years, enjoying the fruits of his prosperous business, and in 1926, Fox had not yet acquired the Roxy and other theaters and properties that were to increase his stature so mightily by 1929. Laemmle and Universal were active and prosperous, but were definitely in the second flight. Loew, Fox, and First National were the only competitors worthy of Zukor's attention in the spring of 1926. A few smaller specialized companies were operating successfully, but there seemed to be nothing in the industry that could seriously annoy Paramount.

Even the First National problem had adjusted itself by one of Zukor's characteristic, far-seeing master-strokes. The Katz-Hoyt plan of merging theaters, studios, and exchanges worked along until there seemed to be a reasonable belief that many, perhaps a majority of members, might agree to it. Then, in 1925-26, Paramount bought control of the Balaban and Katz theaters, and organized "Publix Theaters Corporation," placing the stock of Publix in the treasury of Paramount Famous-Lasky Company, and transferring the theater holdings of Paramount to Publix. Sam Katz was elected president of the theater company and managed its affairs as if it were a separate entity.

In this transaction Zukor accomplished several major objectives:

The loss of Balaban and Katz, foremost exhibitors in the Chicago district, weakened First National's theater position, and strengthened Paramount's;

In obtaining Katz to head the Publix Corporation, Zukor gained a capable, experienced, energetic young manager;

The movement toward amalgamation of First National interests was so effectively weakened and delayed by withdrawal of Katz, that the plan could not be executed, and Zukor and Katz made good use of the situation by acquiring for Publix desirable theaters and circuits which otherwise would probably have been consolidated in the proposed Katz-Hoyt First National; Zukor's industrial strategy in this instance thus enabled Paramount-Publix to establish its theater interests broadly and soundly, and no competition has been able to menace the Zukor group since then;

Politically and legally, Zukor placed his corporations in position to meet an order from the Federal Trade Commission to divorce production and exhibition; if such an order should ever be entered, Paramount Famous-Lasky could obey it by distributing to its stockholders the shares of Publix. Dismemberment of trusts in this manner had never worked to the injury of stockholders, and Zukor now had no particular cause to be worried by any possible order of the commission.

Stanley Mastbaum had died, and Jules Mastbaum, assuming active management of the Stanley Company's affairs, had brought into his corporation various important theater interests. When Katz retired from First National, Mastbaum became the principal individual in that company's administration. Among numerous important houses acquired by the Stanley were the Fabian chain in New Jersey, the Strand in New York (Mitchell Mark having been dead for several years), and circuits in Pennsylvania, Maryland, Delaware, and Washington, D. C. Several votes in First National passed to the Stanley corporation with these houses, and as Mastbaum also acquired other stock relinquished by theater owners who had sold to Paramount or to various combinations, he became the largest single shareholder in First National.

North American Theaters Corporation, organized by Frank R. Wilson, president of Motion Picture Capital Company, and the Jeremiah Milbank group, had purchased the Jensen-Von Herburg and other houses in northwestern states, and the Jensen-Von Herburg vote in First National had passed to North American. The Stanley Company was one of several minority stockholders of the West Coast Company, and Jules Mastbaum, in cooperation with the Wilson-Milbank group, William Fox, and other West Coast stockholders, merged North American and West Coast into a new corporation called "Wesco," of which Harold Franklin, formerly an important Paramount-Publix official, was made chief executive. After this transaction, Stanley had about three hundred and eighty theaters and Wesco about two hundred and seventy-five, and these two corporations had acquired the common stock of so many First National members that now they owned control of the company.

Mastbaum's program was to consolidate as many as possible of the remaining First National owners under Stanley-Wesco control and he was progressing toward this goal when death in the autumn of 1926 brought his labors to an end. With Jules Mastbaum gone, and Sam Katz safely anchored in Publix, the bitter struggle between First National and Paramount began to abate.

THE Federal Trade Commission had found its anti-trust suit against Zukor and his associates a difficult case to bring to completion. The charges settled down to three main counts: the use of oppression and coercion in obtaining theaters, "block booking" to exhibitors, and exclusion from Paramount-controlled theaters of the pictures of other producers.

The charges of oppression, coercion and intimidation arose from exhibitors affected by the operations of Black and Lynch;

such allegations died away after Black and the Lynch wrecking crews obtained the houses they wanted.

"Block-booking" was the system of contract between producers (or, technically, their distributors) and exhibitors, under which the producer agreed to supply the exhibitor with a specified number, "a block," of pictures within a period, and the exhibitor agreed to accept and pay for them. A block might be a dozen, two dozen, or more pictures, "a block" having superseded the program or series system of renting productions. Booking in this manner had become the general custom of all leading producers except United Artists, which rented each picture separately. Specials and other large expensive productions of all manufacturers were not included in the blocks, but were released as individual items.

This system was like a two-edged sword; it could cut both ways. If an exhibitor attempted to supply his theater with pictures booked one at a time, he would be likely to find his competitors contracting for the entire output of Paramount, M-G-M, First National, or other manufacturers, and presently he would be unable to obtain enough first-class pictures to maintain his screen. On the other hand, if he booked a block of a dozen or two dozen pictures before they were made, he was sure to find that some of them were good, others of medium quality, and others bad. Some exhibitors supported the government's attorneys in their plea that block-booking be abolished; others stoutly insisted that block-booking was necessary to insure stability.

Block-booking was inextricably interwoven with the subject of first-run theaters. The government's attorneys contended that Zukor's theaters block-booked Paramount pictures, leaving few or no openings for the exhibition of independent productions. Certainly this was true, and Zukor had acquired control of the houses for that purpose; but it was equally true of Loew, First National, Fox, and Universal.

The government's charge that Zukor controlled the industry was sustained by his ownership of first-run theaters and alliances with owners of other houses. But wherein was the offense against the laws of the United States? Zukor had no control of physical raw materials. For a while he had in his employ a large share of the "raw material" of actors and actresses, but gradually worked away from any attempt to employ the highest priced stars. He had never merged any producing companies except those in the Paramount group. He had no control of patents. Even in his acquisition of theaters he was able to prove that he owned only several hundred in a total of 20,000. The supreme court has never defined the percentage of the whole that constitutes monopoly. William Jennings Bryan once declared that the consolidation of a majority of business concerns into one company should be accepted as evidence of monopoly, but if this rule were applied to Zukor he could reply that he owned only three, or four, or five, percent of the theaters of the country.

Also, he could point out that Loew owned and controlled many houses, that First National through its stockholders and franchise holders indirectly controlled several thousands, that Fox owned many and was buying and building more, that Laemmle had acquired several hundred, that Keith-Albee-Orpheum had merged half a hundred vaudeville-picture houses and joined with Radio and F B O to organize Radio-Keith-Orpheum. Inasmuch as each of these groups followed the practices of block-booking and gave preference in its own houses to its own pictures, Zukor might ask, "if Paramount is a trust, what are these other concerns?"

Nor were these technical points the only obstacles the federal attorneys encountered. They had to carry on their work with no public interest to encourage them. In the successful prosecutions against the oil, tobacco, and sugar trusts, the public had manifested lively interest; newspapers and magazines in those years had given wide publicity to hearings and trials against trusts, and politicians had ridden into office on the wave of public indignation. But the sentiment of the country had undergone many extensive changes since the era of the muckrakers. After the war, the subject of trusts no longer appealed to any section of the public except individuals or groups directly affected by specific mergers, or to the more liberal and radical press. Magazines had forgotten the existence of octopi and malefactors of great wealth, and when government anti-trust litigations appeared from time to time, newspapers for the most part dealt with the subject perfunctorily. The average citizen cared nothing for the government's prosecution of Zukor, and if he thought of the matter at all, it was probably to applaud Zukor's cleverness and initiative in having placed himself in so impregnable a position, or else to make a mental note to buy some Paramount stock.

Within the industry, the government received scant assistance from the producers and exhibitors whose freedom the Trade Commission was trying in vain to save. There was not a trace of the vigorous struggle that accompanied the government's prosecution of Motion Pictures Patents Company and General Film. Manufacturers and distributors testified that theaters were steadily closing to independent product, and that independents would soon be unable to live, but as each nursed the secret belief that he would be able to survive the threatened general catastrophe, and all were too proud to declare frankly that Zukor was surpassing them, their evidence was seldom helpful. The government made the most of instances of oppression of small exhibitors, but Zukor had ceased to buy any but larger houses, and this class of evidence was soon exhausted.

The commission's attorneys labored diligently and conscientiously on the case for eight years, and no conclusion was reached except in regard to block-booking, concerning which the commission issued orders to Paramount to "cease and desist" any use of block-booking for coercive purposes, and to establish practices permitting "exhibitor and manufacturer to cancel a picture in a block in face of racial or religious opposition after arbitration." Exhibitors were also to have the right "to cancel up to ten percent of any block prior to scheduled date of showing upon payment of one-half of the original allocated (rental) cost of the portion cancelled."

THE only cloud on the sky of 1926 was a tendency toward recession in profits in many theaters. Even large houses in leading cities were not maintaining the speed that the industry had come to regard as normal, and in several cities neighborhood theaters were having a hard fight to keep income ahead of outgo. Business was spotty; some theaters were doing well, but too many were barely making expenses. There were various reasons for this general slackening in attendance.

A very successful new form of entertainment, radio broadcasting, had appeared and had achieved enormous success. Radio receiving sets were installed in millions of homes all over the country. Many theater owners were apprehensive that their houses would be deserted when radio began to leap ahead in gigantic strides. For a while radio did affect theater attendance adversely, but not seriously. Soon the public adjusted itself to the newer plaything, and returned to the movie houses except on nights when a particularly thrilling event was on the air, and then the theaters were rather lonesome. But the radio was not the cause of bad business now, any more than the increasing popularity of fiction magazines and national weeklies, detective and mystery novels, or other forms of entertainment were responsible. The causes of unrest were within the film industry, not outside.

There were well-grounded fears that the public was not "as crazy about movies" as it had been. While no perceptible antagonism was present, ticket buyers had grown very discriminating, and there was an increasing luke-warmness that showed itself in empty seats in too many houses whenever the current entertainment was not of the best. A first-run theater's regular receipts of $20,000 to $30,000 a week might rise to $60,000 a week during the run of a Charlie Chaplin film or another attractive picture, only to drop back when the film completed its showing. In neighborhood theaters, conditions were similar: a house would run along for several weeks with moderate patronage, and then suddenly every seat would be filled during the nights a first-run success appeared. Even well-known stars ceased to be a drawing card if the picture itself was inferior.

Several explanations of this situation were advanced, the chief of which were that too many new theaters had been built everywhere in the United States, and that too many pictures were being produced at costs that were too high. Undoubtedly these things were true and were gravely affecting the business, but my opinion is that other reasons must be sought for the reduction of movie attendance. They are closely bound up with one another, but they may be analyzed as follows:

First: prices of admittance had become too high;

Second: good pictures had educated audiences, and the appearance of mediocre films injured the industry;

Third: all pictures were made for the large patronage of first-run houses, and, as audiences now included the entire public, there was definite need of differentiation in both production and distribution.

The public had never before objected to admittance prices. On the contrary, it had supported advances by increased patronage, and external appearances would seem to refute the statement that ticket rates had grown too high. But what economists term "a vicious circle" had been established: studio expenses, mounting higher and higher in the search for "bigger and better" pictures, necessitated corresponding increases in film rentals, which in turn brought about higher levels in ticket rates; round and round the circle traveled the always increasing dollar marks, until the industry as a whole lost sight of its basic function of supplying entertainment to all the people at prices all people can afford to pay.

Young people and other individuals perpetually searching for a "good time," constituted the audiences willing to pay high prices night after night for movie tickets, but family trade calculated carefully before father and mother and two children bought tickets at thirty to sixty cents apiece; each addition to the price reduced the number of their visits to the movies. Americans are generally sensitive about money matters, and they will not frankly admit their inability to afford an expensive necessity or luxury, but will conceal their economies by pretending to prefer the lower priced motor car or radio set. When the price of movie tickets advanced to levels demanding careful consideration, millions of patrons never made open protest to exhibitors, but simply remained away from the theaters unless assured of a very good picture or an exceptional novelty, and camouflaged their thrift by declaring that the star or the story did not appeal to them.

Wide differences in the quality of pictures was the second cause of wavering attendance. Competent studio executives estimated that one-third of the pictures of 1922-26 were especially good, another third mediocre, and the remaining third lower grades of product that could find showings only in rural or back neighborhood houses. The lowest grade may have had its proper place in the movie scheme, but there was no excuse for the middle third which merely disappointed audiences in the better class of theaters and seldom made money for manufacturers or theaters. As one producer described the situation to me, "our good pictures are very, very good, and our theaters are wonderful. A good picture in a fine house establishes a standard so high that the public feels it is not getting its money's worth when a medium-grade picture appears on the same screen the next week. Orchestras and vaudeville can bring regular patrons to the theaters, but nothing but good pictures will induce the great majority to leave their homes and buy tickets. We must have more attendance from these stay-at-homes, and to get it we must have a new method of exhibition, a method that insures longer runs to good pictures, thus shutting out defective product and causing the manufacture of any but good pictures to cease."

This was the common point of view of far-sighted producers with whom I talked in 1926 and '27; they believed that one-third of the pictures then being made could be eliminated with benefit to the industry. Calculating that 600 medium-cost and high-cost features a year were being produced, 400 would supply the theaters if longer runs of quality product should become general. The obstacle in the path of this movement—I am quoting these producers—was the conservatism of exhibitors, who had been in the habit of a weekly change of feature, or a change twice or thrice a week in neighborhood houses, and were reluctant to experiment with a new system. Considered broadly, this was the same obstacle that Hodkinson encountered when he began to select General Film subjects and persuade nickelodeons to run a program two days instead of one, and again when he organized Paramount to secure features that would run as long as a week. In 1926 there was no young Hodkinson, full of zeal and enthusiasm, to sell the idea of a new method to exhibitors, and the industry had to stumble along with its load of waste and its regiments of stay-at-homes while the movement for longer runs spread slowly from house to house.

A third weakness in the situation was that methods of exhibition had not kept pace with better public taste or with progress in the craft of production. Although important sections of audiences were now welcoming broader themes and more sophisticated treatments, all important producers made all pictures solely with the intent of pleasing the assemblies in large theaters; no attention whatever was given to the possibility of developing business by satisfying class audiences in small, select houses. Obviously the intellectual requirements of a first-run screen in a metropolis, playing to 4,000 people a performance, forty to fifty thousand a week, differ materially from those of, say, the Theatre Guild, presenting plays of Ibsen, Shaw, or Eugene O'Neill to 3,000 people a week, or of a village movie house in Mississippi, playing to 300 whites on the first floor and 200 Negroes in the balcony.

The film industry had been created by and for the masses, and as the classes had ignored the screen in its youth, American exhibitors had never become sufficiently interested in analysis of audiences to realize that the more intelligent classes were now represented in the democracy of movie patrons and that their tastes did not jibe with those of the great majority. The industry had no methods of differentiation; its machinery was set to make pictures pleasing to all individuals in the huge first-run audiences, constituting a cross-section of society, in which all ranges of intelligence and taste and mood are represented.

In attempting such a task the producers were striving, of course, to accomplish the impossible. Confusion, bewilderment, and titanic expenditures of money were the inevitable results of such efforts. The movie theater had reached a period in which it should have been divided into classes, as the stage was separated into burlesque, musical comedy, and various types of drama and opera. There should have been small houses in which long runs of the best films could have been presented to discriminating audiences at high prices, houses of medium size at which the middle ranges of mentality could have found entertainment at lower prices than at the "high-brow" houses, and then the huge theaters for everyone at admittance rates graded to fit all purses.

Unquestionably too many theaters had been built nearly everywhere in America. The profits of theater operation had made the field very attractive to real-estate speculators, and many districts were "over-seated." In southern California in 1926, there was a great over-abundance of neighborhood and downtown houses; experts estimated that five years must pass before increased population would absorb all their seating capacity; in Chicago, over-building had forced some theater groups through the drastic reorganization methods of receiverships. Similar conditions existed in many sections, and when the growth in theater attendance failed to maintain its former speed, competition among theaters for the patronage of the public became very expensive. Costly orchestras and vaudeville acts preceding the films became a regular part of the entertainment of most first-run houses, and many neighborhood theaters, striving to maintain large attendance at high admittance prices, added orchestras and vaudeville to their programs.

The old showman adage to the effect that people will always find the money to see a startling novelty was followed by the exhibitors, who combed the world for novelties. The larger houses offered vaudeville acts, condensed versions of light operas, exceptional dancers and eccentric orchestra leaders who hopped and jumped and clowned in mad efforts to interest the ticket buyers. Neighborhood theaters conducted lotteries on Saturday night, giving away prizes contributed or provided at wholesale cost by merchants in the district.

Novelties always draw audiences—for a while. *As long as the novelty effect lasts* the public responds, but as soon as the newness wears off, audiences drop away. The first films themselves were novelties, as was each step forward in the rapid development of movie production and exhibition. Moreover, each new trick, each new improvement in picture quality or picture exhibition, further trained the screen's followers in habits of discrimination and selection that made the problem increasingly more difficult.

Something was needed to stimulate interest in the screen, something so powerful that it would overcome the lukewarmness and the silent antagonism to the price of tickets and draw people in swarms to the box offices. What could that thing be? Better pictures? More vaudeville acts? Or what? The movies found the answer to its problems, and found it in the characteristically romantic manner that has always been the industry's principal charm.

WHEN Edison invented the motion picture machine to be used in conjunction with his talking machine, he had originally intended to combine them in one cabinet. After he lost interest in the commercial development of the movies, his experiments lapsed. The combination of sound and motion pictures, in crude, imperfect form, was achieved in the Edison laboratory, and test talkie-movies were seen and heard there by the scientist and his associates, but nothing but the kinetoscope was carried to conclusion.

During the following thirty years, many other men continued to work in the field of reproducing sound in connection with the movie screen. Some of them tried to synchronize the movement of phonograph and film projector so that sound would be delivered simultaneously with the projection of pictures. Others tried to use a diaphragm and a needle (similar to the diaphragm-and-needle device of the phonograph) to register sound waves on the celluloid of the photographic film. In this latter system, the needle makes a small "sound track" at one side of the picture.

From the early years of screen exhibitions, the movie industry maintained interest in sound pictures, colored pictures, and stereoscopic pictures, the general assumption always being that eventually all three problems would be successfully solved. It was taken for granted that American inventive ingenuity would encounter no insurmountable difficulties in accomplishing these extensions of the film, and movie people confidently awaited the day when audiences would see motion pictures filling the proscenium arch of the stage in natural colors and with stereoscopic depth, and hear faithful reproductions of natural sounds.

Color pictures had been achieved in laboratories, through various processes, and had been exhibited in theaters in 1912-14; although far from perfect, they gave promise of progress. Stereoscopic photography was being studied by a dozen or more investigators in the United States, and many others in Europe labored to fasten two eyes to the one-eyed camera—to make a pair of lenses that would lay hold of the third dimension hidden in the background of photographs, and carry it forward to give depth to screen picturization. The foremost believer was George K. Spoor, pioneer film manufacturer, who organized a laboratory for stereoscopic research in his Chicago studio, and devoted a considerable part of the large fortune accumulated through General Film and Chicago real estate to experiments in the third dimension that continued for more than fifteen years.

Sound received attention from even more scientists, inventors, and engineers than did color photography and stereoscopic lenses. Laboratories announced, from time to time, that the talking picture had been achieved, and occasional exhibitions of sound devices were given, but none of them ever reached a position of practical application.

During the World War great impetus was given to the invention and perfection of all methods of electrical communication. Invention ceased to be a matter of individual ingenuity, and became a scientific operation conducted in large, well-equipped laboratories and shops, where physicists, engineers, and chemists worked together to solve the riddles of electricity, atmosphere, metals, and gases. Such laboratories are owned by the corporations engaged in the telephone, telegraph, and electrical industries, and the patents on devices invented or developed in them usually pass to the ownership of the corporations. The American Telephone and Telegraph Company and its subsidiaries, Western Electric Company, Electrical Research Products, Inc., etc., owned many important patents before the war, and in the years since, this group of corporations had acquired many more. General Electric Company and Westinghouse Electric and Manufacturing Company were very active in the field of wireless telegraphy and radio, and each of these corporations acquired a large group of valuable patents. Lee De Forest and other radio inventors held patents of importance and value.

After the war a condition of confusion resulted from this scattered ownership of thousands of patents, each owner insisting that his rights were being infringed by manufacturers operating under other patents. Radio, the new method of communication and amusement, was threatened with a mass of litigation that would have seriously hampered its progress. The large communication and electrical companies, acting together, organized a new company, called Radio Corporation of America, and turned over to it many patents essential to radio. R. C. A. immediately became the foremost factor in the new industry.

By 1924-25, several inventors and scientists had definitely established the route that talkie-movies had to follow from actor to audience, which may be simply and non-technically described:

First the sound waves must enter a microphone and be carried to a diaphragm and a needle must record the pulsations on a disc, such as the ordinary commercial talking machines use, or on the celluloid of a photographic film; second, after the sound waves are recorded they must be reproduced, and this is accomplished by using a needle and diaphragm, as in the talking machines, or by projecting light through the sound track on the film, causing the recorded sound waves to flash against a diaphragm, which pulsates and starts them on their journey into the auditorium; third, the sound waves, now moving on their journey, must be amplified by tubes similar to those used in radio sets, and carried on by electrical devices similar to those used by telegraph and telephone companies; fourth, at various points in the auditorium at which the sound waves must be delivered to the audiences, other delicate telephonic and radio devices must be employed to deliver the sound waves to the audience, or amplifiers must be placed near the screen, to project the sound waves into the auditorium.

In order to accomplish these various steps in the journey of sound waves from actor to audience, apparatus or methods must be used that were in whole or in part covered by the many patents of American Telephone and Telegraph, General Electric, Westinghouse or Radio Corporation and other owners of communication and electrical patents. Moreover, the talkie inventors had to enter the field covered by the phonograph patents of Edison, Gramophone, Victor Talking Machine, and others. The eventual "discovery" of practical talkie-movies, therefore, was not the dramatic achievement of an individual, but a consummation toward which many engineers and laboratory technicians made their contributions.

Some time before William Fox encouraged his engineer, Theodore W. Case, to experiment with the sound-track-on-the-film in 1925-26, engineers in the Western Electric-Electrical Research-Bell Telephone laboratories, and others in the Victor Talking Machine laboratories, were striving to synchronize the talking-machine disc and the movie film so that dialogue would appear to come from the shadow-players' lips as action flowed along the screen. In the laboratories of the Radio Corporation another group of scientists were trying to make sound tracks on films, reproduce them and distribute the sound waves through an auditorium. In a score of smaller institutions, similar experiments were in progress.

The telephone group of research laboratories developed their method of synchronizing the talking-machine disc with the motion picture film, and following the early practice of using Greek derivatives this invention—or, rather, consolidation of several inventions, processes, and methods—was given the trade name of "Vitaphone."

Fox was the only one of the movie magnates interested in the efforts to produce talkies. Zukor was busy expanding his international empire, Loew had turned over much of his responsibilities to Nicholas Schenck and was enjoying his wealth, Laemmle was bustling from Universal City to New York and to his birthplace in Germany and back again, the heads of First National were intent on their own problems of theater consolidation and studio operation. The business of movie-making had finally become well established and the few corporations remaining in the industry were making large profits; prudent business men would not jeopardize this apparently safe situation by jumping to something radically different from the existing order. When representatives of the Vitaphone offered the device to the screen's principal overlords, the apparatus yielded a squeaky, squawky assemblage of crude noises. They decided its use would be offensive to theater patrons, and, after reasonable consideration, replaced the subject of talkies in the pigeonhole it had occupied for many years.

Years before, the autocrats of General Film had rejected feature pictures because of their conviction that the masses could not assimilate them; the autocrats of 1925-26 rejected talkies because of their conviction that talkies were not good enough to satisfy the same masses. . . . Whatever may be the reason for caution, when the rulers of the movies grow conservative, the Muse of the screen must smile as she rolls back the scroll of three decades of history; a brief scroll, and one that has as its most certain constituent the uncertain, the romantic, the adventurous, the picturesque. The Muse certainly laughed aloud as she recalled the scornful disdain with which General Film magnates had dismissed the upstarts, Carl Laemmle, William Fox, William W. Hodkinson, and Adolph Zukor, with their daring new ideas, only fifteen years earlier. Now those same upstarts were the new overlords who considered the movies tamed, and believed that the tremendous forces wielded by the moviegoing populace were at last safely in leash. Blinded by their own vast empire, by the bricks and mortar of their temple-theaters, by the power of wealth and the adulation of sycophants, they had grown cautious, fearful of endangering the solid position they so comfortably enjoyed. And thus they missed their opportunity and the screen went through still another of the mad gyrations that had made its history the most romantic and unpredictable of all American industrial endeavors.

WARNER BROTHERS—Harry, Sam, Albert and Jack—had followed the trail from nickelodeons to exchanges and state's rights distribution, and finally to the production of pictures. Immediately after the World War, they purchased the remaining forty acres or so of the Beesmyer ranch on Sunset Boulevard, in Hollywood, and built a modern studio. Harry Rapf, successful in vaudeville and picture producing, was engaged as general manager of the studio, and a program of feature pictures began to go through the state's rights exchanges which had been assembled into a national organization by the corporation.

The brothers had no sooner got their business under way when the "battle of the bankrolls" swept all studios into the orgy of out-spending, and they saw their own resources melting away. They had to have more money, or retire from the field with nothing but losses to remember. The days of easy capital had passed; the Warner project was rather too large for private financing and not old enough to enlist Wall Street support. Harry Warner, the oldest of the brothers and the head of the clan, racked his brain in agony and desperation to find a supply of funds.

Although Los Angeles had become the capital of motion picture production, financing for the studios was almost all coming from New York. Los Angeles banks occasionally made loans on individual pictures and to studios and producers, but by and large the movie game was too queer for deposit-bankers to understand, and their cautious, prudent participations in its kaleidescopic changes had permitted New York investment bankers and other financiers to absorb nearly all investments and loans in the industry.

Motley H. Flint, vice-president of the Los Angeles Trust and Savings Bank, was a banker with curiosity and temperament. Interested by the rapid expansion of the movies, he determined to investigate the business to the end that he might learn its peculiarities and make possible and safe the acquisition of motion-picture financing for his bank. He extended his acquaintanceship with producers, visited their studios, and obtained first-hand information regarding production, distribution, and exhibition methods; and soon his bank and its associate, the First National, with the assistance of Harry Chandler, publisher of the Los Angeles *Times,* Thomas H. Ince, and other producers, organized the Cinema Finance Company. Through it and the Flint banking connections, Los Angeles became an active competitor of New York in studio financing. Dr. Giannini, head of the Bank of Italy group of corporations, later expanded his operations in southern California, bringing William G. McAdoo, Joseph Schenck, Cecil DeMille and other picture people into his association. The Giannini interests eventually reached a more important position in movie finance than the Flint group. But, in 1919-20, when Harry Warner and his brothers were staring at the cold face of defeat, Motley Flint was the principal Los Angeles banker to whom the studios had to look for assistance.

It so happened that Harry Chandler, George Young, publisher of the *Examiner,* Henry McKee, banker, and other Los Angeles business men with appreciation of the importance of the studios to their city, and with keen desire to assist the members of the industry in every sensible way, asked me to talk to a group at the Chamber of Commerce. I spoke of the work of Motley Flint and of the services he had rendered to motion pictures and to Los Angeles. George Young printed the speech in the *Examiner*. Harry Warner read it, and, although he had never met Motley Flint, visited the banker and presented arguments to demonstrate that Warner Brothers was an undertaking worthy of banker support. Flint was favorably impressed by the producer, and investigated the corporation carefully; he made it possible for the Warners to borrow $1,000,000 to carry them through the crisis.

The Warners swung their productions into line with the "bigger and better" movement, making a successful star of Irene Rich, a screen actress, and bringing from the stage one of its best known actors, John Barrymore. Their business prospered, and within a few years they were able to enlist the backing of Goldman, Sachs and Company, Wall Street investment bankers, who floated an issue of Warner stock amounting to several million dollars. The money received from this source had to go into the ever-yawning mouth of mounting studio costs, but Warner production and distribution progressed encouragingly until the unanticipated menace of theater concentration spread its paralysis through the ranks of all manufacturers except the few who had safeguarded themselves by buying houses. The brothers had extended their credit and financing possibilities to the utmost in developing their studio and exchange operations, and they lacked sufficient capital to buy a national circuit of first-run theaters.

As theater lines grew tighter and tighter, and one company after another disappeared from production and distribution because of inability to obtain first runs, the condition of the Warners reached its most acute stage. The Flint money was gone; the Goldman Sachs money was invested in production; the Warners were making fairly good pictures, but inch by inch they were slipping down hill because of insufficient theater connections. Apparently they were destined to go the way of the great majority of the fighting army that had passed out of the industry.

After the squeaky talkie-movie of the Bell Telephone engineers had been rejected by the monarchs of the screen, it reached Warner Brothers on its journey around the circle to find a sponsor. Sam Warner went to the Bell laboratories, listened to its demonstrations, examined its mechanisms, and enthusiastically declared to Harry, "It's far from perfect, but it's farther along now than films were when they first swept the country. It can be improved rapidly, and it will sweep the world."

Warner Brothers made a contract with the telephone corporations under the terms of which they were to have exclusive use of the new device for a term of years, and then they attacked the grim task of obtaining enough financing to carry through the experimental period of production and exhibition. With fluency born of desperation they persuaded bankers to advance a limited supply of capital, not enough to make them safe, but, as it was all they could get, it had to suffice. Their initial experiments in producing talkie-movies were in the form of one- and two-reel comedies and vaudeville acts, and several weary, nerve-racking months had to pass before these offerings could be made ready for exhibition or theaters could be wired for their presentation.

Meanwhile Warner pictures were disappearing from more first-run screens; Warner quarterly reports had changed from profits to losses; Warner shares had sunk almost to the vanishing point on the stock exchanges.

Sam Warner died—and Harry aged ten years in three.

In the late spring and early summer of 1926, the Warner Vitaphone and the Fox Movietone appeared on screens simultaneously. The Movietone subjects were similar to the Vitaphone, principally one- and two-reel comedies and acts transferred from the vaudeville stage, and Fox effectively used the Movietone in his news reels. One of the momentous events in motion picture history was the Movietone reproduction of President Coolidge's presentation of the Congressional medal to Charles Lindbergh for his flight to Europe in "The Spirit of St. Louis."

The industry did not instantly awaken to the importance of Vitaphone and Movietone. By the autumn of 1926, talkies were still regarded as an interesting but very imperfect novelty that seemed to have aroused some enthusiasm in the large cities in which a few theaters had been equipped with sound-reproducing apparatus, but there was no general feeling that the screen had entered the most revolutionary period of its existence. Theater owners and managers, watching the patrons of houses using Vitaphone and Movietone, and trying to analyze audience reactions, were confused. The critics of the talkies were outspoken, but the majority of ticket buyers, as usual, had no emphatic comment to offer. The cost of equipping a theater with talking apparatus was ten to thirty thousand dollars, depending on the size of the auditorium and the engineering-acoustical difficulties to overcome; and, as such an investment was not justifiable if the novelty was to be short-lived, many exhibitors hesitated. The few that plunged and installed sound equipment reaped their reward within a few months. By the spring of 1927, the movement of the public toward talkies was unmistakable; by the autumn of 1927 it was a stampede. The manufacturers of equipment could not begin to fill orders, and exhibitors grew frantic because of delays in turning their silent screens into talkies.

Sound pictures proved to be more than an evanescent novelty; they were a new fundamental that aroused such wide-spread, deep interest that stay-at-homes, whose flagging zeal had been disturbing exhibitors and producers for several years, rushed from firesides to ticket windows and caused talkie theaters to boom as theaters had seldom boomed in the past. In every way the reception of sound pictures by the public was a complete and final demonstration of the domination of entertainment by the masses. The Zukor, Loew, First National groups, all the overlords of the screen who had rejected the talkie devices because of their mechanical imperfections and limitations, were proven to have lost their sensitivity to the unspoken desires of the mass of ticket buyers.

The overlords had been right in their anticipation of the disappointment and distress of hundreds of thousands of men and women when their ears were assaulted by the flat, dead tones or the rasping harshness of the early sound-reproducing mechanisms. To these hundreds of thousands, the talkies were canned music and canned dialogue in the most painful form. They missed the restful charm of the silent film, and resented the intrusion of this horrible conglomeration of noises into theaters. Sophisticated screen critics and professional commentators on the movies, who had spent years in perfecting themselves in the art of sneering and jibing at current offerings of the silent drama, suddenly reversed their positions and poured out pæans of praise to the beautiful art that was disappearing before the onward march of the unspeakable talkies. Fan magazines and newspapers conducted voting contests in which their readers were asked to cast ballots for or against the talkies, and many bitter letters condemned the new horror.

In the ten or a dozen years since features had appeared, the chasm between the educated classes and the populace—those who more or less use their brains for thinking and those whose brains are merely beginning to wriggle—had been concealed beneath the assembling of vast audiences in huge first-run theaters. The casual observer might have concluded that no mental differences existed in America; the movies had bridged the gulf and our people, at least so far as entertainment was concerned, were living intellectually in common. But the wide gulf was still in existence, and the talkies tore away the thin veil that concealed it. The great mass of ticket buyers swamped the theaters that offered any sort of noise, reveling in the racket that proceeded from amplifiers and filtered into their ears from all parts of the auditorium. If they could see and hear a vaudeville act two reels in length they enjoyed it; if they got nothing more than the sounds of an aeroplane or a mob cheering at a football game, or the tinny reproduction of an orchestra, they were pleased. They selected for patronage the theater that advertised "SOUND" or "TALKIES" in preference to the one which merely offered old-fashioned silent star pictures—"old-fashioned" only in the sense that six months before the star had been a popular idol.

I venture the suggestion that the great public was unconsciously hungering for sound when the talkies arrived. The phonograph and the radio had created a gigantic appetite for canned noise, just as the spoken stage had for centuries built up an immeasurable desire for entertainment through the canned drama, the "celluloid monstrosities" that so shocked and horrified the intellectuals of 1896 to 1914. The canned noises of 1926 were certainly no worse than the canned dramas of 1906. And the noises had the very important advantage over the early celluloid dramas in that many engineers and scientists and great electric companies were working feverishly to improve them, whereas the films of early years had to make all their progress through the efforts of novices, unprepared in any way to cope with the problems confronting them.

Month by month the sound pictures improved in quality. By 1927, talkies had lost nearly all of their early squeaks and squawks and were delivering to audiences reliable reproductions of music and of the human voice. By 1928, several important, well-made sound pictures reached the screen, and there was no longer any room for doubt about the popular acceptance of talkie-movies.

Fox, with his country-wide chain of theaters, was able to exhibit the Movietone as rapidly as factories could build projecting machines to transmit both sound waves and light waves. The Warners, with only one theater of their own in New York and a few others throughout the country, were dependent on rentals to Paramount, Loew, First National, and other owners of first runs, and for a while they could not exploit their novelty so easily. Although within two years the Warners seemed to have leaped overnight from obscurity and hazard to the heights of glory and rock-ribbed solidity, they encountered many perils before reaching solid ground.

The production of talking pictures required a transformation of studio practices. Sound-proof stages had to be erected at a cost of hundreds of thousands of dollars each. New cameras were required. In the Vitaphone process delicate, costly synchronizing machinery, to time precisely the recording of the picture on the film and the music or the voice on the phonograph disk, had to be installed, and a staff of highly paid engineers was needed to operate it. Directors had to learn how to direct in silence, with the camera and its operators in a glass cage; actors and actresses had to learn the tricks of the microphone, and players whose voices had never been trained had to take lessons in voice culture.

Fresh millions of dollars were required by Warner Brothers and Fox before they could expand their facilities to meet the requirements of this new method of entertainment. Fox was in good condition to meet this strain; but the Warners had extended themselves to the utmost to carry their Vitaphone experiments through the period of initial presentations; even after there was no doubt of the popularity of the Vitaphone, there was much doubt of the Warners' ability to hold on until their talking pictures could fight their way into enough theaters to bring back some of their costs. During the darkest days of their struggle, they conceived a great idea. They had made pictures with dialogue; they were making the first full-length all-talking picture, ("Lights of New York," released in 1928, which, although weak and unimportant as a production, enthralled audiences as the forerunner of a new era); they had experimented with music, instrumental, orchestral, and vocal. Out of their experiments arose the conviction that a film interspersed with songs would provide the most successful talkie-movie entertainment.

They concluded that if they could engage Al Jolson, premier burnt-cork stage comedian and dean of the tribe of Mammy singers, to make a full-length picture, the name of Jolson and the novelty of a talkie-movie with his humorous dialogue and sentimental songs would compel first-run houses to open their screens. Jolson listened, and agreed, and a scenario and music, entitled "The Jazz Singer" (from a play of the same name by Samuel Rafaelson), was prepared. In several months, the production appeared on the screens of the few Warner theaters.

By the time "The Jazz Singer" was ready for release, the principal theater managers throughout the United States had become convinced that talking pictures would work a revolution; enough experiments had appeared to prove that the public had approved sound on the screen, and many exhibitors were ordering apparatus or examining the devices of various manufacturers. "The Jazz Singer" proved to be one of the plays that have occasionally shaken the movie world like an earthquake, people crowding into houses to see it, and leaving the theaters completely converted to the talkies. The Jolson production was the final act in closing the doors of the silent film era and sweeping theaters and studios into a whirlpool of "all-talkie" productions. Thereafter there could be no doubt of the success of Vitaphone or Warner Brothers.

After once turning the corner from hardship to prosperity, the progress of Warner Brothers was very rapid. Their balance-sheets showed losses of millions in 1925-26-27; profits of two or three millions in 1928, and more than seventeen millions, for the enlarged Warner group of theaters and studios, in 1929. Stock dividends, split-ups of the shares, and cash dividends made "Warner Brothers" one of the alluring features of the New York Stock Exchange, to which the shares were transferred early in 1929.

CHAPTER EIGHTEEN
SOUND AND FURY

IN each movie revolution prior to that of talkies, many corporations had disappeared. The talkie upheaval was unique in that no important company was permanently injured by its success. Warner Brothers-Vitaphone entered the movie firmament as a brilliant new star, but its lustre did not dim that of Paramount, Fox, or Loew. The success of Movietone increased the popularity of the Roxy and the other new houses acquired or built by Fox, and the quality of talking pictures produced under Sheehan's management in Hollywood added greatly to the prestige of the Fox name. Although for a year Warner and Fox, as the pioneers in talking-screen entertainment and as the holders of the rights to use the mechanisms of production and reproduction, enjoyed a powerful advantage over Paramount, Loew, First National, Universal, Hearst, United Artists, R-K-O, Columbia, Pathé, and the few other producers still operating, none of these competitors were driven from business.

During that year the progress of other producers was seriously impeded, and their profits diminished by the popularity of Fox and Warner. However, although Warner controlled the Vitaphone, Paramount, Loew, and First National controlled the overwhelming majority of first-run theaters. Compromise followed. Warner and Western Electric granted to Paramount, Loew, and

First National the rights to use the equipment upon the payment of a royalty, based on the gross receipts of their talking pictures for a period of years. The large producer-exhibitor corporations opened their screens to Warner productions, and any decrease in studio profits was more than offset by the increased earnings of their theaters, due to the enlarged box-office receipts brought about by the talkie madness.

RADIO CORPORATION of America, having become a movie owner through its consolidation of Radio-Keith-Orpheum, absorbed the Victor Talking Machine Company, thus enabling Radio to share in the talkies through both the disc and the sound-track-on-film methods. Vitaphone, Movietone, and Radio did not monopolize the sound film field. Lee De Forest, early experimenter in sound-track-on-film, brought suit against Fox and Case on the grounds that they had infringed his patents. De Forest engaged actively in the business of selling producing and reproducing equipment, and a dozen other companies, most of them small, came forth and offered to theaters and studios apparatus for recording and reproducing, which they claimed to be of their own invention.

For a while the talkie branch of the industry was filled with strife. Vitaphone, Movietone, and Radio vigorously fought one another. Western Electric refused to permit its theater apparatus to be used by any other manufacturers; Movietone and Radio made intimations of extensive litigation. The bitterness lasted for a few months until the American Telephone and Telegraph Company, the dominant patent owner and corporation giant of them all, suggested that they make peace and get together towards the common end of selling talkie entertainment to the world. The suit of Lee De Forest against Fox-Case was the only important litigation that continued in the courts.

Vitaphone, Movietone, and Radio agreed that any producer could install the necessary studio apparatus, upon payment of a share of the gross receipts of his talking pictures, and theaters using their equipment could exhibit pictures of any manufacturer. The well-organized studios of Paramount and Metro-Goldwyn-Mayer enabled these corporations to progress rapidly once they entered the talking contest. They first used "sound effects"—music, the roar of mobs, the hum of aeroplanes, the rattle of machine-gun fire and similar sounds—with their silent pictures, but soon swung into all-dialogue or dialogue and vocal music. Within a year or two, Paramount and Metro-Goldwyn-Mayer had transferred all their productions to sound, and maintained in the new field the prestige they had acquired on the silent screen.

Universal, Pathé, Columbia, Tiffany, and R-K-O, almost the only producer-distributors left in the industry aside from the four big groups—Paramount, Fox, Loew and Warner—built sound-proof stages, installed equipment, and made talking pictures. Harold Lloyd, Mack Sennett, Amedee J. Van Beuren, Christie Brothers, Educational Film Corporation, Hal Roach, and other manufacturers of comedies and short subjects put their studios on a talkie basis. All manufacturers had no choice—the silent film was quickly passing into the Great Silence, and if they were to retain positions in the industry they must make talkies or nothing. By the autumn of 1929 the conquest of the talkies was so nearly complete that a silent picture could not be found in any house above the rank of third or fourth run, except in a few small New York theaters that presented European movies.

THE effect of the sound screen on exhibition was materially to accelerate the concentration of theater ownership in a few corporations. At first, exhibitors in general were perplexed by the cost of equipment and the engineering difficulties of operating the equipment so that faithful sound reproduction would reach the audience. The intricate and delicate apparatus required the attention of a competent, expensive engineer and this cost was a burden on the owner of one or a few houses. Fox, Para-

mount, Loew, and Warner could employ staffs of expert engineers and keep them traveling around a circuit. Then, too, as
sound pictures immediately drew large audiences to theaters of
the better grade, many exhibitors who had not brought sound
equipment early enough and had lost business to competing
houses, became disgusted with the complexities of the new era
and were willing to quit the game.

Warner Brothers, Paramount-Publix, and Fox became the
focal points in theater movements, and R-K-O, too, expanded
its holdings extensively. Marcus Loew died in 1926 just at the
time the sound pictures made their entrance, and Nicholas
Schenck succeeded him as president of Loew's, Inc. Loew and
Zukor had been friends and business associates for many years;
Zukor's daughter had married one of Loew's sons; there were
rumors that Paramount and Loew would be merged, and there
were rumors that the Federal Trade Commission, which had
never pushed its suit against Zukor to conclusion, would frown
upon such a consolidation. After Warner Brothers began to rise
in popularity and wealth, gossip connected Warner and Loew
in combination.

The wise heads of the industry did not regard William Fox
as a likely contender for the Loew kingdom. Loew and Fox
had fought each other for a score of years, their first scrimmages
starting in nickelodeons and continuing into struggles for
popular-price vaudeville-film houses, thence progressing through
the years into the era of movie palaces. Theirs was no "friendly
enmity"; they were fighting men who carried on their contest
to the day of Marcus Loew's death. Nevertheless, in the spring
of 1929, Fox purchased from Mrs. Loew and her principal associates, the controlling interest in the great Loew enterprises, at
a price close to $50,000,000. Before he bought control of Loew's,
Inc., Fox had purchased the important Poli Circuit of theaters
in New England—established by an orchestra musician, a Greek
by birth, who started with a small house and ended with a score
of theaters in principal eastern cities for which Fox paid him
more than $20,000,000. At the close of 1929, Fox owned five

hundred or more theaters in America, and controlled the Gaumont chain in the British Isles and enough others throughout Europe to make him a dominant figure in European exhibition.

First National having long ago ceased to be a cooperative protest against Zukor, had continued in practically the same structural condition as existed at the time of Jules Mastbaum's death. It had a large, modern studio at Burbank, California, and its principal stockholders, the Stanley Company, owned or controlled several hundreds of theaters, while several thousand other houses used its pictures.

Warner Brothers, now making millions of net profits a year, and besieged by investment bankers offering unlimited backing, purchased control of the Stanley Company, thereby also acquiring control of First National. Warners later bought Fox's minority interest in First National, as well as other circuits of First National members, thereby completing the final chapter in the history of the exhibitor-producer cooperative movement.

Zukor and his chief theater lieutenant, Sam Katz, president of Publix Theaters, acquired several of the chains built up by First National members and other circuits throughout America and expanded Paramount's list of houses in foreign lands.

At the close of 1930, Paramount-Publix, Fox-Loew, Warner Brothers, and R-K-O owned a total of 2,500 to 3,000 theaters in the United States and Canada. Paramount-Publix was the principal owner of first-run houses of large seating capacity, although Fox-Loew was well represented in all important cities and Warner Brothers were buying theaters rapidly. No other corporations had continued in the contest for theater position; Universal made no attempt to increase its holdings and United Artists retained its circuit of first-runs in large cities and was content.

In 1930, the Hays organization placed the number of theaters in the United States at about 22,000. Although Paramount-Publix, Fox-Loew, Warner Brothers, and R-K-O held only about a tenth of the total, these corporations, through ownership of nearly all first-runs and many of the best second-runs, effectively dominated the industry.

The government of the United States, through the Federal Trade Commission, took cognizance of the increased stature of Fox and Warner Brothers by bringing anti-trust suits under the Clayton Act, in November, 1929, against Fox for having acquired Loew's and the Warners for having bought Stanley-First National.

The commission's bill of complaint declared that Fox and Metro-Goldwyn-Mayer controlled forty percent of the total production of pictures in America, and Warner, with its First National and Vitagraph affiliations, controlled twenty-five percent. Of the remaining thirty-five percent, the government attorneys said that Paramount had approximately two-thirds, or a fourth of the total, leaving ten percent to all other producers. In regard to theaters, the government alleged that Fox, including Loew's, Inc., controlled "a large proportion of the best and largest first-run motion picture theaters throughout the country, and in the New York metropolitan district their theater holdings, embracing most of the first-run houses, total at least fifty percent of the seating capacity of all motion picture theaters of any class."

TALKING pictures brought about drastic changes in studio operation. The principal sufferers were the famous actors and actresses who had maintained the externals of the star system since the fading of the great celebrities, in 1925-27. Thousands of orchestra musicians as well lost employment, while song writers, composers, and dancing and singing girls came into the sunlight of public favor.

The first appearance of sound pictures aroused interest, but no general apprehension, in the studios. Most of the supervisors, writers, directors, craftsmen, and executives, like most of the exhibitors, were mildly excited, but inclined to believe that many years would be required to perfect the mechanical and electrical equipment. A few producers studied the new apparatus and its product carefully, knowing that if the talking screen became a reality instead of a vision, nearly all the labors of twenty years might go to the scrap heap—the art of making movies, slowly, painfully, and expensively developed since 1906, would have to be so completely revised that almost nothing might be salvaged. The players, as a class, were more optimistic, the stars believing that their grip on the public could not be shaken by any novelty.

But the tidal wave of sound burst on Los Angeles even more quickly than the sanguine prophets had predicted. Its effect was seen most clearly on Warner Brothers' lot—a little while ago the Warner plant was in the doldrums; suddenly it was seething with life. Engineers, imported from electrical laboratories in New York, Schenectady, and other eastern cities, began to walk around the stages, and the air was filled with talk of "acoustics," "sound-proofing," "recording," "microphone," "amplifiers," and the like. Carpenters, masons, plasterers, and decorators had to learn new tricks, the object of which was to exclude from a stage all sounds from the outside, and, further, to protect the set on which players were working from every disturbance, however faint, that might creep into a microphone. Scores of players passed through the gate to the dressing-rooms and thence to the new sound-proof stages; and the famous stars observed that many of these were actors and actresses who had never worked in Los Angeles before, or were character or small-part people who had hitherto found only occasional employment. The newcomers were, in the main, vaudeville players summoned to the studio to record in sound-films the acts they had been presenting on variety stages.

The technique of vaudeville is highly specialized and unrelated to the screen. Very few players from variety theaters had ever found places in the studios, and to most vaudevillians, Hollywood had seemed like a faraway Paradise in which lucky actors lived in luxury while they bumped about the country in one-week stands. Then sound arrived; producers learned that vaudeville acts, presented in one- and two-reel talking pictures, were greatly enjoyed by the movie public—and scores of variety players found themselves suddenly transported to Hollywood, with fat contracts in their pockets.

Many of the early Movietone experiments were made in the east, but the transformation of Fox's Los Angeles studios soon followed the changes in Warners'. Almost overnight—at least so it seemed to the bewildered studio colony—Winfield Sheehan started work on sound-proof stages, and began grooming writers and directors in the technique of the new form of entertainment and inviting players to step before the microphone for "voice tests."

Then all studios slowed down on production and marked time. Word was coming from New York that theaters demanded "sound" in pictures. Sound must be had, somehow, some way, or distribution of the films would decrease alarmingly. The silent-film studios—and this included everyone except Warner and Fox—were spending $150,000 to $500,000 on each six or eight-reel negative, while road shows or specials were costing from $1,000,000 to $2,000,000 each. Investments such as these had to move promptly to market at top prices, or the wealthiest studio would soon find its profits changing to deficits. There was a scramble for sound. Pictures that had been completed and sent to the exchanges for distribution were recalled, and sections of music and dialogue were inserted in them. Prologues of talking film, and sometimes epilogues, were tacked to silent films, these expedients saving the lives of numerous expensive pictures during the year or more of transition from silent screen to talkies. Several months passed before the silent-film studios reorganized their stages and equipment for sound pictures—weary, anxious months for members of the nervous film colony.

Many of the actors and actresses had graduated from the stage to the silent screen and understood the use of the voice, but a few of the older players had no knowledge of speaking or singing, or else their voices were undesirable. Many of the younger men and women had never worked on the stage and were not voice trained; nearly all the popular younger stars belonged in this category.

Directors and writers might learn the new tricks demanded by the camera in a glass cage, but the microphone concealed on the set in front of the cage was a horror and a nightmare to the players. The mention of it gave them cold shivers and to endure the test of talking into the little contrivance brought attacks of stage fright worse than appearance before an audience of ten thousand people. A few girls, Bessie Love, Lois Wilson, and one or two others, took advantage of the lull in the studios to jump to the vaudeville stage or stock companies, and obtain work as troupers back of the footlights. They were very wise; their several months of brushing up their voices enabled them to return to the studios and promptly win positions in the talkies. Others enrolled as students with the many voice teachers who flocked to Hollywood to glean quick, easy dollars from players who were beautiful, but could no longer be dumb.

Producers were very cautious about renewing contracts or giving new ones. They could not be sure who would or would not be accepted by the public in this new sound era, and their uncertainty spread misery through the ranks of players. Stage stars, leads, and character people began to augment the vaudeville newcomers in Hollywood, and for a while it appeared to film folk that they were to be replaced in toto by their brethren of the foot-lights.

After several months of uncertainty a new set of conditions settled into form. Talking movies proved themselves a severe taskmaster. The player, in addition to knowing how to act, now had to have a speaking voice, trained to register properly through the microphone, and a singing voice of at least good quality. Scores of screen players submitted themselves to the rigorous demands of the microphone, and after days and weeks of exacting labor developed excellent voices. Improvements in recording apparatus enabled engineers to build up the sound waves of some weak voices or soften the harshness of strident ones, but numerous individuals were unable to come within the limitations of any equipment and for their services there was slight demand.

The silent films had required little or no study of rôles; con-

scientious, ambitious players had made a practice of reading
scenarios carefully and giving careful study to their parts, but
lazy, careless, or overconfident actors skimmed through the
scripts or left their interpretations entirely to the director. The
talkies banished laziness and carelessness. Now every rôle, large
or small, had to be read and rehearsed until each actor and
actress in the cast was proficient in acting and in voice.

Although, after the months of early excitement had passed,
comparatively few of the stage players summoned to Hollywood
had won permanent positions in the studios, the sound films in
other ways thinned the ranks of screen actors and actresses.

First: The methods of story-telling in silent films and talkies
are not analogous. The silent film continuity was longer, often
much longer, than that of the sound film. I have compared the
story-telling of the full-length silent film to a novel or a long
short story; sound-film technique was more closely related to
that of the stage. The goal of the silent screen was to tell the story
with the smallest possible amount of talk or verbal description.
Titles indicating speech were avoided by the best screen writers,
who used them only when necessary for clarity, emphasis, or
emotional effect. The trend of the silent movie was farther and
farther away from speech, and the better players and directors
were approaching a quality of technique that told the story with
a minimum of spoken sub-titles and even a minimum of lip
movement. Charlie Chaplin almost never used speech or the
indication of speech. Jean Hersholt and a few other actors could
convey almost any impression to an audience by pantomime.

Speech, or lip indication, or printed sub-titles halt the action.
Producers learned in 1908-10 that about one-quarter of the
audience could read a printed title in one-third to one-fifth of
the time required by the slower minds in the theater, and they
timed the length of a title's appearance to accommodate inert
mentalities. Action and movement were more easily assimilated;
hence the producer or director who wanted to make rapid-
moving pictures learned to tell his story with few title delays.
The ultimate aim of silent films was, therefore, to avoid speech,

or eventually to do away with it entirely. This was accomplished by the German director, Murnau, in "The Last Laugh," and several Americans were ready to adopt this technique whenever they thought that American audiences were ready for it.

At the opposite extreme, the stage depends almost entirely on dialogue, the players telling the story, portraying characters, and arousing emotions principally by means of conversation. When sound entered pictures, much action had to be eliminated from the films in order to provide time enough for the players to deliver their speeches, and time enough for the audience to absorb what was said. Necessarily this new technique greatly reduced the number of scenes. Sound pictures move more rapidly than stage plays. That is, more action is possible on the talking screen than on the stage, and even in all-talking screen plays, the use of continuous speech was found undesirable, action frequently replacing dialogue without the loss of audience attention. Sound pictures, technically, occupied a position perhaps midway between the silent screen and the spoken stage. Talkie enthusiasts declared that sound films had taken the most desirable elements of each form of entertainment and had merged them into a new, more desirable form.

However, from the viewpoint of screen actors and actresses, talkie technique called for fewer scenes and consequently fewer days of employment. Also, as the microphone could work more efficiently on sound-proof stages than out-of-doors, the talkies reduced or entirely eliminated the out-door sequences that had been a prominent feature of silent films. Work on out-door sets and locations usually called for the use of large mobs, and these sequences were almost invariably expensive. Bringing the pictures indoors reduced camera days and decreased the period of players' engagements. Photographic work on a silent film of standard length in 1925-26 may have averaged eight or ten weeks, while the average stars made four to six pictures a year. Standard sound films went through the studios in two to six weeks of camera time. The average player might get two or three weeks work in the silent, and a week or ten days in the sound, a reduction of one-third or one-quarter in days of employment.

Second: For several years the thinkers in the industry had been insisting that longer runs should be given to the best, or the most entertaining, pictures; they argued that four or five hundred meritorious productions a year would be more acceptable to audiences, and more profitable to the industry, than the six to eight hundred that were being made. When talkies absorbed the screen, in 1927-28, the solidity of this argument quickly manifested itself. Acceptable sound films immediately established long-run practice all over America, and the necessity for producing too many pictures diminished. By 1930, the production of long pictures was well on its way downward toward four hundred, perhaps three hundred, a year.

Longer runs and the enormous enthusiasm of the public for talking pictures intensified the importance of first-run houses. A first-run theater that might have paid a producer $3,000 for a week's exhibition of a silent picture, yielded $10,000, perhaps $25,000, for a run of two weeks to six weeks for a sound film. Many talking pictures each earned $1,000,000 for the producers; earnings up to $2,000,000 were not rare. Another important change was the speed with which returns came back to the manufacturer. A silent film showing one-week runs at say an average of a thousand or two thousand dollars a week in a hundred first-run houses had to be shown for three to six months to earn $100,000 to $200,000. A sound film might show in ten houses in its first month and earn $100,000; within two or three months it might have brought back $500,000 or more. This change in exhibition conditions was the best of good news to the producers but it was not good to the players. Longer runs, reducing the number of pictures made, cut another slice out of the possible weeks of employment per annum. Shortened scenarios made one reduction; long runs, another; competition of a number of vaudeville and stage players, still another. The golden age of film players, that began when Charlotte Pickford decided to get more money for her daughter and Charlie Chaplin demanded and got $10,000 a week, had now passed into history.

Third: There remained another economic bridge for the Hollywood colony to cross. Before the talkie era nearly all of the six hundred to eight hundred features and specials made annually were dramas or melodramas—that is, films that told stories with plot and substance, and called for acting. Chorus girls, dancing girls, and other similar concoctions geared up by stage producers for the benefit of the Tired Business Man and the Out-of-Town Buyer, had occasionally been used in the movies, but the main structure of entertainment was built by actors and actresses portraying characters and telling a story. As it was easier to reproduce music than dialogue, the early sound pictures experimented freely with music; and as music is most readily saleable when decorated with femininity, song-and-dance girls were soon added. A short step farther and the sound films were immersed in the production of girl-and-music shows of the type that had hitherto never been known to the screen but had been sold by the stage in New York at $6.60 to $20.00 per orchestra chair and in other metropolitan centers at the highest rates the traffic would bear.

There must have existed a tremendous longing for such entertainment, hitherto witnessed only by the customers of Florenz Ziegfeld, Earl Carroll, George White, and their stage compeers. The sound-film glorifications of feminine pulchritude were swamped by floods of customers; audiences poured into movie theaters presenting girl-and-music talkies, neglecting or giving second consideration to the dramas and melodramas that recently had been their choicest film fare. The whole country seemed to have gone chorus-girl mad.

This new type of amusement had a marked effect on Hollywood employment conditions. The large out-door and in-door mob scenes of silent films had given casual work to several thousand men and women of all the types imaginable. For a dozen years, Hollywood had been the magnet that drew cowboys from all over the west, and two or three hundred trick rodeo riders, bull-doggers, horse-wranglers, and cow-hands of every sort could be rounded up quickly by a casting director. At the other pole, several hundred women of all ages were available for ballroom scenes, bathing-beach mobs, and so forth. Between were the plain citizens and their wives and children who composed the cheering populace that huzzahed as king or queen rode through the streets in costume plays, or supplied the audiences in theaters or court rooms, or made up throngs wherever they were needed.

As the chorus girls came in, the cowboys faded out. Twinkling slender bare legs, powdered torsos, and marcelled wigs replaced leather or sheephide *chaparreras,* flannel shirts, and ten-gallon Stetson hats. The rude gambling hall and rough saloon of the Golden West were superseded by settings of extravagant night clubs, palatial apartments, intimate boudoirs, and even more intimate dressing-rooms. For a while at least, pictures of the great open spaces, where romance and adventure had a free hand, had lost their power to thrill audiences and there was not much of any place for the rough riders and cowhands who had colonized in Los Angeles and its suburbs. Some day the Golden West might again enthrall screen audiences, but the cowboys could not wait for that time to come. Very few of them could adapt themselves to indoor characterizations; some of them could be used in the rougher types of mob scenes, but most of them faded from studio life into the rodeos or back to the ranches.

The tottering star system received its death blow from the talkies. During all the years of silent films, the lovers inevitably were the center of attraction. Experienced and expert character actors had received little attention—save for a few exceptions—and their value in the market was one-fifth to one-tenth that of the romantic stars. When, however, talkie audiences were able to hear voices as well as watch acting, they broadened their appreciation to non-romantic as well as romantic rôles. The box-office declared that stars, receiving $3,000 to $7,000 a week on yearly contracts, were often worth no more than character players who could be engaged by the week for $1,000 or $2,000.

As promptly as contracts with stars expired, the studio corporations failed to renew them, and almost every celebrated player was soon without employment, or was fortunate to obtain engagement at much lower rates. Nearly all of the "new stars,"—that is, those who had succeeded the great favorites in 1924 to '27—now faded out of fame; there remained only a handful of romantic players who could lay any sort of claim to star glory and numerous new young women and men, working at "practical" salaries, and the character actors who found themselves the recipients of unexpected popularity and attractive wages.

Douglas Fairbanks and Mary Pickford appeared together for the first time, in a talking version of Shakespeare's "Taming of the Shrew," which audiences accepted without noteworthy enthusiasm. Charlie Chaplin declared against the talkies. He produced "The Circus" in 1929 as a silent film, and "City Lights" in 1931, with "sound effects," both of which have been successful despite the public enthusiasm for dialogue. But it is hardly likely that anyone but Chaplin could so successfully have challenged the public will. Harold Lloyd plunged into talkies and retained his adherents; Ronald Colman, Norma Shearer, Greta Garbo, Charles Farrell, Janet Gaynor, Billie Dove, Bebe Daniels, and a few other romantic stars crossed the bridge from silence to sound. Betty Compson, whose career had been dotted with occasional successes and numerous half-failures since "The Miracle Man," was a trouper who could play romantic or character parts at will, and she became one of the outstanding celebrities of the sound screen.

Marie Dressler, now well into the early autumn of life, rose to the top of the box-office list, her success constituting one of the bright romances that dot the pages of the movie record. Miss Dressler, famous in vaudeville and musical comedy, had been one of the earliest screen actresses, appearing in comedies in 1912-14. She had been featured in "Tillie's Punctured Romance," the film in which Chaplin made his start. Returning to the spoken stage, she enjoyed popularity for years, finding the way back to Hollywood in 1926, when the stage no longer offered her high positions and large compensation. Like many artists, she had been liberal with money in the years of easy income, and now in middle age she needed work—and work was hard to get. There were parts, occasionally, for short periods, and the salaries were modest. All in all, the prospect was discouraging; and then sound pictures came, and her splendid acting and strenuous, vibrant voice struck a responsive note with audiences.

Bessie Love, a girl who had left high school to be a Vitagraph star in 1918, and had passed through varying ups and downs in a decade, found herself one of the popular character-romantic actresses of the sound screen, as did Evelyn Brent. Conrad Nagel, Clive Brook, George Bancroft, William Powell, Edmund Lowe, Victor McLaglen, Warner Baxter, and Wallace and Noah Berry were character men to whom the talkies brought generous public approval, even when their rôles were non-romantic. Maurice Chevalier, a French actor and music-hall singer, was imported to the United States, where he learned English, and soon packed the theaters. Ruth Chatterton and Ann Harding, from the Broadway stage, won solid positions for themselves in the talkies.

The broader public viewpoint enabled producers to deal with a larger assortment of story material than hitherto; for example, John McCormack, popular Irish-American tenor who had never appeared in silent films, was successful in sound pictures. Lawrence Tibbett, grand opera star, became a screen lover widely acclaimed, and Jeannette MacDonald, also from the opera stage, was welcomed by the movie throng.

Easy earnings and easy spending in Los Angeles went into the silence with the silent films. The change in economic conditions was so definite by the autumn of 1929, that a Los Angeles journalist, describing the general prosperity of southern California, made this comment on the film colony: "Less money is coming into circulation (in Los Angeles) from the queens and kings of Hollywood. Huge salaries, out of proportion to economic equilibrium, are being sliced; in many cases profitable contracts are not being renewed; budgets are being pared; shut-downs and layoffs are no novelty and additional thousands of extras have been forced to find such work as they could get in the process of readjustment. A good many of them have failed to get any, but the crop is perennial."

The stage was not in condition to use many of the famous volunteers from Hollywood who now found themselves without work. The screen vogue of the vaudeville artists lasted only a year or two, and these players, drifting back to their former positions, absorbed most of the employment opportunities in the theater, which was in a far from flourishing condition. The competition of silent pictures had made serious inroads on the stage and the talkies were now working such injury to stage receipts that the "legitimate" drama was having a hard struggle to live. George Arliss and other stage stars who had never been conspicuous in silent films, transferred their talents to the talking screen, and more and more people were deserting the theater for the bright lure of the talkies.

Lillian Gish was one of the first film stars to leave the screen for the stage, and was one of the few to establish a high position for herself. Dorothy Gish, Colleen Moore, Vilma Banky, Rod LaRocque—the list of those who turned from Hollywood to Broadway was very long, but not many were successful in selling their talents in the declining market-place of the "legitimate drama."

The entertainment group that suffered the most severe losses because of sound films was not the players, but the thousands of musicians employed in hundreds of theater orchestras. Even before the talkies had gone far in the reproduction of the human voice, Movietone, Vitaphone, and other sound devices were selling orchestral programs, from opening overture through the feature picture and to closing selection. As soon as exhibitors became convinced that they could depend on machinery and electricity—some times plus the pipe organ—for their music, they began to dismiss their orchestras, and within two years the sound track had taken the place of orchestra players in nearly all but the largest first-run houses. Many, many musicians,—despite their union, which had been very powerful for several decades—were unable to obtain engagements anywhere.

Prosperity, withdrawing its favor from orchestra players and screen actors, smiled on new groups, notably the "theme song" writers and composers of music for girl shows and arrangers of musical accompaniments for sound film dramas. "Tin Pan Alley" (the Longacre Square district in New York), was the heart of the popular music industry in America. Here are the offices of the music publishers, and to them flocked daily the writers of words and the fabricators of tunes to try out their latest compositions before the publishers. The practice of song makers is to work in pairs, a word-smith and a tune-smith, and the more popular members of the craft usually were under contract to publishers who paid them reasonable advances against royalties. When the screen producers embarked on the theme-song industry, their emissaries scoured Tin Pan Alley for talent, offering salaries and royalty inducements that quickly shifted the center of music-making from Longacre Square to Hollywood Boulevard. Writers of songs, composers, and arrangers of instrumental music to the number of several hundred moved to Los Angeles and assumed the positions of importance, and the salaries, that had hitherto been enjoyed by actors.

The overwhelming vogue of girl-and-music shows passed within two years, and then the tune-smiths found themselves no longer in great demand. A few of them retained their positions; many had to return to Tin Pan Alley.

CHAPTER NINETEEN

TODAY AND TOMORROW

WITHIN a brief two years engineers had made remarkable improvements in sound mechanisms. The cost of sound-reproducing apparatus was reduced to a few thousand dollars for small theaters, and by 1931 nearly every movie house in America was presenting talkies. From 1927 to the summer of 1930, the desire for novelty surmounted objections to high admittance prices, and people paid fifty, sixty, seventy-five cents, and even a dollar for tickets. Very few houses, in city or country, offered good seats at night for less than forty or fifty cents. The show for the poor man and his family seemed never to have existed—or, at any rate, to have disappeared forever.

However, before 1929 had ended, the novelty, merely as a novelty, was beginning to lose its power to draw patronage. The public became lukewarm to girl-and-music shows, theme songs had to be very tuneful indeed to win popular approval, and vaudeville acts were no longer attractive. Audiences again demanded well-written, well-produced plays, equal in quality to the high standards of silent pictures, with the addition of convincing dialogue. Sound now had to be an essential and natural part of the story. The trend of screen dramaturgy moved definitely toward the use of silence wherever possible, dialogue being employed, in the best pictures, only when it would advance the story.

As the musical shows decreased in popularity, among the first plays to return were westerns! They were not as "blood-and-thunder" as the cowboy stories of the early and middle periods, but none the less they were based on the same structural principles that had been so popular for three decades. Modern society plays, too, were successful, and detective and crook stories and all other forms of currently popular literature and stage drama were presented in talking celluloid. Constance Bennett—daughter of Richard Bennett, a favorite of the stage—became a new, bright star of this period, earning with R K O $100,000 per picture. Far removed from Miss Bennett's smartly gowned romances—and illustrating the variety of themes that were popular as talkies—two pictures may be mentioned. Edna Ferber's "Cimarron," a melodramatic novel of the white man's rush to Oklahoma when this land was opened to homesteading; and "All Quiet on the Western Front," a realistic story of the German view of the World War, by Erich Remarque. "Cimarron" was produced by R K O, with Wesley Ruggles as director and Richard Dix in the leading rôle. "All Quiet on the Western Front" came from Universal with an all-star cast headed by Lew Ayres, and directed by Lewis Milestone.

The use of color photography increased materially when theater receipts advanced with the popularity of sound pictures. Photoplays entirely in color were shown and gave promise of soon attaining technical perfection.* The last physical advantage

---

* Progress in color photography may be briefly summarized in three forms: (A) separating the three primary colors—red, blue, and yellow—in camera work, and joining them together again in projection; this process is that known as "Lumière," "Kinemacolor," and by other names, and resembles the systems used in making color half-tones for printing; (B) a method of supplying colors to films by stencils, or by other processes which may be compared to lithography; (C) the application to the celluloid strip of two coatings of film, one in front, the other in back, the back coating carrying the color separations. There are other color processes than these, but this sketchy description is sufficient to indicate the principal methods of movie color in 1931.

That which I have roughly designated as a process somewhat similar to lithography became more generally used than others. "Technicolor" was its principal exponent. Back of Technicolor was the interesting story of William Travers Jerome, famous throughout America in the early years of this century

of the stage, the charm of human beings appearing in person, was now being seriously threatened by the increasing technical accomplishments of the screen. With convincing reproduction of sound, dialogue, and music, and with the improving presentation of natural colors, all that was now lacking was the stereoscopic film, to add a third dimension to the two-dimensional movie. Many experiments with wide film and wide screens were in progress to achieve this end, and it seems probable that in the not too remote future it may become a reality.

The widespread popularity of talkies was reflected in the earnings of the few large corporations remaining in business at the close of 1929. Paramount's balance-sheet for that year showed total assets of $230,000,000, and net income of $15,500,000. Fox's profits amounted to $13,500,000 and Loew's to about $12,000,000. Warner Brothers' net income (including First National) was $17,000,000, and R K O's $2,000,000. The total commerce of the American film industry was probably in excess of a billion and a half dollars a year; some estimates placed it above two billions.

In the autumn of 1929, there came a sharp ending of the gigantic boom in all American industries. The unparalleled prosperity that had persisted, except for the brief deflation of 1921, since Armistice Day, suddenly disappeared. The stock exchanges suffered a collapse that shook the country. This change in business conditions proved to be not a mere readjustment and deflation, such as that of 1921, but an international depression that closed hundreds of factories and threw millions out of employment.

as New York's crusading, fearless district attorney who wrought havoc with the red-light districts and destroyed the infamous "brass check" system of white slavery. Jerome became a political idol, but when he failed to be elected mayor of New York, he retired from public life and concentrated his energies on his hobby of color photography. With the assistance of A. W. Erickson, a wealthy advertising agent, and other capitalists, Jerome, after a dozen years of laboratory experimentation, made possible the commercial success of Technicolor.

The application of a color film—a second coating—to the back of a celluloid strip, was developed by scientists and engineers in the Eastman laboratories. By 1931 it had been successfully applied to the small amateur motion picture cameras, which use film about one-fourth the size required for standard screen projection. Experiments are now in progress to extend the general principles of this and similar methods to standard films.

The United States wrestled with the hardest times it had known in many decades.

Through the final quarter of 1929 and the first four months of 1930, while all other industries were fighting to keep above the floods of disaster, screen theaters rolled up new records of earnings and profits that astonished Wall Street. The financial experts decided that this once chaotic business had been brought under control, and they became so confident of the strength of the movies that some of them, during the Wall Street collapse, considered pictures a "depression-proof industry" and advised investors to place selected film shares on their most preferred lists. In 1909 motion-picture investment was scorned; in 1919 it was a doubtful speculation; in 1929 it had become a favorite of conservative bankers and economists!

Without doubt the investment experts were well within the facts in concluding that organization had replaced individualism in motion pictures. The days of personal grandeur had almost faded from the screen even before sound pictures. Now the huge profits of the talkies and the large investments required by sound mechanisms definitely placed motion pictures among the industries dependent upon Wall Street, and Wall Street, interested only in regular dividends, looks with suspicion on corporation management that seeks personal publicity.

Zukor had made Paramount-Publix an organization comparing favorably with the principal Standard Oil companies, General Electric, United States Steel and other premier industrial corporations. Elek John Ludvigh remained as general counsel, and Jesse L. Lasky as first vice-president. Sidney R. Kent had progressed from a position as salesman to vice-president and general manager. Sam Katz, president of Publix, had charge of the corporation's hundreds of theaters. Benjamin P. Schulberg was the head of Los Angeles studios, and Walter Wanger was in charge of production in New York. Emanuel Cohen was the manager of the newsreels and short subjects.

Loew's, Inc. had been well organized by Marcus Loew and Nicholas Schenck, and after Loew's death the organization, with

Schenck as president and David Bernstein as vice-president, continued its progress unabated. Louis B. Mayer, chief studio executive of Metro-Goldwyn-Mayer, built a production staff— the principal executives of which were Irving Thalberg, Harry Rapf, Hunt Stromberg and Eddie Mannix—that had no superior. Year after year, through the constant changes in audience tastes, M-G-M continued to send to the screen a procession of successful pictures. R K O's affiliation with the large radio, telephone, and electrical manufacturing corporations, gave it standing in Wall Street.

Paramount, Loew's, Inc., Warner Brothers, and Fox each was well established in Wall Street, and Zukor, Loew, Schenck, and the Warners had followed the usual practice of corporation management in permitting the majority of their common, or voting, shares to be distributed to the investing public. William Fox, however, was of different temperament, and had never permitted the controlling stock of his corporations to pass from his hands.

When, in 1926-27, the Movietone and the Vitaphone suddenly rushed into popularity, and theaters and studios clamored for sound equipment, Fox financed his expansion by obtaining loans, aggregating about $30,000,000, from the Bell Telephone interests and the Fox bankers, Halsey, Stuart and Company. These obligations were in the form of "short-time paper," maturing in the winter of 1929-30, and Fox planned to retire them by the sale of additional stock. Arrangements to this end were progressing in the summer of 1929, when, while he was motoring on Long Island one day, an automobile crashed into Fox's car and injured him so severely that for several weeks he was in a hospital. During that time the Wall Street collapse occurred, and the inclination and ability of the investing public to buy securities were seriously weakened.

Then came a series of disagreements between Fox and his bankers, the bankers charging Fox with violations of agreements to permit them to proceed with the new financing, and Fox replying that the bankers and the telephone company were striving to gain control of the Fox corporations and displace him as ruler. In public statements Fox declared that he had built his companies "from their small beginnings with a cash capital of $1,600 to a business of $108,128,313 for the past year," and placed the value of the Fox corporations at more than a quarter of a billion dollars, with net earnings of $17,000,000 a year. In the battle between Fox and the financiers, the latter received the support of Winfield R. Sheehan, vice-president and general manager; Saul E. Rogers, vice-president and counsel; James R. Grainger, general sales manager; C. P. Sheehan, foreign manager; John Zanft, vice-president and general manager of the Theaters Corporation; and Courtland Smith, general manager of the Fox Movietone News.

Mrs. Susie Dryden Kuser, widow of Colonel Anthony N. Kuser, of Newark, New Jersey, who had been one of Fox's early financial associates, joined in a suit for a receivership of the producing and theater corporations. Fox, in an affidavit answering Mrs. Kuser's charges, stated that her husband "was, up to the time of his death, one of my staunchest friends. ... In 1915 he bought preferred stock of the corporation, investing $200,000, for which he received forty percent of the preferred and twenty percent of the common stock. His investment was repaid him in about two years and thereafter he made a large fortune as a result of his original investment, amounting, as we estimate it, to more than $5,000,000."

After several months of intense activity in the courts and extensive publicity in the newspapers, the Fox contests were settled by William Fox selling his stock, for $18,000,000, to Harley L. Clarke, of Chicago, a capitalist of prominence in electrical and allied public utilities and president of the General Theaters Equipment Company. Clarke succeeded Fox as president of the Fox corporations.

William Fox retired from motion pictures. Carl Laemmle, now the sole survivor of pioneer days, remained as the only movie magnate owning the majority stock of a general producing and distributing corporation. Even in the field of short subjects very few individuals had continued to retain control of their companies. Mack Sennett, Christie Brothers, and Hal Roach were almost the only ones in Los Angeles. In the east the only important producer who had continued from the pre-feature era, maintaining his independence of mergers and Wall Street, was Amedee J. Van Beuren. When Pathé left General Film to establish its own business, Van Beuren allied himself with Pathé as an independent producer of travels, comedies, novelties, and other short subjects. His "animated cartoons," were successful as silent films; when talkies entered he caused his lively caricatures to talk and sing and dance, and with the addition of sound they became more popular than ever. After the establishment of R K O, Van Beuren's productions were distributed through R K O-Pathé exchanges.

Unfortunately, the economists and investment experts who praised the movies as a "depression-proof industry," overlooked the human element that dominates the destinies of the screen. The financiers, the economists, and the movie rulers themselves ignored the basic fact that the industry had grown to prodigious size solely because it could provide entertainment for *all* the people—and that the admittance prices of 1929-30 were very high for the hard-times' pocket books of the populace. After the spring of 1930, too many patrons became extremely selective, buying tickets only for exceptionally attractive pictures. Instead of going to the movies once or twice a week they went once or twice a month. The radio took the place formerly held by low-priced film theaters as regular amusement for the entire family.

In 1931 the industry again faced the "spotty" conditions that perplexed its leaders in 1926-27, before sound films drew the stay-at-homes to the playhouses. A few theaters were enjoying good business; some were just holding their own; and too many were suffering losses. Although the film business was maintaining a position comparing favorably with that of other industries during the general depression, even the large producing and theater corporations showed severe reductions in earnings. Movie shares on the stock exchanges went down with those of railroads, public utilities, and the other industries that had not won the award of "depression-proof."

Officials of film corporations sought frantically for methods to retain and to increase the popularity and the profits of their products. Every department of each branch of the industry was scrutinized for weaknesses and for new ways to insure the stability of picture entertainment. The principal source of dissatisfaction was with studio costs and the entertainment quality of the pictures themselves. The cost situation was very irregular; a few program negatives came through at $150,000 each, many at nearer $300,000, and some at about $500,000. Comparatively few specials, or pictures with high-priced stars, were appearing, and their cost might be anything from a million to four million dollars.

The box-office appeal of too many pictures was very low. In some productions the actual technical quality was so inferior that New York executives, after viewing the films, laid them on the shelf, preferring to lose the negative costs rather than risk injury to theater attendance by exhibiting a feeble talkie. One prominent executive told me in 1931: "We have learned that a poor picture will keep audiences away from a theater for several weeks. Our theater investments are so great that we simply can't gamble with danger by offering the public a picture that isn't at least fairly good. A good play draws crowds not only while it is running; during the following weeks it will keep attendance up until a poor one comes along. No matter what they cost, it is economy to throw away the bad pictures."

Another able producer told me: "Negative costs are simply insane extravagance. Players' salaries are not high now. None of the items in actual studio expense are as high as they were a few years ago. The one new cost is that of sound-recording, and that has been offset by reductions in other items. It would easily be possible to save $150,000 to $200,000 on nearly every program picture without even slightly decreasing the quality. The only reason for this present crazy condition is that most of the studios in Los Angeles are rotten with carelessness and inefficiency, and the Los Angeles managers persistently defy the instructions of New York officials to reduce costs. Poor quality in most of the studios' output is due to politics, favoritism, and downright lack of ability to engage competent men and women." This man declared that the corporation of which he was a prominent executive could add $5,000,000 to $7,000,000 a year to its net earnings by the elimination of avoidable studio extravagance.

Still another man, highly placed in the industry, made this diagnosis: "The trouble with picture-making is that it is located in Hollywood. The Hollywood colony is small, and the principal studio people are so clannish and so divided into small cliques that they never see beyond the boundaries of the tiny world they've built around themselves. They've simply 'gone Hollywood,' as some white men in Oriental countries 'go native,' and in 'going Hollywood' they have lost touch with the public and with good business sense. It is literally true that New York officials are not able to control the studios. My own men out there give me reasons galore why costs do not come down and quality does not go up, and that's all they give me. I'm just about ready to close our Los Angeles studios and move all our productions to New York. This town (New York) is so big that they can't get together in clans and cliques, and here they will at least occasionally see and hear something that's different from the constant chatter of Hollywood."

In the searching analysis of depression days the theater branch of the industry received its share of readjustment. One decision, upon which all the large corporations apparently agreed, was that in acquiring hundreds of theaters they had attempted an impracticable objective. Entertainment is too personal and too intimate—even too whimsical—for any one man in New York, Chicago, or Los Angeles to manage a national chain. Each city, almost each neighborhood, demands special consideration. When the movie officials reached these conclusions, decentralization of theater control began to replace the rapid centralization of a few years earlier. Houses were sold or leased to individuals. Large circuits were divided into small ones. Every effort was directed toward restoration of personal management, or at least close, intimate supervision, of each theater.

Revision in admittance rates was usually downward in 1931, but important changes in exhibition methods may attract larger audiences in the near future by increasing the prices in some houses, and lowering them in others. Small, beautiful, well-constructed theaters may be organized for long runs of serious or intellectual dramas, operas, or the more technical forms of music and the ballet in sound pictures; patrons of such theaters will expect the finest forms of screening and sound reproduction; they will expect reserved seats; and they will pay prices high enough to justify producers in making screen entertainment to please them. Next in the price list can come large first-run, centrally located theaters in which scales of fifty cents to a dollar will obtain. A third classification may be large but older houses, in downtown districts or neighborhoods, that can operate as second or third runs, with admittance ranging from fifty cents down to twenty-five or fifteen.

In twenty-five years the American people—and large sections of the public in other lands—have learned to enjoy theaters more than any other form of amusement, entertainment, or mental recreation. They like to be part of a crowd at a theater. As long as our present form of civilization continues these desires and habits will endure, and the screen will broaden and modify its methods and prices to provide whatever manner of theatrical exhibitions the public will patronize.

LOOKING backward for a moment, as we review these comments on studio quality and costs and the decentralization of theater management, and try to peer into the future of the movies, we are reminded of the thoughts expressed by various film leaders in the years gone by. Hodkinson insisted that production, distribution, and exhibition should be kept separate. Aitken avoided theater ownership except in New York City, and that was only for the purpose of advertising Triangle films. Williams and Tally believed that exhibitors could distribute pictures, but that good production could be insured only by encouraging independent manufacturers. Zukor tried in several ways to avoid the burden of theater responsibility. In 1921, at the Minneapolis convention, he agreed—despite his determination to hold first place in the industry—that independent production was essential to the progress of the movies. Cecil DeMille, D. W. Griffith, Samuel Goldwyn, Douglas Fairbanks, Charles Chaplin, Mary Pickford, and many other men and women had insisted upon and fought for independence in production.

During the happy-go-lucky years of freedom—from 1896 to 1920-21, when the formation of large theater circuits began to close the screen to independents—each of the producers, the directors, and the writers who had made important contributions to film progress was either a tyro or a daring adventurer when he attempted the innovation that broke down established customs and won public approval. During these years the man or the woman with a new or different idea merely had to induce a distributor or the head of a producing corporation to permit him to try the experiment. Then he was free to proceed. If his undertaking was a failure—and of course most new ideas always are failures—some money was lost. If his scheme was successful, new waves of attendance flooded the theaters, and large profits rewarded the movie magnate who had sponsored the innovation.

Such practices were unbusiness-like. Often they appeared amateurish and silly to the efficiency engineers and financiers who dominated nearly all other American industries. However, in some mysterious manner, this loose-jointed operation of democracy in production, ruled by numerous "big bosses" in distributing corporations, each of whom had autocratic power in his own little kingdom, succeeded in creating craftsmanship and entertainment that pleased the public.

When the merging of studios, exchanges, and theaters into a few large corporations, and the extravagances of the "out-spending era," had brought an end to independent production, the inelastic methods of bureaucracy replaced the loose practices of democracy in picture making. Now a new idea, instead of having to win the "O. K." of one autocrat of a little kingdom, had to run the gauntlet of editorial boards, production committees, and conferences of various sorts. A multitude of alleged experts awaited the fellow with the new thought, and when his innovation had completed the circuit of the studio's intricate system there was seldom a trace of originality or novelty left in it. The sharp shears and heavy smoothing-irons of the experts had transformed the wild, crazy idea to one of the rigid patterns in favor, at the time, with the studio head and his yes-men and yes-women. The good pictures of 1930-31 were usually the work of an individual to whom authority had been given, or of a small group powerful enough to control the system.

The movie problems in 1931 were not unlike those the industry faced in 1909 when the Motion Pictures Patents Company and General Film seemed likely to control its destinies. In 1931, bureaucracy and theater control had reduced the constant flow of ideas, inspirations, defeats and triumphs that had made the screen a most vibrant instrument of modern civilization. The movies found the way to destroy the grasp of the patents-film trust. I have no doubt that they will find the way to break down the restrictions of studios and theater systems and again make the screen free to men and women with new thoughts or novel methods of expressing old ones. Indeed, the most significant trend of 1931 was the indication of the return of independent production. Several of the largest corporations were opening their screens to picture makers not connected with their studios. Even Poverty Row in Hollywood enjoyed a renascence, and cheap "quickies" were once again finding acceptance in playhouses that wanted to revive their box-offices with alluring melodramas and low prices for tickets.

The movie magnates and their Wall Street allies were becoming convinced that large, beautiful playhouses and huge studios are, after all, mere assemblages of bricks and mortar and steel. Great capital investments and the trading in shares on stock exchanges cannot exist unless the business back of them maintains public interest at high pitch. That interest can only be maintained by the constant discovery and development of fresh ideas. The movies are in danger of stagnation, and the return of independent production is an encouraging sign that the revivifying flood of new inspiration will bring the screen an even greater popularity than it has enjoyed in the past.

I HAVE treated at some length the effect of motion pictures on the minds of the people, and these past events throw a clear light on the pathway that the movies will follow in the years to come. The screen has brought such wide enjoyment and relaxation to countless millions throughout the world, that the ideas presented by the printed page and the spoken word have been made to live. Joy follows the sensation of acquiring information and knowledge through the medium of entertainment. The means to advance civilization rapidly and effectively by the use of films is now merely awaiting the necessary organization to extend its beneficial influence to the farthermost settlements of mankind. Everywhere that movies have gone they have been welcomed by the populace; in China men gather in gardens to witness the marvels of the screen, and in India railroad cars, outfitted as miniature theaters, carry the movies into remote and backward districts. The Japanese have already become successful producers of pictures, and studios are being established in many other countries. Wherever movies appear, imaginations are stimulated, inert mentalities are aroused, and the prejudices and superstitions fostered by ignorance are broken down. The opportunity of the movies to spread entertainment and to disseminate education enjoyably is almost unlimited. Pictures are the "universal language" that philosophers and idealists have long held to be prerequisite to the universal brotherhood of mankind.

It seems safe to predict that the principal extensions of the movies in the near future will be in fields that heretofore have made progress slowly: first, educational, or teaching, films; second, non-theatrical, or scientific, pictures—those midway between general entertainment and teaching; third, the organized use of the screen in presenting a variety of information, including subjects as diversified as scientific and mechanical technologies, household and agricultural management, religion, morals, and ethics; fourth, a large development in manufacture, in foreign countries, of movies and talkies specifically adapted to the desires and needs of all nationalities and all races.

Teaching films, for schools and colleges, involve large investments of capital in their preparation and extensive organization to distribute them to our 250,000 schools; not until 1929-30 had there been anything further than pioneer work in this important direction. No department of movie endeavor has received more of the attention and enthusiasm of Will H. Hays than the efforts to develop films for classrooms. In 1931, the Hays organization was cooperating with numerous groups of educators, scientists, and business men to find the right methods of bringing text-books and text-films into harmonious relationship and general use.

George Eastman has established at Rochester, New York, a studio for the production of educational films, with Dr. Thomas E. Finegan, former commissioner of education of New York and Pennsylvania, at the head. A staff of educators is making schoolroom films linked up with text-books, so that after the student has read his lesson he can see the text come to life on the screen. The film is made in small size, requiring only a moderate investment in projection apparatus and screen. Eastman, in a few years, has supplied the corporation with more than a million dollars. Electrical Research Products, Inc., an associate of the American Telephone and Telegraph Company, has created an educational department to develop schoolroom films. The Fox corporations, Pathé, and other companies in the entertainment field have entered into "educationals." Publishers of school text-books are conducting experiments with films to be used in connection with the printed page.

Experiments to determine the effectiveness of classroom films have been conducted by the National Educational Association in twelve states, involving about eleven thousand pupils and two hundred teachers, pictures of geography and general science being used in the tests. The pupils pursuing each of the courses were divided into two groups, one known as the "experimental" or "film" group, the other as the "control" group. The use of motion pictures in the control group was prohibited.

The report of the association stated that "the children in the film group who studied geography showed a gain of thirty-three percent over their competitors in the second group; in general science the increased proficiency of the film group was fifteen percent. In addition, the film-taught pupils exhibited an increased interest in school work, greater originality, ability to think more accurately and reason more soundly, an increase in the quantity and an improvement in the quality of their reading, marked improvement in vocabulary, a clearer appreciation of environment, an extension of experiences beyond immediate environment."

Educational and teaching methods seemed in 1931 to be ready for revolutionary changes. Dr. William John Cooper, United States Commissioner of Education, in an address before the Department of Superintendents of the National Educational Association, at Atlantic City, voiced the opinion of many leading educators when he said: "Collegiate and professional education is rapidly shifting from Old World traditions to New World conditions.... The public school system itself manifests an activity which presages rapid changes within the near future. Not the least noteworthy among evidences that American education moves ahead are efforts of school men to adopt new tools to their use." Dr. Cooper selected "for specific praise the utilization of such schoolroom instruments as the talkie-movie and the radio.... Already the possibilities of the talking picture in recording the operations of great surgeons have been demonstrated. Men like the Mayos, who cannot be had for the faculties of our medical colleges, may perform their operations under the camera, explain them in detail, and send them not only into the medical schools but into every city and hamlet of the land to keep the medical profession up to date and alert."

"Non-theatrical" is a term usually used in the industry to describe pictures that are semi-entertaining and semi-educational. Films made by travelers and explorers, films made by the United States Government to show processes of farming, mining, and other activities, films made by manufacturers to show factory processes or to advertise their products before conventions of salesmen, are among these classes. Thousands of reels of interesting, informative, and useful movies lie in warehouses in the United States merely because no adequate facilities for distributing and exhibiting them have been devised. Within the next few years small theaters, halls, churches, school auditoriums, lodge rooms, hotels, and other places of congregation will be organized with screens and projection machines, and the business of distributing and exhibiting these varied classes of pictures will probably reach a volume of $500,000,000 to $1,000,000,000 a year within the next decade.

The experience of the American Museum of Natural History in New York typifies the fate of the average non-theatrical picture in the past. The museum constantly sends expeditions to the farthest quarters of the globe to carry on zoological, anthropological, ethnological, and archeological work. An expedition's motion pictures are exhibited at the museum, and are offered to other museums, schools, and colleges, but the limited use of this splendid material has been a constant cause of disappointment to Dr. Henry Fairfield Osborn, president of the institution, who has insisted that if methods of exhibition could be devised, millions of Americans, instead of thousands, would enjoy these remarkable movies.

In 1928, Mr. and Mrs. Martin Johnson returned from an expedition to Africa which had lasted about two years and had cost nearly a quarter of a million dollars. Daniel E. Pomeroy, George Eastman, and other capitalists who had financed the undertaking, shared with Dr. Osborn his keen disappointment that the splendid film record of the explorers' labors should slumber in vaults after a handful of people had seen the pictures on museum screens. Pomeroy and Dr. Osborn brought the Johnson movies to the attention of Frank R. Wilson, who was associated with the Jeremiah Milbank group in various picture matters. Wilson had been deeply impressed by the success of a few films of travel and exploration that had won success as theatrical exhibitions. The most important of these were "Nanook of the North," made by Robert J. Flaherty, and "Grass" and "Chang," each a six-reel movie record of the journeys of two camera men, Ernest B. Schoedsack and Merian C. Cooper in Asiatic lands. None of these pictures told a story in accordance with the accepted patterns of the studios, and yet each attracted large audiences.

Wilson was so pleased with the Johnson films that he selected six reels from the total of nearly two hundred, and exhibited the picture under the title of "Simba." "Simba" earned about $2,000,000 in America and abroad. The experience induced Wilson to resign from all other motion picture connections and organize "Talking Picture Epics, Inc." for the purpose of distributing non-theatricals. Among the first subjects offered by the Epics exchanges, in addition to "Simba," were Donald Mac-Millan's North Pole pictures, Dr. Robert Cushman Murphy's "The Bird Islands of Peru," Harold McCracken's films of the Aleutian Islands, James L. Clark's journey through the center of Asia, Dr. Ernest Cadle's two expeditions into Western Africa, and the nature and travel films of Captain Bob Bartlett, Dr. Raymond L. Ditmars, Roy Chapman Andrews, and William Beebe.

The extent of the field for these non-theatrical semi-educational pictures is indicated by Wilson's statement that "while there are approximately 20,000 motion picture theaters in the United States and Canada, there are 246,000 schools, 210,000 churches, approximately 15,000 business organizations which meet weekly, such as Chambers of Commerce, Rotary Club, and Kiwanis Club . . . 14,000 women's clubs, and 1,400 Y. M. C. A.'s."

The future extension of movies into many other fields of interest and usefulness presents enormous possibilities. The sale of "home study" courses to ambitious men and women who cannot afford to go to college or technical school has grown to be a large business in the United States. Scores of thousands of students are enrolled in correspondence schools, and many of the graduates of these home study institutions have won high positions in business, the professions, and in technological work. Experiments have already been made with talkie-movies in home study, and although each student has to rent a projector and screen, involving considerable expense for an individual, these courses are being eagerly sought. Perhaps this form of education will be accomplished by renting a hall, or any small auditorium, and bringing the students of a neighborhood together for group study in the various courses offered.

The use of films in medicine and surgery is not a matter of the future. As Dr. William John Cooper indicated in the address from which I have quoted, such movies are already in service. In 1926-27, Will H. Hays aroused the interest of the American College of Surgeons in preparing motion pictures for use in medicine and surgery. To cooperate with the Hays organization the college appointed as a committee such eminent members of the profession as Dr. J. Bentley Squier, Dr. W. W. Chipman, Dr. Franklin Martin, Dr. Allan Craig, Dr. Bowman Crowell, Dr. Malcolm McEachern, Dr. C. H. Mayo, and Dr. George W. Crile. George Eastman supplied the money for the studies of the American College of Surgeons and for a series of pictures made under the direction of the committee. These films were made available for doctors, hospitals, and nurses throughout the world.

Will Hays has enlisted the cooperation of European physicians and surgeons, and films showing the technique of the greatest practitioners in both continents are being shown at home and abroad. Noteworthy results have already been accomplished, as evidenced by this quotation from an official report: "Through use of the close-ups, the moving picture can bring the student intimately in contact with the operating table. He is, in fact, closer to the table than he could be in the classroom, and the details of the operation, whether they be arterial, nerve, or intestinal, the grafting of bones, or the work of tendons and muscles, are brought directly to his attention. Already where pictures of this nature have been shown in classrooms the average mark per student has been higher than by any other method."

The production of pictures directly for religious, moral, and ethical purposes, has been discussed in many quarters, but only a few attempts at such films have been made. These classes of movies—like all others in the non-theatrical, educational, and scientific sections—may be advanced by the lower cost of film machinery that began to be marketed generally in 1930-31. Cameras and projectors using small film—approximately one-quarter the size of standard negative—had been made practicable. Picture making and projection was less expensive, and, too, the cameras could be used successfully by amateurs.

That religious, moral, and ethical films can benefit mankind has been convincingly demonstrated by the result obtained solely as a by-product of the general amusement pictures shown in theaters. The two worst social evils in American life—the saloon and the white slave traffic—received a severe check through the early motion pictures; the latter has never been able to recover its lost ground, and beverage alcohol has been saved from extinction only by our well-intentioned but unscientific and unfortunate experiment with the eighteenth amendment to the Constitution. Sociologists had known for years that commercialized prostitution received most of its recruits from the army of lonely, entertainment-hungry girls employed in factories, stores, offices, and domestic services. Girls seldom wilfully entered the oldest profession; ordinarily they drifted along the streets in the evening, seeking companionship and amusement, and the drifting led step by step downward. Street-walking practically disappeared when five-cent store-shows spread across the United States by thousands, the girls finding in the movies amusement and recreation and a new outlook on life that propelled them away from the red-light district and into homes of their own or toward business or professional ambitions.

The cheap movie theaters lured so many husbands and fathers away from bar-rooms that thousands of saloons had to close their doors, and manufacturers and purveyors of alcohol became bitterly hostile to this winning competitor for the small coins of the masses. Farsighted brewers, convinced that the movie habit would supply to the temperance movement the force needed to destroy the political and financial power of the saloon, urged their fellows to withdraw from alliance with distillers and wine growers, and to save beer by placing it in a class by itself. In many large cities wealthy brewers maintained saloons on nearly every corner of business streets; soon after the nickel odeons and store-shows swung into their stride, hundreds of these choice locations ceased to be profitable as saloons and the brewers rented them to merchants. At a dinner given to President Wilson by the Motion Picture Board of Trade, in New York City on January 17, 1916, J. Stuart Blackton, the toastmaster, presented statistics concerning the effect of movies on the saloon industry. In one district, for example, the Wilkes-Barre section of eastern Pennsylvania, there were 10,000 saloons in 1906 and 1,400 in 1916. According to Commodore Blackton, such figures were typical of conditions throughout all America.

THE future of American films abroad is an interesting subject of speculation as the last pages of this book are being written. Can Yankee talkies maintain the international supremacy enjoyed by our silent movies, or will sound pictures produced in other countries reduce the popularity of American films? American commerce in general has been greatly benefited by the exhibition of our pictures everywhere in the world. Will the demand for American manufactures decline if foreign audiences learn to enjoy their own talkies in preference to ours? If we review briefly the existing conditions at the close of 1931, we may find the material upon which to base guesses concerning the future.

Sound movies traveled round the world almost as quickly as they had conquered America. As soon as sound apparatus became fairly reliable, American equipment was installed in numerous European theaters, and, with little delay, in the larger cities of the other continents. The novelty of pictures with sound effects created a sensation. People thronged the theaters in all countries to hear the new wonder, and when the Yankee talkies appeared they continued to draw crowds, despite their dialogue in English.

In 1931 several thousand theaters throughout the world were presenting sound, and the boys and girls in Berlin, Paris, Buenos Aires, Rome, Bombay, Shanghai, Los Angeles, and London were singing the same songs—the theme tunes they had heard in the talkies. The internationalism of the screen could be appreciated by a glance any week at *Variety,* the American trade journal of the entertainment industries. In 1930 its correspondents told stories of movie talkies in the world's principal countries, and if the screen had not yet become a common meeting-place for all peoples, it seemed to be rapidly approaching that position. *Variety's* Tokio correspondent reported, for example, late in 1931: "The biggest song hit in Japan this year has been the French *Sous les Toits de Paris.* Moreover, the theme song has gone like wildfire. Everybody can hum that tune. All the phonograph companies released it and all the music publishers jumped on it separately, so that there are probably nine sets of Japanese lyrics, all different. Perhaps No. 2 attraction of 1931 has been *The Blue Angel,* * with *Falling in Love Again* a song favorite, although not in the class of *Roofs of Paris."*

Soon after American sound equipment began to be installed in foreign theaters, European electrical and phonograph manufacturers—principally in Germany—produced sound-recording

---

* "The Blue Angel" was produced by Ufa, in Germany, with Emil Jannings and Marlene Dietrich in the principal rôles, and distributed in America by Paramount. *Sous les Toits de Paris* was a French comedy-talkie directed by René Clair.

and projecting machines and entered into competition with the Americans for this new form of business. Threats of lawsuits flew back and forth across the Atlantic for several months, until Will Hays went to Europe and assisted the principal patent owners of America and Europe to reach an agreement. This compact followed the general lines of the peace settlement made among themselves by Western Electric, Radio Corporation of America, and other companies in this country.

But apart from the problems of patents and of competition in manufacturing equipment, American producers had to consider a new phase of mass psychology which arrived with the talking pictures. Perhaps the universal acceptance of American silent movies could be attributed to their having created, in foreign minds, an almost perfect illusion. It was at least so nearly complete that even the presentation of a scheme of life unlike their own failed to destroy it. Perhaps the spectators' imaginations temporarily carried them into a dream world in which they accepted the alien presentation as a realistic experience of which they were participants. When the movies began to talk, the novelty of speech coming from the shadow players' lips was enjoyable, but nevertheless the sound of a foreign language reduced the illusion of reality. The dream world faded. The talking photoplay appeared as a counterfeit of life, and the instinctive clan feeling, the pride of race and nation, which might be forgotten while viewing a silent film, was aroused against the alien speech. The talking screen excited the caution, the suspicion, that comes—often subconsciously—with the arrival of a stranger. As was to be expected, audiences soon wanted to hear plays in their own languages.

American producers employed several methods in dealing with this new condition. Printed titles, in the language of the country in which the film was to be exhibited, continued to be used in some instances. Voices were "doubled" in Los Angeles studios —a sound track made by foreign actors in German, French, Spanish, or other languages, replaced the English sound track on the disc or on the film. A few of the largest studios employed complete casts of foreign players and made versions of their most important films for each principal country. Paramount opened a studio in France. In 1931 other American manufacturers were carefully surveying the foreign situation to determine whether or not they should establish plants abroad. The principal American corporations have theater affiliations in all countries where screen entertainment has acquired any considerable size, and their exchanges have been thoroughly organized all over the world. It is therefore possible for them to open studios wherever there arises a sufficient demand for home-produced talkies.

Progress in the production of talkies by the peoples of foreign lands has been restricted by the world-wide depression of 1930-31 and the political unrest that prevails in many countries. When better economic and political conditions appear, the installation of sound-reproducing apparatus in foreign theaters will advance rapidly. Talkies have already gone far enough to prove that all members of the human race are alike in at least one respect—they all enjoy screen shows, and sound pictures give them more pleasure than silent ones.

It seems reasonable to believe that the desire of audiences for talkies of their own will benefit the film industries of all large countries more effectively than kontingents, quotas, or tariffs against American movies have operated in the past, but it is hardly likely that the progress of foreign talkies will work any serious dislocation of the American industry. The solid commercial position of the Americans throughout the world will enable them to participate in foreign developments for themselves, or as partners of foreigners in production, distribution, and exhibition. Therefore, when the business of any country moves ahead, the Americans will share in its progress. Nor is it likely that American exports will be injured by any future advance in foreign films. Such advance must necessarily be slow, extending over two or three decades before it becomes widely effective, and before its influence injures our general commerce, our manufacturers will have had time to adjust their affairs to new conditions.

Success of the principal nationals in talkies will probably be acquired by following lines similar to those that built the American movie industry—that is, by the manufacture of cheap sound films and their exhibition in cheap playhouses. While millions of people in many lands have already learned to enjoy the screen, many more millions would become regular theater-goers if the cost of the entertainment were reduced. The huge success of American movies at home was due to the cheap films and cheap show-shops, presenting quality that was never too far ahead of the populace. If taxation in foreign lands does not impose an insuperable burden on low-cost talkies and cheap theaters, their film industries ought to grow steadily. Once quantity is achieved (to enable the studios to operate profitably), quality will follow.

Internationalism, or at least the beginnings of friendship between nations and peoples, has been measurably advanced by the universal acceptance of film entertainment. Jealousy, fear, and hatred, born of insularity and ignorance, have been diminished by the spread of the movies. Little by little, all peoples have been unconsciously acquiring knowledge—never before available—of their fellow men of other races and other nationalities, and knowledge must inevitably be followed by understanding and toleration.

The period of depression through which we are now going has been a most severe teacher, but it has taught men and women everywhere that the whole world is irrevocably united in this age of machinery, chemistry, and electricity. The American wheat farmers and cotton growers, the makers of motor cars and of all other products of factories, have learned that their prosperity is inextricably interwoven with the economic and social welfare of workmen and peasants on every continent. The "brotherhood of man," which, only a few years ago, seemed to be an impracticable dream of idealists, now has become a business necessity. War, poverty, disease, and crime will have to disappear from life, not because poets and visionaries declare that all mankind is entitled to enjoy a happy civilization, but because agriculture, industry, and finance can no longer endure these horrors.

In the remaking of world civilization that lies just ahead of us the talkies and the movies will serve humanity as the pioneer force, the advance guard, that arouses backward minds into action. The multiplicity of tongues, the myriad languages and dialects, are the barriers that have stood between peoples and nations from the beginning of time, constituting the foundation upon which are built the superstitions, the errors, and the evils that restrain civilization. These barriers have already been weakened by the universal language of the silent films. Talkies will advance the work begun by the movies. Talkies will appear, within one or two generations, in, let us say, a dozen or so of the world's principal languages and dialects. They will *not* be presented in the hundreds of tongues that now plague mankind. The enjoyment of screen entertainment will spread farther and farther into the minds of all masses, and the world will settle down to the use of the languages employed by the screen. And finally, before many generations have passed, one common tongue will dominate the globe. The radio will follow closely on the pathway of the talkie, and these two modern forms of amusement will be assisted by television. Hand in hand with them the products of the printing press will complete the processes of stimulation and education. Youth everywhere will be trained in schools by the union of these several instrumentalities and schooling will be joyous, practical, and helpful, designed to enable mankind so to live as to derive the utmost from life. We have the instruments, ready to do the work, and we have at least the foundation of an organization that could be used in its accomplishment —the League of Nations.

In closing this story of the movies—this tale of the one triumph of democracy in creating an effective agency of its very own— I am reminded of a remark of Walter Wanger, one of the keenest minds in American studios, who said: "Why not put the

League of Nations to work? If the League would appoint a committee to encourage, and finally to supervise, the production of text-films and text-books, to be used all over the world, the problems of mankind could be settled within three generations. Why don't we stop talking about this 'brotherhood of man' idea —why not make it a fact, instead of a dream?"

INDEX

INDEX

Aaronson, Max, see *Anderson, G. M.*
Abbot, George, Pl. 104B
Abrams, Hiram, 119, 161-163, 228, 229, 234, 235, Pl. 66
Acord, Art, Pls. 19B, 29
Adam's Rib, 249
Adams, Claire, Pl. 62B
Adams, Maude, 88
Adelphi, The, 354
Admirable Crichton, The, 220
Adopted Son, The, Pl. 51A
Adorée, Renée, Pls. 86, 87B
Adventures of Sandy McGregor, The, 38
Æsop's Fables, Pl. 116B
Aiglon, L', 52
Aitken, Harry, 81, 102, 117, 128, 130, 141-145, 150, 163, 178, 202, 235, 415
Alco Film Corp., 131, 132
All Quiet on the Western Front, 407, Pl. 110A
Allied Artists, 234
Allison, May, 166, Pl. 50B

American College of Surgeons, 423
American Film Manufacturing Co., 103
American International Corp., 243
American Museum of Natural History, 421
American Studio, 82, 102
American Telephone and Telegraph Co., 376-378, 389, 419
American Theater, St. Louis, 258
American Tobacco Co., 150, 289
Among Those Present, Pl. 67A
Amusement Finance Corp., 255
Anderson, G. M., 35, 78, 86, 88, 124, 155, 190, 191, 339, Pls. 22A, 22B, 37
Anderson (de Novarro), Mary, 142
Anderson, Mary, Pl. 23
Anderson, Maxwell, 341, Pl. 92
Andrews, Del, Pl. 102A
Andrews, Roy Chapman, 422
animated cartoons, 412, Pls. 116A, 116B
Anna Christie, Pls. 80A, 111A

435

Annabelle the Dancer, 11 footnote
Apostle of Vengeance, The, Pl. 42A
Arbuckle, Roscoe ("Fatty"), 163, 188, 284-289, 295, 296, Pls. 9B, 52
Arlen, Michael, Pl. 109A
Arliss, George, 404, Pl. 68A
Armat, Thomas, 10, 11, 20, 64
Armistice Day, 201
Artcraft Pictures Corp., 163-165, 167, 174-176, 179-182, 185-188, 190-193, 195, 228, 234, 239, Pls. 46B, 50A, 56, 61A
Ascher, Nathan, 135
Ascher Brothers, 135, 264, 275
Associated Exhibitors, 247, 319 footnote
Astor Theater, New York, 107, 341, 342
Atkinson, J. J., Pl. 75
Avenging a Crime, or Burned at the Stake, 39
Ayres, Agnes, Pl. 68B
Ayres, Lew, 407, Pl. 110A

Bacon, Lloyd, Pl. 107B
Badger, Clarence, Pls. 53A, 87A, 96A
Balaban, Barney, 274, 275
Balaban and Katz, 275, 363, 364
Bancroft, George, 403, Pl. 94B
Bank of Italy, 380
Banky, Vilma, 404, Pl. 93B
Banzhof, H. T., Pl. 66
Bara, Theda, 88, 123, 166, 220, 335, 336, Pls. 47, 48
Barnum, P. T., 12
Barrie, Sir James Matthew, 220
Barrier, The, 137

Barrymore, John, 344, 345, 381, Pls. 61A, 107B
Barrymore, Lionel, 206
Bartlett, Captain Bob, 422
Barthelmess, Richard, Pls. 65A, 65B
Battle Cry of Peace, The, 194, Pls. 35A, 35B
Bauman, Charles O., 81, 82, 141, 155, Pl. 49A
Baxter, Warner, 403
Bayne, Beverly, Pls. 25, 51A
Beach, Rex, 126, 137, 178, 317, Pl. 74B
Bearded Bandit, The, Pl. 22B
Beau Geste, 342, Pl. 93A
Beaumont, Harry, Pl. 104A
Beban, George, 234
Beebe, William, 422
Beery, Noah, 322, 403, Pl. 93A
Beery, Wallace, 403, Pls. 25, 73, 91A
Beetson, Fred, 297-299
Behind the Front, Pl. 91A
Behn, Harry, 341
Belasco, David, 26, 54
Bell Telephone Co., 377, 410
Ben Hur, 16, 35, 173, 237, 342, 343, Pls. 89A, 89B, 90A, 90B
Bennett, Constance, 407, Pl. 109B
Bennett, Enid, Pl. 82
Bennett, Joan, Pl. 107B
Bennett, Richard, 407
Bennett, Whitman, 206
Bergman, Henry, Pl. 40A
Bernhardt, Sarah, 52, 110, Pl. 26
Bernstein, David, 410
Berst, J. A., 63, 126, 247, Pl. 20
Besserer, Eugenie, Pl. 19B
Beware of Boarders, Pl. 45B

Big Game, Pl. 116B
Big Kick, The, Pl. 108A
Big Parade, The, 341, 342, 350, Pl. 86
Binney, Constance, 246
biograph, 8
Biograph Co., 8-10, 17-21, 24, 30, 31, 49, 55, 56, 66, 69, 87, 92, 105, 106, 116, 126, 146, 147, Pls. 3, 7A, 7B, 10A, 10B, 27A, 27B
bioscope, 8
Bird Islands of Peru, The, 422
Birth of a Nation, The, 128-130, 137, 140, 141, 173, 178, 193, 194, 219, 236, 237, 306, 342, Pls. 33A, 33B
Bison Life Motion Pictures, 82
Black, Alfred S., 253, 254, 257, 264, 265, 272, 273, 365, 366
Black Pirate, The, 234
Blackton, J. Stuart, 22-24, 96, 127, 136, 188, 425, Pls. 8, 20, 35A
Blank, A. H., 177, 274
Blinn, Holbrook, Pl. 36
Block, Harry, *xiv*
Blue Angel, The, 426 and *footnote*
Blue Envelope Mystery, The, Pl. 39A
Blue, Monte, 144, Pl. 84A
Blumenthal, A. C., 332-334, 336
Boardman, Eleanor, Pl. 102B
Bohème, La, Pl. 87B
Bolton, Guy, Pl. 106A
Borzage, Frank, 324, Pl. 96B
Bosworth, Hobart, 120, 202, Pls. 5, 9A, 13, 19B, 109A
Bow, Clara, 317, Pl. 96A
Bowes, Edward, 260
Brabin, Charles, 336, Pl. 51A
Brady, William A., 183, 288

Brandt, Joseph, 27, 322, 323
Brenon, Herbert, 137, Pls. 43, 44A, 44B, 93A
Brent, Evelyn, 403, Pl. 94B
Brian, Mary, Pl. 112B
Broadway, Pl. 104B
Broadway Melody, The, 324, Pl. 104A
Brockwell, Gladys, 335, 336, Pl. 96B
Broken Blossoms, 219
Broncho Billy, see *Anderson, G. M.*
Broncho Billy's Adventure, Pl. 22A
Brook, Clive, 403, Pl. 94B
Brown, Clarence, Pls. 109A, 111A, 117B
Brown, Hiram C., 320
Browne, Porter Emerson, 123
Bruce, Kate, Pl. 27B
Brulatour, Jules, 134
Brunton, Robert, 112-116, 199, 205, 217, Pl. 28
Brunton Co., Robert, 205
Bryan, William Jennings, 367
Bunny, John, 56, 88, 157, 190, 191, Pl. 23
Burkan, Nathan, Pl. 66
Burke, Billie, 142
Burke, Thomas, 219
Burnett, R. W., Pl. 111B
Bushman, Francis X., Pls. 25, 37, 51A, 90B
Butler, David, Pl. 114A

Cabiria, 104
Cadle, Ernest, 422
California Theater, San Francisco, 258
Calvert, Catherine, 142
Camille, 342

Capitol Theater, New York, 260, 264, 330-334

Carewe, Edwin, Pl. 94A

Carmen, Pl. 5

Carroll, Earl, 400

Carroll, Nancy, Pl. 112A

Case, Theodore W., 336, 377, 389

Casler, Herman, 8

Castle, Irene, 324

Central Park Theater, Chicago, 275

Certain Rich Man, A, Pl. 62B

Chamberlin, Joseph Edward, 227

Chambers, Robert W., 178, 246, Pl. 109B

Chandler, Harry, 380

Chaney, Lon, 217, 341, Pls. 55, 61B, 107A

Chang, 422, Pls. 95A, 95B

Chaplin, Charles Spencer, 82, 124, 142, 145, 155-158, 166, 180-182, 190, 191, 200, 205, 206, 218, 224, 229, 230, 232-234, 238, 249, 284, 333, 335, 344, 369, 397, 399, 402, 416, Pls. 37, 38, 40A, 40B, 54, 60, 63, 77, 85

Chaplin, Syd, 156, Pls. 54, 66

Charleson, Mary, Pl. 15A

Chase National Bank, 244

Chatterton, Ruth, 403

Chevalier, Maurice, 351, 403, Pl. 114B

Chicago, Pl. 100A

Chicago, Ill., 77, 78, 135, 274, 275, 364

Chicago World's Fair, 5

Chipman, Dr. W. W., 423

Christian Science Church, 217

Christie, Al, 115, 314, 320, 321

Christie, Charles, 314, 320, 321

Christie Brothers, 390, 412

Christie Comedies, 217

Cimarron, 407, Pls. 113A, 113B

Cinderella, Pl. 34A

cinema, 9

Cinema Finance Co., 380

cinematograph, 9

Circle Theater, Indianapolis, 258

Circle Theater, New York, 325

Circus, The, 402

City Lights, 402

Clair, René, 426 *footnote*

Claire, Ina, Pl. 112B

Clansman, The, 128

Clark, James L., 422

Clark, Marguerite, 166, Pl. 53B

Clarke, Harley L., 411

Clarke, James B., 131

Clayton Act, 241, 242, 393

Cleopatra, Pl. 48

Clifton, Elmer, 317

Clodhopper, The, Pl. 45A

Clune's Auditorium, Los Angeles, 128

Cochrane, Robert, 27, 81, 87, 90, 102, 133, 321, Pl. 75

Code of Honor, The, Pl. 13

Cody, Lew, Pl. 109B

Cohan, George M., 107, 181, 216

Cohen, Emanuel, 409

Cohen, Sydney S., 261, 263-265, 267-269, 271

Cohens and the Kellys, The, 321, Pl. 91B

Cohn, Harry, 27, 322, 323

Cohn, Jack, 27, 322, 323

Colbert, Claudette, Pl. 114B

Cole, Rufus C., Pl. 75

Collier, William, Sr., 142

Collins, Frederick, 178

Colman, Ronald, 345, 351, 402, Pls. 93A, 93B

Columbia Broadcasting Co., 320 *footnote*

Columbia Pictures Corp., 320, 322, 323, 340 *footnote*, 388, 390
Common Law, The, 246, Pl. 109B
Compson, Betty, 217, 322, 402, Pl. 55
Conklin, Chester, Pl. 45B
Connecticut Yankee, A, Pl. 114A
Connelly, Edward, Pl. 44B
Connick, A. G., 243
Conway, Jack, Pl. 106B
Coogan, Jackie, 206, 238, Pl. 60
Coolidge, Calvin, 383, Pl. 99
Cooper, Gary, Pl. 110B
Cooper, Merian C., 422, Pls. 95A, 95B
Cooper, William John, 420, 423
Corbett, James J., 134
Cosmopolitan Productions, Inc., 188, 207, 323, 324, Pls. 71B, 104A
Costello, Maurice, 56, 86, Pls. 15A, 15B
Covered Wagon, The, 340, Pl. 81
Cowl, Jane, 178
Crafts, Rev. Wilbur Fisk, 293, 294, 302
Craig, Dr. Allan, 423
Crawford, Joan, Pl. 106B
Crile, Dr. George W., 423
Crisp, Donald, Pl. 78B
Criterion Theater, Los Angeles, 240
Crosland, Alan, Pl. 101A
Crosman, Henrietta, Pl. 112B
Crowd, The, Pl. 102B
Crowell, Dr. Bowman, 423
Cruze, James, 139, 340, Pl. 81
Cukor, George, Pl. 112B
Culver City, 144, 199, 205, 319, 323, Pl. 120
Cure, The, Pl. 40B

Daguerre, 3
Dalton, Dorothy, Pls. 69A, 69B
Dana, Viola, 178
Daniels, Bebe, 246, 402, Pl. 58A
Darmond, Grace, Pl. 51B
D'Arrast, Harry, Pl. 112A
Daughter of the Gods, A, Pl. 43
Davies, Marion, 323, 324, Pl. 71B
Davis, Harry, 44, 45, 47
Davis, Mildred, Pl. 67A
Davy Crockett, 16
Deadwood Coach, The, Pl. 84B
Dearden, Harold, Pl. 103B
De Forest, Lee, 336, 376, 389
Delmonico's, 291, 292
Del Rio, Dolores, 337, Pls. 92, 94A
DeMille, Cecil B., 114, 115, 117, 119, 139, 151, 162, 181, 194, 195, 202, 206, 209, 214, 218-224, 235, 237, 249, 250, 306, 319, 320, 340, 343, 380, 416, Pls. 29, 50A, 56, 58A, 76, 97A
DeMille, Henry C., 114
DeMille, William C., 114, 224, Pl. 58A
Desert Gold, 208
Dewey, John, *xiii*
Dexter, Elliott, 142, Pl. 78A
Diamond from the Sky, The, 103
Dickson, W. K. L., 7, 8, 10, 64
Dietrich, Marlene, 350, 426 *footnote*, Pl. 110B
Dillon, John Francis, Pl. 78A
Disney, Walt, Pl. 116A
Disraeli, Pl. 68A
Ditmars, Raymond L., 422
Dix, Richard, 407, Pl. 113A
Dixon, Thomas, 128, 129
Donohue, Joe, Pl. 46A
Don't Change Your Husband, 249

Doro, Marie, 142, 246
Dorothy Vernon of Haddon Hall, 232
Dove, Billie, 402
Dowling, Joseph, 217, Pl. 55
Down to the Sea in Ships, 317
Dr. Jekyll and Mr. Hyde, Pl. 61A
Dr. Lafleur's Theory, Pl. 15B
Dressler, Marie, 142, 402, 403, Pls. 12, 111A
Drew, Mr. and Mrs. Sidney, Pl. 39B
Drury Lane Theatre, London, 112
Dryden, John F., 102, 244
Du Barry, 238, see *Passion*
Duke, James B., 184, 241
Dunne, Irene, Pl. 113A
Dunning, Philip, Pl. 104B
Duponts, the, 245
Duse, Eleanora, 52
Dwan, Allan, Pl. 73
Dyer, Frank L., Pl. 20

East Orange, N. J., 7
Eastman, George, 6, 419, 421
Eastman Kodak Co., 126, 408 *footnote*
Eddy, Mrs. Mary Baker, 217
Edison, Thomas A., 6-11, 20, 22, 23, 37, 64, 65, 121, 124, 374, Pl. 20
Edison Co., 11, 12, 17-25, 34, 64-66, 73, 75, 77, 96, 101, 104, 126, Pls. 2, 24
Edison Wargraph Co., 37
Educational Film Co., 320, 390
educational films, see *non-theatrical films*
Edwards, J. Gordon, Pl. 48
Edwards, Walter, Pl. 53B

Electric Theater, Los Angeles, 44, 99, 100
Electrical Research Products, Inc., 376, 377, 419
Elliott, Maxine, 178
Elmer, Billy, Pl. 29
Emanuel Presbyterian Church, Los Angeles, 295
Emerson, John, 188
End of St. Petersburg, The, 350
End of the Tour, The, Pl. 50B
Engel, Joseph, 132, 228
Epoch Film Corp., 128, 130, Pls. 33A, 33B
Erickson, A. W., 408 *footnote*
Essanay Film Manufacturing Co., 35, 66, 78, 92, 151, 155-157, Pls. 22A, 22B, 25, 37, 38
Eternal Flame, The, Pl. 71A
Evening Mail, New York, 227
Evil Men Do, The, Pl. 15A
Examiner, Los Angeles, 380, 381
Exhibitor's Herald, 293

Fabian theaters, 177, 364
Fair, Elinor, 217
Fairbanks, Douglas, 142, 143, 145, 163, 181, 188, 206, 218, 229-235, 237, 245, 248, 249, 284, 285, 343, 344, 402, 416, Pls. 63, 66, 73, 79
Fairbanks, John, Pl. 66
Fall of the Romanoffs, The, 137, Pl. 44B
"Falling in Love Again," 426
Famous Players Canadian Corp., 258
Famous Players Film Co., 110, 111, 131, 132, 137, 140, 147-149, 156, 159, 160, 162, 228, 243, 244, 362, Pl. 34A
Famous Players-Lasky Corp.,

162-164, 195, 206, 228, 240, 259, 260

Farnum, Dustin, 114, 142, 143, Pl. 29

Farnum, William, 123, 166, 335, 336, Pls. 42B, 114A

Farrar, Geraldine, 178, 181, Pl. 50A

Farrell, Charles, 337, 402, Pl. 96B

Father's Flirtation, Pl. 23

Fatty in Coney Island, Pl. 52

Faust, Pl. 4

Fawcett, George, 142

Fazenda, Louise, Pl. 30

Federal Trade Commission, 213, 241, 276, 277, 279, 280, 364-368, 391, 393

Fejos, Paul, Pl. 104B

Ferber, Edna, 407, Pls. 112B, 113A, 113B

Ferguson, Elsie, 181, 245

Fields, Lew, 144

Fighting Blood, Pl. 42B

Film Booking Office of America, 320, 367

Finch, Flora, Pl. 23

Finegan, Dr. Thomas E., 419

Finkelstein and Rubin, 176, 274

Firebug, The, or A Night of Terrors, 39

Fire Chief's Daughter, The, Pl. 19A

First National Bank, Los Angeles, 380

first-run theaters, 95, 122, 172-177, 182, 191, 197, 204, 237, 238, 240-243, 260, 261, 273, 326, 329-334, 369, 373, 388, 392, 393, 415

First National Exhibitors' Circuit, 176, 177, 179-182, 185, 187-190, 192, 193, 195, 196, 200, 205, 206, 212, 230, 234, 235, 238, 242, 245, 247, 248, 250-252, 254-265, 268, 274-276, 278, 279, 304, 314, 317, 318, 327, 329, 335, 358, 363-367, 378, 383, 385, 388, 389, 392, 393, 408, Pls. 54, 57, 60, 62A, 65B, 71A, 78A, 80A, 111B, 125

Fiske, Minnie Maddern, 88

Flaherty, Robert J., 422, Pls. 72, 88A, 88B

Flaming Youth, Pl. 78A

Flint, Motley H., 380, 381

Florida, 76

Flugrath sisters, see *Dana, Viola,* and *Mason, Shirley*

Folies Bergères, New York, 113

Fontanne, Lynn, Pl. 118A

Fool There Was, A, 123

Foolish Wives, Pl. 70A

Forbes, Ralph, Pl. 93A

Forbidden Fruit, 249

Ford, Harrison, Pl. 53B

Ford, Henry, 337

Forest, Hal de, Pl. 43

Fort Lee, N. J., Pl. 36

Four Horsemen of the Apocalypse, The, 260, 306, 310, 350, Pls. 64A, 64B

Fox, William, 26, 80, 81, 101, 102, 123, 124, 141, 179, 185, 200, 202, 205, 274, 275, 317, 329, 332-338, 341, 342, 363, 366, 367, 377-379, 382, 385, 386, 388, 389, 391-393, 395, 410, 411, Pl. 75

Fox Film Corp., 92, 109, 123, 124, 141, 162, 175, 179, 200, 205, 239, 244, 251, 261, 317, 320, 408, 410, 411, 419, Pls. 42B, 43, 47, 48, 84B, 92, 96B, 114A, 119

Fox Movietone News, 411, Pl. 99

Fox Theaters Corp., 411
Foy, Brian, Pl. 101B
Franklin, Harold, 365
Franklin, Sidney, Pl. 118A
Frederick, Pauline, 166, Pl. 59B
Free Soul, A, Pl. 117B
Freuler, John R., 81, 102, 157,
    158, 166, 180, 181, Pl. 40B
Friend, Arthur, 113, 114
Frohman, Daniel, 110, 111
*From Christiana to the North
    Cape,* 38
Front Page, The, Pl. 115B

Gable, Clark, Pls. 117B, 118B
Gaige, Crosby, 178
Gammon, Frank R., 10
Garbo, Greta, 336, 351, 402, Pls.
    109A, 118B
Garbutt, Frank C., 120, 162, 289,
    295
Gardner, Cyril, Pl. 112B
Garson, Harry, 246
Gaumont, Leon, 18
Gaumont theaters, 392
Gaynor, Janet, 337, 402, Pl. 96B
General Electric Co., 376, 377,
    409
General Film Co., 69-77, 80, 84,
    85, 87, 89-92, 95-97, 99, 101-
    110, 117, 120, 122, 140, 141,
    147, 159, 179, 189, 195, 212,
    319-321, 335, 368, 372, 375,
    378, 379, 412, 417, Pls. 8, 20
General Theaters Equipment Co.,
    411
Georgia Enterprises, Inc., 255
Giannini, Dr. A. H., 380
Gibson, Hoot, Pl. 102A
Gilbert, John, Pls. 42A, 86, 87B,
    109A
Girls, Pl. 53B

Gish, Dorothy, 56, 166, 234, 404,
    Pl. 70B
Gish, Lillian, 56, 166, 234, 404,
    Pls. 65A, 70B, 87B
Glaum, Louise, 143
Glazer, Benjamin, 337
Glyn, Elinor, Pl. 96A
Godsol, Frank Joseph, 244, 247,
    260, 264, 265, 308-311, 317, 319
Gold Rush, The, 233, 333, Pl. 85
Golden Bed, 249
Goldfish, Samuel, see *Goldwyn,
    Samuel*
Goldman, Sachs and Co., 381
Goldwyn, Samuel, 113-115, 117,
    119, 151, 162, 175, 178-181,
    185, 187, 202, 205, 244, 247,
    250, 251, 275, 293, 312, 314,
    317, 319, 351, 416, Pls. 75, 117A
Goldwyn Pictures Corp., 178,
    217, 239, 244, 260, 264, 308-
    310, 312, 317, Pls. 53A, 59B,
    61B, 74B, 83
Goodwin, Hannibal, 6
Gordon, Kitty, 247
Gordon, Nate, 177, 254, 257, 279
Gordon, Vera, Pl. 91B
Gore, Abe, 259
Gore, Mike, 259
Gore Brothers, 257, 274
Gowland, Gibson, Pl. 83
Gradwell, Ricord, 135
Grainger, James R., 411
Grass, 422
Grauman's Million Dollar The-
    ater, Los Angeles, 240, 243
Gray, William P., 254, 257, 265
Graybill, Joe, Pl. 7B
Great Train Robbery, The, 31,
    39, 40, 110, Pl. 2
Greed, 309 and *footnote,* Pl. 83,
    see also *Life's Whirlpool*
Green Hat, The, Pl. 109A

Greene, Walter, 119, 161, 163, 165
Grey, Jane, 142
Grey, Zane, 126, 208, 340
Griffith, Corinne, 246, 344, 345
Griffith, David Wark, 49-53, 55, 56, 60, 61, 87, 89, 105, 106, 116, 117, 128, 130, 137, 139, 141, 143, 163, 178, 188, 202, 206, 207, 218, 219, 224, 229, 231, 233, 234, 248, 306, 344, 416, Pls. 7A, 10A, 10B, 33A, 63, 65A, 66, 70B
Griffith, Raymond, Pl. 87A
Guardsman, The, Pl. 118A
Guinan, Texas, 142
Gun Fighter, The, Pl. 49B
Guthman, William, 328

Hackett, James K., 111
Hagedorn, Herman, 341
Hale's Tours, 183
Hale, Creighton, Pl. 65A
Hale, Georgia, Pl. 85
Hallelujah, Pls. 105A, 105B
Halsey, Stuart and Co., 337, 410, 411
Hamilton, Neil, Pl. 93A
Hammerstein, Elaine, 246
Hammons, E. V., Pl. 75
Hampton, Benjamin Boles, *ix, x,* 150-161, 267-272, 289-293, Pl. 62B
Hampton, Jesse Durham, 217, 230, 317, Pl. 74B
Hands Up, Pl. 87A
Hansen, Juanita, 296
Harding, Ann, 403
Harding, Warren G., 297
Hardy, Oliver, Pl. 108B
Harper, Glenn, 289
Harriman, E. H., 184

Harris, John P., 44, 45, 47
Harris, Mitchell, Pl. 114A
Harris, Sam H., 107
Harron, Robert, 129
Hart, William S., 35, 124, 142, 163, 166, 188, 191, 207, 245, 339, 340, 345, Pls. 42A, 49B
Harte, Betty, Pl. 9A
Hatton, Raymond, Pls. 50A, 91A
Havemeyer, Henry O., 184, 241
Haver, Phyllis, Pls. 67B, 100A
Hay, Mary, Pl. 65A
Hayden, Stone and Co., 278
Haynes, Daniel, Pl. 105A
Hays, Will H., *xiv,* 297 299, 302, 303, 340, 342, 392, 419, 423, 427, Pl. 75
Hearst, William Randolph, 103, 188, 207, 320, 321, 323-325
Hecht, Ben, Pls. 94B, 115B
Hell's Angels, Pl. 115A
Hendershot, Ed, Pl. 102A
Hergesheimer, Joseph, Pl. 65B
Hernández, George, Pl. 9B
Herne, James, 16
Hersholt, Jean, 345, 397, Pls. 62B, 83
Hertz, John, 274
Hess, Gabriel L., 178, 297
Hickman, Alfred, Pl. 44B
Hill, Percival S., 150-152
Hillyer, Lambert, Pl. 74B
His Wife Knew About It, Pl. 39B
Hitchcock, Raymond, 143
Hodkinson, William W., 61, 89, 97, 98, 108, 109, 116-120, 131, 137, 147-150, 152-154, 157, 159-163, 175, 178-181, 187, 199, 202, 228, 235, 239, 244, 247, 250, 251, 254, 260, 264, 270, 289, 317, 319, 362, 372, 379, 415

Hodkinson Co., W. W., 319, Pl. 62B

Hollywood, 103, 112-116, 199, 200, 207-211, 222, 223, 287, 297, 298, 400, 401, 414, Pls. 28, 119, 121, 123, 125

Hollywood, 211

Holmes, Taylor, 142

Holt, Jack, Pl. 69B

Hope, Sir Anthony, 111, 246, Pl. 74A

Hopper, De Wolf, 142, 144

Hopper, Hedda, Pl. 109B

Horsley, David, 115

Horton, Edward Everett, Pl. 87B

Hough, Emerson, 340, Pl. 81

Howard, Leslie, Pl. 117B

Hoyt, Richard, 278, 279, 363, 364

Huber, Peter, Pl. 20

Hughes, Howard, 345, Pls. 115A, 115B

Hughes, Rupert, 289, 295

Hulsey, E. H., 177, 255-257, 279

Humoresque, 324

Hurst, Brandon, Pl. 114A

Hutchinson, Samuel S., 81, 82, 102

Ibáñez, Vicente Blasco, 260, Pls. 64A, 64B

Ibsen, 372

Idols of the North, Pl. 69A

Immigrant, The, Pl. 40A

Impossible Voyage, 38

In the Days of the Thundering Herd, Pl. 18B

In the Latin Quarter, Pl. 31A

In Wolf's Clothing, Pl. 34B

Ince, Thomas H., 82, 137, 139, 141, 143, 163, 188, 207, 380, Pl. 49A

Inceville, Santa Monica, Cal., Pl. 49A

Independent Motion Pictures Producers and Distributors of America, 81, 87, 146

Indians and Cowboys, 39

Ingram, Rex, 260, Pls. 21, 64A, 74A

Interference, Pl. 103B

International Film Co., 103

International Reform Bureau, 293

Intolerance, 219, 231

Iron Strain, The, 143

Irving, Sir Henry, 112

Irwin, Walter, 127, 163, 179, 185, 241, 242, 256-258

Isaacs, John D., 4, 5

It, Pl. 96A

Italian Barber, The, Pl. 7B

Jackson, Joe, 142

James, Arthur, 132, 293

Janis, Elsie, 246

Jannings, Emil, 349, 350, 426 *footnote,* Pl. 103A

Jazz Singer, The, 387, Pl. 101A

Jenkins, C. Francis, 10, 11 and *footnote,* 24

Jensen and Von Herburg, 176, 274, 365

Jerome, William Travers, 407 *footnote,* 408 *footnote*

Johnson, Arthur, Pl. 10B

Johnson, Mr. and Mrs. Martin, 421, 422

Johnson, Orrin, 142

Johnston, William Allen, 293

Jolson, Al, 386, 387, Pl. 101A

Jones, Aaron, 135

Jones, Buck, 340 *footnote*

Jones, Linick and Schaefer, 135, 175, 176, 275

Joyce, Alice, 56, 166, Pls. 34B, 46A

Judith of Bethulia, 105, 106, Pls. 27A, 27B

Judy of Rogues' Harbor, Pl. 59A

Julian, Rupert, Pl. 107A

K̲ahn, Otto H., 151, 242

Kalem Co., 35, 66, 76, 92, 99, 126, Pl. 34B

Kane, Arthur S., 246

Karger, Max, 132

Karno, Fred, 155

Katz, Sam, 274, 275, 278, 279, 363-365, 392, 409

Kaufman, George S., Pl. 112B

Keaton, Buster, Pls. 52, 78B

Keenan, Frank, 142, 145, 247

Keith-Albee-Orpheum, 320, 367

Kellermann, Annette, Pl. 43

Kennedy, Jeremiah J., 18, 69, Pl. 20

Kennedy, Joseph, 320

Kennedy, Madge, 178

Kent, Sidney R., 409

Kenyon, Doris, Pl. 103B

Kessel, Adam, 81, 82, 141, 155, Pl. 49A

Keystone Comedies, 82, 155, Pls. 30, 31B

Kid, The, 206, 238, Pl. 60

Kinema Theater, Los Angeles, 240, 257

Kinemacolor, 407 *footnote*

kinetoscope, 7-10, 21

King, Charles, Pl. 104A

King, Henry, 354, Pls. 65B, 93B

King of Kings, The, 342, 343, Pls. 97A, 97B

Kingston, Winifred, Pl. 29

Kinograms, 320

Kipling, Rudyard, 123

Kit Carson, 39

Klauber, Adolph, 178

Klaw and Erlanger, 35

Kleine, George, 20 and *footnote,* 21, 29, 35, 66, 104, 106, 107, 237, 362, Pl. 20

Knickerbocker Theater, New York, 142, 143

Kolker, Henry, Pl. 68A

Koopman, E. B., 8

Kosloff, Theodore, Pl. 50A

Koster and Bial's Music Hall, 11

Ku Klux Klan, 129

Kuhn, Loeb and Co., 102, 242, 243, 318

Kunsky, John, 177, 274

Kuser, Anthony N., 411

Kuser, Mrs. Susie Dryden, 411

L̲aemmle, Carl, 26, 27, 61, 80, 81, 87, 90, 102, 103, 133, 134, 141, 146, 185, 199, 202, 275, 314, 321, 340 *footnote,* 349, 358, 359, 363, 367, 378, 379, 411, Pl. 75

Laemmle, Carl, Jr., Pls. 104B, 110A

La Marr, Barbara, 327, 336

Lamb, The, 143

Lambda Co., 10, 11, 18-20, 34

Langdon, Harry, Pl. 108A

La Rocque, Rod, 404, Pl. 94A

Lasky, Blanche, 113-116

Lasky, Jesse L., 113-117, 119, 161, 162, 194, 195, 202, 207, 235, 249, 293, 314, 409

Lasky Feature Play Co., Jesse L., 113-117, 119, 131, 137, 151, 153, 154, 162, 199, 205, Pls. 28, 29

Last Command, The, Pl. 103A

Last Laugh, The, 349, 350, 398

Latham, Woodville, 10, 18, 34, 64

Laughter, Pl. 112A
Laurel, Stan, Pl. 108B
League of Nations, The, 430, 431
Le Baron, William, Pls. 106A, 113A, 113B
Leiber, Fritz, Pl. 48
Leigh, Frank, Pl. 80B
Leonard, Robert Z., Pls. 13, 118B
Leroux, Gaston, Pl. 107A
LeRoy, Mervyn, Pl. 111B
Lesser, Sol, 135, 238, 257, 259, 274, 289
Levee, M. C., 116
Levy theaters, 274
Lewis, Mitchell, Pl. 69B
Lewis, Ralph, 129
Lichtman, Alexander, 111, 131, 163, 165
Lieber, Robert, 258
Life of Moses, The, 104, Pl. 8
Life's Whirlpool, Pl. 36
Lights of New York, 386, Pl. 101B
Lindbergh, Charles A., 383, Pl. 99
Little Caesar, Pl. 111B
Livingston, Crawford, 102, 151, 242
Lloyd, Frank, 206, Pls. 59B, 71A
Lloyd, Harold, 247, 284, 317, 320, 321, 344, 345, 390, 402, Pl. 67A
Lockwood, Harold, 166, Pl. 50B
Locomotive Races: Electricity vs. Steam, 38
Loeb, Albert, 274
Loew, Arthur, 259
Loew, Marcus, 26, 107, 108, 110, 135, 136, 141, 183, 185, 204, 244, 259-261, 263-265, 268, 271, 272, 275, 276, 317, 318, 329, 334, 349, 363, 391, Pl. 75
Loew, Mrs. Marcus, 391

Loew's, Inc., 259, 265, 304, 317-319, 329, 335, 338, 358, 363, 366, 367, 383, 385, 388-393, 408-410
Long, Samuel, 35, 99, Pl. 20
Loos, Anita, 163, 188
Los Angeles, 44, 77-80, 82, 111, 112, 199, 200, 205, 210, 214, Pl. 122
Los Angeles Trust and Savings Bank, 380
Lost Child, The, 38
Love, Bessie, 396, 403, Pl. 104A
Love, Montagu, Pl. 97B
Lowe, Edmund, 337, 403, Pl. 92
Lowry, Ira M., 152, 156-158
Lubin, Herbert, 326-329, 331-334
Lubin, Sigmund, 24, 34, 66, 127, 151, 152, 189, 326, Pls. 16, 20
Lubitsch, Ernst, 350, Pls. 57, 80B, 84A, 114B
Ludvigh, Elek John, 110, 159, 160, 409
Lumière, Auguste, 9, 18, 20, 24
Lumière color photography, 407 *footnote*
Lunt, Alfred, Pl. 118A
Lynch, Stephen E., 254-257, 264, 265, 272-274, 365, 366
Lynch Enterprises, Inc., S. E., 255

MacArthur, Charles, Pl. 115B
MacDonald, Jeannette, 403
MacDonald, Katherine, 206, 235
MacKinnon, B. A., 290
MacMillan, Donald, 422
MacPherson, Jeanie, 194, 209, 219, 220, 228, Pl. 97A

McAdoo, William Gibbs, 229, 230, 235, 380, Pl. 66
McAvoy, May, Pl. 101A
McCardell, Roy, 30, 103, 123, 158
McCarthy, Neil, 209
McClure's, 329
McCormack, John, 403
McCracken, Harold, 422
McCrea, Joel, Pl. 109B
McEachern, Dr. Malcolm, 423
McGee, James, Pl. 4
McGrail, Walter, Pl. 46A
McKee, Henry, 380
McKeesport, Pa., 44, 45
McKenny, Nina May, Pl. 105A
McKenzie, Maurice, *xiv*
McKim, Robert, Pl. 62B
McKinley, funeral of President, Pl. 1
McLaglen, Victor, 337, 403, Pl. 92
McManus, Edward A., 103
McTeague, 309 *footnote*, Pls. 36, 83
Mace, Fred, 143, Pl. 31B
Mack, Willard, 142
Madame X, Pl. 59B
Magic Flame, The, Pl. 93B
magic lantern, 3, 4
Major, Charles, 232, Pl. 71B
Male and Female, 220, 249, Pl. 56
Man Who Wouldn't Tell, The, Pl. 51B
Mandelbaum, Emanuel, 259
Mannix, Eddie, 410
Manslaughter, 249
March, Fredric, Pls. 112A, 112B
Marinoff, Fania, Pl. 36
Marion, Frank J., 35, 99, Pl. 20
Marion, George, Pl. 80A
Mark, Mitchell, 89, 100, 117, 127, 364

Markey, Enid, 143
Marriage Circle, The, Pl. 84A
Marsh, Mae, 129, 166, 178
Martin, Dr. Franklin, 423
Marvin, Henry N., 8, 18, 30, 49, Pl. 20
Mason, Shirley, 178
Mastbaum, Jules, 176, 177, 189, 317, 364, 365
Mastbaum, Stanley, 176, 177, 189, 317, 364
Mathis, June, 260, 306, 310-312, Pl. 64A
Matin, Le, 353
Maugham, W. Somerset, 342, Pl. 100B
Mayer, Louis B., 131, 132, 206, 217, 235, 314, 319, 343, 410, Pl. 62A
Mayflower Pictures, 188, 207, 217, Pl. 55
Mayo brothers, 420
Mayo, Dr. C. H., 423
Mayo, Margaret, 178
Meighan, Thomas, 217, 220, 345, Pls. 55, 56, 58A
Melford, George, Pl. 68B
Melies Co., 24, 63, 66, 126
Melville, Herman, Pl. 107B
Mendes, Lothar, Pl. 103B
Menjou, Adolphe, 233, Pl. 77
Merrill, Lynch and Co., 126
Metro Pictures, 132, 137, 162, 179, 180, 199, 239, 250, 259, 304, 310, 317, 319, Pls. 50B, 51A, 64A, 74A
Metro-Goldwyn-Mayer, 107, 141, 319-321, 323, 329, 341, 343, 351, 366, 390, 393, 410, Pls. 78B, 82, 86, 87B, 89A, 102B, 104A, 105A, 106B, 108A, 108B, 109A, 111A, 117B, 118A, 118B, 120
Metropolis, 358

Michael Strogoff, 359
Mickey Mouse, Pl. 116A
Milbank, Jeremiah, 244, 247, 319, 365, 422
Miles, Harry, 28
Miles, Herbert, 28
Milestone, Lewis, 407, Pls. 110A, 115B
Miller Brothers' 101 Ranch and Wild West Show, 34, 336
Milliken, Carl Elias, 297
Million and One Nights, A, xiii
Minnie Mouse, Pl. 116A
Minter, Mary Miles, 246, 286, Pl. 59A
Miracle Man, The, 216-218, 402, Pl. 55
Missouri Theater, St. Louis, 258
Mix, Tom, 34, 35, 88, 124, 166, 191, 335, 336, 339, 340 and *footnote,* 344, Pls. 18B, 84B
Moana, Pls. 88A, 88B
Moby Dick, Pl. 107B
Molnar, Ferenc, Pl. 118A
Moonshiners, The, 39
Moore, Colleen, 345, 404, Pl. 78A
Moore, Owen, 246, 284, 285, Pl. 34A
Moreno, Antonio, Pls. 31A, 96A
Morocco, Pl. 110B
Morosco, Oliver, 120
Morosco Pictures, 120, 151, 162
Motion Picture Board of Trade, 425
Motion Picture Capital Co., 365
Motion Picture Patents Co., 66-69, 80, 84, 96, 101, 140, 195, 228, 319, 335, 368, 417, Pl. 20
Motion Picture Producers and Distributors of America, Inc., 297-299, Pl. 75
Motion Picture Producers' Association, 289

Motion Picture Theater Owners of America, 261-273, 278
Motion Picture World, 293
Movie Fans, Pl. 67B
Movietone, 382, 383, 385, 388, 389, 395, 404, 410
Mullikan and Roberts, 329
Munroe, F. L., 319
Munsey's Magazine, 329
Murnau, F. W., 350, 398
Murray, Charles, 142, Pl. 91B
Murray, James, Pl. 102B
mutoscope, 8
Mutual Film Co., 80-82, 87, 102, 103, 109, 123, 124, 140, 141, 156-158, 162, 179, 242, 321, Pls. 40A, 40B
Muybridge, Eadweard, 4, 5
My Valet, 143
Myers, Carmel, Pl. 89A

Nagel, Conrad, 403
Nanook of the North, 422, Pl. 72
Nathanson circuit, 258
National Broadcasting Co., 320 *footnote*
National Educational Assn., 420
National Picture Theaters, Inc., 247
Navigator, The, Pl. 78B
Nazimova, Alla, 137, Pl. 44A
negative costs, 118, 130, 167, 168, 173, 180, 192, 194, 195, 205, 211, 212, 217, 219, 231, 237, 238, 246, 248, 249, 306, 308-310, 313, 318, 321, 324, 341-344, 357, 395, 413
Negri, Pola, 238, 336, 345, 346, 349, Pl. 57
neighborhood theaters, 177, 191, 197, 204, 237, 238, 415

Neilan, Marshall D., 206
Neill, R. William, Pl. 69A
New York Central Railroad, 38
Newmeyer, Fred, Pl. 67A
news reels, 37, 320, 321, 323, 382, 383
Niblo, Fred, 206, Pls. 82, 89A
nickelettes, 45 footnote
nickelodeons, 45-47, 57-62, 138, 190
Night in a Music Hall, A, 155
Night Out, A, Pl. 38
Nilsson, Anna Q., Pl. 74B
non-theatrical films, 420-425
Normand, Mabel, 143, 286, Pl. 53A
Norris, Frank, 309 footnote, Pls. 36, 83
North American Theaters Corp., 365
Novarro, Ramon, Pls. 74A, 89A

Oberammergau Passion Play, 31
O'Brien, Dennis F., Pl. 66
O'Brien, Eugene, 246
Ochs, Lee, 247
October, 350
Old Homestead, 16
Old Ironsides, 342
Old Wives for New, 194, 195
On the High Seas, Pl. 69B
O'Neil, Barry, Pl. 36
O'Neill, Eugene, 372, Pls. 80A, 111A
Only a Farmer's Daughter, 16
Oriental Theater, Chicago, 275
Orphans of the Storm, 234, Pl. 70B
Osborn, Henry Fairfield, 421, 422
Owen, Seena, 143

Packard, Frank L., 216
Page, Anita, Pl. 104A
Palisades Park, N. J., 136
Pallas Pictures, 120, 151, 162
pantopticon, 10, 11 footnote
Paralta Plays, 199, 205
Paramount Pictures Corp., 118-124, 130-132, 137, 147-149, 151, 152, 154, 156, 157, 159-164, 166, 174-179, 181, 182, 185-187, 188, 190, 193-195, 206, 211, 212, 217, 222, 228, 230, 234, 235, 238, 239, 241-243, 250, 251, 254-256, 258-261, 264-268, 272-277, 279, 304, 313, 314, 317-321, 323, 329, 340-342, 345, 358, 362-368, 372, 388, 389, Pls. 45B, 52, 53B, 55, 58A, 61A, 67B, 68B, 69A, 69B, 71B, 76, 81, 87A, 88A, 88B, 91A, 93A, 94B, 95A, 95B, 96A, 98, 103A, 103B, 110B, 112A, 112B, 114B, 121
Paramount Publix Corp., 363-365, 385, 390-393, 408-410, 428
Paramount Theater, New York, 329, 334
Pardon Us, Pl. 108B
Parrott, James, Pl. 108B
Passion, 238, 349, 350, 358, Pl. 57
Pathé-DeMille, Pls. 97A, 97B, 100A
Pathé-Dupont Film Manufacturing Co., 126
Pathé Exchange, Inc., 126, 179, 187, 244, 247, 251, 264, 317, 320, 412, Pls. 67A, 72
Pathé Frères, 18, 24, 63, 66, Pl. 32
Paul, Robert, 9
Pawley, Raymond, 119, 161, 162, 178, 319
Pearson, Elmer, 126
Peerless Co., 134

Penalty, The, Pl. 61B
penny arcades, 9, 12, 45, 47
Perils of Pauline, The, Pl. 32
Pertwee, Roland, Pl. 103B
Petrova, Olga, 178
Pettijohn, Charles, 247, 297
Phantom of the Opera, The, 341, 342, Pl. 107A
Philbin, Mary, Pl. 107A
Phillips, David Graham, Pl. 118B
photography, invention of, 3, 4
Photoplay, xiii, xiv, 293
Pickford, Charlotte, 49, 53, 54, 146-150, 158-160, 164, 165, 192, 197, 229, 230, 235, 399, Pl. 41
Pickford, Jack, 53, 54, 206
Pickford, Lottie, 53, 54
Pickford, Mary, 49, 52-56, 85-88, 111, 146-150, 156-160, 163-166, 168, 174, 176, 179-182, 190-192, 194-196, 200, 205, 206, 218, 224, 227-234, 238, 249, 284, 285, 335, 344, 402, 416, Pls. 7B, 10A, 10B, 34A, 41, 46B, 63, 66, 80B
Pickford Pictures Corp., Mary, 158
Pictorial Review, 290, 291, 293
Pinchot, Amos, *xiii*
Pitts, Zasu, Pl. 83
Pittsburgh, Pa., 44, 45
Plumes, 341, Pl. 86
Poli theaters, 275, 391
Pollard, Harry, Pl. 91B
Pomeroy, Daniel E., 421, 422
Pomeroy, John J., Pl. 103B
Pomeroy, Roy, 341
Poor Little Rich Girl, The, Pl. 46B
Pope, Richardson and Co., 329
Porter, Edwin S., 31, 39, 110, 228, Pl. 2
Potemkin, 350

Powell, Frank, 123
Powell, William, 403, Pls. 93A, 103B
Powers, Patrick A., 28, 80, 81, 124, 133, 134, 179, 185
Preferred Pictures, Inc., 235
Prevost, Marie, Pl. 84A
Price, Kate, Pl. 91B
Price, Oscar A., 229, Pl. 66
Prisoner of Zenda, The, 111, Pl. 74A
Producers Distributing Co., 319, 320
Progressive Exchanges, 99
projectoscope, 37
Publix Theaters Corp., 363-365, 391, 392, 409
Purviance, Edna, 233, Pls. 40A, 54, 77

Q*ueen Elizabeth,* 110, Pl. 26
Quigley, Martin, 293
Quirk, James R. *xiii,* 293
Quo Vadis, 104, 106-108, 137, 236

R*ace for a Kiss, A,* 39, 41
Radio Corporation of America, 321 and *footnote,* 367, 376, 377, 389, 427
Radio-Keith-Orpheum, 320 and *footnote,* 367, 388-392, 407, 408, 410, 412
Raff, Norman C., 10
Rain, 342
Ramona, Pl. 10A
Ramsaye, Terry, *xiii*
Randolf, Anders, Pl. 46A
Rapf, Harry, 311, 312, 379
Raphaelson, Samson, 387
Rappe, Virginia, 284, 285, 296
Rawhide Kid, The, Pl. 102A

Rawlinson, Herbert, Pl. 19B
Ray, Charles, Pl. 45A
Realart Pictures Corp., 246, Pl. 59A
Red Lily, The, Pl. 82
Reed, Luther, Pl. 106A
Reid, Wallace, 206, 296, Pl. 33B
Remarque, Erich Maria, 407, Pl. 110A
Republic Pictures, 245, 247
Resurrection, Pl. 94A
Revillon Frères, Pl. 72
Rex Pictures, 228
Reynolds, Lynn, Pl. 84B
Reynolds, W. J., 289, 295
Rialto Theater, Los Angeles, 240
Rialto Theater, New York, 240, 243, 260, 261, 329, 330, 334, 358
Rice, Elmer, Pl. 117A
Rich, Irene, 381
Richardson, Charles, 329
Richardson, "Daddy," Pl. 19B
Ringling, John, 336
Rio Rita, Pl. 106A
Riviera Theater, Chicago, 275
Rivoli Theater, New York, 240, 261, 329, 333, 334
R-K-O-Pathé Pictures, Inc., 320, 388, 390, 419, Pls. 106A, 109B, 113A, 113B, 122
Roach, Hal, 314, 320, 321, 390, 412, Pls. 67A, 108A, 108B
road-show theaters, 236, 238
Roberts, Harold, 329
Roberts, Theodore, Pl. 59A
Robertson, John, Pl. 61A
Robertson-Cole, 179, 187, 239, 250, 320, Pl. 49A
Robin Hood, 231, 234, Pl. 73
Robinson, Edward G., Pl. 111B
Rock, William, 23, 24, Pl. 20
Rockefeller, John D., 184, 241

Rogers, Saul E., 335, 411
Rogers, Will, 289, 295, Pl. 114A
Roman, The, Pl. 9A
Roosevelt, Theodore, 188, 341
Roosevelt Theater, Chicago, 264
Rosenthal, Moritz, 135, 151
Rosita, Pl. 80B
Roth, Eugene, 100, 175, 258
Rothapfel, Gustav, 330
Rothapfel, Samuel, 330, 331
Rothschild, Golden and Rothschild, 258
Rough Riders, The, 341, 342
Rowland, Richard, 28, 131, 132, 137, 179, 185, 259, 260, 310
Rowland and Clarke, 119, 131, 177
Roxy, see Rothapfel, Samuel
Roxy Theater, New York, 326-334, 388
Royal Family of Broadway, The, Pl. 112B
Rubens, Alma, 324
Rubin, Robert, 132
Ruggles, Wesley, 407, Pl. 113A
Rupert of Hentzau, 246
Ryan, Thomas Fortune, 184

Sadie Thompson, 342, Pl. 100B
Saenger Amusement Co., 252, 254, 274, 279
Sag Harbor, 16
salaries, 55, 75, 87, 91, 114-149, 156-158, 166-169, 179-182, 192, 194-196, 205, 217, 230, 236, 307, 355, 399-403, 407
Salisbury, Monroe, Pl. 29
San Fernando Valley, 199
San Francisco, Cal., 78, 97, 98
Sanger-Jordan theaters, 177
Sanitarium, The, Pl. 9B
Santa Barbara, Cal., 82, 102

Santa Monica, Cal., see *Inceville*
Santschi, Tom, Pls. 4, 19B
Sawyer, Herbert, 327
Sawyer-Lubin, 327
Saxe, Thomas, 274
Schenck, Joseph M., 116, 135-137, 185, 206, 238, 284, 314, 344, 380, Pl. 71A
Schenck, Nicholas, 135-137, 185, 378, 391, 409, 410
Schertzinger, Victor, Pl. 45A
Schildkraut, Joseph, Pl. 97A
Schildkraut, Rudolph, Pl. 97B
Schoedsack, Ernest B., 422, Pls. 95A, 95B
screen writing, 30, 43, 48, 55, 103, 207-209, 216, 219, 220, 224, 228, 260, 307, 309-312, 338-341, 344-347, 397
Schulberg, Benjamin P., 110, 162, 206, 227-229, 234, 235, 314, 409
Schulberg Productions, Inc., B. P., 235
Schwalbe, Harry, 177, 179, 192, 206, 235
Sea Beast, The, Pl. 107B
Seeley, Walter Hoff, 131
Seelye, C. R., 247
Select Pictures Corp., 186-188, 244-246
Selig, William N., 24, 34, 35, 66, 77-79, 86, 92, 94, 103, 124, 126, 127, 151, 207, 336, Pls. 4, 5, 6, 9A, 13, 17, 18A, 18B, 19A, 19B, 20, 74B
Selwyn, Archie, 178
Selwyn, Edgar, 178
Selznick, David, 319 and *footnote*
Selznick, Lewis J., 132-137, 163, 175, 180, 181, 185-188, 239, 244-247, 250, 251, 260, 264, 319 and *footnote*, Pl. 75

Selznick, Myron, 244, 246, 319 and *footnote*, Pl. 75
Selznick Pictures Co., Lewis J., 135, 162, 175, 178-181, 206, 238, 239, Pls. 44A, 44B
Selznick Select Pictures Corp., 245, 311
Sennett, Mack, 82, 141-143, 145, 155, 163, 188, 207, 220, 234, 314, 390, 412, Pls. 7B, 31B, 45B, 67B
Seventh Heaven, 337, Pl. 96B
Shakespeare, 35, 402
Shaw, George Bernard, 372
Shearer, Norma, 402, Pl. 117B
Sheehan, C. P., 411
Sheehan, Winfield, 80, 81, 335-338, 342, 388, 395, 411, Pl. 75
Sheer, William, Pl. 30
Sheik, The, Pl. 68B
Shepard, Ira, Pl. 19B
Sherman Anti-Trust Law, 67, 125, 162, 241, 242, 277
Sherman, Lowell, Pl. 65A
Sherry, W. L., 119, 161
Shields and Co., 321
Shoulder Arms, 206, Pl. 54
Sidney, George, Pl. 91B
Sienkiewicz, Henryk, 106
Sievers, William, 258
Sills, Milton, 317, Pl. 74B
Simba, 422
Simon and Schuster, *xiii*
Singhi, William, Pl. 20
Smiling Lieutenant, The, Pl. 114B
Smith, Albert Edward, 22-24, 64, 96, 127, 137, Pl. 20
Smith, Charlotte, see *Pickford, Charlotte*
Smith, Courtland, 411, Pl. 75
Smith, Gladys, see *Pickford, Mary*

Smith, Dr. Herbert Booth, 295
Smithers and Co., 151
Sohn, Monte, 266
Sothern, E. H., 88, 140
Sous les Toits de Paris, 426 and footnote
Southern Enterprises, Inc., 255
Southern Enterprises of Texas, Inc., 256
Sowing the Wind, Pl. 62A
special pictures, 236, 238, 246, 248, 250, 306, 395
Spiegel, Arthur, 134, 135
Spiegel, May and Stern, 134
Spivey, Victoria, Pl. 105D
Spoilers, The, 126, 127, 130, 137, 193, 194, 317, Pl. 74B
Spoor, George K., 24, 35, 67, 127, 155, 375, Pl. 20
Squaw Man, The, 114, 115, 194, 195, Pl. 29
Squier, Dr. J. Bentley, 423
Stage Rustler, The, Pl. 7A
Stahl, John M., Pl. 62A
Stallings, Laurence, 341, Pls. 86, 92
Standard Oil Co., 142, 409
Standing, Joan, Pl. 83
Stanford, Leland, 4
Stanley Booking Company of America, 189, 190
Stanley Co., 177, 189, 252, 254, 275, 279, 364, 365, 392, 393
Stanley, Forrest, Pl. 71B
star system, 86-92, 129, 140-142, 163, 171, 175, 176, 179, 182, 193-195, 198, 202, 213-216, 218, 234, 337, 344, 401, 402
Stedman, Myrtle, Pl. 62A
Steele, James, 119, 161
Stein, Paul, Pl. 109B
stereopticon, 3-5

Sternberg, Josef von, 350, Pls. 94B, 103A, 110B
Stevenson, Robert Louis, Pl. 61A
Stewart, Anita, 56, 166, 206, Pl. 62A
Stillman, J. D. B., 4
Stillman Theater, Cleveland, 243, 259
Stoddard, Henry, 227
Stone, Lewis, Pl. 74A
Stowe, Harriet Beecher, 321
Strand Theater, New York, 117, 127, 130, 137, 172, 240, 261, 329, 330, 333, 334, 364
Straus, S. W. and Co., 329
Street Scene, Pl. 117A
Striker, Joseph, Pl. 97A
Stroheim, Erich von, 306, 308, 309, Pls. 70A, 83
Stromberg, Hunt, 410
Strong, Austin, 337, Pl. 96B
Strongheart, 114
Suburbanites, The, 38
Sunshine, Marion, Pl. 7B
Super-pictures Co., 178
Susan Lenox: Her Fall and Rise, Pl. 118B
Sutherland, Edward, Pl. 91A
Swain, Mack, Pl. 40A
Swanson, Gloria, 163, 220, 342, 344, 345, Pls. 56, 58A, 58B, 100B
Sweet, Blanche, 56, 166, Pls. 27A, 27B, 80A
Swickard, Josef, Pl. 62A

Talking Picture Epics, Inc., 422
Tally, Thomas L., 28, 44, 61, 89, 99, 100, 117, 175-177, 179, 181, 192, 206, 235, 240, 256, 257
Talmadge, Constance, 56, 136,

137, 166, 206, 238, 246, 345, Pl. 31A

Talmadge, Mrs. M., 136

Talmadge, Norma, 56, 136, 137, 166, 206, 238, 246, 293, 342, 344, 345, Pls. 35A, 71A

Taming of the Shrew, The, 402

Taylor, William Deane, 285-289, Pl. 59A

Tearle, Conway, Pls. 44B, 71A

Technicolor, 407 *footnote*, 408 *footnote*

Ten Commandments, The, 209, 341, Pl. 76

Ten Nights in a Bar Room, 16

Terry, Alice, 260, Pl. 64A

Thalberg, Irving, 410

Thanhauser Film Corp., 81

Theatre Guild, 372

Thief of Bagdad, The, 231, 234, 344, Pl. 79

Thomas, Olive, 244, 246, 285

Thompson, Denman, 16

Thompson, Fred, Pl. 106A

Tibbett, Lawrence, 403

Tiffany Productions, Inc., 320, 390

Tillie's Punctured Romance, 142, 402

Times, Los Angeles, 380

Tin Pan Alley, 405

Todd, Harry, Pl. 4

Tol'able David, Pl. 65B

Tolstoy, Leo, Pl. 94A

Tourneur, Maurice, 207, 46B

Trail of '98, The, 342

Trained Monkey, The, 39

Tree, Sir Herbert Beerbohm, 142, 144

Triangle Film Corp., 140-146, 149, 150, 156, 158, 162-164, 166, 188, 199, 205, 220, 242, 243, Pls. 33A, 33B, 42A

Triangle-Ince-Kay Bee, Pls. 45A, 49B

Trip to the Moon, A, 38

Tucker, George Loane, 139, 188, 217, Pl. 55

Turner, Florence, 56, 86

Turner and Dankin, 175, 176, 257

Turpin, Ben, Pls. 25, 38

Twain, Mark, Pl. 114A

Ufa, 349, 426 *footnote*

Uncle Josh Spruceby, 16

Uncle Tom's Cabin, 15, 16, 321

Underworld, Pl. 94B

United Artists, 229, 230, 233-235, 238, 248, 319, 320, 344, 345, 366, 388, 392, Pls. 63, 65A, 66, 68A, 70B, 73, 77, 79, 80B, 85, 93B, 94A, 100B, 115A, 115B, 123

United Theaters, Inc., 247

Universal City, 103, 314, 359, 378, Pl. 124

Universal Pictures Corp., 81, 82, 92, 103, 109, 123, 124, 132-134, 141, 156, 162, 175, 179, 199, 205, 217, 228, 239, 251, 306, 308, 319-321, 358, 363, 366, 388, 390, 392, Pls. 11, 70A, 75, 91B, 102A, 104B, 107A, 110A

Universal Theaters Corp., 321

Untamed, Pl. 106B

Urban, Charles, 24

Urban, Joseph, 324, 325

Urson, Frank, Pl. 100A

Vadja, Ernst, Pl. 114B

Valentino, Rudolph, 260, 346, Pls. 64A, 64B, 68B

Van Beuren, Amedee, J., 320, 390, 412, Pl. 116B

Van Vechten, Carl, Pl. 36
Varconi, Victor, Pl. 97B
Variety, 349, 358
Variety (publication), 362, 426
vaudeville artists, 373, 374, 394-396
vaudeville theaters, 11, 12, 14, 16, 47, 57
Vengeful Vagabonds, Ye, Pl. 18A
Venus Model, The, Pl. 53A
Verne, Jules, 38
Versatile Villain, A, Pl. 30
Victor Talking Machine Co., 377, 389
Vidor, King, 341, Pls. 86, 87B, 102B, 105A, 105B, 117A
Vignola, Robert G., Pl. 71B
Vitagraph, Inc., 23, 24, 31, 39, 66, 86-88, 92, 96, 135-137, 140, 151, 157, 188, 199, 206, 239, 242, 250, 260, 320, 393, Pls. 8, 14, 15A, 15B, 21, 23, 31A, 35A, 35B, 39A, 39B, 46A, 51B
Vitaphone, 378, 382, 383, 386-389, 404, 410
vitascope, 10-12, 18, 21
V L S E, 127, 137, 151, 152, 154-157, 159, 161-163, 175, 179, 242, 289

Wagner, Bob, 289, 295
Walker, James J., 263-265, 268, 269, 271
Walker, Lillian, Pls. 21, 39A
Wallace, General Lew, 35, Pls. 89A, 89B, 90A, 90B
Walsh, George, Pl. 80B
Walsh, Raoul, Pls. 79, 92, 100B
Walthall, Henry B., 129, Pls. 27A, 97A
Waltz-Dream, Pl. 114B

Wanger, Walter, 409, 430
War Brides, 137, Pl. 44A
Ward, Jean, Pl. 4
Ware, Helen, 142
Warfield, David, 26
Warner, Albert, 379
Warner, Harry, 141, 379-382
Warner, Jack, 379
Warner, Sam, 379, 382
Warner Brothers, 141, 311, 320, 379-382, 385-395, 408, 410, Pls. 84A, 101A, 101B, 107B, 125
Warren, Frederick Blount, 178
Warrens of Virginia, The, 114
Warwick Trading Company, 24
Waters, Percy, 18
Watkins, Maurine, Pl. 100A
Way Down East, Pl. 65A
Weber, Joe, 144
Weber and Fields, 142, 144
Wellman, William, Pl. 98
Wesco, 365
West Coast Theaters, Inc., 257, 259, 274, 365
Western Electric Co., 376, 377, 389, 427
Westinghouse Electric and Manufacturing Co., 376, 377
What Price Glory?, 337, 341, 342, 350, Pl. 92
When Knighthood Was in Flower, 324, Pl. 71B
White, George, 400
White, Leo, Pl. 38
White, Pearl, Pl. 32
White, William Allen, Pl. 62B
Why Change Your Wife?, 224, 249, Pls. 58A, 58B
Wilbur, Crane, 142
Wilkenning, Cora C., 156-158
Willat, Irvin, Pl. 69B
Williams, Earle, 166, Pls. 21, 51B
Williams, John D., 176, 177, 179,

181, 185, 188, 192, 206, 235, 238, 270, 278, Pl. 75

Williams, Kathlyn, 34, 35, Pl. 19A

Wilson, Frank R., 365, 422

Wilson, Lois, 396

Wilson, Woodrow, 229, 425

Wilstach, Frank J., xiv

Windsor, Claire, 322

Wings, 342, Pl. 98

Within the Law, Pl. 46A

Wolheim, Louis, Pl. 110A

Wolper, Isaac M., 216, 217

Woman God Forgot, The, Pl. 50A

Woman of Affairs, A, Pl. 109A

Woman of Paris, A, 233, Pl. 77

Woodruff, Henry, 142

Woods, A. H., Pl. 44B

Woods, Frank A., 128, 289

World Films Corp., 134, 135, 157, 162, 243, 245, Pl. 36

World War, 197-199, 201, 202

Worsley, Wallace, Pl. 61B

Wray, John Griffith, Pl. 80A

Wren, P. C., Pl. 93A

Writers' Club, Hollywood, 289

Young, Clara Kimball, 56, 135, 186, 246, Pl. 15B

Young, George, 380, 381

Young, James, Pl. 51B

Young Pictures Co., Clara Kimball, 135

Zanft, John, 411

Ziegfeld, Florenz, 400

Ziegfeld Follies, 244

Ziegfeld Theater, New York, 325

zoopraxiscope, 5

Zukor, Adolph, 26, 89, 100, 108-111, 117, 119, 130, 131, 137, 140, 141, 147, 149-151, 153, 154, 157, 159-165, 174-190, 192-196, 202, 206, 207, 213, 228, 235, 239-247, 249, 254-273, 275-281, 289, 314, 317, 318, 320 *footnote,* 335, 338, 349, 359, 362-368, 378, 379, 383, 391, 392, 409, 410, 416, Pls. 26, 41, 75

Zukor, Mrs. Adolph, 183

Zukor, Arthur, 183

A CATALOGUE OF SELECTED DOVER BOOKS
IN ALL FIELDS OF INTEREST

A CATALOGUE OF SELECTED DOVER BOOKS
IN ALL FIELDS OF INTEREST

AMERICA'S OLD MASTERS, James T. Flexner. Four men emerged unexpectedly from provincial 18th century America to leadership in European art: Benjamin West, J. S. Copley, C. R. Peale, Gilbert Stuart. Brilliant coverage of lives and contributions. Revised, 1967 edition. 69 plates. 365pp. of text.
21806-6 Paperbound $3.00

FIRST FLOWERS OF OUR WILDERNESS: AMERICAN PAINTING, THE COLONIAL PERIOD, James T. Flexner. Painters, and regional painting traditions from earliest Colonial times up to the emergence of Copley, West and Peale Sr., Foster, Gustavus Hesselius, Feke, John Smibert and many anonymous painters in the primitive manner. Engaging presentation, with 162 illustrations. xxii + 368pp.
22180-6 Paperbound $3.50

THE LIGHT OF DISTANT SKIES: AMERICAN PAINTING, 1760-1835, James T. Flexner. The great generation of early American painters goes to Europe to learn and to teach: West, Copley, Gilbert Stuart and others. Allston, Trumbull, Morse; also contemporary American painters—primitives, derivatives, academics—who remained in America. 102 illustrations. xiii + 306pp. 22179-2 Paperbound $3.50

A HISTORY OF THE RISE AND PROGRESS OF THE ARTS OF DESIGN IN THE UNITED STATES, William Dunlap. Much the richest mine of information on early American painters, sculptors, architects, engravers, miniaturists, etc. The only source of information for scores of artists, the major primary source for many others. Unabridged reprint of rare original 1834 edition, with new introduction by James T. Flexner, and 394 new illustrations. Edited by Rita Weiss. 6⅝ x 9⅝.
21695-0, 21696-9, 21697-7 Three volumes, Paperbound $13.50

EPOCHS OF CHINESE AND JAPANESE ART, Ernest F. Fenollosa. From primitive Chinese art to the 20th century, thorough history, explanation of every important art period and form, including Japanese woodcuts; main stress on China and Japan, but Tibet, Korea also included. Still unexcelled for its detailed, rich coverage of cultural background, aesthetic elements, diffusion studies, particularly of the historical period. 2nd, 1913 edition. 242 illustrations. lii + 439pp. of text.
20364-6, 20365-4 Two volumes, Paperbound $6.00

THE GENTLE ART OF MAKING ENEMIES, James A. M. Whistler. Greatest wit of his day deflates Oscar Wilde, Ruskin, Swinburne; strikes back at inane critics, exhibitions, art journalism; aesthetics of impressionist revolution in most striking form. Highly readable classic by great painter. Reproduction of edition designed by Whistler. Introduction by Alfred Werner. xxxvi + 334pp.
21875-9 Paperbound $3.00

VISUAL ILLUSIONS: THEIR CAUSES, CHARACTERISTICS, AND APPLICATIONS, Matthew Luckiesh. Thorough description and discussion of optical illusion, geometric and perspective, particularly; size and shape distortions, illusions of color, of motion; natural illusions; use of illusion in art and magic, industry, etc. Most useful today with op art, also for classical art. Scores of effects illustrated. Introduction by William H. Ittleson. 100 illustrations. xxi + 252pp.

21530-X Paperbound $2.00

A HANDBOOK OF ANATOMY FOR ART STUDENTS, Arthur Thomson. Thorough, virtually exhaustive coverage of skeletal structure, musculature, etc. Full text, supplemented by anatomical diagrams and drawings and by photographs of undraped figures. Unique in its comparison of male and female forms, pointing out differences of contour, texture, form. 211 figures, 40 drawings, 86 photographs. xx + 459pp. 5⅜ x 8⅜.

21163-0 Paperbound $3.50

150 MASTERPIECES OF DRAWING, Selected by Anthony Toney. Full page reproductions of drawings from the early 16th to the end of the 18th century, all beautifully reproduced: Rembrandt, Michelangelo, Dürer, Fragonard, Urs, Graf, Wouwerman, many others. First-rate browsing book, model book for artists. xviii + 150pp. 8⅜ x 11¼.

21032-4 Paperbound $2.50

THE LATER WORK OF AUBREY BEARDSLEY, Aubrey Beardsley. Exotic, erotic, ironic masterpieces in full maturity: Comedy Ballet, Venus and Tannhauser, Pierrot, Lysistrata, Rape of the Lock, Savoy material, Ali Baba, Volpone, etc. This material revolutionized the art world, and is still powerful, fresh, brilliant. With *The Early Work*, all Beardsley's finest work. 174 plates, 2 in color. xiv + 176pp. 8⅛ x 11.

21817-1 Paperbound $3.00

DRAWINGS OF REMBRANDT, Rembrandt van Rijn. Complete reproduction of fabulously rare edition by Lippmann and Hofstede de Groot, completely reedited, updated, improved by Prof. Seymour Slive, Fogg Museum. Portraits, Biblical sketches, landscapes, Oriental types, nudes, episodes from classical mythology—All Rembrandt's fertile genius. Also selection of drawings by his pupils and followers. "Stunning volumes," *Saturday Review*. 550 illustrations. lxxviii + 552pp. 9⅛ x 12¼.

21485-0, 21486-9 Two volumes, Paperbound $10.00

THE DISASTERS OF WAR, Francisco Goya. One of the masterpieces of Western civilization—83 etchings that record Goya's shattering, bitter reaction to the Napoleonic war that swept through Spain after the insurrection of 1808 and to war in general. Reprint of the first edition, with three additional plates from Boston's Museum of Fine Arts. All plates facsimile size. Introduction by Philip Hofer, Fogg Museum. v + 97pp. 9⅜ x 8¼.

21872-4 Paperbound $2.00

GRAPHIC WORKS OF ODILON REDON. Largest collection of Redon's graphic works ever assembled: 172 lithographs, 28 etchings and engravings, 9 drawings. These include some of his most famous works. All the plates from *Odilon Redon: oeuvre graphique complet*, plus additional plates. New introduction and caption translations by Alfred Werner. 209 illustrations. xxvii + 209pp. 9⅛ x 12¼.

21966-8 Paperbound $4.50

DESIGN BY ACCIDENT; A BOOK OF "ACCIDENTAL EFFECTS" FOR ARTISTS AND DESIGNERS, James F. O'Brien. Create your own unique, striking, imaginative effects by "controlled accident" interaction of materials: paints and lacquers, oil and water based paints, splatter, crackling materials, shatter, similar items. Everything you do will be different; first book on this limitless art, so useful to both fine artist and commercial artist. Full instructions. 192 plates showing "accidents," 8 in color. viii + 215pp. 8⅜ x 11¼. 21942-9 Paperbound $3.50

THE BOOK OF SIGNS, Rudolf Koch. Famed German type designer draws 493 beautiful symbols: religious, mystical, alchemical, imperial, property marks, runes, etc. Remarkable fusion of traditional and modern. Good for suggestions of timelessness, smartness, modernity. Text. vi + 104pp. 6⅛ x 9¼.
20162-7 Paperbound $1.25

HISTORY OF INDIAN AND INDONESIAN ART, Ananda K. Coomaraswamy. An unabridged republication of one of the finest books by a great scholar in Eastern art. Rich in descriptive material, history, social backgrounds; Sunga reliefs, Rajput paintings, Gupta temples, Burmese frescoes, textiles, jewelry, sculpture, etc. 400 photos. viii + 423pp. 6⅜ x 9¾. 21436-2 Paperbound $5.00

PRIMITIVE ART, Franz Boas. America's foremost anthropologist surveys textiles, ceramics, woodcarving, basketry, metalwork, etc.; patterns, technology, creation of symbols, style origins. All areas of world, but very full on Northwest Coast Indians. More than 350 illustrations of baskets, boxes, totem poles, weapons, etc. 378 pp.
20025-6 Paperbound $3.00

THE GENTLEMAN AND CABINET MAKER'S DIRECTOR, Thomas Chippendale. Full reprint (third edition, 1762) of most influential furniture book of all time, by master cabinetmaker. 200 plates, illustrating chairs, sofas, mirrors, tables, cabinets, plus 24 photographs of surviving pieces. Biographical introduction by N. Bienenstock. vi + 249pp. 9⅞ x 12¾. 21601-2 Paperbound $4.00

AMERICAN ANTIQUE FURNITURE, Edgar G. Miller, Jr. The basic coverage of all American furniture before 1840. Individual chapters cover type of furniture—clocks, tables, sideboards, etc.—chronologically, with inexhaustible wealth of data. More than 2100 photographs, all identified, commented on. Essential to all early American collectors. Introduction by H. E. Keyes. vi + 1106pp. 7⅞ x 10¾.
21599-7, 21600-4 Two volumes, Paperbound $11.00

PENNSYLVANIA DUTCH AMERICAN FOLK ART, Henry J. Kauffman. 279 photos, 28 drawings of tulipware, Fraktur script, painted tinware, toys, flowered furniture, quilts, samplers, hex signs, house interiors, etc. Full descriptive text. Excellent for tourist, rewarding for designer, collector. Map. 146pp. 7⅞ x 10¾.
21205-X Paperbound $2.50

EARLY NEW ENGLAND GRAVESTONE RUBBINGS, Edmund V. Gillon, Jr. 43 photographs, 226 carefully reproduced rubbings show heavily symbolic, sometimes macabre early gravestones, up to early 19th century. Remarkable early American primitive art, occasionally strikingly beautiful; always powerful. Text. xxvi + 207pp. 8⅜ x 11¼. 21380-3 Paperbound $3.50

ALPHABETS AND ORNAMENTS, Ernst Lehner. Well-known pictorial source for decorative alphabets, script examples, cartouches, frames, decorative title pages, calligraphic initials, borders, similar material. 14th to 19th century, mostly European. Useful in almost any graphic arts designing, varied styles. 750 illustrations. 256pp. 7 x 10.   21905-4 Paperbound $4.00

PAINTING: A CREATIVE APPROACH, Norman Colquhoun. For the beginner simple guide provides an instructive approach to painting: major stumbling blocks for beginner; overcoming them, technical points; paints and pigments; oil painting; watercolor and other media and color. New section on "plastic" paints. Glossary. Formerly *Paint Your Own Pictures.* 221pp.   22000-1 Paperbound $1.75

THE ENJOYMENT AND USE OF COLOR, Walter Sargent. Explanation of the relations between colors themselves and between colors in nature and art, including hundreds of little-known facts about color values, intensities, effects of high and low illumination, complementary colors. Many practical hints for painters, references to great masters. 7 color plates, 29 illustrations. x + 274pp.
                                                        20944-X Paperbound $2.75

THE NOTEBOOKS OF LEONARDO DA VINCI, compiled and edited by Jean Paul Richter. 1566 extracts from original manuscripts reveal the full range of Leonardo's versatile genius: all his writings on painting, sculpture, architecture, anatomy, astronomy, geography, topography, physiology, mining, music, etc., in both Italian and English, with 186 plates of manuscript pages and more than 500 additional drawings. Includes studies for the Last Supper, the lost Sforza monument, and other works. Total of xlvii + 866pp. 7⅞ x 10¾.
                            22572-0, 22573-9 Two volumes, Paperbound $10.00

MONTGOMERY WARD CATALOGUE OF 1895. Tea gowns, yards of flannel and pillow-case lace, stereoscopes, books of gospel hymns, the New Improved Singer Sewing Machine, side saddles, milk skimmers, straight-edged razors, high-button shoes, spittoons, and on and on . . . listing some 25,000 items, practically all illustrated. Essential to the shoppers of the 1890's, it is our truest record of the spirit of the period. Unaltered reprint of Issue No. 57, Spring and Summer 1895. Introduction by Boris Emmet. Innumerable illustrations. xiii + 624pp. 8½ x 11⅝.
                                                        22377-9 Paperbound $6.95

THE CRYSTAL PALACE EXHIBITION ILLUSTRATED CATALOGUE (LONDON, 1851). One of the wonders of the modern world—the Crystal Palace Exhibition in which all the nations of the civilized world exhibited their achievements in the arts and sciences—presented in an equally important illustrated catalogue. More than 1700 items pictured with accompanying text—ceramics, textiles, cast-iron work, carpets, pianos, sleds, razors, wall-papers, billiard tables, beehives, silverware and hundreds of other artifacts—represent the focal point of Victorian culture in the Western World. Probably the largest collection of Victorian decorative art ever assembled— indispensable for antiquarians and designers. Unabridged republication of the Art-Journal Catalogue of the Great Exhibition of 1851, with all terminal essays. New introduction by John Gloag, F.S.A. xxxiv + 426pp. 9 x 12.
                                                        22503-8 Paperbound $5.00

A HISTORY OF COSTUME, Carl Köhler. Definitive history, based on surviving pieces of clothing primarily, and paintings, statues, etc. secondarily. Highly readable text, supplemented by 594 illustrations of costumes of the ancient Mediterranean peoples, Greece and Rome, the Teutonic prehistoric period; costumes of the Middle Ages, Renaissance, Baroque, 18th and 19th centuries. Clear, measured patterns are provided for many clothing articles. Approach is practical throughout. Enlarged by Emma von Sichart. 464pp. 21030-8 Paperbound $3.50.

ORIENTAL RUGS, ANTIQUE AND MODERN, Walter A. Hawley. A complete and authoritative treatise on the Oriental rug—where they are made, by whom and how, designs and symbols, characteristics in detail of the six major groups, how to distinguish them and how to buy them. Detailed technical data is provided on periods, weaves, warps, wefts, textures, sides, ends and knots, although no technical background is required for an understanding. 11 color plates, 80 halftones, 4 maps. vi + 320pp. 6⅛ x 9⅛. 22366-3 Paperbound $5.00

TEN BOOKS ON ARCHITECTURE, Vitruvius. By any standards the most important book on architecture ever written. Early Roman discussion of aesthetics of building, construction methods, orders, sites, and every other aspect of architecture has inspired, instructed architecture for about 2,000 years. Stands behind Palladio, Michelangelo, Bramante, Wren, countless others. Definitive Morris H. Morgan translation. 68 illustrations. xii + 331pp. 20645-9 Paperbound $3.00

THE FOUR BOOKS OF ARCHITECTURE, Andrea Palladio. Translated into every major Western European language in the two centuries following its publication in 1570, this has been one of the most influential books in the history of architecture. Complete reprint of the 1738 Isaac Ware edition. New introduction by Adolf Placzek, Columbia Univ. 216 plates. xxii + 110pp. of text. 9½ x 12¾. 21308-0 Clothbound $12.50

STICKS AND STONES: A STUDY OF AMERICAN ARCHITECTURE AND CIVILIZATION, Lewis Mumford.One of the great classics of American cultural history. American architecture from the medieval-inspired earliest forms to the early 20th century; evolution of structure and style, and reciprocal influences on environment. 21 photographic illustrations. 238pp. 20202-X Paperbound $2.00

THE AMERICAN BUILDER'S COMPANION, Asher Benjamin. The most widely used early 19th century architectural style and source book, for colonial up into Greek Revival periods. Extensive development of geometry of carpentering, construction of sashes, frames, doors, stairs; plans and elevations of domestic and other buildings. Hundreds of thousands of houses were built according to this book, now invaluable to historians, architects, restorers, etc. 1827 edition. 59 plates. 114pp. 7⅞ x 10¾. 22236-5 Paperbound $3.50

DUTCH HOUSES IN THE HUDSON VALLEY BEFORE 1776, Helen Wilkinson Reynolds. The standard survey of the Dutch colonial house and outbuildings, with constructional features, decoration, and local history associated with individual homesteads. Introduction by Franklin D. Roosevelt. Map. 150 illustrations. 469pp. 6⅝ x 9¼. 21469-9 Paperbound $5.00

THE ARCHITECTURE OF COUNTRY HOUSES, Andrew J. Downing. Together with Vaux's *Villas and Cottages* this is the basic book for Hudson River Gothic architecture of the middle Victorian period. Full, sound discussions of general aspects of housing, architecture, style, decoration, furnishing, together with scores of detailed house plans, illustrations of specific buildings, accompanied by full text. Perhaps the most influential single American architectural book. 1850 edition. Introduction by J. Stewart Johnson. 321 figures, 34 architectural designs. xvi + 560pp.

22003-6 Paperbound $4.00

LOST EXAMPLES OF COLONIAL ARCHITECTURE, John Mead Howells. Full-page photographs of buildings that have disappeared or been so altered as to be denatured, including many designed by major early American architects. 245 plates. xvii + 248pp. 7⅞ x 10¾.

21143-6 Paperbound $3.50

DOMESTIC ARCHITECTURE OF THE AMERICAN COLONIES AND OF THE EARLY REPUBLIC, Fiske Kimball. Foremost architect and restorer of Williamsburg and Monticello covers nearly 200 homes between 1620-1825. Architectural details, construction, style features, special fixtures, floor plans, etc. Generally considered finest work in its area. 219 illustrations of houses, doorways, windows, capital mantels. xx + 314pp. 7⅞ x 10¾.

21743-4 Paperbound $4.00

EARLY AMERICAN ROOMS: 1650-1858, edited by Russell Hawes Kettell. Tour of 12 rooms, each representative of a different era in American history and each furnished, decorated, designed and occupied in the style of the era. 72 plans and elevations, 8-page color section, etc, show fabrics, wall papers, arrangements, etc. Full descriptive text. xvii + 200pp. of text. 8⅜ x 11¼.

21633-0 Paperbound $5.00

THE FITZWILLIAM VIRGINAL BOOK, edited by J. Fuller Maitland and W. B. Squire. Full modern printing of famous early 17th-century ms. volume of 300 works by Morley, Byrd, Bull, Gibbons, etc. For piano or other modern keyboard instrument; easy to read format. xxxvi + 938pp. 8⅜ x 11.

21068-5, 21069-3 Two volumes, Paperbound $10.00

KEYBOARD MUSIC, Johann Sebastian Bach. Bach Gesellschaft edition. A rich selection of Bach's masterpieces for the harpsichord: the six English Suites, six French Suites, the six Partitas (Clavierübung part I), the Goldberg Variations (Clavierübung part IV), the fifteen Two-Part Inventions and the fifteen Three-Part Sinfonias. Clearly reproduced on large sheets with ample margins; eminently playable. vi + 312pp. 8⅛ x 11.

22360-4 Paperbound $5.00

THE MUSIC OF BACH: AN INTRODUCTION, Charles Sanford Terry. A fine, nontechnical introduction to Bach's music, both instrumental and vocal. Covers organ music, chamber music, passion music, other types. Analyzes themes, developments, innovations. x + 114pp.

21075-8 Paperbound $1.50

BEETHOVEN AND HIS NINE SYMPHONIES, Sir George Grove. Noted British musicologist provides best history, analysis, commentary on symphonies. Very thorough, rigorously accurate; necessary to both advanced student and amateur music lover. 436 musical passages. vii + 407 pp

20334-4 Paperbound $2.75

JOHANN SEBASTIAN BACH, Philipp Spitta. One of the great classics of musicology, this definitive analysis of Bach's music (and life) has never been surpassed. Lucid, nontechnical analyses of hundreds of pieces (30 pages devoted to St. Matthew Passion, 26 to B Minor Mass). Also includes major analysis of 18th-century music. 450 musical examples. 40-page musical supplement. Total of xx + 1799pp.

(EUK) 22278-0, 22279-9 Two volumes, Clothbound $17.50

MOZART AND HIS PIANO CONCERTOS, Cuthbert Girdlestone. The only full-length study of an important area of Mozart's creativity. Provides detailed analyses of all 23 concertos, traces inspirational sources. 417 musical examples. Second edition. 509pp.   21271-8 Paperbound $3.50

THE PERFECT WAGNERITE: A COMMENTARY ON THE NIBLUNG'S RING, George Bernard Shaw. Brilliant and still relevant criticism in remarkable essays on Wagner's Ring cycle, Shaw's ideas on political and social ideology behind the plots, role of Leitmotifs, vocal requisites, etc. Prefaces. xxi + 136pp.

(USO) 21707-8 Paperbound $1.50

DON GIOVANNI, W. A. Mozart. Complete libretto, modern English translation; biographies of composer and librettist; accounts of early performances and critical reaction. Lavishly illustrated. All the material you need to understand and appreciate this great work. Dover Opera Guide and Libretto Series; translated and introduced by Ellen Bleiler. 92 illustrations. 209pp.

21134-7 Paperbound $2.00

BASIC ELECTRICITY, U. S. Bureau of Naval Personel. Originally a training course, best non-technical coverage of basic theory of electricity and its applications. Fundamental concepts, batteries, circuits, conductors and wiring techniques, AC and DC, inductance and capacitance, generators, motors, transformers, magnetic amplifiers, synchros, servomechanisms, etc. Also covers blue-prints, electrical diagrams, etc. Many questions, with answers. 349 illustrations. x + 448pp. 6½ x 9¼.

20973-3 Paperbound $3.50

REPRODUCTION OF SOUND, Edgar Villchur. Thorough coverage for laymen of high fidelity systems, reproducing systems in general, needles, amplifiers, preamps, loudspeakers, feedback, explaining physical background. "A rare talent for making technicalities vividly comprehensible," R. Darrell, *High Fidelity*. 69 figures. iv + 92pp.   21515-6 Paperbound $1.25

HEAR ME TALKIN' TO YA: THE STORY OF JAZZ AS TOLD BY THE MEN WHO MADE IT, Nat Shapiro and Nat Hentoff. Louis Armstrong, Fats Waller, Jo Jones, Clarence Williams, Billy Holiday, Duke Ellington, Jelly Roll Morton and dozens of other jazz greats tell how it was in Chicago's South Side, New Orleans, depression Harlem and the modern West Coast as jazz was born and grew. xvi + 429pp.

21726-4 Paperbound $3.00

FABLES OF AESOP, translated by Sir Roger L'Estrange. A reproduction of the very rare 1931 Paris edition; a selection of the most interesting fables, together with 50 imaginative drawings by Alexander Calder. v + 128pp. 6½x9¼.

21780-9 Paperbound $1.50

AGAINST THE GRAIN (A REBOURS), Joris K. Huysmans. Filled with weird images, evidences of a bizarre imagination, exotic experiments with hallucinatory drugs, rich tastes and smells and the diversions of its sybarite hero Duc Jean des Esseintes, this classic novel pushed 19th-century literary decadence to its limits. Full unabridged edition. Do not confuse this with abridged editions generally sold. Introduction by Havelock Ellis. xlix + 206pp.   22190-3 Paperbound $2.00

VARIORUM SHAKESPEARE: HAMLET. Edited by Horace H. Furness; a landmark of American scholarship. Exhaustive footnotes and appendices treat all doubtful words and phrases, as well as suggested critical emendations throughout the play's history. First volume contains editor's own text, collated with all Quartos and Folios. Second volume contains full first Quarto, translations of Shakespeare's sources (Belleforest, and Saxo Grammaticus), Der Bestrafte Brudermord, and many essays on critical and historical points of interest by major authorities of past and present. Includes details of staging and costuming over the years. By far the best edition available for serious students of Shakespeare. Total of xx + 905pp.
21004-9, 21005-7, 2 volumes, Paperbound $7.00

A LIFE OF WILLIAM SHAKESPEARE, Sir Sidney Lee. This is the standard life of Shakespeare, summarizing everything known about Shakespeare and his plays. Incredibly rich in material, broad in coverage, clear and judicious, it has served thousands as the best introduction to Shakespeare. 1931 edition. 9 plates. xxix + 792pp.   (USO) 21967-4 Paperbound $3.75

MASTERS OF THE DRAMA, John Gassner. Most comprehensive history of the drama in print, covering every tradition from Greeks to modern Europe and America, including India, Far East, etc. Covers more than 800 dramatists, 2000 plays, with biographical material, plot summaries, theatre history, criticism, etc. "Best of its kind in English," *New Republic.* 77 illustrations. xxii + 890pp.
20100-7 Clothbound $8.50

THE EVOLUTION OF THE ENGLISH LANGUAGE, George McKnight. The growth of English, from the 14th century to the present. Unusual, non-technical account presents basic information in very interesting form: sound shifts, change in grammar and syntax, vocabulary growth, similar topics. Abundantly illustrated with quotations. Formerly *Modern English in the Making.* xii + 590pp.
21932-1 Paperbound $3.50

AN ETYMOLOGICAL DICTIONARY OF MODERN ENGLISH, Ernest Weekley. Fullest, richest work of its sort, by foremost British lexicographer. Detailed word histories, including many colloquial and archaic words; extensive quotations. Do not confuse this with the Concise Etymological Dictionary, which is much abridged. Total of xxvii + 830pp. 6½ x 9¼.
21873-2, 21874-0 Two volumes, Paperbound $7.90

FLATLAND: A ROMANCE OF MANY DIMENSIONS, E. A. Abbott. Classic of science-fiction explores ramifications of life in a two-dimensional world, and what happens when a three-dimensional being intrudes. Amusing reading, but also useful as introduction to thought about hyperspace. Introduction by Banesh Hoffmann. 16 illustrations. xx + 103pp.   20001-9 Paperbound $1.00

POEMS OF ANNE BRADSTREET, edited with an introduction by Robert Hutchinson. A new selection of poems by America's first poet and perhaps the first significant woman poet in the English language. 48 poems display her development in works of considerable variety—love poems, domestic poems, religious meditations, formal elegies, "quaternions," etc. Notes, bibliography. viii + 222pp.

22160-1 Paperbound $2.50

THREE GOTHIC NOVELS: THE CASTLE OF OTRANTO BY HORACE WALPOLE; VATHEK BY WILLIAM BECKFORD; THE VAMPYRE BY JOHN POLIDORI, WITH FRAGMENT OF A NOVEL BY LORD BYRON, edited by E. F. Bleiler. The first Gothic novel, by Walpole; the finest Oriental tale in English, by Beckford; powerful Romantic supernatural story in versions by Polidori and Byron. All extremely important in history of literature; all still exciting, packed with supernatural thrills, ghosts, haunted castles, magic, etc. xl + 291pp.

21232-7 Paperbound $2.50

THE BEST TALES OF HOFFMANN, E. T. A. Hoffmann. 10 of Hoffmann's most important stories, in modern re-editings of standard translations: Nutcracker and the King of Mice, Signor Formica, Automata, The Sandman, Rath Krespel, The Golden Flowerpot, Master Martin the Cooper, The Mines of Falun, The King's Betrothed, A New Year's Eve Adventure. 7 illustrations by Hoffmann. Edited by E. F. Bleiler. xxxix + 419pp. 21793-0 Paperbound $3.00

GHOST AND HORROR STORIES OF AMBROSE BIERCE, Ambrose Bierce. 23 strikingly modern stories of the horrors latent in the human mind: The Eyes of the Panther, The Damned Thing, An Occurrence at Owl Creek Bridge, An Inhabitant of Carcosa, etc., plus the dream-essay, Visions of the Night. Edited by E. F. Bleiler. xxii + 199pp. 20767-6 Paperbound $1.50

BEST GHOST STORIES OF J. S. LEFANU, J. Sheridan LeFanu. Finest stories by Victorian master often considered greatest supernatural writer of all. Carmilla, Green Tea, The Haunted Baronet, The Familiar, and 12 others. Most never before available in the U. S. A. Edited by E. F. Bleiler. 8 illustrations from Victorian publications. xvii + 467pp. 20415-4 Paperbound $3.00

MATHEMATICAL FOUNDATIONS OF INFORMATION THEORY, A. I. Khinchin. Comprehensive introduction to work of Shannon, McMillan, Feinstein and Khinchin, placing these investigations on a rigorous mathematical basis. Covers entropy concept in probability theory, uniqueness theorem, Shannon's inequality, ergodic sources, the E property, martingale concept, noise, Feinstein's fundamental lemma, Shanon's first and second theorems. Translated by R. A. Silverman and M. D. Friedman. iii + 120pp. 60434-9 Paperbound $2.00

SEVEN SCIENCE FICTION NOVELS, H. G. Wells. The standard collection of the great novels. Complete, unabridged. *First Men in the Moon, Island of Dr. Moreau, War of the Worlds, Food of the Gods, Invisible Man, Time Machine, In the Days of the Comet.* Not only science fiction fans, but every educated person owes it to himself to read these novels. 1015pp. (USO) 20264-X Clothbound $6.00

LAST AND FIRST MEN AND STAR MAKER, TWO SCIENCE FICTION NOVELS, Olaf Stapledon. Greatest future histories in science fiction. In the first, human intelligence is the "hero," through strange paths of evolution, interplanetary invasions, incredible technologies, near extinctions and reemergences. Star Maker describes the quest of a band of star rovers for intelligence itself, through time and space: weird inhuman civilizations, crustacean minds, symbiotic worlds, etc. Complete, unabridged. v + 438pp. (USO) 21962-3 Paperbound $2.50

THREE PROPHETIC NOVELS, H. G. WELLS. Stages of a consistently planned future for mankind. *When the Sleeper Wakes,* and *A Story of the Days to Come,* anticipate *Brave New World* and *1984,* in the 21st Century; *The Time Machine,* only complete version in print, shows farther future and the end of mankind. All show Wells's greatest gifts as storyteller and novelist. Edited by E. F. Bleiler. x + 335pp. (USO) 20605-X Paperbound $2.50

THE DEVIL'S DICTIONARY, Ambrose Bierce. America's own Oscar Wilde— Ambrose Bierce—offers his barbed iconoclastic wisdom in over 1,000 definitions hailed by H. L. Mencken as "some of the most gorgeous witticisms in the English language." 145pp. 20487-1 Paperbound $1.25

MAX AND MORITZ, Wilhelm Busch. Great children's classic, father of comic strip, of two bad boys, Max and Moritz. Also Ker and Plunk (Plisch und Plumm), Cat and Mouse, Deceitful Henry, Ice-Peter, The Boy and the Pipe, and five other pieces. Original German, with English translation. Edited by H. Arthur Klein; translations by various hands and H. Arthur Klein. vi + 216pp.
20181-3 Paperbound $2.00

PIGS IS PIGS AND OTHER FAVORITES, Ellis Parker Butler. The title story is one of the best humor short stories, as Mike Flannery obfuscates biology and English. Also included, That Pup of Murchison's, The Great American Pie Company, and Perkins of Portland. 14 illustrations. v + 109pp. 21532-6 Paperbound $1.25

THE PETERKIN PAPERS, Lucretia P. Hale. It takes genius to be as stupidly mad as the Peterkins, as they decide to become wise, celebrate the "Fourth," keep a cow, and otherwise strain the resources of the Lady from Philadelphia. Basic book of American humor. 153 illustrations. 219pp. 20794-3 Paperbound $1.50

PERRAULT'S FAIRY TALES, translated by A. E. Johnson and S. R. Littlewood, with 34 full-page illustrations by Gustave Doré. All the original Perrault stories— Cinderella, Sleeping Beauty, Bluebeard, Little Red Riding Hood, Puss in Boots, Tom Thumb, etc.—with their witty verse morals and the magnificent illustrations of Doré. One of the five or six great books of European fairy tales. viii + 117pp. 8⅛ x 11. 22311-6 Paperbound $2.00

OLD HUNGARIAN FAIRY TALES, Baroness Orczy. Favorites translated and adapted by author of the *Scarlet Pimpernel.* Eight fairy tales include "The Suitors of Princess Fire-Fly," "The Twin Hunchbacks," "Mr. Cuttlefish's Love Story," and "The Enchanted Cat." This little volume of magic and adventure will captivate children as it has for generations. 90 drawings by Montagu Barstow. 96pp.
22293-4 Paperbound $1.95

THE RED FAIRY BOOK, Andrew Lang. Lang's color fairy books have long been children's favorites. This volume includes Rapunzel, Jack and the Bean-stalk and 35 other stories, familiar and unfamiliar. 4 plates, 93 illustrations x + 367pp.

21673-X Paperbound $2.50

THE BLUE FAIRY BOOK, Andrew Lang. Lang's tales come from all countries and all times. Here are 37 tales from Grimm, the Arabian Nights, Greek Mythology, and other fascinating sources. 8 plates, 130 illustrations. xi + 390pp.

21437-0 Paperbound $2.50

HOUSEHOLD STORIES BY THE BROTHERS GRIMM. Classic English-language edition of the well-known tales — Rumpelstiltskin, Snow White, Hansel and Gretel, The Twelve Brothers, Faithful John, Rapunzel, Tom Thumb (52 stories in all). Translated into simple, straightforward English by Lucy Crane. Ornamented with headpieces, vignettes, elaborate decorative initials and a dozen full-page illustrations by Walter Crane. x + 269pp.

21080-4 Paperbound **$2.00**

THE MERRY ADVENTURES OF ROBIN HOOD, Howard Pyle. The finest modern versions of the traditional ballads and tales about the great English outlaw. Howard Pyle's complete prose version, with every word, every illustration of the first edition. Do not confuse this facsimile of the original (1883) with modern editions that change text or illustrations. 23 plates plus many page decorations. xxii + 296pp.

22043-5 Paperbound $2.50

THE STORY OF KING ARTHUR AND HIS KNIGHTS, Howard Pyle. The finest children's version of the life of King Arthur; brilliantly retold by Pyle, with 48 of his most imaginative illustrations. xviii + 313pp. 6⅛ x 9¼.

21445-1 Paperbound $2.50

THE WONDERFUL WIZARD OF OZ, L. Frank Baum. America's finest children's book in facsimile of first edition with all Denslow illustrations in full color. The edition a child should have. Introduction by Martin Gardner. 23 color plates, scores of drawings. iv + 267pp.

20691-2 Paperbound $2.50

THE MARVELOUS LAND OF OZ, L. Frank Baum. The second Oz book, every bit as imaginative as the Wizard. The hero is a boy named Tip, but the Scarecrow and the Tin Woodman are back, as is the Oz magic. 16 color plates, 120 drawings by John R. Neill. 287pp.

20692-0 Paperbound $2.50

THE MAGICAL MONARCH OF MO, L. Frank Baum. Remarkable adventures in a land even stranger than Oz. The best of Baum's books not in the Oz series. 15 color plates and dozens of drawings by Frank Verbeck. xviii + 237pp.

21892-9 Paperbound $2.25

THE BAD CHILD'S BOOK OF BEASTS, MORE BEASTS FOR WORSE CHILDREN, A MORAL ALPHABET, Hilaire Belloc. Three complete humor classics in one volume. Be kind to the frog, and do not call him names . . . and 28 other whimsical animals. Familiar favorites and some not so well known. Illustrated by Basil Blackwell. 156pp.

(USO) 20749-8 Paperbound $1.50

EAST O' THE SUN AND WEST O' THE MOON, George W. Dasent. Considered the best of all translations of these Norwegian folk tales, this collection has been enjoyed by generations of children (and folklorists too). Includes True and Untrue, Why the Sea is Salt, East O' the Sun and West O' the Moon, Why the Bear is Stumpy-Tailed, Boots and the Troll, The Cock and the Hen, Rich Peter the Pedlar, and 52 more. The only edition with all 59 tales. 77 illustrations by Erik Werenskiold and Theodor Kittelsen. xv + 418pp.   22521-6 Paperbound $3.50

GOOPS AND HOW TO BE THEM, Gelett Burgess. Classic of tongue-in-cheek humor, masquerading as etiquette book. 87 verses, twice as many cartoons, show mischievous Goops as they demonstrate to children virtues of table manners, neatness, courtesy, etc. Favorite for generations. viii + 88pp. 6½ x 9¼.
22233-0 Paperbound $1.25

ALICE'S ADVENTURES UNDER GROUND, Lewis Carroll. The first version, quite different from the final *Alice in Wonderland,* printed out by Carroll himself with his own illustrations. Complete facsimile of the "million dollar" manuscript Carroll gave to Alice Liddell in 1864. Introduction by Martin Gardner. viii + 96pp. Title and dedication pages in color.   21482-6 Paperbound $1.25

THE BROWNIES, THEIR BOOK, Palmer Cox. Small as mice, cunning as foxes, exuberant and full of mischief, the Brownies go to the zoo, toy shop, seashore, circus, etc., in 24 verse adventures and 266 illustrations. Long a favorite, since their first appearance in St. Nicholas Magazine. xi + 144pp. 6⅝ x 9¼.
21265-3 Paperbound $1.75

SONGS OF CHILDHOOD, Walter De La Mare. Published (under the pseudonym Walter Ramal) when De La Mare was only 29, this charming collection has long been a favorite children's book. A facsimile of the first edition in paper, the 47 poems capture the simplicity of the nursery rhyme and the ballad, including such lyrics as I Met Eve, Tartary, The Silver Penny. vii + 106pp. (USO) 21972-0 Paperbound $1.25

THE COMPLETE NONSENSE OF EDWARD LEAR, Edward Lear. The finest 19th-century humorist cartoonist in full: all nonsense limericks, zany alphabets, Owl and Pussycat, songs, nonsense botany, and more than 500 illustrations by Lear himself. Edited by Holbrook Jackson. xxix + 287pp.   (USO) 20167-8 Paperbound $2.00

BILLY WHISKERS: THE AUTOBIOGRAPHY OF A GOAT, Frances Trego Montgomery. A favorite of children since the early 20th century, here are the escapades of that rambunctious, irresistible and mischievous goat—Billy Whiskers. Much in the spirit of *Peck's Bad Boy,* this is a book that children never tire of reading or hearing. All the original familiar illustrations by W. H. Fry are included: 6 color plates, 18 black and white drawings. 159pp.   22345-0 Paperbound $2.00

MOTHER GOOSE MELODIES. Faithful republication of the fabulously rare Munroe and Francis "copyright 1833" Boston edition—the most important Mother Goose collection, usually referred to as the "original." Familiar rhymes plus many rare ones, with wonderful old woodcut illustrations. Edited by E. F. Bleiler. 128pp. 4½ x 6⅜.   22577-1 Paperbound $1.00

Two Little Savages; Being the Adventures of Two Boys Who Lived as Indians and What They Learned, Ernest Thompson Seton. Great classic of nature and boyhood provides a vast range of woodlore in most palatable form, a genuinely entertaining story. Two farm boys build a teepee in woods and live in it for a month, working out Indian solutions to living problems, star lore, birds and animals, plants, etc. 293 illustrations. vii + 286pp.

20985-7 Paperbound $2.50

Peter Piper's Practical Principles of Plain & Perfect Pronunciation. Alliterative jingles and tongue-twisters of surprising charm, that made their first appearance in America about 1830. Republished in full with the spirited woodcut illustrations from this earliest American edition. 32pp. 4½ x 6⅜.

22560-7 Paperbound $1.00

Science Experiments and Amusements for Children, Charles Vivian. 73 easy experiments, requiring only materials found at home or easily available, such as candles, coins, steel wool, etc.; illustrate basic phenomena like vacuum, simple chemical reaction, etc. All safe. Modern, well-planned. Formerly *Science Games for Children.* 102 photos, numerous drawings. 96pp. 6⅛ x 9¼.

21856-2 Paperbound $1.25

An Introduction to Chess Moves and Tactics Simply Explained, Leonard Barden. Informal intermediate introduction, quite strong in explaining reasons for moves. Covers basic material, tactics, important openings, traps, positional play in middle game, end game. Attempts to isolate patterns and recurrent configurations. Formerly *Chess.* 58 figures. 102pp. (USO) 21210-6 Paperbound $1.25

Lasker's Manual of Chess, Dr. Emanuel Lasker. Lasker was not only one of the five great World Champions, he was also one of the ablest expositors, theorists, and analysts. In many ways, his Manual, permeated with his philosophy of battle, filled with keen insights, is one of the greatest works ever written on chess. Filled with analyzed games by the great players. A single-volume library that will profit almost any chess player, beginner or master. 308 diagrams. xli x 349pp.

20640-8 Paperbound $2.75

The Master Book of Mathematical Recreations, Fred Schuh. In opinion of many the finest work ever prepared on mathematical puzzles, stunts, recreations; exhaustively thorough explanations of mathematics involved, analysis of effects, citation of puzzles and games. Mathematics involved is elementary. Translated by F. Göbel. 194 figures. xxiv + 430pp. 22134-2 Paperbound $3.50

Mathematics, Magic and Mystery, Martin Gardner. Puzzle editor for Scientific American explains mathematics behind various mystifying tricks: card tricks, stage "mind reading," coin and match tricks, counting out games, geometric dissections, etc. Probability sets, theory of numbers clearly explained. Also provides more than 400 tricks, guaranteed to work, that you can do. 135 illustrations. xii + 176pp.

20335-2 Paperbound $1.75

MATHEMATICAL PUZZLES FOR BEGINNERS AND ENTHUSIASTS, Geoffrey Mott-Smith. 189 puzzles from easy to difficult—involving arithmetic, logic, algebra, properties of digits, probability, etc.—for enjoyment and mental stimulus. Explanation of mathematical principles behind the puzzles. 135 illustrations. viii + 248pp.
20198-8 Paperbound $1.75

PAPER FOLDING FOR BEGINNERS, William D. Murray and Francis J. Rigney. Easiest book on the market, clearest instructions on making interesting, beautiful origami. Sail boats, cups, roosters, frogs that move legs, bonbon boxes, standing birds, etc. 40 projects; more than 275 diagrams and photographs. 94pp.
20713-7 Paperbound $1.00

TRICKS AND GAMES ON THE POOL TABLE, Fred Herrmann. 79 tricks and games—some solitaires, some for two or more players, some competitive games—to entertain you between formal games. Mystifying shots and throws, unusual caroms, tricks involving such props as cork, coins, a hat, etc. Formerly *Fun on the Pool Table*. 77 figures. 95pp.
21814-7 Paperbound $1.00

HAND SHADOWS TO BE THROWN UPON THE WALL: A SERIES OF NOVEL AND AMUSING FIGURES FORMED BY THE HAND, Henry Bursill. Delightful picturebook from great-grandfather's day shows how to make 18 different hand shadows: a bird that flies, duck that quacks, dog that wags his tail, camel, goose, deer, boy, turtle, etc. Only book of its sort. vi + 33pp. 6½ x 9¼. 21779-5 Paperbound $1.00

WHITTLING AND WOODCARVING, E. J. Tangerman. 18th printing of best book on market. "If you can cut a potato you can carve" toys and puzzles, chains, chessmen, caricatures, masks, frames, woodcut blocks, surface patterns, much more. Information on tools, woods, techniques. Also goes into serious wood sculpture from Middle Ages to present, East and West. 464 photos, figures. x + 293pp.
20965-2 Paperbound $2.00

HISTORY OF PHILOSOPHY, Julián Marías. Possibly the clearest, most easily followed, best planned, most useful one-volume history of philosophy on the market; neither skimpy nor overfull. Full details on system of every major philosopher and dozens of less important thinkers from pre-Socratics up to Existentialism and later. Strong on many European figures usually omitted. Has gone through dozens of editions in Europe. 1966 edition, translated by Stanley Appelbaum and Clarence Strowbridge. xviii + 505pp.
21739-6 Paperbound $3.50

YOGA: A SCIENTIFIC EVALUATION, Kovoor T. Behanan. Scientific but non-technical study of physiological results of yoga exercises; done under auspices of Yale U. Relations to Indian thought, to psychoanalysis, etc. 16 photos. xxiii + 270pp.
20505-3 Paperbound $2.50

Prices subject to change without notice.
Available at your book dealer or write for free catalogue to Dept. GI, Dover Publications, Inc., 180 Varick St., N. Y., N. Y. 10014. Dover publishes more than 150 books each year on science, elementary and advanced mathematics, biology, music, art, literary history, social sciences and other areas.